Understanding
Software Dynamics

The Pearson Addison-Wesley Professional Computing Series

Brian W. Kernighan, Consulting Editor

Visit **informit.com/series/professionalcomputing**
for a complete list of available publications.

The **Pearson Addison-Wesley Professional Computing Series** was created in 1990 to provide serious programmers and networking professionals with well-written and practical reference books. Pearson Addison-Wesley is renowned for publishing accurate and authoritative books on current and cutting-edge technology, and the titles in this series will help you understand the state of the art in programming languages, operating systems, and networks.

Make sure to connect with us!
informit.com/socialconnect

Understanding Software Dynamics

Richard L. Sites

✦Addison-Wesley

Boston • Columbus • New York • San Francisco • Amsterdam • Cape Town
Dubai • London • Madrid • Milan • Munich • Paris • Montreal • Toronto • Delhi • Mexico City
São Paulo • Sydney • Hong Kong • Seoul • Singapore • Taipei • Tokyo

For information about buying this title in bulk quantities, or for special sales opportunities (which may include electronic versions; custom cover designs; and content particular to your business, training goals, marketing focus, or branding interests), please contact our corporate sales department at corpsales@pearsoned.com or (800) 382-3419.

For government sales inquiries, please contact governmentsales@pearsoned.com.

For questions about sales outside the U.S., please contact intlcs@pearson.com.

Visit us on the Web: informit.com/aw

Library of Congress Control Number: 2021944164

ISBN-13: 978-0-13-758973-9
ISBN-10: 0-13-758973-5

1 2021

Dedicated to the memory of Chuck Thacker,
a true Friend of the Electron who could do more
performance analysis in his head than most mortals.

Contents at a Glance

Contents

Foreword

Dick Sites approaches problem-solving in a way that is shockingly rare these days: he finds it almost personally offensive to make guesses, and instead he insists on understanding a phenomenon before trying to fix it. When faced with the complexity of modern computer systems, including their hardware and software, most programmers approach performance debugging armed with a hunch about what is happening and proceed to "try this, try that" with the hope that this might yield a shortcut to a solution. Those of us who use this method are implicitly giving up on the possibility of truly grasping the complex interactions that could cause a program to underperform. The idea that something computer related is beyond understanding certainly doesn't occur to Dick. Often it is the case that basic tools that provide telemetry on a program's behavior are missing. In those cases Dick does the obvious thing (for Dick), which is to build them, including the visualization framework that compresses essential information about program execution into readable charts that shine a bright light into program dynamics.

When you go through Dick's remarkable career, it becomes clear why he is confident in his ability to understand complex computing systems. He became a programmer at age 10 in 1959, and his curiosity about computing resulted in a career where he studied or worked closely with giants of our field such as Fran Allen, Fred Brooks, John Cocke, Don Knuth, and Chuck Seitz, to name just a few. His accomplishments in industry are impressively broad: from co-designing the DEC Alpha Architecture to working on Adobe's Photoshop and speeding up Google web services such as Gmail.

When I met Dick (joining DEC in 1995), he was already a legend of our field, and I had the unique pleasure of spending time with him during his Google tenure and witnessed his problem-solving approach firsthand. Readers of this book will delight in the clarity of Dick's writing and how performance debugging problems are described as mysteries to be solved through his knowledge of hardware/software interactions and sequences of clues unveiled by observing detailed traces of program execution. This is a book that will be immensely useful for programmers and computer designers alike, in no small part because there is no other book to compare it with. It is as unique as its author.

—Luiz André Barroso, Google Fellow

Preface

Understanding the performance of complex software is difficult. It is even more difficult when that software is time-constrained and mysteriously exceeds its constraints now and then. Software professionals have pictures in their heads of their software's *execution dynamics*: How the various pieces work and interact together over time and estimates of how long each piece takes. (Sometimes they even document those pictures.) But when time constraints are not met, we have few tools for understanding *why*—for finding the root cause(s) of delay and other performance anomalies. This is a textbook for software developers and advanced students who work on such software.

Software dynamics refers not just to the performance or execution time of a single program thread but to the interactions between threads, between unrelated programs, and between an operating system and user programs. Delays in complex software often are caused by these interactions—code blocking and waiting for other code to wake it up, runnable code waiting for the scheduler to assign it a CPU to run on, code running slowly due to shared-hardware interference from other code, code not running at all because an interrupt routine is using its CPU, code invisibly spending much of its time in operating-system services or in page-fault handling, code waiting for I/O devices or network messages from other computers, and so on.

Time-constrained software handles repeated tasks that have periodic deadlines or tasks that have an aperiodic arrival rate of new requests each with a deadline. These tasks can have *hard* deadlines for sending control signals to moving machinery (airplanes, cars, industrial robots), *soft* deadlines such as for converting speech to text on the fly, or just *aspirational* deadlines such as for customer database lookup or web-search response times. Time-constrained also applies to phone/tablet/desktop/game user-interface responses. The term *time-constrained* is broader than the term *real-time*, which often implies hard constraints.

In each case, software tasks have a stimulus or request and a result or response. The elapsed time between the stimulus and result, the *latency* or *response time*, has some deadline. Tasks that exceed their deadlines fail, sometimes in catastrophic ways and sometimes in merely frustrating ways. You will learn how to find the root causes for these failures.

The individual tasks within such software can be called *transactions*, *queries*, *control-responses*, or *game-reactions* depending on the context. Here we will use the term *transactions* to encompass all of these. Often an end-to-end task is composed of several sub-tasks, some of which run in parallel and some of which depend on the completion of other subtasks. Sub-tasks may be CPU-bound, memory-bound, disk-bound, or network-bound. They may be executing but more slowly than expected due to interference across shared hardware resources or due to power-saving strategies in modern CPU chips. They may be waiting (i.e., not executing) for software locks or for responses from other tasks or other computers or external devices. There may be unexpected delays or interference from the underlying operating system or its kernel-mode device drivers, rather than in the programmer's user-mode code.

In many situations the software involved consists of a dozen or more *layers* or subsystems, all of which may contribute to unexpected delays and all of which may be running on separate networked computers. For example, a Google web search may spread the query across 2,000 computers, each of which does a small portion of the search and then the results are passed back and prioritized. An email message arrival in the cloud may trigger subsystems for databases, network disk storage, indexing, locking, encryption, replication, and cross-continent transmission. An automobile-driving computer may be running 50 different programs, some of which interact on every video frame coming from a half-dozen cameras, plus radar returns, changing GPS coordinates, changing 3D acceleration forces on the vehicle, and feedback about rain, visibility, tire slippage, etc. A small database system might have query optimization and disk-access subsystems using a dozen disks spread across several networked computers. A game can have subsystems for local computation, graphics processing, and networked interactions with other players.

You will learn in this book how to design in observability, logging, and timestamps for such software, how to measure CPU/memory/disk/network behavior, how to design low-overhead observation tools, and how to reason about the resulting performance data. Once you have an accurate picture of the actual elapsed-time tasks and sub-tasks for normal transactions and also for slow ones, you can see how that reality differs from the picture in your head. At that point, substantially improving the slow transactions may take only 20 minutes of software changes. But without a good picture of reality, programmers are reduced to guessing and "trying things" to reduce long delays and improve performance. This book is about not guessing, but knowing.

All of the examples, programming exercises, and supplied software in this book are written in C or C++, based on the Linux operating system running on 64-bit AMD, ARM, or Intel processors. The reader is assumed to be familiar with developing software in this environment. We assume further that the reader has some software that is time-constrained and has performance issues that the reader wants to fix. The software should already be functional and deemed debugged, with acceptable average performance—the problem is just unexplained performance variance. The reader is assumed to have an in-the-head picture of how the software runs and can on request sketch how the pieces are *supposed* to interact in a typical transaction. Finally, the reader is assumed to know a little about CPUs, virtual memory, disk and network I/O, software locks, multi-core execution, and parallel processing. Together, we will take it from there.

We explore three major themes: Measure, Observe, and Reason.

Measure. The starting place for any performance study is to measure what is happening. A numerical measurement—transactions per second, 99th percentile response time, or dropped video frame count—tells you only what is happening but not why.

Observe. To understand why some measurement is unexpectedly slow or otherwise bad but measuring the same work again is fast, it is necessary to observe in close detail where all the time is going or what processing is being done for both normal and slow instances. For the hard case of unexpectedly bad behavior that only occurs under heavy live load, it is necessary to observe over a substantial enough time interval to have a high probability of observing several slow instances and to do so in situ with minimal distortion while running full live loads.

Reason (and fix). Once careful observations are available, you need to reason about what you see—how are slow instances different from normal ones, how do software and hardware interactions produce slow instances, and how can you improve the situation? In the last part of the book, we go through case-study examples of such reasoning and some of the fixes.

Following these themes, the book material is organized into four parts, including a part about building the low-overhead KUtrace observation tool:

- Part I (Chapters 1–7), **Measurement**—how to do careful measurements of the four fundamental computer resources: CPU, memory, disk/SSD, and network.

- Part II (Chapters 8–13), **Observation**—normal observation tools: logging, dashboards, counting/profiling/sampling, and tracing.

- Part III (Chapters 14–19), **Kernel-User Trace**—the design and construction of a running low-overhead Linux tracing tool that records what every CPU core is doing every nano-second, along with postprocessing programs to create dynamic HTML pages that display the resulting timelines and interactions.

- Part IV (Chapters 20–30), **Reasoning**—case studies of reasoning about the interference underlying unusual delays observed in: excess execution, slow instruction execution, waiting for CPU, memory, disk, network, software locks, queues, and timers.

Using these ideas, you will be able to turn this picture of unexplained delay:

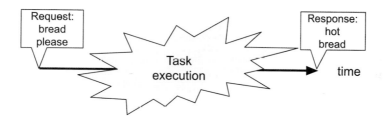

into the following detailed picture showing which subtasks happened when, which happened in parallel, which depended on another step finishing, and thus exactly *why* it took three hours:

The same ideas can turn an example software delay into this picture of the remote-login ssh daemon on CPU 2 waking up `gedit` on CPU 1:

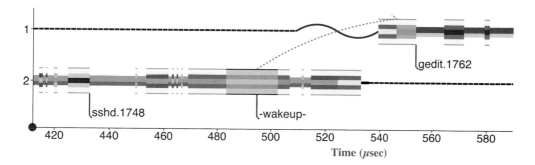

(In Part III you will learn how to create this last kind of picture for your arbitrary software.)

This book is intended especially for engaged readers who do the included programming assignments and who implement portions of the software observation tools described.

Layered throughout this book are comments about modern complex processor chips and their performance-enhancing mechanisms. Accidently defeating these mechanisms can create surprising delays. The careful reader will gain a deeper understanding of computer architecture and microarchitecture, along with everything else.

This is a textbook for software professionals and advanced students. But it also covers material of interest to computer hardware architects, operating system developers, system-architecture IT professionals, real-time system designers, and game developers. Its focus on understanding user-facing latency will develop skills that enhance any programmer's career.

Accessing the Source Code

The book uses several computer programs: mystery1, mystery2, and so forth. The source code for these programs is available for download from Addison-Wesley at informit.com/title/9780137589739.

Register your copy of *Understanding Software Dynamics* on the InformIT site for convenient access to updates and/or corrections as they become available. To start the registration process, go to informit.com/register and log in or create an account. Enter the product ISBN (9780137589739) and click Submit. Look on the Registered Products tab for an Access Bonus Content link next to this product, and follow that link to access any available bonus materials. If you would like to be notified of exclusive offers on new editions and updates, please check the box to receive email from us.

Acknowledgments

Many people have helped along the path to this book. Amer Diwan, V. Bruce Hunt, Richard Kaufmann, and Hal Murry have actively read and provided feedback on the text. Connor Sites-Bowen, J. Craig Mudge, Jim Maurer, and Rik Farrow provided thoughtful reviews and encouragement for earlier versions and related articles. Brian Kernighan did a thorough reading of the manuscript and made suggestions to materially improve the final product.

Much of the material here was developed from graduate courses I taught after retiring from Google in 2016. I am grateful for the opportunities and the student feedback arranged by Michael Brown at the National University of Singapore; Jim Larus and Willy Zwaenepoel at Ecole Polytechnique Federale de Lausanne; Christos Kozyrakis at Stanford University; and Kevin Jeffay and Fred Brooks at the University of North Carolina.

Joshua Bakita, Drew Gallatin, and Hal Murray have done ports of KUtrace to different Unix flavors. Jim Keller and Pete Bannon provided me the opportunity to do a port at Tesla Motors. Sandhya Dwarkadas asked the key question about detecting cache interference that led to my adding instructions-per-cycle counting to KUtrace.

My early career became focused on CPU performance and tracing through the influence and guidance of Elaine Bond, Pat Goldberg, Ray Hedberg, Fran Allen, and John Cocke at IBM; Don Knuth at Stanford; and Joel Emer, Anita Borg, and Sharon Perl at Digital Equipment Corporation.

My wife of 37 years, Lucey Bowen, has been especially gracious and supportive while I spent too much time focused on completing the book.

My editor, Greg Doench, has been particularly helpful in bringing this project to a smooth completion. He took time in the early months to arrange trial runs of importing text and the extensive figures into the publishing workflow, saving time and grief near the end of the process. My copy editor, Kim Wimpsett, did a fantastic job inserting literally thousands of small improvements.

—Richard L. Sites, September 2021

About the Author

Richard L. Sites wrote his first computer program in 1959 and has spent most of his career at the boundary between hardware and software, with a particular interest in CPU/software performance interactions. His past work includes VAX microcode, DEC Alpha co-architect, and inventing the performance counters found in nearly all processors today. He has done low-overhead microcode and software tracing at DEC, Adobe, Google, and Tesla. Dr. Sites earned his PhD at Stanford in 1974; he holds 66 patents and is a member of the US National Academy of Engineering.

Part I

Measurement

Understanding variation is the key to success in quality and business.

—W. Edwards Deming

Measurement is the act of ascertaining the size, amount, or degree of something. Careful measurements are the underpinning of understanding software performance.

This first part describes a complex hardware and software environment, the book's emphasis on transaction latency, the concept of latency distributions, and the consequences of long 99th percentile latencies.

Our overall goal is to understand the root causes of *variance* in transaction latency—the apparently random unexpectedly long response times in complex software.

The datacenter environment is a superset of the environment you might have set up when exploring the performance of database transactions, desktop software delays, dedicated controller delays, or game delays. This part also introduces the important practice of estimating within a factor of 10 how long pieces of code should take. As an underpinning for the rest of the book, it leads readers through detailed measurements of CPU, memory, disk, and network latencies. These chapters use pre-supplied but flawed programs that every reader can run and get some insight and then can modify as directed to fix the flaws and gain substantially more insight. The resulting measurements will start to show the sources of latency variation in simple programs.

The first part serves to bring readers with varying backgrounds to a common base of knowledge about performance measurement, user- and kernel-mode software interactions, cross-thread and cross-program software interference, and interactions between complex software and computer hardware. At the end of this part, every reader will be able to make informed estimates of how long a piece of code *should* take.

Chapter 1

My Program Is Too Slow

Someone walks into my office and says "My program is too slow." After a pause, I ask "How slow should it be?"

A good programmer has a ready answer to this question, as she describes the work to be done and estimates of how long each portion should take. Perhaps she says "This database query accesses 10,000 records of which about 1,000 turn out to be relevant; each access should take about 10 milliseconds and they are spread across 20 disks, so 10,000 accesses should be about 5 seconds total. There is no network activity and the CPU processing and memory use are small and simple—all much faster than the disk access time. The actual query is taking about 15 seconds, which is too slow."

A sloppier programmer might answer "I wrote 1,000 lines of code all night using lots of existing libraries, and it all works but takes about 15 seconds per query, and I want it to take 1/10 of a second. One of those libraries must be too slow; how can I find it?" When asked, he has no idea whether 1/10 of a second is a reasonable expectation, no idea how long each library call should take, no idea if he is using the libraries appropriately, and no designed-in way to observe the dynamics of his code to determine where the time really goes. We will explore all these issues in this book.

1.1 Datacenter Context

We introduce some terms and concepts from a complex software environment. Your environment may be much simpler, but the ideas carry over almost exactly. The terminology is from datacenters, but the ideas also apply to database, desktop, vehicle, gaming, and other time-constrained environments.

A *transaction* or *query* or *request* is an input message to a computer system that must be dealt with as a single unit of work. Each computer processing transactions is termed a *server*. The *latency* or *response time* of a transaction is the time elapsed between sending a message and receiving its result. The *offered load* is the number of transactions sent per second; when this exceeds the number of transactions processed per second, response time suffers, sometimes dramatically. A *service* is a collection of programs that handle one particular kind of transaction. Large datacenters process transactions for dozens of different services simultaneously, and each service has a different offered load and a different latency goal.

Transaction latency is not constant—it has a probability distribution taken over thousands of transactions per second. *Tail latency* refers to the slowest transactions in this distribution. A simple way to summarize the tail latency is to state the 99th percentile latency—the time that is exceeded by the slowest 1% of all transactions, i.e., by 50 transactions every second if the offered load is 5,000 transactions per second.

By the *dynamics* of a program or collection of programs we mean the activity over time—what pieces of code run when, what they wait for, what memory space they take, and how different programs affect each other. As programmers, we imagine in our heads simple dynamics for a program, but in reality the program may (occasionally) behave much differently than that picture and perform much more slowly than expected. If we can observe the true dynamics, we can adjust our mental picture and usually improve the code's performance with simple changes.

We are interested in user-facing transactions in complex software—the datacenter half of cell phones, for example. We are particularly interested in transactions that are usually fast but occasionally take much longer—enough that the end user sees an annoying delay. In datacenters, the hardware budget for each service is often determined by how many transactions per second each server can "handle." This target number is determined *empirically* by increasing the offered load until some tail-latency time constraint is exceeded, and then the target load is backed off a little.

If we can understand and then reduce the number of too-long transactions, the same hardware can handle larger loads within the tail-latency goal, at no additional cost. This is worth a lot of money. A skilled and somewhat lucky performance engineer can occasionally make a simple software change that saves enough money to pay for 10 years of salary. Companies and customers like such people.

Time-constrained transaction software is fundamentally different from batch or offline software (or most benchmarks). The important metric for transaction software is response time, while the important metric for batch software is usually efficient hardware utilization. For transactions, it is not the *average* response time that matters, but the slowest times, the tail latency.

> In a datacenter, a higher average latency but shorter tail latency is usually preferred over a lower average latency and longer tail latency. Most commuters prefer the same thing—a route that takes a few minutes longer but always takes about the same time is better than a slightly faster route that occasionally has unpredictable hour-long delays.

For batch software, having the CPUs 98% busy on average can be good; for transaction software, 98% busy is a *disaster*, and even CPUs 50% busy on average might be too much, because it produces long response times whenever the offered load spikes for a few seconds to 3x above the average. When I first joined Google in 2004, the average datacenter CPU was 9% busy and 91% idle. The 9% busy was too low. Increasing that to 18% without increasing tail latency doubled the efficiency of all those datacenters. Doubling again to 36% busy would be good, but doubling a third time to 72% busy would likely ruin too many transactions' time constraints.

In looking at the performance of complex transaction-oriented software, we assume in this book that the programs involved fundamentally work and that on average they work quickly enough.

We won't discuss designing or debugging such software, nor understanding or improving its average performance. We also assume that always-slow transactions have been identified and fixed in offline test/debug environments that have no time constraints, leaving us just with occasionally slow transactions. We focus on the mechanisms that make occasional transactions slow, on how to observe these mechanisms, and on how to interpret the observations.

When you use a cell phone to send a text message, read a post, search the web, look at a map, stream a video, use an app, or even dial a telephone number, there is a datacenter somewhere that responds to your requests. If these responses are annoyingly slow and some competing app or service is faster, you may well switch to that one, or at least use the slow one less often. Everyone in a time-constrained ecosystem has an incentive, often financial, to reduce annoying delays. Few people have the skills to do so.

It is the goal of this book to teach a few more people how.

1.2   Datacenter Hardware

Large datacenters have something like 10,000 servers in a building, with each server a PC about the size of a desktop PC but without the case. Instead, about 50 server boards are mounted in a rack, and there are 200 racks spread around a very large room. A typical server has 1–4 CPU chip sockets with 4–50 CPU cores each, a boatload[1] of RAM, a couple of disks or *solid-state drives* (SSDs), and a network connection to a datacenter-wide switching fabric set up so that any server can communicate with any other server, and at least some of the servers can also communicate with the Internet and hence your phone. Outside the building, there are big generators that can run the entire building, including air conditioning, for days or weeks when there is a power outage. Inside, there are batteries that can run the servers and network switches for tens of seconds while the generators start up.

Each server runs multiple programs. It usually doesn't make business sense to dedicate some servers to just doing email, others to just map tiles, and others to just instant messages. Instead, each server runs multiple programs, and each of those programs likely has multiple *threads*. For example, an email server program might have 100 worker threads processing email requests for several thousand users simultaneously, most of whom are typing or reading, with many of the active threads waiting for disk accesses or for other software layers. The worker threads take incoming requests, do whatever is asked, respond, and then go on to another pending request from another user. During the busiest hour of the day almost all the worker threads are busy, while during the slowest hour of the day at least half of them will be idle, waiting for work. There is a constant boom-and-bust cycle of offered work at almost all time scales—microsecond, millisecond, second, and minute. There is even a seven-day cycle with lower activity on Saturday and Sunday (for Western work weeks).

To control response times, it is important to have spare hardware resources available for user-facing transactions, since the user load tends to spike now and then based on physical-world events. But it is also economical to have some non-user-facing batch programs to run when there are otherwise idle processors. In addition to user-facing foreground programs and batch

---

[1] A computer science technical term, 10^{12}

background programs, there are always a few supervisory programs running on each server, keeping track of how busy that server is, how many errors it is getting, how much disk space is left, etc. These supervisory programs deal with machine health and rebooting/reconfiguring individual machines and with starting/stopping /restarting the various software programs. It turns out to be a complex environment just on a single server. This complexity is then multiplied by 10,000 for a roomful of servers.

1.3   Datacenter Software

Datacenter software is quite different from self-contained programs and benchmarks. It consists of *layers and layers* of subsystems, many running in parallel, each handling requests from multiple services and multiple instances of single services, and each trying to respond quickly enough to each request to meet its individual latency goals. Often, the layers serving one user request will all be running on different servers. To improve performance, many layers will include software caches holding recent data or calculated results. Finding and reusing software-cached data is termed a *hit* and not finding it a *miss*. The dynamics of software caches can affect transaction latency in unexpected ways, as we shall see.

A user requesting the text of an email message would first have that request routed to a datacenter containing the primary mail repository for that user and then go through a load-balancing server that forwards the request to a less busy one of hundreds of email front-end servers. The front-end software layer manages the request and eventually constructs the HTML or app API result. It requests the mail message itself from a back-end layer, which calls a *database layer*, which calls a database caching layer and upon software-cache miss calls a replication layer (to access or update a secondary mail repository in another datacenter), and eventually there is a call to a disk-server layer that reads the mail message from one of several redundant disks, as shown in Figure 1.1. Results are then returned up the call tree, possibly being modified as they go.

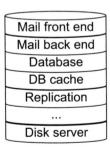

Figure 1.1   **Layers of a software example**

Some form of network message passing or remote procedure call ties all this activity together. We will use the term *remote procedure call* and its abbreviation RPC throughout this book. RPCs from one layer to another may be synchronous, with the caller waiting for a response, or asynchronous with the caller continuing to execute and quite possibly doing other RPCs that all execute in parallel on many different servers. It is this parallel execution of small portions of work that allows datacenter software to perform massive amounts of work for one request and still finish in a fraction of a second. A single user-facing transaction may easily fan out to use 200–2,000 different servers.

Figure 1.2 shows a small example RPC tree, in the style of [Sigelman 2010]. Server A might call B synchronously and then after B returns call C. Server C might call D and E in parallel and then wait for both to return.

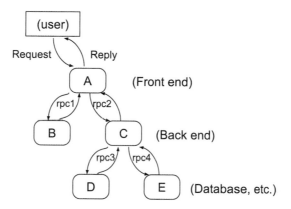

Figure 1.2   **RPC tree across five servers A–E**

Each user request and each RPC sub-request has a response-time goal. If the user request at an email front-end layer has a 200-millisecond goal, the back-end layer might be given a 160 millisecond goal, the database layer a shorter goal, and so on down to a disk-server goal of 50 milliseconds. Whenever a sub-request responds too slowly, each of the layered callers is also exposed to responding too slowly. For a set of parallel executions, the term *execution skew* describes the variation in completion times.

If many RPCs are done in parallel, it is usually the slowest of these that determines the overall response time. Thus, if we execute 100 RPCs in parallel, it is the 99th percentile slowest response time that sets the overall response time. Execution skew makes understanding and controlling long response times important.

1.4   Long-Tail Latency

Latency is the elapsed wall-clock time between two events. When carefully discussing latency, be sure to specify which two events. For example, "the latency of an RPC" might mean the time between a user-mode program (client in client-server terminology) sending a request and that program receiving the corresponding response. Or it might mean the time from when the called user-mode program (server in client-server terminology) receives a request to when it sends the corresponding response. These two different definitions of latency, client and server, may sometimes differ by 30 milliseconds or more for the same RPC, with some mystery involved about where the extra time goes and on which computer or network hardware.

We will focus by default on *server* RPC latency except when we are discussing discrepancies such as the 30 milliseconds earlier.

Multiple RPC requests to a service will have different latencies, but they often will cluster near similar values for similar requests. In general, this can be summarized by a histogram of latency values—a little graph showing latency buckets on the x-axis and count of RPCs with that latency on the y-axis.

For datacenter transactions, these latency histograms have one or more peaks for normal cases but often have a *long tail* of substantially slower responses for unusual cases [Blake 2015, Hoff 2012, Weaveworks 2017, Dean 2013]. The disk server histogram in Figure 1.3 has three peaks at about 1, 3, and 20 milliseconds for three different kinds of normal cases, and then a long tail that extends out beyond 1,500 milliseconds. The desired response time is 50 milliseconds or less. This book is about understanding and reducing the long tail. The barely visible peaks soon before 250, 500, 750, etc., milliseconds are indications of an underlying performance mystery, which we will resolve in Part II.

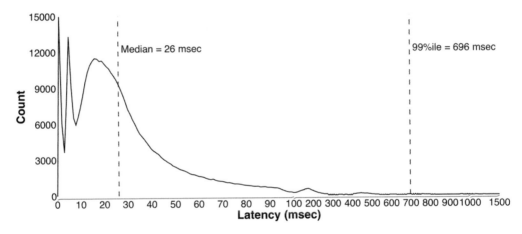

Figure 1.3 **Histogram of disk-server accesses with long tail on the right**

It is useful to describe a latency histogram with just a few numbers, instead of 500 numbers if the histogram has 500 buckets. What number should we use?

The median (or similar average) latency is a particularly ill-suited description of a skewed or multi-peak distribution because it rarely is near many of the actual values and it tells us nothing about the shape and size of the long tail—our topic of interest. In the graph in Figure 1.3 the median latency is 26 milliseconds, telling us nothing about the peaks or the tail. The maximum latency is also ill-suited because there might be one extremely slow RPC in a day (associated with a recovered memory or disk hardware error, for example) and all the others are tens to hundreds of times faster.

Instead we turn to percentiles. If our latency histogram has 50,000 measurements, then the shortest 500 of these are the fastest 1% and the longest 500 are the slowest 1%. The numeric boundary between the fastest 99% and slowest 1% is the 99th percentile value—99 percent of the sorted measurements are less than or equal to this value. (There are many such values, all lying between the 49,500th and 49,001st sorted measurements; any of these numbers will do, but conventionally the exact 49,500th sorted value will be used.) A quick but useful way to describe a long-tail distribution is to give the 99th percentile value, or 95th, 99.9th, etc. The 99th percentile value for the histogram in Figure 1.3 is 696 milliseconds, which is much too large compared to the 50-millisecond goal. It represents a serious performance bug.

> In Chapter 9, we will learn what caused this particular long tail, how it was fixed, and the eventual new 99th percentile of about 150 milliseconds. That simple change paid for 10 years of my salary.

1.5   Thought Framework

In thinking about tail latency and related performance issues, we will follow the programmer's discipline of first estimating how long some work should take, then observing how long it actually does take, and then thinking about any differences. Figure 1.4 shows this framework.

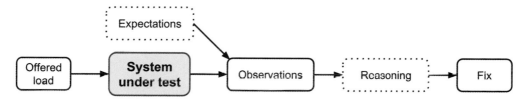

Figure 1.4   **Framework for examining the performance of complex software**

The framework consists of a software and hardware system under test, some offered load for that system, a human's expectations of the performance of the system for such a load, software performance-tool observations of the actual dynamics and performance, human reasoning about what is happening, and eventually fixes or changes to improve the performance.

1.6   Order-of-Magnitude Estimates

In looking at software performance, part of "How slow should it be?" is estimating how long various pieces of work should take. These estimates can be very rough and still give useful insight. Performance-aware programmers do order-of-magnitude estimates in their heads all the time while designing and writing serious programs.

The phrase *order of magnitude* refers to an approximate measure of the size of a number. A *decimal* order of magnitude gives an estimate that is the nearest power of 10 (1, 10, 100, ...), while a *binary* order of magnitude gives an estimate that is the nearest power of 2 (1, 2, 4, 8, and so on). Occasionally, you will see decimal half-orders—1, 3, 10, 30, etc. In this book, we use decimal orders of magnitude unless otherwise qualified, using the notation *O(n)* for "on the order of *n*," with the *units* always specified. It matters a lot whether you are talking about O(10) nanoseconds or O(10) milliseconds or O(10) bytes. From here on in the book, we will also use *nsec, usec,* and *msec* to abbreviate nanoseconds, microseconds, and milliseconds, respectively.

In Table 1.1 you will find a series of estimates that every serious programmer should be familiar with. It is from a 2009 talk by Jeff Dean, one of the very few Google Fellows. The numbers have not changed much since then. I have added a column of just order-of-magnitudes.

Table 1.1   **Numbers Everyone Should Know [Dean 2009]**

Action	Time	O(n)
L1 cache reference	0.5 nsec	O(1) nsec
Branch mispredict	5 nsec	O(10) nsec
L2 cache reference	7 nsec	O(10) nsec
Mutex lock/unlock	25 nsec	O(10) nsec
Main memory reference	100 nsec	O(100) nsec
Compress 1K bytes with Zippy	3,000 nsec	O(1) usec
Send 2K bytes over 1 Gbps network	20,000 nsec	O(10) usec
Read 1 MB sequentially from memory	250,000 nsec	O(100) usec
Round trip within same datacenter	500,000 nsec	O(1) msec
Disk seek	10,000,000 nsec	O(10) msec
Read 1 MB sequentially from disk	20,000,000 nsec	O(10) msec
Send packet CA->Netherlands->CA	150,000,000 nsec	O(100) msec

Doing an order-of-magnitude estimate of expected times in various parts of a program makes it easy, when you get real measurements of those times, to spot ones that differ substantially from your expectations. **This is where the learning is.** Sometimes your estimate will be quite wrong and you get to learn something subtle about how computers or programs work. Sometimes your estimate will be about right but the program is doing something much different than the picture in your head, and that unexpected faster or slower behavior needs fixing. As you practice and get better at estimating, more and more of the discrepancies you find will be real performance bugs.

Knowing the estimates in Table 1.1 will also guide you in identifying the likely source of a performance bug. If some program fragment takes 100 msec more than you expect, the problem is unlikely to be related to branch misprediction, whose effect is 10,000,000 times smaller than 100 msec. It is more likely related to disk or network times, or as we will see in later chapters, to long lock-holding times or to waiting on long RPC sub-requests.

We will design and build observation tools and data displays. As you use them, get in the habit of predicting within an order of magnitude what you expect to see. Once you are practiced at this prediction-observation-comparison loop, you will rapidly start spotting the odd stuff.

1.7   Why Are Transactions Slow?

Recall that we are particularly interested in transactions that are usually fast but occasionally take a lot of extra time—enough that the end user sees an annoying delay. In particular, slow transactions are those that violate a written response-time goal. What can cause such delays; i.e., what can cause varying latency and especially long-tail latency?

The clue here is that a transaction or transaction type is usually fast. When it is slow, that indicates the normal transaction execution time plus some unknown delay. If we can identify the source of the delay, we can usually make simple code changes that remove most of that delay and thus shorten the long-tail latency.

In heavily layered software, the most common source of delay in one layer is that it is waiting for a response from a lower layer. The lowest slow layer could be slow for its own reasons, or it could be slow because it is swamped by *unreasonable offered load*. Be sure when you develop response-time goals to simultaneously develop offered-load goals, or more precisely *constraints*.

Changing one layer's code won't help if it is simply waiting on a lower layer. We need to find the lowest layer that is actually too slow and work on improving it. To do so, we will want to design in ways to observe how long each layer is taking and to turn those measurements into displays that make it quickly clear where the bottlenecks are. A simple such display shows the actual offered load vs. the offered-load goal and the actual response time vs. the response-time goal at each layer or each RPC interface.

If the offered load to a layer N is acceptable and that layer is not waiting excessively on a lower-level layer N+1 but layer N's response time is too slow, then we have RPCs to layer N running on a single server whose latency is often normal but occasionally is much longer. We want to observe that particular server in more detail. Either the slow RPCs are doing *extra work* that is not normally done or they are doing normal work but *executing slowly*—more slowly than usual.

Doing extra work is based on the branching structure of code and the state that it keeps. Programs vary enormously in how they can end up doing extra work, but they usually have the property that this extra work is done even if the program runs standalone on a server all by itself, with no other programs running. Such performance bugs are relatively easy to find by running the code offline in a test-bed environment, giving it clones or recordings of live traffic requests but running with extra instrumentation to find the errant branching pattern. Running on testing machines allows use of standard performance tools that slow down processing by 2x or even 20x or more. The book by Brendan Gregg [Gregg 2021] discusses many observation tools that are appropriately used in such an environment.

The more interesting case, and the subject of this book, is an RPC doing just the normal work but more slowly than usual. In other words, something is *interfering* with the RPC's normal work on a single server, slowing down its completion. We call these *hindered* transactions. Their delays usually do not occur in offline testing, but instead occur only when running a live user-facing load, often only during the busiest hour of the day. We want to find the source(s) of interference and remove or at least minimize them. Unfortunately, in this live environment, observation tools that slow down processing by 2x or even by 10% are too slow to be used. We need observation techniques and tools with less than 1% overhead if they are to be deployed in live datacenters (or in vehicles or in heavy multiplayer gaming, etc.). There are very few of these available in our industry. Part III of this book introduces one.

Recall that in a datacenter environment, each server runs multiple programs, and each of those programs likely has multiple threads. Interference on a single server must come from something on that server (including incoming and outgoing network traffic). Interference in this environment comes almost exclusively from contention for a shared resource.

1.8   The Five Fundamental Resources

There are only four computer hardware resources shared between unrelated programs running on a single server:

- CPU
- Memory
- Disk/SSD
- Network

If a program has multiple cooperating threads, there is a fifth fundamental resource:

- Software critical section

A critical section is a piece of code that accesses shared data in a way that would not behave correctly if more than one thread does so concurrently. These code sections are protected by software locks so that only one thread at a time may execute them, with any other thread forced to wait to enter the critical section.

To spot interference you need an understanding of normal execution. The starting point is learning how to carefully measure each of the five fundamental resources. The remaining chapters of Part I cover the four hardware resources, but we defer covering software locks to Chapter 27, after we have developed an appropriate observation tool. If a slow RPC is trying to use any of these five resources and some other program or thread is also using it, our RPC will have to wait. This is the fundamental mechanism of interference or hindering.

1.9   Summary

This book is about understanding the dynamics of datacenter, database, desktop, gaming, and dedicated controller software transactions, especially ones that occasionally take much longer than usual. A good programmer can estimate within an order of magnitude how long any piece of code she writes should take and therefore can notice and fix code that is always too slow. We assume in this book that always-slow code has already been fixed. We are interested in the much harder to understand occasionally slow code.

On a datacenter server running thousands of transactions per second, some transactions will be slow occasionally and will be fast if run again. A histogram of transaction times will show a long tail of slow performers, and these will disproportionately affect the overall response times for users and will disproportionately reduce the amount of work a given server can do. These slow transactions are suffering some form of interference, but with heavily layered datacenter software it is often difficult to determine which layer is actually slow for a particular transaction, and it is therefore difficult to know where to look for the interference.

Using order-of-magnitude estimates such as those in Table 1.1 can guide you in identifying likely sources or mechanisms for a performance bug, but usually cannot pin down the exact piece of slow code. For that, we will need to design in proper observation tools for layered software and for servers running many unrelated programs that can interfere with each other.

Overall, a transaction on a single server is either executing normally, executing slowly, or waiting for something on that server. The last two are caused by interference. We will explore the mechanisms for these last two and explore how to observe them *in situ*.

That's it. To solve occasionally slow transaction performance problems, all we have to do is (i) identify which layer of code is slow and then (ii) identify what is interfering with it and then (iii) fix that. The rest of this book is devoted to learning how to do these three simple steps. Unfortunately, the first two are hard.

- We focus on understanding occasionally slow RPC transactions.
- For 100 RPCs done in parallel, the 99th percentile slowest time sets the *overall* response time.
- Datacenter software is rife with execution skew—a long tail of substantially slower responses.
- Slower or hindered transactions mean that something is interfering with the RPC.
- Interference comes from sharing the five fundamental resources.
- Interference is hard to observe *in situ*; we will build some missing observation tools.
- Be sure to do order-of-magnitude estimates of expected times to more easily spot unexpected ones.

Chapter 2

Measuring CPUs

In this chapter and the following ones, you will learn how to measure each of the four fundamental hardware resources on x86 processors running Linux and using the gcc compiler, as described in Appendix A. The ideas here carry over to other processors and other software environments, but the numbers will vary somewhat.

Rather than encouraging you to just memorize Table 1.1 from Chapter 1, we will actively measure most of those values on computers you use. Along the way, you will learn the basics of designing measurements and also learn something about the subtleties of modern computers. When we are done, you will have a stronger underpinning for estimating how much time various pieces of code should take. These chapters also allow readers of varying backgrounds to fill in a few gaps in their knowledge of computers and software.

The first fundamental resource to measure is CPU time—how long real computer instructions take. A simple measurement of how long an add instruction takes is surprisingly subtle. What does "how long" mean in this context?

Modern CPUs can issue one or more instructions every CPU clock cycle, but an individual instruction may take several cycles to complete. If a particular type of instruction can issue every cycle but takes three cycles to produce a result that is available to a subsequent instruction, do we want "long" to mean one cycle or three cycles? Some instructions can take dozens of cycles, and these delay subsequent instructions that need their results. These delays may in fact be the performance problem we are trying to find. So we want "how long" to mean the *latency* of an instruction—the time in CPU clock cycles from issuing the instruction to a subsequent instruction being able to use its result.

If you are not very familiar with the terms *instruction fetch*, *pipelining*, *cache* memory, and (for the next chapter) *virtual memory*, now would be a good time to review a computer architecture textbook, such as Hennessy and Patterson [Hennessy 2017].

2.1 How We Got Here

In the golden age of computing, the 1950s, with CPU clock cycle and *core memory* (see the next chapter) cycle times being identical, simple instructions took two cycles to complete. Cycle 1 fetched and decoded the instruction word from memory, and cycle 2 accessed (read or write) a data word in memory as part of the instruction execution, as shown in Figure 2.1a. A *word* on a popular machine of the time, the IBM 709 [Wikipedia 2020a], was 36 bits.

To speed things up, later machines such as the IBM 7094 II [Wikipedia 2021a] fetched an even-odd pair of instructions from memory at once, with the second held in a temporary instruction register while executing the first. The CPU then executed the second directly without another instruction fetch; thus, two simple instructions executed sequentially one at a time, but in three cycles instead of four, as shown in Figure 2.1b.

Another speedup technique had two or more independent core memory units, arranged so that the execution of instruction N could be overlapped with the fetch of instruction N+1 if they were accessing different memory units.

With the advent of transistors, CPU cycle times got faster, but core memory access times did not. To speed up processing, the CPU and memory clocks were decoupled, with the CPU running faster and each memory reference taking multiple CPU cycles. At the same time, more registers were added inside the CPU so that some instructions could do register-to-register operations that did not need to wait for a data access in memory, as shown in Figure 2.1c with a register write done in the last CPU cycle. Instructions with complex processing, such as `multiply`, could take several execution cycles before writing a result, as shown in Figure 2.1d.

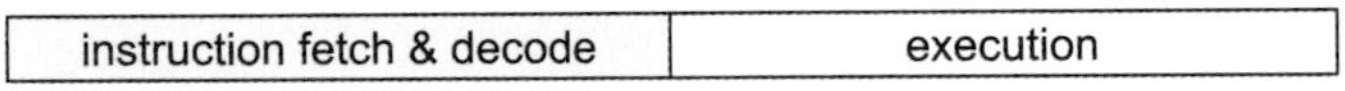

instruction fetch & decode	execution

Figure 2.1a   **Simple fetch/execute in two CPU cycles**

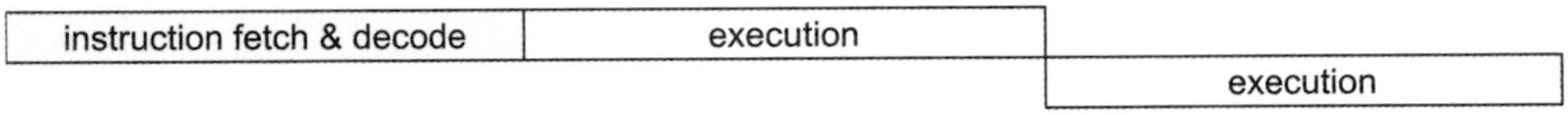

instruction fetch & decode	execution
	execution

Figure 2.1b   **Fetch pair and execute each**

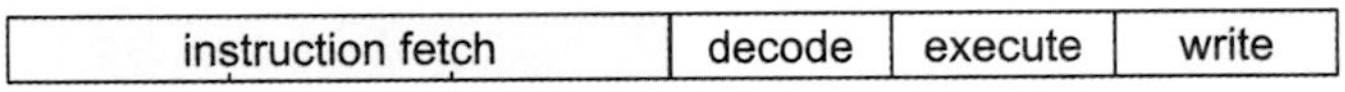

instruction fetch	decode	execute	write

Figure 2.1c   **Fetch/decode/execute/write result in six faster cycles**

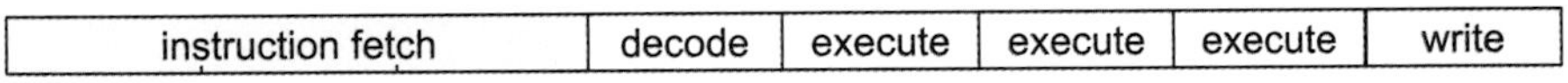

instruction fetch	decode	execute	execute	execute	write

Figure 2.1d   **Multiple execute cycles before write result**

The earliest machine to use many of these ideas was the IBM Stretch (IBM 7030) designed in 1956–1960 and first shipped in 1961 [Wikipedia 2021b]. It was a tour de force in speedup techniques: the first machine with instruction pipelining, multiple execution units, speculative execution beyond conditional branches, multiple (more than three) data registers, and multiple memory banks. It also could pack two instructions per 64-bit word. Its explicit goal was to speed up processing by 100x over the prior IBM 704. This required decoupling CPU cycles from the 6x slower memory access cycles and required multiple memory accesses in parallel. The computer industry is still on this path 60 years later. Stretch itself was slower than promised and too expensive to build, so only nine copies were delivered.

The slightly later CDC 6600 in 1964 [Wikipedia 2021c] was a simpler and faster computer with a CPU cycle time of 100 nsec and a memory cycle time of 1000 nsec, a 10x ratio. Multiple pipelined execution units ran in parallel, with instructions allowed to complete out of order. Up to four instructions could be packed into a single word of 60 bits; there were eight data registers and eight address registers. The 6600 also had a loop buffer that could hold a small loop of 31 instructions entirely inside the CPU, completely avoiding instruction fetches after the first iteration. The 6600 was faster than the Stretch, causing IBM much anguish and driving the launch of the System 360/91 design [Wikipedia 2020b]. You may enjoy reading about the subsequent IBM-CDC litigation and antitrust case [Krohnke 2011].

The Manchester Atlas machine in 1962 [Wikipedia 2021d] was the first commercial machine with paged virtual memory, allowing a small 16K word (48 bits each) physical main memory to be used as though it were a larger 96K-word but somewhat slower memory. Pages of 512 words were moved on demand between main memory and rotating drum. The GE 645 in 1965 [Wikipedia 2020c] was another early paged virtual memory machine, running the Multics operating system developed at MIT. IBM's response to losing this prestigious MIT sale was the IBM 360/67 in 1966 [Wikipedia 2021e] with virtual memory hardware and microcode. The subsequent System/370 machines in 1970 initially shipped with no virtual memory, but that was added (or more precisely, turned on) in 1972.

Using a *translation lookaside buffer* (TLB) to do address mapping from virtual to physical addresses on every memory access initially slowed down CPU cycle times slightly, but it also allowed large programs with large data to run faster than using manual instruction and data overlay I/O techniques of the time for moving bytes between main memory and backing disk or drum. Address mapping also introduced per-page memory protection, allowing multiple programs to run on a single machine but with their memory accesses protected from each other and with all user-mode accesses protected from touching kernel-mode pages. Protection bits could also mark individual pages as no-write or no-execute, increasing program security.

Starting in 1961 as Stretch was finishing, a small IBM team worked on the ACS-1 computer design [Wikipedia 2019a] to explore yet-faster machines. Although it never shipped, many of its innovations are used throughout the industry. One of its main goals was to break the instruction-issue-rate barrier by issuing more than one instruction each clock cycle. Figure 2.2 shows two instructions, A and B, being fetched and executed in parallel starting in the first cycle. This is now called a *superscalar* design. Figure 2.2 also shows instructions C and D starting a cycle later, before the first two have finished, a *pipelined* design. ACS-1 used both techniques.

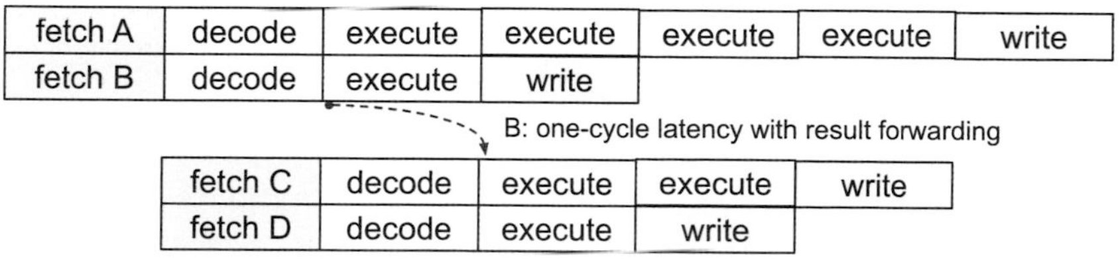

| fetch A | decode | execute | execute | execute | execute | write |
| fetch B | decode | execute | write | | | |

B: one-cycle latency with result forwarding

| fetch C | decode | execute | execute | write |
| fetch D | decode | execute | write | |

Figure 2.2   **Superscalar and pipelined instruction execution**

The final ACS-1 design was capable of having up to seven instructions in flight at once. In 1968 IBM redirected the effort to become System/360-compatible, ACS-360, and that design effort became progressively slower and slower; it was canceled a year later. However, the superscalar design ideas remained and eventually first shipped commercially 22 years later in the 1990 IBM RISC System/6000 [Wikipedia 2021f]. Almost immediately, all other major microprocessor chip designs switched to superscalar, including the 1991 MIPS R4000 [Wikipedia 2021l], the 1992 Digital Equipment Corporation DEC Alpha 21064 [Wikipedia 2021g], and the 1993 Pentium [Wikipedia 2021h].

To further decouple CPU speed from main memory speed, the IBM 360/85 in 1968 [Wikipedia 2020d, Liptay 1968] introduced cache memory, with an 80 nsec cache and 1040 nsec core main memory, an access-time ratio of 13:1. In today's processor chips that ratio is closer to 200:1. The 360/85 was estimated to run at about 0.8 of the speed of a machine with 100% fast 80 nsec main memory, so a small amount of cache memory gave a substantial speedup compared to accessing everything from a 13x slower main memory. (The one-cycle instruction fetch in Figure 2.2 assumes an instruction cache, and the one-cycle write assumes either a register result or a data cache.) The 360/85 had a single-level cache, backed by main memory.

All of these speedup techniques were carried over into microprocessor chip designs throughout the following decades. Today's microprocessor chips have multi-level on-chip caches, typically a pair of small, fast, first-level L1 caches per CPU core—one for instructions L1-Icache and one for data L1-Dcache; a medium-size medium-speed combined instruction+data second-level L2 cache shared across one or more cores; and a larger, slower L3 or last-level cache (LLC) shared across all cores.

With the performance of single CPU cores starting to level off by the late 1990s, the IBM Power4 chip in 2001 [Wikipedia 2021i] introduced multiple (two) CPU cores on a single chip. Each core had its own L1-I and L1-D caches, but they shared lower-level caches. Combined with operating systems that allowed multiple programs and multiple software threads within a program, multiple CPU cores per chip gave more total processing power at relatively low net cost.

Early in the 21st century, *simultaneous multithreading* (SMT or Hyper-Threading Technology, Intel's proprietary name for SMT) was introduced [Wikipedia 2021j]. The Intel Xeon and Pentium 4 processors shipped in 2002 with simultaneous multithreading. There had been earlier designs with SMT in the ACS-360 and Alpha 21464 [Wikipedia 2020e] projects, but they were not brought to market. SMT allows each physical CPU core to have multiple (typically two, four, or eight) program counters (PCs) and associated data/address registers, but only one set of execution units and caches. With only a tiny increase in chip area, SMT fundamentally makes additional instructions available for execution while other instructions are blocked, typically waiting for memory access. A processor core using two program counters (CPU threads) can usually perform 30–50% more total computation than the same core using just one program counter. This allows a single physical core to look like two logical cores, each an average of about 0.7 the speed of the physical one.

2.2   Where Are We Now?

Most modern processor chips now use *all* these speedup techniques:

- CPU and memory clocks decoupled
- Multiple memory banks
- Multiple data registers
- Multiple instructions per word
- Instruction pipelining
- Multiple execution units
- Speculative execution
- Multiple instruction issue
- Out-of-order execution
- Cache memory
- Paged virtual memory
- Simultaneous multithreading

Figure 2.3 shows the overall flow of execution in a fast modern microprocessor, with the instruction-fetching front end on the left, multiple instruction issue slots (the point at which fetched instructions are committed for execution) in the middle, and the execution back end on the right.

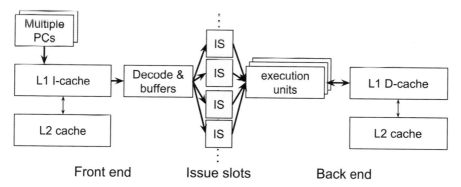

Figure 2.3   **Fast microprocessor CPU core**

As you can see, the instruction execution environment is quite complex, and measuring execution times requires some careful thought. Software that accidentally defeats some of these speedup mechanisms can run unexpectedly slowly, producing performance surprises.

> People who are more than casually interested in computers should have at least some idea of what the underlying hardware is like. Otherwise the programs they write will be pretty weird.—Don Knuth

2.3   Measuring the Latency of an `add` Instruction

Definitions are important here. The *latency of an instruction* is normally defined as the number of CPU cycles from its first "execute" cycle to the first "execute" cycle of a subsequent instruction that uses the result. In Figure 2.2, if instruction B is an `add` instruction and instruction C uses the sum without having to wait, C's first "execute" cycle starts one cycle later than B's first "execute" cycle, so the execution latency of B is *one cycle*. In this case, C's execute cycle overlaps with B's write cycle. Fast hardware implementations accomplish this timing by sending B's result at the end of B's last execute cycle to B's register-result writing hardware and also forwards it directly to C's execution hardware. Slower hardware loses a cycle or two by requiring B's register write to finish before C's read of that register starts. Note that the latency of an instruction usually does not include its fetch and decode time, nor its result-write time (if results are forwarded without losing cycles).

However, the latency of a *branch* instruction is the number of CPU cycles from fetching the instruction to fetching its successor. If the fetch, decode, and conditional-branch decision stages take multiple cycles, these all can appear as part of the branch latency. A branch instruction whose successor is not perfectly predicted by the hardware may have a latency of 3–30 cycles in today's processors, enough that good branch prediction is essential to high performance.

The straightforward approach to measuring the latency of an `add` instruction is to do something like this:

```
Read the time
  Execute an add instruction
Read the time
  Subtract
```

but this fails badly in a modern execution environment. We will explore each step in a bit more detail.

What does "read the time" mean? We would like to count exact CPU cycles so that we calculate a difference of 1 for an `add` instruction that takes one CPU cycle to execute. Some computers have a cycle counter that increments by one each cycle, exactly for this purpose. Other machines have a "cycle" counter that increments only by, for example, 30 once every 30 cycles. Others have a 10 or 32 or 100 MHz counter that does not count cycles at all but counts elapsed time.

The Cray-1 in 1976 [Wikipedia 2021k] had the ideal cycle counter—incrementing by one every CPU cycle and readable in one cycle by user-mode code. That design was carried over to the DEC Alpha 21064 chip in 1992. A year later, a cycle counter was added via the read timestamp counter instruction (RDTSC) in the Pentium P5 chip and then soon appeared across the industry. Reading the cycle counter, doing some work, reading the cycle counter, and subtracting became a normal way to measure elapsed time for pieces of code.

Counting cycles and counting elapsed time are the same thing except for a constant factor. To turn cycles into wall-clock time, one needs to multiply by (pico)seconds per cycle. However, this is true *only* if the cycle rate (clock frequency) remains constant.

CPU clock frequencies were constant for a while in the industry, but with the 2002 advent of power-saving techniques that dynamically slow down the CPU clock, users found that their calculated execution times could vary substantially from actual times, depending on whether power-saving was happening. This led eventually to defining a so-called "constant-rate" time-stamp counter that, for example, always increments by 24 every 10 nsec (i.e., at 100 MHz) on a nominal 2.4 GHz chip instead of incrementing by 1 at 2.4 GHz. Even if that chip is actually running at 800 MHz or is overclocked at 2.7 GHz, the rate remains constant, incrementing by 24 100M times per second. This gives consistent elapsed-time measurements but no longer counts actual CPU cycles. It also decreases the resolution by more than an order of magnitude, from changing the count at 2.4 GHz to changing it at 100 MHz.

Using such a time base, we need to do tens to thousands of cycles of work between RDTSC instructions to get meaningful results, and we need to measure only when the CPU is busy enough to avoid power-saving states. At the execution of an RDTSC, it is unpredictable when the next 10 nsec increment will occur, so there is an inherent 10 nsec ambiguity in each read. To keep the distortion from this less than about 1%, the amount of work between reads needs to be at least 1000 nsec, or about 2400 cycles at 2.4 GHz. So instead of measuring a single add, we need to measure a burst of thousands of them. Something like this

```
Read time
  Execute N adds
Read time
Subtract and divide by N
```

can give a reasonable average time per add, but that time may be far from the single-add latency that we wish to measure. Why is that?

2.4   Straight-Line Code Fail

In a C program, we might do 5,000 adds by having no loop but instead 5,000 lines of straight-line code:

```
sum += 1;
sum += 1;
sum += 1;
sum += 1;
...
```

However, it might well turn out that this sequence does not measure adds at all but instead measures instruction-fetch rate from the instruction cache or memory for 1,000+ sequential instructions or measures time to load and store sum in the first-level data cache.

2.5   Simple Loop, Loop Overhead Fail, Optimizing Compiler Fail

Instead of sequential instructions, more likely we would write a loop

```
start = RDTSC();
for (int n = 0; n < 5000; ++n) {
  sum += 1;
}
delta = RDTSC() - start;
```

and then divide by 5,000. But there are many more instructions than a single add inside the loop—the increment, compare, conditional-branch instructions for the loop counter n.

Take a moment now and write down (just for yourself) your order-of-magnitude estimate of how long you *expect* an add to take: 1, 10, 100, ... cycles.

Now take a look at the flawed measurement program mystery0.cc in Code Sample 2.1.

Code Sample 2.1   **mystery0.cc**

```
// Flawed sample mystery program to measure how long an add takes.
// dick sites 2016.06.25

#include <stdint.h>
#include <stdio.h>
#include <time.h>
#include <x86intrin.h>

static const int kIterations = 1000 * 1000000;

int main (int argc, const char** argv) {
  uint64_t startcy, stopcy;
  uint64_t sum = 0;

  startcy = __rdtsc();                    // starting cycle count
  for (int i = 0; i < kIterations; ++i) { // loop kIterations times
    sum += 1;                             // the add we want to measure
  }
  stopcy = __rdtsc();                     // ending cycle count

  int64_t elapsed = stopcy - startcy;
  double felapsed = elapsed;
  fprintf(stdout, "%d iterations, %lu cycles, %4.2f cycles/iteration\n",
          kIterations, elapsed, felapsed / kIterations);
  return 0;
}
```

It uses the gcc intrinsic (built-in routine) __rdtsc() to read the so-called cycle counter.

Compile and run this via

```
gcc -O0 mystery0.cc -o mystery0
./mystery0
```

and see what you get. The little sample server (see Appendix A) Intel i3 box got

```
1000000000 iterations, 6757688397 cycles, 6.76 cycles/iteration
```

The 6.76 cycles includes time for the loop-overhead code (see Table 2.1). We could try to reduce this by asking the compiler to optimize the loop.

Table 2.1   **Imperfect Measurements of add Time**

Compile	Iterations	Cycles	Cycles/Iteration
gcc -O0 mystery0.cc -o mystery0	1000000000	6757688397	6.76
gcc -O2 mystery0.cc -o mystery0_opt	1000000000	120	0.00

Now compile and run mystery0.cc optimized via

```
gcc -O2 mystery0.cc -o mystery0_opt
./mystery0_opt
```

and see what you get. The sample server box got

```
1000000000 iterations, 120 cycles, 0.00 cycles/iteration
```

What is going on here? The total cycles changed from 6.7 billion to 120!

Code Sample 2.2 is the unoptimized code generated by gcc.

Code Sample 2.2   **mystery0.cc compiled unoptimized**

```
  rdtsc                              read timestamp counter
  salq $32, %rdx                     shift left quadword (64 bits)
  orq %rdx, %rax                     or quadword
  movq %rax, -32(%rbp)               move quadword rax to startcy in memory
  movl $0, -44(%rbp)                 move longword 0 to i in memory (32 bits)

.L4:
  cmpl $999999999, -44(%rbp)         compare i to constant
  jg .L3                             conditional branch greater-than
  addq $1, -40(%rbp)                 sum += 1; sum is in memory at -40(%rbp)
  addl $1, -44(%rbp)                 ++i;        i is in memory at -44(%rbp)
  jmp .L4                            jump to top of loop

.L3:
  rdtsc                              read timestamp counter
  salq $32, %rdx                     shift left quadword
  orq %rdx, %rax                     or quadword
```

The __rdtsc() intrinsic compiles into three instructions rdtsc, salq, orq because of the history of rdtsc starting out in 1993 as a 32-bit instruction that is now used to get a single 64-bit result from two 32-bit pieces. The unoptimized inner loop highlighted at label .L4: has five instructions, three of which access memory by three reads (cmpl, addq, addl) and two writes (addq, addl). So most of what we are measuring is in fact memory accesses, specifically to the L1 data cache. Our actual add is the 64-bit addq instruction.

Now look at the optimized code generated by gcc in Code Sample 2.3.

Code Sample 2.3   **mystery0.cc compiled optimized**

```
rdtsc
movq %rax, %rcx
salq $32, %rdx
orq %rdx, %rcx

rdtsc
pxor %xmm0, %xmm0
movq stdout(%rip), %rdi
salq $32, %rdx
movl $1, %esi
orq %rdx, %rax
```

Where did the loop go? All we have is the two __rdtsc() expansions plus some move and xor instructions that are getting ready for the later fprintf() call.

The gcc optimizer constant-folded all the billion increments of 1 into just a constant result of 1,000,000,000 *pre-calculated* at compile time, effectively:

```
sum = 1000000000;
```

The 120 cycles are just measuring the time between the two rdtsc instructions, keeping in mind that the rdtsc instruction results are all multiples of 39 or some such on our sample server's ~3.9 GHz processor chip.

2.6   Dead Variable Fail

To defeat the optimizer, we could use a constant that the compiler does not know. This little dodge is occasionally handy for that purpose:

```
time_t t = time(NULL);  // The compiler doesn't know t
int incr = t & 255;      // Unknown increment 0..255
```

Unfortunately for our narrow purpose, the gcc compiler *also* optimizes this loop away, effectively into

```
sum = 1000000000 * incr;
```

Even if we turn the sum calculation into something that cannot be easily predicted, the gcc compiler *still* optimizes the loop away. Why?

A standard compiler optimization removes *dead code*—calculations whose result is never used elsewhere in the program. Since sum is never used later, the compiler optimizes away everything that contributes to its calculation, so the loop becomes empty. A second optimization removes code that has no effect, thus deleting the entire loop.

If we really want the compiler to preserve the loop, we can make the sum *live* by using it later, for example by printing it, or by pretending to print it only when time() == 0, since that test is true only when the time is midnight January 1, 1970, the Unix epoch, but the compiler doesn't know that.

```
bool nevertrue = (time(NULL) == 0);
if (nevertrue) {
    fprintf(..., x, y, z);    // Makes x y and z live
}
```

The lesson here is that it is quite easy to construct a measurement program that measures something other than what you think it is measuring—memory access time, compiler smartness, not measuring anything at all, etc. We will see this again in the Chapter 22 Whetstone benchmark.

You have more control over the code being measured when you write directly in assembly language, but we want to measure code written in higher-level compiled languages such as C or C++.

2.7 Better Loop

We can force the compiler to perform the full loop by declaring sum or increment as *volatile*, meaning that its value may change at any time due to shared access by some other code. In this case, the compiler does no constant analysis and always reads and writes the value in its (presumably shared) memory location. This does not fix the problem of also measuring loop overhead, but it helps keep the loop itself around.

To reduce the distortion of the loop overhead, some modest loop unrolling can help, as in Code Sample 2.4. Unrolling four times reduces the effect of the loop overhead by a factor of four.

Code Sample 2.4   **mystery0.cc loop unrolled four times**

```
for (int i = 0; i < kIterations; i += 4) {
    sum += 1;
    sum += 1;
    sum += 1;
    sum += 1;
}
```

To effectively remove the loop overhead, a useful technique is to time two different loops, one with N1 adds inside the loop and one with N2 adds. Subtracting the two times gives a pretty good approximation of the time for N2 – N1 adds, with the loop overhead cancelled out. If you do this, keep N1 and N2 larger than 2, since the compiler may well generate different faster loop code for N=0, 1, or 2. In our current example, unrolling four times and also eight times might be good. Unrolling 10 times and 20 might be incrementally better, unless it causes the loop to no longer fit in a CPU loop buffer or otherwise causes too much instruction-fetch time.

When you are done measuring and have a number like 1.06 cycles per iteration for integer add, keep in mind that real instructions take integer numbers of cycles: 0, 1, 2, 3, . . . CPU cycles. They do not take fractions of a CPU clock cycle. So a result like 1.06 cycles represents an *average* of many iteration times, all of which are integers. A few of these iteration times may well be thousands of cycles instead of single-digit cycles. The long times can come from timer and other interrupts delivered to the CPU core you are running on, from interference by an unrelated program's hyperthread running on the same physical core, or from the operating system scheduler time-slicing your program and running some other program now and then. These effects can be minimized by running on an otherwise idle machine and by constructing your loop to run well under the timer-interrupt interval, which is typically 1..10 msec.

Running for about 1/4 of the timer interrupt interval means that approximately three times out of four when you run the program your measurement loop will not encounter a timer interrupt. It is best to run a few times and take the *fastest* values you observe.

Alternately, running for about 10x the timer interrupt interval means that you likely will see 9, 10, or 11 timer interrupts when you run the program. But if your loop is long and the timer interrupt processing time is short, the overall distortion from the interrupts can be quite small.

2.8 Dependent Variables

Are we there yet? Not quite. Remember that we started out interested in measuring the latency of an add instruction, the time from issuing the instruction to its results being available to a subsequent instruction. Consider how Code Sample 2.5 differs from Code Sample 2.4.

Code Sample 2.5   **mystery0.cc loop unrolled four times, with some result dependencies removed**

```
for (int i = 0; i < kIterations; i += 4) {
  sum += 1;
  sum2 += 1;
  sum += 1;
  sum2 += 1;
}
```

It uses two independent sums. This means on a superscalar CPU that the first two add instructions could issue simultaneously in one cycle, and the next pair one or more cycles later. A billion of these pairs might take 500,000,000 cycles, giving an average add (issue) time of 0.5 cycle. Note that an average time of 0.5 cycle on a multi-issue machine does not mean that an individual add takes half a cycle—it means that some adds take one cycle and due to overlap the others effectively take zero additional cycles. In any case, all we are measuring is issue time, not execution latency. If these were divide or multiply operations, they might issue at the same rate, even though those instructions likely have long execution latencies.

2.9 Actual Execution Latency

To measure execution latency instead of issue rate, we need to make sure that each measured instruction is *dependent* on the result of the previous one. We did this without thinking much when we started, but it is important to do this explicitly.

An aggressive optimizing compiler can reorder computations for associative operators, such as integer add and multiply. Consider the loop in Code Sample 2.6.

Code Sample 2.6 **Unrolled product loop**

```
volatile uint64_t incr0 = ...;
uint64_t prod = 1;
for (int i = 0; i < kIterations; i += 4) {
    prod *= incr0;
    prod *= incr1;
    prod *= incr2;
    prod *= incr3;
}
```

You might expect the inner loop to do four dependent multiplies, each using the previous result

```
prod = (((prod * incr0) * incr1) * incr2) * incr3;
```

but in fact gcc -O2 for 64-bit x86 by default rearranges this into

```
temp = ((incr0 * incr1) * incr2) * incr3;
prod = prod * temp;
```

The difference is that the temp calculation is a loop constant. Only the final `prod = prod * temp` depends on the previous iteration. With multi-issue and instruction pipelining, the sample server CPU hardware can in fact keep at least four iterations of the loop in flight at once, with the multiplies overlapped. So long as the actual integer multiply latency is 4 cycles or less, the effective execution time of one iteration of four multiplies can be 4 cycles, giving a misleadingly fast apparent multiply time of 1 cycle.

2.10 More Nuance

To defeat this rewriting of the calculation, you may need to use the obscure gcc `-fno-tree-reassoc` command-line flag. Doing so on the sample server produces a more accurate timing of three cycles per multiply, which is still impressively (to me) fast.

Finally, consider the actual data values that participate in your measurements. Some data values might be implemented in especially fast or especially slow ways that are not representative of "ordinary" computation. For example, adding 0, multiplying by 0 or 1 or –1, or dividing by 1 or –1 could all be implemented especially quickly or even suppressed if the answer is constant (think A * 0). At the other end of the performance scale, some loops may produce overflowed or underflowed floating-point results whose subsequent use continues but is handled by 10x slower microcode paths instead of direct hardware.

Here are the instruction measurements I made on a sample server:

```
gcc -O2  -fno-tree-reassoc mystery1_all.cc -o mystery1_all_opt
  addq 1000000000 iterations, 1136134399 cycles, 1.14 cycles/iteration
  mulq 1000000000 iterations, 3012984427 cycles, 3.01 cycles/iteration
  divq 1000000000 iterations, 31808957519 cycles, 31.81 cycles/iteration
  fadd 1000000000 iterations, 4025330656 cycles, 4.03 cycles/iteration
  fmul 1000000000 iterations, 4022046375 cycles, 4.02 cycles/iteration
  fdiv 1000000000 iterations, 14576505981 cycles, 14.58 cycles/iteration
```

2.11 Summary

We set out to measure the execution time of a simple add instruction. But to do so we had to explore time bases, loop overhead, compiler optimization, and the overriding issue of measuring what we think we are measuring, not something completely different. We learned a little about loop unrolling, dead code, dependent calculation, and carefully defining the instruction latency start/end points that we want to measure. We learned a little along the way about the complexity of modern microprocessor speedup techniques.

Some software performance issues are imaginary, revealed by mistaken measurements. Others are real but hidden by mistaken measurements. That is the reason for our emphasis throughout this book on making estimates in your head of expected performance and comparing observations to those expectations.

Measuring the speed of an individual instruction will not directly help us in investigating transactions that are slow by tens or hundreds of milliseconds, but the measurement design issues encountered here will recur in the upcoming more complex software environments.

- Choose your time base carefully and understand its limitations.

- Estimate what you expect to see.

- Compare your measurements against expectations.

- There is always learning in the discrepancies.

- Software that accidentally defeats some chip speedup mechanism can run unexpectedly slowly.

Exercises

In these exercises, "explain" means "Write just a sentence or two describing what you believe is happening." It does not mean "Write three or four paragraphs of detail and philosophy that will not be read in their entirety by someone who is grading 25 papers of 10 such answers each."

In these exercises, when giving numeric answers, do not give excess precision such as 1.062735591. Instead, give about three digits of precision: 1.06 or 1.063. Your measurements will not be more accurate or more repeatable than this anyway. When giving order-of-magnitude estimates, round values less than 3.16 (10**0.5) down to 1 and above 3.16 up to 10. If you feel strongly inclined, use half-order-of-magnitudes and round midrange numbers to 3.

2.1 If you have not already, write down your estimate of the latency in cycles for an add instruction: 0.1, 1, 10, 100. Even if you are uncomfortable estimating something you know nothing about, you will soon realize that you can bound the possibilities to only about three or four reasonable values. Pick one of them and then go back and look at Table 1.1 in Chapter 1.

2.2 Compile and run mystery1.cc both unoptimized –O0 and optimized –O2. Explain the differences.

2.3   Uncomment the last `fprintf` in mystery1.cc and run again both –O0 and –O2. Explain any changes or lack of change.

2.4   Declare the variable `incr` in mystery1.cc as volatile and run again both –O0 and –O2. Explain any changes or lack of change.

2.5   Make your own copy of mystery1.cc and modify it along the lines discussed in this chapter to give a reasonable measurement of the latency in cycles of a 64-bit integer add. Write down your numeric answer.

2.6   Experiment with the number of loop iterations in your mystery1.cc: 1, 10, 100, . . . 1000000000. Explain why some values do not produce meaningful results.

2.7   Write down your order-of-magnitude estimates of the latency in cycles for 64-bit integer multiply and divide and double-precision floating-point add, multiply, and divide. You actually know these. For example, multiplies are likely to consume at least one bit of multiplicand per cycle, so are unlikely to take more than 64 cycles plus a little startup time. Similarly, divides are likely to produce at least one bit of quotient per cycle. Either may in fact process 2, 3, or 4 bits per cycle.

2.8   Add code to your mystery1.cc to measure the latency of 64-bit integer multiply and divide and double-precision add, multiply, and divide. Write down the five numeric answers. You might want to reduce the number of loop iterations by 10x or so, based on what you learned in Exercise 2.6. For the floating-point calculations, keep your data values away from the extremes of overflow/underflow, but also not exactly 1.0 or 0.0.

2.9   (Optional) Deliberately have your double-precision multiply and divide loops above drift into overflow and underflow ranges for the data values (i.e., larger than $10^{**}306$ or less than $1/10^{**}306$ for IEEE double-precision), printing out the observed latency perhaps every 10,000 iterations. If the cycle latencies suddenly change, explain what is going on.

Chapter 3

Measuring Memory

In the previous chapter, we explored measuring CPU performance, the first of the four fundamental hardware resources.

The second fundamental resource to measure is memory access latency—how long do real computer reads and writes take, for each level of the memory hierarchy? A simple measurement of the latency of a single data load is even more subtle than the measurement of arithmetic instructions. The goal in this chapter is to measure the size and organization of the typical four-level memory subsystem in modern machines.

3.1 Memory Timing

This is the most complex topic in Part I. We will examine several design layers, each with its own concepts and constraints. Because main memory is so much slower than CPUs, modern processors have many speedup mechanisms. Like the girl with a curl on her forehead, when they are good they are very, very good, and when they are bad they are horrid [Longfellow 1904]. Sometimes software will have memory access *patterns* that defeat the speedup mechanisms or cause them to do substantial unneeded work, producing bad performance. At the end of this chapter, you will have a much better understanding of today's complex computer memory systems.

Many different design layers interact to produce memory access patterns and to deliver data with varying amounts of delay. These layers include

- C programmer
- Compiler
- Assembly language
- CPU instructions
- Virtual memory
- Several levels of cache memory
- Main-memory DRAMs

Our two sample-server processors (Appendix A) have an Intel i3 chip and an AMD Ryzen chip, each with three levels of cache on chip and 8GB of *dynamic random-access memory* (DRAM) off chip in two *dual-inline memory modules* (DIMMs). Each i3 chip has two physical cores hyper-threaded to present the illusion of four cores. Each Ryzen processor chip has four physical cores. For both chips, each physical core has a dedicated L1 instruction cache and dedicated L1 data cache, plus a dedicated L2 combined cache. Each processor has a single L3 cache shared across all cores.

A datacenter server processor will have more complex chips with more cache and may have multiple processor chips per server. A desktop or embedded processor may have smaller and simpler caches. However, the measurements done here can also be performed on other processors. Along the way, you will learn more about memory hierarchies, and that in turn will inform your work on understanding software performance.

3.2   About Memory

As you recall from the previous chapter, in the 1950s golden age of computing simple instructions took two cycles to execute, one for instruction fetch and one for instruction execution that typically included a single memory access for data. This made sense when the CPU clock cycle time and core memory access times were identical.

At that time, main memories were constructed from ferrite cores (little 0.4mm iron-oxide donuts) with wires going through the holes (Figure 3.1), one core per bit of memory. Pulsing a positive current spike through a core magnetized it clockwise, and a negative spike magnetized it counterclockwise. The magnetization remained forever with no power supplied, providing a way to remember a single bit: 0 for one magnetic direction and 1 for the other.

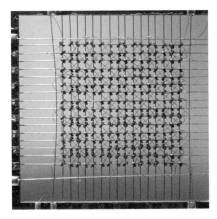

Figure 3.1   **Ferrite core memory [Wikimedia 2010]**

Memories were arranged as words, not bytes (byte addressing arrived in 1964 [Amdahl 1964]). Depending on the computer, a word might be 36 bits or 48 or some other number. Core memories were physically arranged as a dense plane of wires and cores for a single bit of each memory word: all bit<0> cores for all memory words in one plane, all bit<1> cores in another plane, etc. A number of these planes were then stacked together to make a complete memory. For example, the IBM 7090 had 32K words of memory, each 36 bits. The 36 planes each contained 32,768 cores (there was no parity or *error correction code*, ECC).

Reading was done by pulsing a horizontal and a vertical wire in each plane to drive all the cores in a word to zero and then looking at the resulting electrical waveforms via the diagonal threaded sense wire to see if each addressed core switched magnetic state. If so, it had been a 1, and if not, it had been a 0. The readout was thus *destructive*. After reading, the bits read were then always *restored*—written back into the just-zeroed cores. Core memory cycle times for read + restore ran from 10 usec down to about 1 usec.

In 1964, John Schmidt at Fairchild Semiconductor invented the transistorized *static random-access memory* (SRAM) [ChipsEtc 2020a, Schmidt 1965, Schmidt 1964]. With six transistors per bit, SRAM is fast but somewhat expensive. With no magnetic state, the data in an SRAM disappears when power is removed.

The very first cache memory, in the 1968 IBM 360/85, was SRAM, called *monolithic memory* in the IBM papers [Liptay 1968] of the time.

Just two years after SRAM, Robert Dennard at IBM invented the dynamic random-access memory (DRAM) in 1966 [ChipsEtc 2020b, Wikipedia 2021m]. With just one transistor per bit, DRAM is much denser (and therefore cheaper) than SRAM, but slower to access.

In September 1970, the IBM System 370/145 was announced [IBM 1970]—the first commercial machine to switch to solid-state DRAM main memory, using IBM's internally manufactured chips. The following month, Intel introduced the first commercially available dynamic random-access memory chip, the Intel 1103 DRAM (Figure 3.2), created by William Regitz and Joel Karp [Wikipedia 2020f]. By 1972 it was the best-selling semiconductor memory chip in the world—leading to the demise of core memory. (SRAM was too expensive to displace 1970s core memory.)

Figure 3.2   **DRAM memory [Wikimedia 2016]**

As in core memory, DRAM reading is destructive. Each read drains charge from the single storage transistor per bit, and the bits read are then written back to those transistors. Unlike SRAM memory, DRAM bits leak away after several milliseconds even with power supplied. DRAMs thus need to have every location *refreshed*—read and re-written—every 2 msec or so.

The performance of these various memory technologies interacts with programs' access patterns to provide varying execution performance. This chapter covers measuring elements of a processor's memory hierarchy, and the next chapter covers changing access patterns to take advantage of this hierarchy to speed up execution, or more often to avoid patterns that severely slow down execution.

3.3 Cache Organization

Today's datacenter CPUs have a *memory hierarchy* consisting of several layers of cache memory plus a very large main memory, as shown in Figure 3.3. Each physical CPU core in a multicore processor chip has its own Level-1 instruction (L1i) and data (L1d) caches, each built out of very fast SRAM cells. These caches can usually access a new memory word or even two words every CPU cycle, with cycle times now around 0.3 nsec, about 250 times faster than the original 80 nsec cache in the IBM 360/85. Main memory cycle times have increased only by about a factor of 20 over the same time period.

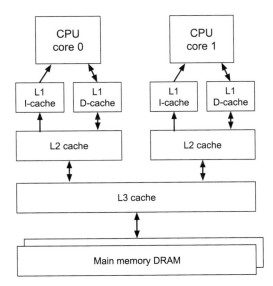

Figure 3.3 **Typical multi-level cache memory organization for two CPU cores**

Level-1 instruction and data caches typically are filled from a larger but slower combined Level-2 (L2) cache, sometimes one per physical CPU core, as in Figure 3.3, and sometimes shared across a few CPU cores. In turn, the Level-2 caches are filled from a larger and slower Level-3 (L3) cache that is on-chip and shared across all the cores. Some processors may even have a Level-4 cache.

A single large cache level would be best if it could be simultaneously fast enough, big enough, and shared enough. Unfortunately, that isn't possible since semiconductor memory access times always get longer as the memory size gets bigger. Modern cache designs thus represent an engineering balance that delivers high performance with relatively low cost, *so long as the memory-access patterns include a fair number of repeated accesses to the same locations*. Over time, the details of this balance will change, but the general picture may not.

With L1 caches able to start one or two new low-latency accesses every CPU cycle and each bank of main memory systems unable to start a new access more often than about every 50–100 CPU cycles, the placement of data and instructions in the cache hierarchy has a huge effect on overall CPU performance. Some patterns are very, very good, while others are horrid.

Cache memory is organized as *lines* (or blocks) of several bytes each, with all the bytes of a line brought into or moved out of the cache together. Each cache line has an associated *tag* specifying the main memory address for its data (shown at the top of Figure 3.4). To find data in a cache, the cache hardware compares the memory address involved against one or more tags. If a match is found, termed a cache *hit*, the corresponding data is accessed quickly. If no match is found, termed a cache *miss*, the data must be accessed more slowly from a lower level of the memory hierarchy.

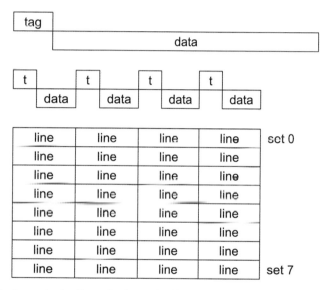

Figure 3.4 **Cache organization: single cache line (top), a four-way associative cache set with four cache lines (middle), cache with eight sets, each four-way, tags not shown (bottom)**

The minimum useful amount of data per cache line is two machine words, with a word most often the size of a pointer; this means for chips with 64-bit addresses, that two 8-byte pointers or 16 bytes total is the minimum practical cache line size. Smaller lines would spend too much hardware on tags and not enough on data. The maximum useful line size is one page in a virtual memory system, which means 4KB in most current chips. Thus, the only reasonable cache-line data sizes are

16, 32, 64, 128, 256, 512, 1024, 2048, and 4096 bytes

The most common choices in the industry are 64 and 128 bytes, but 32 and 256 bytes are sometimes seen. (The first cache in the IBM 360/85 had sixteen 1KB cache sectors and hence only 16 tags, but filled them in pieces by transferring 64-byte subblocks/sublines from main memory.)

In a *fully associative* cache, data at a given main memory address can be stored in any line in the cache. To find which one, the memory address is compared against *all* the tags in the cache. For a 32KB cache with 64B lines, this means comparing against all 512 tags at once—a lot of fast hardware. If one tag matches, then the corresponding line's data are quickly accessed. If none matches, the data are accessed from a slower memory, typically also doing a *fill*—replacing some cache line so that a subsequent access to the same or nearby data will hit. (If more than one tag matches, there is a serious hardware bug.)

In contrast, a *direct-mapped* cache allows data at a given main memory address to be stored in exactly one possible cache line, usually chosen by low memory address bits to spread successive memory locations around the cache as much as possible. Direct-mapped caches perform poorly whenever two frequently accessed data items map to the same cache line: each access to one item removes the other one from the cache, so alternating accesses *thrash* the cache with 100% misses to slower memory.

A middle-ground design is the *set-associative* cache [Conti 1969]. Data at a given main memory address are stored in exactly one possible set of N cache lines for an N-way associative cache. Within each set, the memory address is compared against all the N tags. Typical values of N range from 2 to 16. In a four-way set-associative cache, each set contains four cache lines, as shown in the middle of Figure 3.4. Caches often have 2^k sets so that the set selection can be done directly with low memory address bits; otherwise, some simple *hash* of the memory address is used to select the set. The bottom of Figure 3.4 shows a small four-way associative cache with eight sets total. For simplicity, the 32 tags are not shown. Three address bits are used to select the set, and then all four tags in that set are compared to the memory address being accessed. Note that sequential memory accesses would land within a cache line in some set and then move down, not sideways, in this picture to a line in the next set—for example, first accessing a line in set 0, then a line in set 1, etc. This design spreads sequential accesses across all sets. Common set-associative caches have 64 or more sets.

3.4   Data Alignment

In the following discussion, the term *aligned* is prominent. An *aligned* reference to a 4-byte item is at a byte address that is a multiple of 4. An aligned reference to an 8-byte item is at a byte address that is a multiple of 8, etc. Actual cache and memory accesses are done only in aligned quantities. Unaligned references are done by accessing two aligned locations and doing some byte shifting and merging to select the referenced bytes. When done in hardware, unaligned references are often a few cycles slower than aligned accesses. If done in a software unaligned-access-trap routine, unaligned references often take 100 cycles or more.

3.5   Translation Lookaside Buffer Organization

In addition to caches for instructions and data, modern processors provide virtual memory mapping and have *translation lookaside buffers* (TLBs) to hold frequently used virtual-to-physical mappings. In some cases, TLBs are constructed as a small Level-1 TLB per CPU core and a larger slower Level-2 TLB, either per core or shared across several cores. All this mechanism increases speed but also adds complexity and variability to CPU performance.

TLBs and cache designs interact. Most caches are *physically addressed*, meaning that set selection and tag values are from physical memory addresses, after translation from virtual addresses. The alternate design of *virtually addressed* cache is occasionally used, with set selection and tag values taken from the unmapped virtual address. This design has difficulties if two distinct virtual addresses map to the same physical address, since the different virtual addresses would map to different cache lines. Such duplicate mappings are not a problem if the data are read-only (such as instruction streams), but are an issue if data is written via one virtual address and then read via a different virtual address.

With a physically addressed cache bigger than one page, the virtual-to-physical mapping must be completed before cache tag comparisons can be started, and tag comparisons must be completed before cached data can be accessed by the CPU. These steps usually use the fastest possible hardware for L1 cache accesses, so can take noticeable amounts of power and chip area. To gain some speed, it is common to use unmapped lower-order virtual address bits to choose the right cache set before the virtual-to-physical mapping is completed. The number of unmapped low-order address bits thus determines the maximum size of a fast L1 cache—one of the under-appreciated costs of small pages.

Cache set choice based on unmapped address bits works only if the number of sets is small enough. For example, with a 4KB page, the low-order 12 address bits are unmapped. With a 64-byte cache line, the six lowest bits select a byte within a line, so at most the other six unmapped bits are available to select a cache set, so exactly 64 sets maximum. If the L1 cache is direct-mapped, it can be at most 64 sets of *one* line each, or 4KB total. If it is four-way associative, it can be at most 64 sets of *four* lines each or 16KB total. In general, overlapping the time for address mapping and tag access works only if the maximum L1 set-associative **cache size is less than or equal to pagesize * associativity.**

This unfortunate coupling means that small page sizes such as 4KB require small L1 caches. Eventually, the industry will need to move to larger page sizes, with more unmapped bits and hence an opportunity for modestly larger L1 caches. For a datacenter machine with 256GB of main-memory RAM, managing it as 4KB pages means there are *64 million* pages of main memory, an excessively large number. It would be better and faster to have a somewhat larger page size and fewer total pages.

3.6   The Measurements

It is possible to look up in (often obscure) manufacturer literature such as a chip datasheet what the actual cache organization is for a given processor, but we want to find out via programs that can run on a wide variety of machines.

In this chapter we seek to measure the performance of each layer of the memory hierarchy and in the process gain some insight to the dynamics of single and multiple instruction threads as they compete for shared memory resources. Our objective is for you to learn techniques to tease out memory performance characteristics so that you can better understand and estimate program performance and better understand what is happening when access patterns defeat the speedup normally provided by a cache hierarchy.

Our measurement will be done in three steps, the first two of which are done in the supplied mystery2.cc program:

1. Determine the cache line size.

2. Determine the total size of each level of cache.

3. Determine the associativity of each layer of cache.

As with measuring instruction latency in the previous chapter, the straightforward approach to measuring memory parameters is to do something like

1. Read time.

2. Access memory in some pattern.

3. Read time.

4. Subtract.

However, this is tricky in a modern execution environment. We will explore each step in a little more detail.

For concreteness, the details in the following discussion are based on a sample server (Appendix A) with a representative processor, the Intel i3. Other processors have similar memory hierarchies but the speeds, sizes, and organization may differ.

3.7   Measuring Cache Line Size

How can we have a program discover the cache line size? There are several design choices and several available dead-ends. One choice is to start with a cache containing *none* of the data we are about to access, load an aligned word at location X, and then load the word at X + c, where c is a possible cache line size.

If X is aligned on a cache line boundary and c is less than the line size, loading X + c will hit in the cache because it was brought in as part of a single cache line when X was brought in. Figure 3.5 shows twelve sequential accesses and where they land in the four-way eight-set cache of Figure 3.4. In Figure 3.5a, c is 1/4 of the line size, so the first four accesses are in the same line, the next four in the next line, etc. The twelve accesses thus cover three cache lines and therefore encounter just three misses. In Figure 3.5b, c is 1/2 of the line size, so pairs of accesses are in the same line, encountering six cache misses total for our twelve accesses. In Figures 3.5c and 3.5d, all twelve accesses miss.

If X is aligned on a cache line boundary and c is greater than or equal to the line size, then loading X + c will not hit in the cache. Assuming that cache misses are on the order of 10 times slower than cache hits, we can time a loop doing a few hundred loads to different possible increments (*strides*) and distinguish those values of c that are fast and those that are slow. *The smallest slow c is the cache line size.*

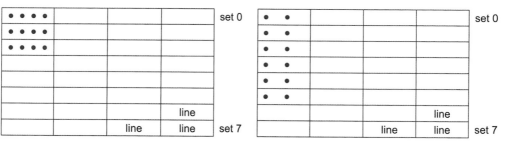

Figure 3.5a   **Accesses spaced 1/4 of a cache line apart and therefore landing in three lines in three successive sets**

Figure 3.5b   **Spaced 1/2 a cache line apart, landing in six lines in three sets**

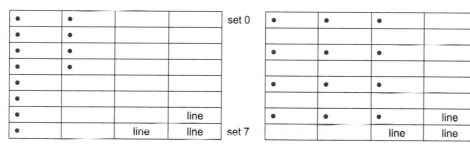

Figure 3.5c   **Spaced one cache line apart, landing in twelve lines across the eight sets but with multiple lines in some sets**

Figure 3.5d   **Spaced two cache lines apart, landing in twelve lines across just four sets, three lines per set of the four-way associative choices**

What would we expect to see? It is an important professional design discipline to ask this question at this point in your thought process and to *write down or sketch for yourself* what you expect. Only then can you react quickly to finding something quite different. Assume for a moment that the real cache line size is 128 bytes. For accesses to an array of items spaced 16 bytes apart (a stride of 16), the first eight items all fit into one cache line, the second eight into another, etc. If we fetched 200 consecutive items, we would expect to see 200/8 = 25 cache misses. If instead we access stride-32 items, we would expect to see 200/4 = 50 cache misses. For stride-128 items and greater, we would expect to see 200 cache misses every time. If we sketch a graph of the time per access (load), we might expect something like Figure 3.6, where the *average* time per load starts out as 1/8 the real miss time, then 1/4, then 1/2, then all the rest are the real miss time, 100% misses.

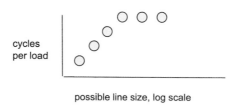

possible line size, log scale

Figure 3.6   **Sketch of expected access times vs. stride**

3.8 Problem: N+1 Prefetching

This sequential-stride design choice of using addresses X, X + c, X + 2c, ... sounds good but turns out to be too simplistic. Modern caches often *prefetch* line N + 1 when line N is accessed, removing all but the first cache miss in our access pattern. Also, modern CPUs do out-of-order execution, launch multiple instructions per CPU cycle, and may well have 5–50 outstanding loads waiting in parallel for memory responses. The effect can be to make many cache misses take about the same time as just one miss, reducing the apparent miss time by over a factor of 10.

The supplied program mystery2.cc implements this choice of sequential-stride accesses in the routine NaiveTiming(), so you can see that it gives uniformly misleading results that are too fast. The inner loop accesses 16-byte items spaced pairstride apart. The caller varies the stride, clearing the cache between calls by loading 40MB of unrelated data. I picked 40MB because it is somewhat larger than the largest expected cache size of 32MB. This number may have to be increased for future chips with larger caches. Nothing here attempts to defeat prefetching or parallel misses. See Code Sample 3.1.

Code Sample 3.1 **Naive load loop**

```
// We will read and write these 16-byte pairs, allocated at different strides
struct Pair {
  Pair* next;
  int64 data;
};

int64 NaiveTiming(uint8* ptr, int bytesize, int bytestride) {
  const Pair* pairptr = reinterpret_cast<Pair*>(ptr);
  int pairstride = bytestride / sizeof(Pair);
  int64 sum = 0;

  // Try to force the data we will access out of the caches
  TrashTheCaches(ptr, bytesize);

  // Load 256 items spaced by stride
  // May have multiple loads outstanding; may have prefetching
  // Unroll 4 times to attempt to reduce loop overhead in timing
  uint64 startcy = __rdtsc();
  for (int i = 0; i < 256; i += 4) {
    sum += pairptr[0 * pairstride].data;
    sum += pairptr[1 * pairstride].data;
    sum += pairptr[2 * pairstride].data;
    sum += pairptr[3 * pairstride].data;
    pairptr += 4 * pairstride;
  }
  uint64 stopcy = __rdtsc();
  int64 elapsed = stopcy - startcy;      // Cycles

  // Make sum live so compiler doesn't delete the loop
  if (nevertrue) {
```

```
        fprintf(stdout, "sum = %ld\n", sum);
    }
    return (elapsed >> 8);                // Cycles per one load
}
```

3.9 Dependent Loads

Another design choice is to build a linked list of items in memory, with each item the size of a possible cache line and aligned on a cache line boundary. Each item contains a pointer to the next sequential item, as shown in Figure 3.7a. Then if `ptr` points to the first item, a loop of `ptr = ptr->next` will do a series of loads, but the address for each load depends on the value fetched by the previous load, so they must be executed strictly sequentially, defeating out-of-order execution, multiple instructions per CPU cycle, and multiple parallel outstanding loads. This design also allows us to see how long the load-to-use latency is for each level of the memory subsystem.

The supplied program mystery2.cc implements this choice in the routine `LinearTiming()`, so you can see that it gives better but also misleading results. One remaining problem is that the linked lists do not defeat cache prefetching.

To attempt to defeat prefetching, we can build the linked lists so that the items are scrambled around in the address space, as shown in Figure 3.7b.

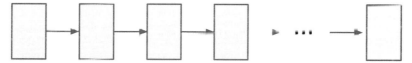

Figure 3.7a   **Linear list of items**

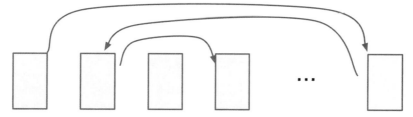

Figure 3.7b   **Scrambled list of Items**

This helps but is not sufficient. When the leftmost scrambled item is in fact the line size, fetching it may still cause the hardware to prefetch the next-to-leftmost item. Even though this item is not accessed immediately, it will be accessed later and can therefore be a hit when we are hoping the design produces a miss.

3.10   Non-random Dynamic Random-Access Memory

It turns out there is another complication. We count cache misses by timing a few hundred memory loads and expect twice as many misses to take about twice as long. But when you look at main memory DRAM designs, you find a surprise. Access times are not random (in spite of "random" in the name). Actual DRAM chips first *access a row* of a big array of bits inside the chip and then *access a column* of bytes from that row. A so-called *precharge cycle* precedes the row access, to set the internal data lines to about half the power-supply voltage, so that reading only a little charge in a bit cell is enough to get the data lines off dead center quickly. Sense amplifiers within the chip quickly drive these small read changes to full zero or one voltage levels. Each of the precharge, row access, and column access cycles takes about 15 nsec.

Rows are typically 1,024 bytes, and a dual inline memory module (DIMM, memory card) typically has eight DRAM chips cycled in parallel to produce eight bytes at once, driving an 8-byte-wide memory bus to the CPU chip. In this case, the effective row size across the eight DRAM chips is 8 *1,024 = 8,192 bytes. A CPU with two memory buses connected to two DIMMs usually stores successive cache lines in alternating DIMMs to achieve a 2x bandwidth improvement when accessing multiple sequential cache lines. In this case, the effective row size is 2 * 8KB = 16KB. Our sample server has this organization.

If two successive accesses to a DRAM are in two different rows, the sequence

```
precharge, row access, column access
```

occurs for each. But if the second access is to the *same* row as the first one, the CPU and DRAM hardware implement a shortcut; just the

```
column access
```

occurs for the second one. This is approximately three times faster than the full sequence. A 3x variation in memory access time is a large amount of distortion if we are trying to measure a 2x difference in total time. So we may also have to defeat the DRAM shortcut timing.

We do this when building the linked lists by flipping the 16KB address bit in *every other* list item, explicitly putting successive items into different DRAM rows. In the supplied mystery2.cc program, routine MakeLongList(), this is the purpose of the variable extrabit.

The supplied program mystery2.cc implements all this in the routine ScrambledTiming(), so you can see that it gives better results that finally look a bit like our earlier sketch. There are a few more details to consider in the exercises at the end of this chapter.

In Figure 3.8 we see one set of results. Your results will differ somewhat. The scrambled cycles per load shows the expected approximate doubling per 2x stride change, flattening off at about 200 cycles for stride 128 bytes and above. The actual line size is 64 bytes, but even our scrambled measurement did not completely defeat the cache prefetcher(s) and same-row DRAM access optimization. The linear measurement is distorted by prefetching all the way out to 512 byte stride, while the naive measurement is not measuring load latency at all. The extra cycles at stride 4,096 bytes most likely reflect 100% TLB misses.

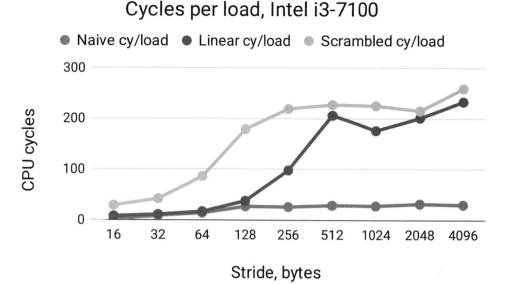

Figure 3.8 **Cycles per load for different strides and different measurement techniques. Compare to the sketch in Figure 3.6.**

Virtual-to-physical address mapping means that all the pictures in our heads about cache layout are too simplistic. The physical addresses that the caches see match our pictures only for the low-order 12 address bits —all the higher physical address bits are unpredictable, adding noise to most of our measurements and making timing changes less sharp.

3.11 Measuring Total Size of Each Cache Level

Once we have the cache line size, we next want to know for each level of the cache hierarchy how big it is. The total size of the L1 cache informs data structure designs that have working sets that likely fit into the L1 cache and hence are faster than designs that don't fit. The same consideration applies to L2 and L3.

Our strategy for finding the size of each cache level is to read N bytes into the cache and then reread, looking at timings. If all N bytes fit in the cache, then the rereads will be fast. If the bytes don't fit, then some or all of the rereads will miss and be filled from the next level down, assuming (as is always the case) that each level is bigger than the previous one. In contrast to the previous section, where we were either hitting in the L1 cache or going to main memory that is O(100) times slower, our measurements in this section will be comparing L1 hits to L2 hits, or L2 hits to L3 hits, etc., where each level is only O(5) times slower than the previous one.

Timings on real machines and operating systems are rarely exactly repeatable. External interrupts, network traffic, humans typing, and background programs such as browsers or display software all contribute to small time variations in multiple runs of the same program. Our timing data will thus always be a bit noisy. The relatively small difference in adjacent memory-level times will make timings somewhat harder to evaluate.

What would we expect to see? For N <= L1 cache total size, we would expect the re-reads to be fast at just a few cycles per load, the L1 access time. For L1size < N <= L2size, we would expect to see mostly the somewhat slower L2 access time, etc. The result may look like the Figure 3.9 sketch, with L1 cache hits in the bottom row, L2 in the middle row, L3 in the top row, and main memory not shown but above the top row.

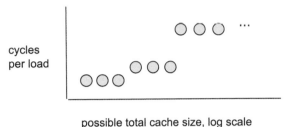

possible total cache size, log scale

Figure 3.9   **Sketch of expected access times vs. number of bytes accessed**

Since there will be some noise in this measurement, it is helpful to run each experiment several times. The supplied mystery2.cc routine `FindCacheSizes()` does each timing measurement in four passes, using simple linear stride. The first time initializes the cache by loading from main memory so is always slow and is to be ignored here. The next three times should all be similar and show the time difference we seek. The program results are given in count of cache lines, not kilobytes. I multiplied by an assumed or previously measured 64B per cache line to get the graph in Figure 3.10, which shows one set of measured results.

Loading 1KB of data into the cache and then re-reading it is fast, at about four cycles per load. The same is roughly true for 2–16KB. At 32KB, things slow down a little to about eight cycles per load. For 64–256KB, loads take about 14 cycles each. For 512–2048KB, loads take 20–24 cycles each. Above 2048KB (2MB) the load time quickly rises to 70–80 cycles each. The actual L1 cache on this chip is 32KB and has a three- or four-cycle load-use latency. The L2 cache is 256KB and about 14 cycles, and the L3 cache is 3MB and roughly 40 cycles. The 3MB size falls between the 2MB and 4MB measurements we made in Figure 3.10.

The timing of about eight cycles per load for 32KB of data should be closer to four cycles in a fully used 32KB cache. Why? We implicitly assumed that accessing 32KB of data would exactly fill the 32KB L1 data cache. This assumption depends on there being nothing else accessed in the L1 cache and depends on the allocation policy being true least recently used (LRU), or true round-robin. In reality, the mystery2.cc program itself has a few variables that use the L1 cache, and the cache replacement policy is not perfect LRU, leading to some underutilization of the cache and thus some misses out to the L2 cache. Both of these make the measurement somewhat slower when our total data is just under the total cache size.

A different phenomenon occurs at 64KB and 512KB, just above the size of the L1 and L2 caches, respectively. In a not-perfect-LRU environment, some of the 64KB of data expected to be found in L2 is instead found in the L1 cache because it happened not to be replaced. This gives a slightly fast overall average load time at 64KB, and similarly for some of the 512KB of data found in the L2 cache instead of L3. As you should expect by now, our measurement and hence our graph do not have the sharp step-function boundaries we had in the Figure 3.9 sketch.

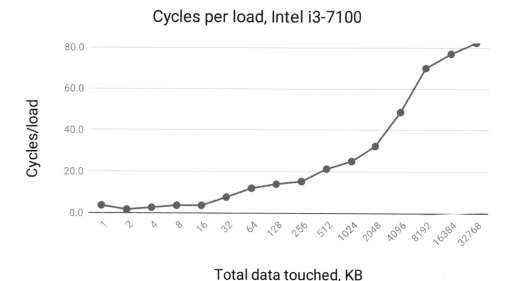

Figure 3.10   **Cycles per load for different total sizes touched. Compare to Figure 3.9.**

3.12   Measuring Cache Associativity of Each Level

Once we have the line size and the total size of each cache level, we can find the associativity of each cache. In a fully associative cache, a given cache line can go any place at all in the cache. In a set associative cache, a given cache line can go in a small number of places, within just one set. If a given cache line can go only one place in the cache, the set size is 1, and the cache is direct mapped or one-way associative. If a cache line can go two places in the cache, it is two-way associative, etc.

An N-way associative cache usually accesses all N possible tags and data locations in parallel (using almost N times as much electrical power as accessing one location). If one of the tags matches the given address, there is a cache hit, and the corresponding data is used. If none matches, there is a cache miss at that level.

Our strategy for finding the cache associativity at each cache level is to read a list consisting of addresses in A distinct lines with those addresses repeated many times, e.g. for A=4,

   0 4K 8K 12K 0 4K 8K 12K 0 4K 8K ...

The addresses are picked so they all go into **just** set[0] of the cache. Then re-read the list, looking at timings. If all A distinct lines fit into set[0], then the re-reads will be fast. If they don't fit, then the re-reads will miss and be filled from the next level down. The largest number A that fit at once is the cache associativity. The supplied mystery2.cc program does not measure cache associativity. In the exercises, you get to do this one.

If the L2, etc., caches have higher associativity than the L1 cache, you should be able to find the L2, etc., values. But if they have less associativity than the L1 cache, hits in L1 may obscure the timing you would like to see for the other cache levels. In that case, you could look for an address pattern that spreads across a small number of associative sets in the L2 cache but all land in a single set in the L1 cache, overwhelming the L1 associativity and forcing misses out to L2.

3.13   Translation Buffer Time

We aren't quite done with complications. While accessing memory in today's processors, we are also accessing the virtual-memory page tables. Reading tens of megabytes of data to trash the caches also trashes the hardware TLB in a CPU core. Some subsequent memory accesses must first do a page-table memory access to load the corresponding TLB entry, at least doubling the total access time for those.

If there are 16-byte items being accessed, i.e., stride 16, then 256 of these fit in a single 4KB page, so accessing all 256 involves just one TLB miss. But if there are 4KB items being accessed, stride 4KB, loading from 256 of these will get 256 TLB misses, not just one. The TLB miss times thus may distort all our earlier measurements, but in a predictable way.

3.14   Cache Underutilization

The final complication we discuss is that of cache underutilization. Normally, the lowest bits of a memory address are used to pick which bytes to use in a cache line. If the line size is 64 bytes, this would be the lowest 6 bits. The next higher bits are used to select the associative set. If a tiny cache is 2KB organized as 64-byte lines, there are 32 cache lines total. If these are organized four-way associative, then there are eight sets of four cache lines each, as in Figures 3.4 and 3.5. With the low six address bits selecting a byte within a line, the next higher three address bits would be used to select the set, and the remaining higher bits would be compared against four tags in that set to determine a hit.

If we load data into a cache with 64-byte lines, but *only* load data spaced at multiples of 128 bytes, one of the address bits used to select a set will always be 0. So set[0], set[2], set[4], etc., will be used, but the other 1/2 of the sets will not be used. This means that the effective cache size is not 2KB but only 1KB. This is something to keep in mind when accessing regular address patterns. Figure 3.5d shows this effect, with the odd-numbered sets not used and shown in gray. We will see more of this effect in the next chapter when accessing columns of an array. For now, just keep in mind that underutilized cache equals slower execution.

3.15   Summary

In this chapter we examined and measured memory hierarchies consisting of multiple levels of cache plus DRAM main memory. Hierarchies are needed to strike an engineering balance between fast access at nearly CPU speed and the much slower access time inherent in very large DRAM memories. We explored some of the many speedup mechanisms used in modern CPUs while accessing memory and then defeated some of these to try to get meaningful measurements of just the memory access times for various patterns. Carefully chosen patterns inform us of the memory system organization. They also inform us about access patterns that will create performance problems.

- Estimate what you expect to see.

- Page size limits physically addressed L1 cache size.

- Stride patterns reveal cache organization.

- Total-size patterns reveal cache sizes.

- Prefetching, multi-issue, out-of-order execution, and non-dependent loads make careful memory measurements difficult.

- Virtual-address mapping makes patterns inexact.

- TLB misses distort cache timings.

- Patterns that produce cache underutilization can produce performance problems.

- Compare your measurements against expectations. There is always learning in the discrepancies.

Exercises

Starting with the supplied mystery2.cc program *compiled optimized*, –O2, answer some questions, do some modifications, and then answer some more questions. You shouldn't need to spend more than about two hours on the initial questions 3.1 through 3.7, plus maybe two more on question 3.8. If you are spending much more time, set it aside and do something else, or chat with a friend about the problem.

You will find it helpful to use a spreadsheet such as Microsoft Excel or Google Charts to turn the numbers into graphs so you can compare them to your sketches and think about what the patterns are telling you. *Always* label the x- and y-axis of your graphs, giving the units: counts, cycles, msec, KB, etc. Do this even if you are the only one looking at the graph. At some point, it will save you from making an order-of-magnitude error or from coming to a completely false conclusion. Once you develop this habit, it will save time.

Before you change things, rerun mystery2.cc a few times to see what the inherent variation is like in the cycle counts.

3.1   In the first part of mystery2.cc that looks at cache line size timings, what do you think the cache line size is, and why? If you have access to sample servers with more than one type of CPU chip, be sure to specify *which server* you measured.

3.2   In the first part of mystery2.cc that looks at cache line size timings, explain a little about the three timings for a possible line size of 256 bytes. These are the ones that should be about 30, 80, and 200 cycles per load.

3.3   In the first part of mystery2.cc that looks at cache line size timings, make a copy of the program, and in routine `MakeLongList()`, add a line after

```
int extrabit = makelinear ? 0 : (1 << 14);
```

that defeats the DRAM different-row address patterns:

```
extrabit = 0;
```

Explain a little about the changes this produces in the scrambled timings, especially for possible line size of 128 bytes. Keep in mind that the virtual-to-physical address mapping will somewhat corrupt the alternate different-row pattern before your change and will somewhat corrupt the same-row pattern afterward.

3.4   In the second part that looks at total cache size `FindCacheSizes()`, what do you think are the total sizes of the L1, L2, and L3 caches?

3.5   What is your best estimate of the load-to-use time in cycles for each cache level?

3.6   To run on a CPU with a non-power-of-2 cache size, such as an Intel i3 with 3MB L3 cache, how would you modify the program slightly to test for somewhat-common not-power-of-2 sizes? (You need not do the modification; just explain what you would do.)

3.7   In the second part that looks at total cache size `FindCacheSizes()`, explain a bit about the variation in cycle counts *within* each cache level. The ones that barely fill a level are somewhat faster than the ones that completely fill a level. Why could that be?

3.8   Implement `FindCacheAssociativity()`. What is the associativity of each cache level?

Chapter 4

CPU and Memory Interaction

We have now measured CPU instruction times and memory access times. How do these interact?

Consider a matrix multiply program working on two double-precision arrays of dimension 1024 x 1024, writing to a third array of the same size, and running on our sample server as described in Appendix A—an x86 CPU with

32KB 8-way L1 data cache,

256KB 8-way L2 cache, and

12-way 3MB L3 cache,

all with a line size of 64 bytes. Figure 4.1 shows the L1 cache layout, consisting of 64 sets, each 8-way associative. For 64-byte lines, address bits <5:0> are the byte within a line, and address bits <11:6> select a set. A given memory line can go into any of the eight *ways* within that set. Each vertical way in this L1 cache holds 4KB, and the eight ways total 32KB.

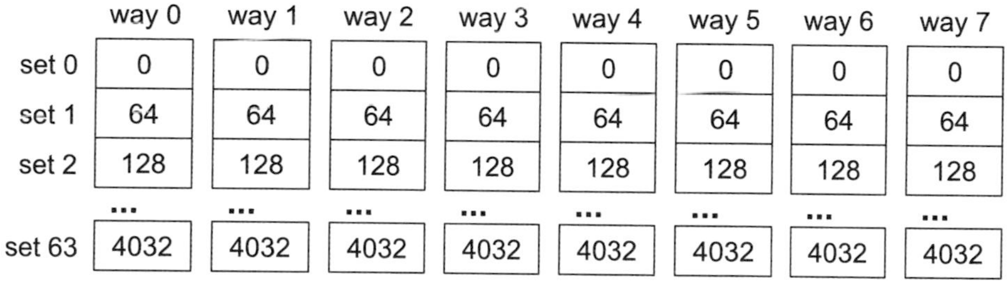

	way 0	way 1	way 2	way 3	way 4	way 5	way 6	way 7
set 0	0	0	0	0	0	0	0	0
set 1	64	64	64	64	64	64	64	64
set 2	128	128	128	128	128	128	128	128
	...	...	...	...	...	...	...	...
set 63	4032	4032	4032	4032	4032	4032	4032	4032

Figure 4.1   **Set-associative L1 cache with 64 sets, 8-way associative, 64-byte lines**

4.1   Cache Interaction

Because the L1 hardware uses low address bits to select a set, consecutive memory locations are spread across all 64 sets, but by the same token memory locations that differ by multiples of 4KB all fall into the *same* set. Accessing 4KB of consecutive bytes can fill up way 0 of all 64 sets, and then accessing the next 4KB can fill up way 1 of all 64 sets, etc., for a total of 512 cache lines (32KB) held in the L1 cache. But accessing just the first few bytes of a 4KB region and then skipping to the first few bytes of another 4KB region, etc., can use only set 0 way 0 and then set 0 way 1, etc., for a total of just eight cache lines (512 bytes) held in the L1 cache. Subsequent accesses 4KB apart still fall into set 0, so they have to start replacing the previous eight lines. For this access pattern, the other 63 sets of the cache are unused—the useful part of the cache is just 512B instead of 32KB. Such an access pattern leads to substantially more cache misses than the consecutive access pattern.

Matrices are typically stored in row-major order, meaning that elements within a row are in consecutive memory locations, while elements in a column are spaced apart by the length of one row. (Older FORTRAN programs stored matrices in column-major order.) Figure 4.2 shows a 3x3 matrix of 8-byte double-precision floats stored in row-major order. Elements A–H fill one cache line and element I starts the next cache line.

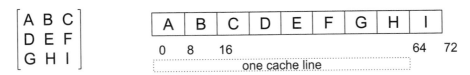

Figure 4.2   **Simple 3x3 matrix stored in row-major order**

In our 1024 x 1024 example for this chapter, one matrix row is 8KB long, i.e., 1,024 times 8 bytes per double-precision floating-point number. With 64-byte cache lines, eight values fit in a cache line, so a single row can fit in 128 cache lines, if and only if a row starts at an address that is a multiple of 64, i.e., the row is cache-line-aligned. Otherwise, it is spread across 129 cache lines, with some bytes of the first and last lines not in the row at all. The program matrix.cc that goes with this chapter in fact aligns the arrays on 4KB boundaries. With 8KB rows spread perfectly across all 64 cache sets, a 32KB cache can hold four entire rows totaling 4,096 double-precision elements.

The elements of a column are spaced 8KB apart for the row length of 8KB. Because they are not contiguous, the 1,024 elements of a column occupy 1,024 different cache lines. Those lines also contain seven other columns of data, which may or may not be useful to us.

Because the row length of our example matrix is an exact multiple of 4KB, the elements of a column *all land in the same L1 cache set*. This means that at most *eight elements* of a given column can be in the L1 cache at once, since the L1 cache is eight-way associative. Accessing all the 1,024 elements of a column in sequential order will therefore get nearly 100% L1 cache misses.

If the row length were 1,024 + 8 elements, successive elements of a column would fall in different cache sets, and 64 consecutive elements of a column would be in 64 cache lines that spread across all 64 different sets of our L1 cache. To see the unvarnished effects of memory access patterns, we use the bad-case row length of 1,024 elements in this chapter.

With 1,024-element rows, one way to spread out column elements into many cache sets is to make the set selection a function not of just a few low-order address bits but a hash function of many more address bits. This is usually not done for L1 caches because the translated high-order physical address bits are not available soon enough. Even if hashing were done, for our current example one entire column of our matrix would fit into 1,024 different cache lines, twice as many as our L1 cache has. Even with hashed set selection, accessing an entire column will get at least 50% L1 cache misses. Hashed set selection will help us in the L3 cache, however, as we will see in the following sections.

Careful consideration of access patterns can maximize cache hits and hence maximize performance. Keep in mind that array dimensions that are exact powers of 2 are more prone to underutilization of cache space by creating *set access bias*—overutilizing some sets and not touching others.

Each entire matrix in our example is 8MB so does not even fit into the 3MB L3 cache. In addition to looking at the dynamics of accessing elements of a single matrix, we need to consider the interactions—how the dynamics of accessing all three matrices can produce even more cache misses and main memory traffic.

4.2 Simple Matrix Multiply Dynamics

A simple matrix multiply algorithm has the three nested loops of Code Sample 4.1.

Code Sample 4.1   **Simple matrix multiply algorithm**

```
// Multiply matrix a times b giving c.
// All arrays are 1024 x1024 in this example
for (int row = 0; row < 1024; ++row) {
  for (int col = 0; col < 1024; ++col) {
    double sum = 0.0;
    for (int k = 0; k < 1024; ++k) {
      sum += a[row, k] * b[k, col];
    }
    c[row, col] = sum;
  }
}
```

Looking just at the innermost loop, the accesses to array **a** go across a row, so we expect them to touch 8KB of contiguous memory locations. One row fits easily into the L1 data cache. The accesses to array **b**, however, go down a column. Those elements are spaced 8KB apart so land in 1,024 different cache lines, all of which belong to the *same* L1 cache set and to only *four* different L2 cache sets. We expect almost all the array **b** references to be cache misses.

4.3 Estimates

How long should this matrix multiply take? There are 1024x1024x1024 = 1 billion multiplies and also 1 billion adds. As we saw in Chapter 2, a double-precision multiply takes about four CPU cycles on our sample server, as does a double-precision add. Ignoring memory accesses for a moment, one billion multiplies at four cycles each and 3.9 GHz is about one second, and the same for the adds, for two seconds total. This is before accounting for overlaps. If the multiplies and adds overlap perfectly and if the loop is unrolled and successfully overlaps four iterations, the total computation could be done in as little as 1/4 second.

On our sample server, just doing the multiplies and adds in an unrolled loop takes a measured 0.274 seconds.

Reading one entire array of 8MB means accessing 128K cache lines of 64 bytes each. At a minimum, we should see 128K cache misses for each of the arrays **a**, **b**, and **c**. But with the simple access pattern shown previously, we should expect to see 1 billion cache misses for array **b** —1,024 misses per inner loop times 1 million instances of the inner loop. If each miss takes 200 cycles or 50 nsec at 3.9 GHz, that would total 50 seconds of cache miss time, plus tiny amounts for arrays **a** and **c**. This is before accounting for overlaps. If the misses were a little faster and many of them were overlapped or fetched sequentially, we might expect 10x faster memory time, or about 5 seconds.

Our estimates suggest that the memory access pattern will be key to the performance of this program. Overall, we might expect somewhere between about 5 and 50 seconds for the full matrix multiply.

Keep in mind that there is an underlying virtual-to-physical address mapping that will distort the distribution of addresses that the caches see, compared to simple virtual-address pictures.

4.4   Initialization, Cross-Checking, and Observing

To measure a real matrix multiply, we need to initialize the **a** and **b** arrays with 1M values each. What values should we use? The standard choices in computer science are 0, 1, and random. Values of 0 and 1 are likely to trigger any available computation shortcuts in our CPU chip, so we want to avoid them. Random values are plausible, but they may introduce run-to-run variation and may accidentally trigger floating-point overflow/underflow and any related slow or extra processing.

Instead of these three, we choose to initialize the array elements each with a known value close to 1.0, specifically

```
1.0 + ((row * 1024 + col) / 1000000.0)
```

giving a range of 1.0 to just over 2.0 and an average value near 1.5. Each inner loop sum should then be about 1,024 * 1.5 * 1.5, or about 2,300.

It is easy in rearranging matrix code loops to make mistakes. So we will include a simple plausibility check: summing all the elements of the result **c** matrix. This should be about 2300 * 1 million or about 2.3 billion. If it is 10,000 instead, we will know something is terribly wrong. If the simplest matrix technique gives a checksum S0 and a fancy technique gives a checksum S1 equal to S0, we know the fancy one is likely to be correct. If S1 differs from S0 but not by much, we see that slightly different roundoff behavior has been introduced by rearranging the computation. If S1 and S0 differ substantially, we know something is wrong.

Since the memory access pattern affects the computation time so much, we also instrument the code to optionally count simulated L1, L2, and L3 cache misses. We will run with this code turned off to get performance times and run with it turned on to get miss counts. The cache simulation and counting will slow down the matrix computation by 10x or more, so we can't do both measurements at once.

4.5 Initial Results

Casting Code Sample 4.1 into valid C code with the two-dimensional subscript computations explicitly exposed and with compile-time constants for the dimensions allows the compiler to optimize out much of the loop overhead work. Running the simple triple-nested loops shown earlier on our sample server produces the output shown in Timing Result 4.1.

Timing Result 4.1   **Simple matrix multiply time and misses**

```
SimpleMultiply              6.482 seconds, sum=2494884076.030955315
Misses L1/L2/L3             1077341184 1058414205  886641817
```

This result agrees somewhat well with our estimates:

- Total runtime of 6.5 seconds vs. 5–50 seconds estimated

- Sum across the result matrix c of 2.5 billion vs. 2.3 billion estimated

- Miss counts in L1 and L2 of about 1 billion and a little less in L3 of 0.89 billion vs. 1 billion estimated

Well done! You can produce these times on your test machine by compiling and running matrix.cc twice, once with TRACK_CACHES set to 0 and once with it set to 1, both times with HASHED_L3 set to 0 and with gcc optimization set to -O2. Timing results for different computers will vary somewhat.

Looking more carefully at the loop structure in Code Sample 4.1, you might notice that col changes more quickly than row, with col different for every iteration of the inner loop. It is possible that swapping the order of the outer two loops will change the total time because of the change in access pattern for **b[k, col]**. Based on expected cache misses, estimate whether the program in Code Sample 4.2 will run faster or slower than Code Sample 4.1. What do you think?

Code Sample 4.2   **Simple matrix multiply algorithm with column number changing more slowly than row number**

```
// Multiply matrix a times b giving c.
// All arrays are 1024 x1024 in this example
for (int col = 0; col < 1024; ++col) {
  for (int row = 0; row < 1024; ++row) {
    double sum = 0.0;
    for (int k = 0; k < 1024; ++k) {
      sum += a[row, k] * b[k, col];
    }
    c[row, col] = sum;
  }
}
```

Looking at the inner loop, we see it scans across one row sequentially and one column vertically. As discussed, the one row of 8KB fits easily into the L1 cache spread across 128 lines and all 64 sets, but the column is all mapped to a single set so misses almost always. With the Code Sample 4.1 loop ordering, 1,024 iterations of the inner loop access the same row, while the Code Sample 4.2 loop ordering keeps changing rows. We might therefore expect the original Code Sample 4.1 loop's ordering to have fewer cache misses and to be somewhat faster.

Running the simple triple-nested loops of Code Sample 4.1 on our sample server produces Timing Result 4.2.

Timing Result 4.2   **Simple matrix multiply time and misses, row changing more quickly than column**

```
SimpleMultiplyColumnwise      5.115 seconds, sum=2494884076.030955315
Misses L1/L2/L3               1209008128 1209008128 1092145348
```

The checksum is identical, as we would expect. This loop ordering has about 20% more cache misses, as expected. But it is somehow faster, not slower! What could be going on?

If you look more carefully at the source code for matrix.cc, you will notice several discrepancies in the cache-miss-counting simulations. First, it is using the program's user-mode virtual addresses, not the physical address these are mapped to. We can't do much about that except hope that our simulated cache counts are similar to the real ones. Second, note that the L3 cache simulation is for a 2MB 16-way cache, not the real 3MB 12-way one on our sample server. But that turns out to be minor since rows fit in L3 in both cases and arrays do not.

The real sample server L3 cache does not index its sets by address bits<16:6> but by an undocumented hash of this along with some of the high-order address bits. For our program, the effect of this hashing is to *spread out columns across all the L3 cache sets*. This matters, and in fact is why the hashing is done in the L3 hardware. We should expect this real hardware to have fewer L3 cache misses than our simplistic count, perhaps even enough to make the Code Sample 4.2 loops faster than the Code Sample 4.1 loops.

To approximate this behavior, the L3 cache simulation optionally XORs in high bits when selecting the cache set. Re-running the Code Sample 4.1 and Code Sample 4.2 loops on our sample server but with HASHED_L3 set to 1 produces the additional "-hashed" results shown in Timing Result 4.3 (total time varies slightly from run to run, as you should always expect).

Timing Result 4.3   **Simple matrix multiply time and misses, with hashed L3 set selection**

```
SimpleMultiply                6.482 seconds, sum=2494884076.030955315
Misses L1/L2/L3               1077341184 1058414205  886641817

SimpleMultiplyColumnwise      5.115 seconds, sum=2494884076.030955315
Misses L1/L2/L3               1209008128 1209008128 1092145348

SimpleMultiply                6.458 seconds, sum=2494884076.030955315
Misses L1/L2/L3-hashed        1077341184 1058414205  751193415

SimpleMultiplyColumnwise      5.211 seconds, sum=2494884076.030955315
Misses L1/L2/L3-hashed        1209008128 1209008128  184542843
```

Now we see the columnwise estimated L1 and L2 cache miss counts increased by 20% as before, but the L3 miss count for Code Sample 4.2 ordering is about four times lower than the Code Sample 4.1 count. With L3 misses of perhaps 100–200 CPU cycles each, this is enough to tilt the total runtime to be about 20% faster instead of about 20% slower. From the CPU's point of view, 1 billion cache misses in Code Sample 4.1 take an average of about 25 cycles each (6.4 seconds * 4B cycles / 1 billion misses) and in Code Sample 4.2 only an average of about 20 cycles each.

Keep in mind that all the cache miss counts here are simply software simulations, not exact reality. On some machines it might be possible to read a performance counter of exactly L3 cache misses, but usually reading this is not exposed to user-mode code, and the counter may be polluted by kernel code or other programs or by partial execution on each of several different CPU cores. We will discuss performance counters further in Chapter 11. Even with exact miss counts, the total runtime is not fully determined. Some L3 misses might take the worst-case time to access DRAM, while others are perfectly predicted by hardware prefetchers and effectively take zero time.

For now, just keep in mind that cache behavior matters and that modern processor chips have sometimes quite complex ways of improving performance. Execution patterns that end up accidentally defeating these performance improvements can contribute to excess transaction latency, not just for matrix manipulation but also for any program that accesses significant amounts of scattered memory (think big hash tables) per transaction.

4.6 Faster Matrix Multiply, Transpose Method

How could we speed up matrix multiply? Our goal should be to increase the reuse of array elements that are brought into a cache. We look at two approaches to this, one involving transposing array **b** and one involving rearranging square subblocks of all three matrices.

The transpose approach notes that array **b** is accessed in column order, and that order produces bad cache behavior when the row size is a multiple of 4KB. What would it cost to *transpose* array **b** to array **bb**, and then access **bb** in row order, and hence with an excellent cache pattern?

Transposing **b** involves reading elements of **b** in row order for 128K cache misses and writing **bb** in column order for 1M cache misses, or about 1.2M total. But we do this just *once*, better than the 1 billion misses above by almost a factor of 1,000.

To cross-check the transpose code, we transpose an array twice and check that the result is exactly equal to the original. Running this check produces, for direct and hashed L3 set selection, Timing Result 4.4.

Timing Result 4.4 **Transpose-twice miss counts, without and with hashed L3 set selection**

Transpose Misses L1/L2/L3	2359296	2359258	**2342724**
Transpose Misses L1/L2/L3-hashed	2359296	2359258	**943198**

The total L1 and L2 misses for two transposes closely match double our estimate for one transpose, and the L3 misses drop substantially when hashing to choose the set, all as expected.

The modified matrix multiply transposes **b** to **bb** and then multiplies **a** by **bb**. We expect the inner loop to get 128 misses on a row of **a** and 128 misses on a row of **bb**, and this loop is run 1M times. This should give a total of about 256M misses. Running the modified multiply produces, for direct and hashed L3 set selection, Timing Result 4.5.

Timing Result 4.5   **Transposed matrix multiply time and misses, without and with hashed L3 set selection**

```
    SimpleMultiplyTranspose      1.138 seconds, sum=2494884076.030955315
    Misses L1/L2/L3              269018803  148146944  142050176

    SimpleMultiplyTranspose      1.144 seconds, sum=2494884076.030955315
    Misses L1/L2/L3-hashed       269018803  148146944  133124904
```

Wow! About 6x faster than Timing Result 1. The total L1 misses closely match our estimate, the L2 misses are about 2x better, and the L3 misses drop only a little more when hashing to choose the set.

We can do somewhat better. Transposing **b** more quickly involves reading 8x8 blocks of elements (based on eight-way associativity and eight elements per cache line) and writing each of these transposed, filling every **bb** cache line with eight elements per miss instead of just one element. In addition, the transpose loop can be unrolled 4x to reduce loop overhead. We expect about 128K misses for reading and about 128K misses for writing, or about 256K misses total, 5x better than simple transpose. Running the transpose-twice check produces, for direct and hashed L3 set selection, Timing Result 4.6.

Timing Result 4.6   **Transpose- and block-transpose-twice miss counts, without and with hashed L3 set selection**

```
    Transpose      Misses L1/L2/L3          2359296    2359258    2342724
    BlockTranspose Misses L1/L2/L3           552960     524395     522240

    Transpose      Misses L1/L2/L3-hashed   2359296    2359258    1019221
    BlockTranspose Misses L1/L2/L3-hashed    552960     524395     522427
```

The block transpose in fact has about 4.5x fewer misses and is insensitive to the L3 set selection algorithm.

The inner loop of the matrix multiply can also be unrolled 4x to reduce loop overhead and offer more opportunities to do adds and multiplies in parallel. Putting all this together produces, for direct and hashed L3 set selection, Timing Result 4.7.

Timing Result 4.7   **Faster transposed matrix multiply time and misses, without and with hashed L3 set selection**

```
    SimpleMultiplyTransposeFast 0.586 seconds, sum=2494884076.030954838
    Misses L1/L2/L3                 268100748  147229568  141132672

    SimpleMultiplyTransposeFast 0.579 seconds, sum=2494884076.030954838
    Misses L1/L2/L3-hashed          268100748  147229568  132811796
```

This is 10x faster than Timing Result 4.1 and 2x faster than Timing Result 4.5. The total miss counts have dropped by only about 1 million each from Timing Result 4.5, so the bulk of the speedup comes from unrolling. Note that the checksum has changed slightly vs. Result 4.5, by about 1/2 in the 17th digit. This is not because of the transposing but because of the 4x unrolling of the inner loop, producing four sums in parallel that are added together once at the end.

4.7   Faster Matrix Multiply, Subblock Method

A completely different approach is to rearrange square subblocks of all three matrices so that each subblock is brought into the cache once and used in its entirety. Subblocks could be 8x8, 16x16, 32x32, 64x64, etc. For the sample server's cache design, 32x32 turns out to be the fastest.

Figure 4.3 shows the rearrangement of an example 4x4 subblock taken from four columns of four rows in the big 1024x1024 matrix. The original 16 elements all map into *the same* L1 cache set, while the rearranged ones fill consecutive memory locations spread across *different* cache sets.

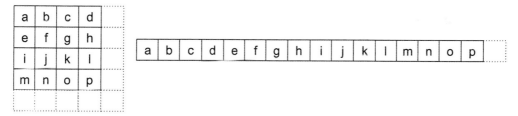

Figure 4.3   **Rearranging a subblock of a big matrix to put each subblock into consecutive memory locations that cache and prefetch well**

In matrix.cc each 32x32 element subblock is read once in row-major order and written sequentially to a new array. Instead of 32 discontiguous rows of 32 elements, the copied subblock is one contiguous run of 1,024 elements (8KB). Copying takes only 128K + 128K misses per array, or about 256K misses total, just like transpose.

The copied subblocks can then be processed with the (unrolled) inner loop of 32 elements repeated 32x32 times, producing one subblock of partial sums for **cc**, all using just the L1 cache. The full multiply involves remapping **a** to **aa** and **b** to **bb**, multiplying **aa** and **bb** to produce **cc**, and then reverse-mapping the subblocks of **cc** to produce **c**. Putting all this together gives, for direct and hashed L3 set selection, Timing Result 4.8.

Timing Result 4.8   **Subblock remapped matrix multiply time and misses, without and with hashed L3 set selection**

BlockMultiplyRemap	**0.373** seconds, sum=2494884076.030955315		
Misses L1/L2/L3	**26161141**	8116254	5228737
BlockMultiplyRemap	**0.392** seconds, sum=2494884076.030955315		
Misses L1/L2/L3-hashed	**26161141**	8116254	5243627

The total misses are down by another factor of 10, but the total time drops only by a factor of 1.5. The L3 hashing actually increases the small number of L3 misses slightly, which also increases the runtime slightly. In either case, we are approaching the time it takes just for the arithmetic, measured separately as 0.274 seconds. That means it is time to stop optimizing memory access patterns.

> It is only by fluke that the 32x32 subblock checksum is exactly the same as for simple multiply—other subblock sizes give slightly different results in the 15th digit.

4.8   Cache-Aware Computation

This chapter presents a case study of tuning code to improve cache behavior and hence to improve runtime. Using the results from Chapter 2's measurement of add and multiply times and Chapter 3's measurement of cache dimensions and memory access times, we explored four different ways to arrange the loops and memory access patterns of matrix multiplication. Along the way, we did a little explicit loop unrolling to pick up a factor of 2 in performance. The final result is about 17 times faster than the initial result on our sample server.

> Many of you are aware of the SPEC benchmarks [Dixit 1991], which attempt to measure CPU performance in reasonably representative ways. The initial SPEC89 benchmark suite included the program 030.matrix300, a FORTRAN program to multiply matrices of dimension 300x300. The introduction of compiler optimizations to rearrange the cache accesses in this program [Keatts 1991] produced a 10x performance improvement in this benchmark for those companies that included such an optimization, causing all major hardware venders to approach Kuck Associates about buying that compiler technology and causing the SPEC consortium to drop matrix300 from the subsequent SPEC92 suite.

During the exploration, we estimated time and cache misses and then measured the real code explicitly to see how well it conformed to our estimates. We also introduced a simple mechanism, a full-array checksum, to cross-check that the computation results from the different methods were plausibly similar. We stopped optimizing memory access when the time approached our estimate and measurement of the minimum possible pure-computation time. All of these are important habits for software professionals.

4.9   Summary

When dealing with large amounts of data, cache-friendly organization can substantially improve performance compared to a not-thought-out organization. Keeping data that are accessed together in time also together in memory helps.

This applies not only to matrices, but also to hash tables, B-trees, linked-list nodes, network messages, and many other data structures. For example, instead of 16-byte linked-list nodes with an 8-byte pointer and 8 bytes of data, it may improve cache performance 4x by having 64-byte nodes with 1 pointer and 4+ sets of data.

Exercises

4.1 You might enjoy trying to further reduce the matrix multiply time by 20% or so.

Chapter 5

Measuring Disk/SSD

The third fundamental hardware resource to measure is disk/SSD latency—how long do real storage-device reads and writes take? In contrast to the previous chapters that do CPU and memory measurements of average latency over thousands of identical operations, we will look at the internal dynamics of a single long disk/SSD read or write, revealing a wealth of substructure and a few surprises.

What really happens when you do a disk read or disk write? As shown in Figure 5.1, there are several layers of software involved, including the operating system and the file system. At least the file system and the drive itself have caches of disk data. The file system in general will prefetch and cache read data and buffer writes, committing them to disk at leisure, attempting to write fewer bigger transfers to disk. Modern disk drives *also* all include on-drive prefetching caches, holding data from at least the current disk track and often from multiple tracks, and on-drive write buffers, holding write data that the drive itself commits to the disk surface at leisure.

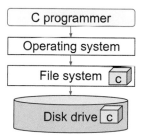

Figure 5.1 **Software and hardware involved in accessing a disk drive. Boxes [c] indicate caches.**

As usual, to do good timing we will need to defeat some of these prefetching, caching, and buffering performance mechanisms. But first a little background about disk and SSD operation.

5.1   About Hard Disks

Today's normal 3-1/2 inch hard drive holds 1TB or so and inside usually has one to four disk platters: the one in Figure 5.2 looks like it has three platters. Both surfaces of a platter record data, so for three platters there are six read/write heads at the ends of the long arms; Figure 5.3 shows a pair of heads. The arms all move together to put the read/write heads at a particular radial position on the disks. The circle of data passing under one read/write head is a single *track*, as shown in Figure 5.4. The vertical stack of tracks passing (more or less) under all the read/write heads at once is called a *cylinder*. Within a single track, there are a few hundred 4KB disk blocks or *sectors* of data. Because the outer tracks of a disk are physically longer than the inner tracks, most disks now vary the number of sectors per track, storing more on the outer tracks and fewer on the inner tracks. This also means that the transfer rate is faster on the outer tracks (more bytes transferred per constant-rate revolution).

Figure 5.2   **A 3.5" hard drive [Wikimedia 2013]**

⊢ **1 mm**

Figure 5.3   **Drive heads [Wikimedia 2012]**

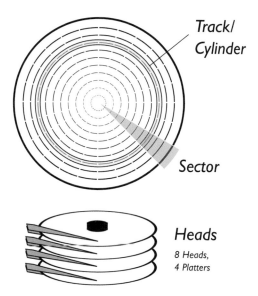

Figure 5.4   **Diagram of sector, track, cylinder [Wikimedia 2005]**

The active part of a read/write head is quite small, about the width of a single track. Usually, the write head is the width of a single track, and the read head is a bit narrower so it can be positioned in the middle of a track for picking up the best signal. Tracks are *tiny*— over 200,000 tracks per inch (80,000 per cm). About 1000 tracks would make up the width of one human hair.

When you read from a disk location, the command sent to the disk has a *Logical Block Address* (LBA). The drive maps an LBA into a particular cylinder, track within the cylinder, and 4KB block or sector within the track. It then starts a seek that moves the arms to that cylinder and simultaneously switches electronically to listen to the appropriate read head. As the seek finishes, the drive is reading the bits passing under the selected read head, looking for specific embedded-servo patterns that are on each track between blocks. These patterns tell the drive what track it is currently over, even as the arm is still moving radially. During the final part of the seek, the drive locks on to the desired track, gets centered on it, and then is ready to read or write data. Rubtsov has a nice discussion of disk physical layouts [Rubstov 2021].

> Tracks are so tiny that when read head 0 is centered on its track, the other read heads will be vaguely near the corresponding track on their surfaces but not exactly on them. If the other heads were off radially by the width of a human hair, they would be 1,000 tracks away. At any given time, just one read head is over the right track. At these tiny dimensions, tracks are also not perfect circles but are slightly off-center or out-of-round. The center of a track varies in and out as the disk rotates. A servo mechanism is therefore always active, moving the read/write head in and out by tiny amounts to stay centered on a track.

When the seek finishes and locks on track, the drive waits until the desired block passes under the read head and then either copies read data from the surface or writes new data to the surface. A seek might take 4–15 msec, depending on how far away the arm starts out from the desired cylinder. A typical 7200rpm disk rotates at 7200/60 = 120 revolutions per second, so each revolution is 8.33 msec. On average, the drive will have to wait half a rrevolution—for example, ~4 msec after the seek before the desired block rotates under the head.

> If some outside force vibrates a disk, the heads will move slightly, and the drive may detect that it is off-track and then stop reading or writing and wait a revolution and try again. By design, writing is more sensitive to this than reading. The effect in a datacenter environment with many disks packed close together can be that when disk D is writing, substantial seek activity at an unlucky resonant frequency [YouTube 2016] on nearby disks can cause D to lose revolutions and preferentially make writing slow, but *only* when completely unrelated nearby disks have just the right activity pattern. If you have 100,000 disks and poor vibration isolation, this can happen fairly frequently and entirely mysteriously. As computer scientists, we tend to think of the world as clean 1s and 0s, but this is just a digital abstraction—the real world remains analog and breaks the abstraction now and then in vicious ways.

If you read data that crosses a track boundary, there will head-switching time between the last block of one track and the first block of the next. This time will include switching the read electronics to the next read head, but also will necessarily involve a small servo seek and time to settle onto the middle of the desired track on the new disk surface. In early disk designs, it would also involve waiting for the disk to rotate nearly all the way around to get to the first block of the new track, because it was directly underneath the first block of the old track and would always have rotated a bit past the head before the settling finished. In today's disks, the first block of each track is offset from the previous one by perhaps 1/5 of a revolution so that it comes under the read head just after the track-to-track settling time.

5.2 About SSDs

Solid-state disks have flash memory instead of rotating disk platters. They are more expensive per gigabyte than hard drives, so will not immediately displace hard drives in datacenters. They, however, are rapidly replacing hard drives in portable, battery-powered devices such as iPods (the original had a tiny hard drive), tablets, notebooks, and of course cell phones.

Each bit in a flash memory chip is stored in a single transistor by injecting or draining change on a floating gate, via a control gate above it. In this context, *floating* means that the gate is not connected to anything—it is fully insulated, as shown in Figure 5.5. Once the charge is injected or drained, the gate will hold its value for years with no power applied.

Draining charge from the floating gate involves a higher than normal voltage, about 12V with a nominal power supply of 3.3V driven with one polarity to force electrons out and with the other polarity to attract electrons in. This is done on-chip, but it takes a while to boost the voltage, and

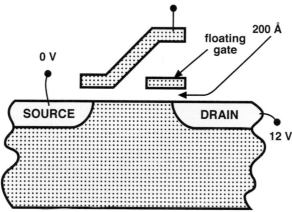

Programming via hot electron injection

Figure 5.5 **Flash memory bit [Wikimedia 2006]**

during this time the chip cannot do anything else. Because of electrical considerations and the voltage-boost delay, the design style is to occasionally drain charge from all the bits of a block of memory at once, perhaps 4–16KB. The *erase cycle* sets the values of all the bits to 1. Writing is done by block erase to 1s followed any time later by selective injection to write 0s. Typically writes are done for an entire 4KB block *write cycle* at once, mimicking a disk drive.

Reads use lower voltages to sense the charge on the floating gate without disturbing it. The access time to read a bit is O(100) usec so is 1000x slower than DRAM but 100x faster than a hard drive. Like DRAMs, thousands of bits are read at once. After the 100 usec "seek time," an SSD connected as a *serial AT attachment* (SATA, "AT" from the IBM Personal Computer AT model) bus can deliver about 500–600 MB/sec, the SATA III design limit. Compared to a hard drive's 100 MB/sec, this is about 5x faster. Connections via the faster *peripheral component interconnect express* (PCIe) bus can transfer data at over 1 GB/sec. As in hard drives, writes are buffered up in SSDs and then applied a little later (to pre-erased blocks). Erasing a block is slow, taking O(10) msec. Writing a block is somewhat faster, O(1) msec. Both of these are significantly slower than reading. Unlike hard drives, the mapping of LBAs to actual memory blocks is quite dynamic, with the SSD controller assigning new blocks on the fly from a large pool of pre-erased blocks.

Some SSD controllers not only rearrange the mapping of LBAs to physical blocks; they compress data before writing, using up fewer blocks, and then decompress it as part of reading. For some controllers, writing 100 blocks of zero might assign just one physical block of zeros and then map 100 LBAs to it! This is the reason in testing read/write speeds we prefer to fill up data blocks with pseudorandom bits instead of simple patterns like all-zero or all-one. The pseudorandom bits defeat any SSD compression shortcuts.

Flash memories inside SSDs usually start out with many bad bits—floating gates that do not hold charge reliably or are shorted to ground or otherwise dysfunctional. Under normal use, the remaining bits are also a little flaky, so extra ECC bits and multi-bit error correcting codes are used throughout. In addition, bits wear out under use; they have a limited number of erase/write cycles. For expensive flash bits, 30,000 write cycles is typical, while for cheap ones 3,000 writes might be the limit. To avoid wearing out one block quickly while having others stable for years, the SSD controller keeps track of the lifetime writes per block and spreads around the block assignment to try to write each block about the same number of times. This process is called *wear-leveling*. Overall, an SSD drive has a finite lifetime of GB that can be written to it, so these drives may not be appropriate to use for high and steady rates of write traffic over time.

> Thousands of reads to a single flash location can in fact start disturbing the charge on nearby transistors, so some SSD controllers also do a simple form of read wear leveling in addition to the standard write wear leveling.

Cheap SSDs have another property that makes them flaky. Instead of storing just a single bit per transistor, some *multi-level cell* (MLC) drives use four different levels of charge to store two bits, and most common cheap SSDs today store eight levels of charge and thus three bits per transistor. This cuts into the analog noise margin by a factor of eight, making it more likely that some bits are mis-read and then (with luck) fixed by the ECC logic. But such a flash chip holds three times as many bits per transistor so is cheaper per bit. At every new chip fabrication generation, the actual transistors get smaller, the amount of charge stored gets smaller, the noise levels go up, and the signal levels go down.

The net effect is that SSDs are faster than hard drives but are not magic storage solutions.

We will see the effect of these details when we discuss the results of disk and SSD timing in later sections. Now back to software programs.

5.3   Software Disk Access and On-Disk Buffering

When you first access a file on a disk, i.e., open it, the file system will look up the filename in a directory, which is just a specialized disk file. The directory will say where the file data is, by ranges of Logical Block Numbers. Depending on how it was written, a file may be stored on disk in one *file extent* or in multiple scattered extents, each of which is a set of consecutive LBAs.

> While a set of consecutive LBAs are usually mapped to physically contiguous disk blocks, the drive may occasionally remap a block to a nearby location in order to replace a bad block on the disk surface with a good spare.

The file system software will turn your request to read N blocks into one request if N is not too large and the blocks are all in the same extent, and into multiple requests totaling N blocks if N is large or the blocks span multiple extents. Because the drive will need to seek between extents, a badly fragmented file with lots of extents is slow to read. Defragmentation software copies files around, trying to make each into a single extent.

Directories have all sorts of other metadata about a file, including file size, read/write/execute access permissions, owner, creation time, and last-accessed time.

This last item, called *atime*, is updated every time a file is accessed, meaning that reading one byte from a file or even just opening it can cause the corresponding directory entry to be read, modified, and rewritten to disk. This can turn one disk access into three, a potential performance disaster. At least one file system implements "approximate atime" by default, doing the directory file update at most once per day. That is sufficient to see how many months it has been since a file was last used or last backed up.

Fortunately, the open( ) system call in Linux has an O_NOATIME parameter that may defeat this update. "May" because file systems are allowed (by the open system call definition) to ignore the option. In Linux, only the owner of a file can open it with O_NOATIME.

The open( ) system call in Linux also has an O_DIRECT parameter that may defeat most of the file system buffering and caching. We will use both of these.

> From the man page: "O_DIRECT (since Linux 2.4.10) Try to minimize cache effects of the I/O to and from this file. In general this will degrade performance, but it is useful in special situations, such as when applications d their own caching. File I/O is done directly to/from user- space buffers."

It is also possible on some disks to turn off the on-disk write buffering and read caching, but doing so is *almost always a performance disaster,* so we leave them on. (The superuser-only command is hdparm -W0 to disable write buffering, hdparm -A0 to disable readahead caching.) With readahead off, two reads of, say, 64KB will likely not get the second read sent to the disk soon enough and therefore will lose a revolution (8.33 msec at 7200rpm) before doing it. With write buffering off, two writes of, say, 64KB will likely not get the second write sent to the disk soon enough and therefore will lose a revolution also. Both of these are performance disasters. *Don't do this.*

With the *read caching* in the disk drive working as intended, the slightly delayed second 64KB read is served from the readahead cache, which is always copying whatever is under the disk's read head. This is always good.

With the *write buffering* in the disk drive working as intended, the disk *lies* about the first 64KB write, signaling completion of the write as soon as the last byte is buffered, well before the seek and data transfer to the actual disk surface have finished, maybe even before the seek has started. This gives the operating system plenty of time to send the second 64KB write, and then both are done together when the seek finishes. This buffering is somewhat good—it makes multiple writes more efficient.

But if you intermix reads and writes, as is completely normal in a datacenter, an unfortunate thing happens. Suppose program A sends 10 different and physically scattered 1MB writes to a disk drive, and then program B tries to read 64KB from that drive. Assuming no reordering of requests within the drive, the first write from A goes into the on-drive write buffer, the seek for it is started, and the drive lies and says the write is completed. The other nine writes are also simply buffered, and the drive says they are all completed early. Then the read for B arrives at the drive. The drive may well first complete all the writes, along with their 10 seeks, taking around 400 msec total, delaying B's read by a factor of 10 compared to reading from an idle drive. This is a performance disaster for real-time user-facing software with a 200 msec response-time goal.

Drives that reorder requests may improve the average performance, but do not remove the 10x bad cases, and in fact may make user-visible disk latency occasionally worse. With reordering, the earlier read may bypass the buffered writes and get its own seek and read started promptly, but there is a hidden cost. With reads bypassing writes, but new writes also arriving, eventually the write buffer gets full. At this point, the drive has to stop bypassing reads and actually do some of the writes. One design choice is to completely empty the entire write buffer at that point, and another design choice is to just do one write and then go back to reading. The first is much simpler for disk drive firmware and is the one generally done. When this happens, *all* reads (which user code probably assumes will be served immediately) are locked out for the worst possible amount of time for the user code—emptying a completely full write buffer. Even worse, when the writes are from other programs, the time at which this happens is *completely arbitrary* from the point of view of the program doing reads. Another performance disaster for real-time user-facing traffic.

For latency-sensitive applications with intermixed reads and writes, some attention must be paid to preventing write buffering from ruining read latency. One approach is to keep the on-disk write buffers nearly empty by not starting another disk operation until the disk has had enough time to copy the buffer to the surface.

Because the erase cycle for a block on an SSD is slow and locks out all other chip activity, flash drives also introduce unexpected delays for reads when intermixed with writes, changing 100 usec read seek time into 10 msec (10,000 usec) seek time now and then if the SSD just started an erase cycle. Again, the time at which this happens is *completely arbitrary* from the point of view of the program doing reads. So writes are a potential performance disaster for real-time user-facing traffic, even though the absolute time scale is a bit better for SSDs than for disks.

5.4 How Fast Is a Disk Read?

To measure the speed of a disk read that really gets data from the surface of the disk and not from the on-disk read cache, we will use a strategy similar to Chapter 3's strategy for timing memory. We create a disk file that is bigger than the largest expected on-disk cache, expecting most of the early data to be evicted and just some of the final data to be left in the cache. Then we read and time starting with the early data.

Because the time scale involved is microseconds to milliseconds, we don't need sub-nanosecond cycle counts as our time base. The standard `gettimeofday()` call, which internally does a system call of perhaps 100 nsec, will be fine. It returns the current time of day in two `int`s: seconds and microseconds. Using two pieces is an artifact from the days of 32-bit processors. In the provided mystery3.cc code, the `GetUsec()` routine uses `gettimeofday()` and immediately puts those two pieces back together into a single 64-bit microsecond count so we can subtract easily.

To get the overall disk transfer rate, we could read the time, read a few megabytes, and read the time and subtract. But this won't tell us anything about the details: time spent seeking vs. time spent transferring data, multiple seeks for multiple extents, time spent changing tracks or changing cylinders, etc. To look a bit more closely, we instead read a lot of megabytes into an array and record *the time at which each 4KB block arrives in memory*. The strategy looks like this:

1. Write and fsync a 40MB file (bigger than a possible 32MB on-disk cache) of non-zero words, trashing the on-disk cache.

2. Reopen it specifying O_DIRECT and O_NOATIME.

3. Record the start time.

4. Read the file into an all-zero array via an **asynchronous** read.

5. *While* the read is happening, look at the first word of each 4KB block to see if it is still zero. If not, record the time at which it changed from zero to non-zero.

When we are done, we will have a start time and 10,000 timestamps, one for each 4KB block showing when it arrived at our user-mode array.

What do we expect to see?

Disk transfer rates are O(100) MB/sec, and probably in the range 50–200MB/sec. So reading all 40MB should take about 400 msec. If we see 40 msec or 4 seconds, something is wrong. But what *pattern* do we expect to see within the 40MB?

Where is the disk arm when we start the timed 40MB read? The last thing we did at the disk was to write the 40MB, so we expect the arm to be near the last MB of the file. Thus the first thing should be a seek of about 40MB (or more if multiple extents) and a delay for that seek of O(10) msec. Then what? Figure 5.6 shows examples of a shorter read of 100 disk blocks, 400 KB.

The simplest pattern, Figure 5.6a, is that after the seek, block 0 of the file arrives in memory, and then successive data blocks arrive sequentially in our array at regular intervals, spread across ~4 msec. The figure shows a seek time of about 16 msec before block 0 arrives and then 99 more blocks spaced about 40 usec apart, i.e., at a rate of about 100 MB/sec. The seek time is the horizontal time from 0 to the first block at about 0.016 seconds. The transfer rate is the slope of the diagonal line (which is actually 100 distinct dots, one for each block).

> Note that reading random 400KB pieces of data from such a disk spends about 80% of the time seeking (16msec) and only 20% doing useful work transferring data (4msec). If your program reads random 4KB blocks from disk, the ratio is even worse, with over 99% of the time seeking and less than 1% transferring data.

A good rule of thumb for efficiency in the presence of latency is to strive for doing useful work at least half the time—the *Half-Useful Principle*—in this case transferring for 16 msec after seeking for 16 msec. That would be about 1.6MB of data for each seek; transferring only 4KB for 40 usec after a 16 msec seek is a violation of the Half-Useful Principle. Few programs or database designs pay enough attention to this.

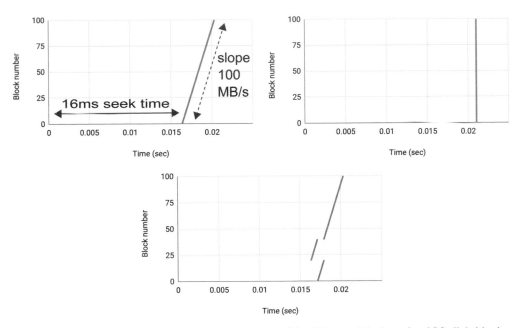

Figure 5.6abc   **Sample charts showing some possible disk read timings for 100 disk blocks**

> **Half-Useful Principle**
>
> After a startup latency T, work for at least time T—
> to do useful work at least half the time.

Another possible pattern, Figure 5.6b, is that nothing arrives for a long time, and then after ~21 msec of seek plus transfer, *all* the blocks arrive in the user buffer at once. This could happen if the operating system reads all the data into a kernel buffer and then delivers it into user space by rewriting page table entries.

Yet another pattern, Figure 5.6c, is that the read picks up somewhere in the middle, perhaps near the front of the file, fills in the very front a bit later, and then continues with the rest of the file. This could happen if the disk optimizes reading just after the seek by not waiting for the very first block to rotate into position but instead starts delivering at whatever block passes the read head first, wrapping around to the initial blocks when they pass by later.

If the file is stored in two extents with a seek in between, what else would you expect to see? Part of the file will be read, then there will be an extra delay for the seek/rotate to the second extent, and then the rest of the file will be read.

If the file has a bad block that the disk drive internally replaces with a reserved one on the same disk cylinder (no long seek, but a different track and different sector position), what else would you expect to see? Part of the file will be read, then there will be a short seek/rotate within the cylinder to get to the replacement block, and then a short seek/rotate to get back to continue the main file.

Note that if you don't see the pattern for multiple extents or the pattern for bad blocks, then (by logical exclusion) there definitely must be exactly one extent and exactly zero bad blocks.

5.5 A Little Back-of-the-Envelope Calculation

About how long should it take to transfer a single 4KB disk block? At O(100) MB/sec, a disk transfers O(100) bytes in a microsecond, so 4KB should take roughly 40 usec. For our slow disks, it might be closer to 60 usec. The total time for 10,000 blocks should be about 600 msec.

How long will each iteration of our "look at the first word of each 4KB block" loop take? These items are all 4KB apart so will not spread out well in a CPU L1 or L2 or even L3 cache, using just a few of all the cache associativity sets, and will therefore likely *all be cache misses*. And remember that the I/O hardware is simultaneously accessing the *same* data, so might be further delaying any imagined CPU cache behavior. If a main memory access takes about 50 nsec, then one pass of 10,000 of them will take about 500 usec. But we expect blocks to arrive about every 60 usec. Do you see the problem?

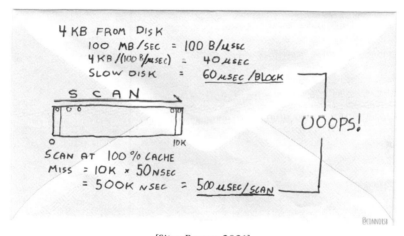

[Sites-Bowen 2021]

To get more accurate successive-block timings, we also look at the *expected* very-next-block every other time instead of just once per 10K blocks. To avoid giving crummy time resolution while also avoiding spending all the time in `gettimeofday()` system calls, we strike a balance and renew the time of day every 256 scanned items of the 10K total, or roughly once every 20 usec.

It is time to go compile and run mystery3.cc and see what pattern you get. Note that the disks on the sample servers are very cheap and rotate at only 5400 rpm (not 7200). They don't seek very fast either. You should derate your time expectations appropriately. The SSDs on the sample servers are also cheap; you might see average transfer rates faster than disks but still only about 400–800 MB/sec.

The program mystery3.cc takes as a command-line argument the name of the 40MB file to write. Our sample servers have a second disk drive *just* for data (no interfering operating-system activity) mounted as /datadisk/dserve. Put your temp file there, using something like

```
g++ -O2 mystery3.cc -lrt -o mystery3
./mystery3 /datadisk/dserve/xxxxx.tmp
```

where "xxxxx" is your login name or something else unique. The g++ (not gcc) command allows full C++ language constructs, and the -lrt flag allows the proper library support for asynchronous I/O. The program will write a JavaScript object notation (JSON) output file, based on the input filename. In this case,

```
/datadisk/dserve/xxxxx_read_times.json
```

It contains 10,000 pairs of time and block#, where time is seconds and a microsecond fraction from the start of the asynchronous read/write.

One of our sample servers also has a cheap SSD drive *just* for data, mounted as /datassd/dserve. Run it via something like

```
./mystery3 /datassd/dserve/xxxxx.tmp
```

producing

```
/datassd/dserve/xxxxx_read_times.json
```

You will find these SSD timings to be quite different, and not quite as simple as you might have expected.

As always, you will get somewhat different times and likely different patterns if you run on other computers or with other operating systems, disks, or SSDs. Every machine is a little different.

5.6   How Fast Is a Disk Write?

To measure the speed of a disk write, we will use a similar strategy, except this time we want to timestamp when each block is copied *out* of our buffer to the disk. The modified strategy looks like this:

1. Set up by filling a 40MB array with non-zero words; then go back and set the first int64 of each 4KB block to zero.

2. Open a file for write specifying O_DIRECT and O_NOATIME.

3. Record the start time in a variable.

4. Write the file via an *asynchronous* write.

5. *While* the write is happening, repeatedly scan the array, setting the first int64 of each 4KB block to the current time. One of these values for each block will be copied out to disk.

After the write finishes, read all 40MB back from disk. Look through the array to see what timestamp was actually copied to disk for each 4KB block (or, more exactly, the time at which it was copied out of the user-mode array).

When we are done, we will have a start time and 10,240 copy-out times. What pattern do you expect to see, or what possible patterns?

You get to finish this question in the later exercises, based on completing the `TimeDiskWrite()` routine in mystery3.cc. Make a copy, edit it to complete, and run it on both kinds of devices to get the write times.

5.7 Results

You should now have four result files:

```
/datadisk/dserve/xxxxx_read_times.json
/datadisk/dserve/xxxxx_write_times.json
/datassd/dserve/xxxxx_read_times.json
/datassd/dserve/xxxxx_write_times.json
```

To the extent that blocks arrive out of order, the times in these will be out of order. We need to re-sort them before displaying the results. To preserve the intended JSON initial and final lines, the sorting needs to be strictly by byte value including spaces, not by alphabetic name. The Linux command

```
$ export LC_ALL=C
```

sets the proper sorting algorithm. Follow this with

```
$ cat /datadisk/dserve/xxxxx_read_times.json |sort \
  |./makeself show_disk.html >xxxxx_disk_read.html
```

and similar commands for disk write, SSD read, and SSD write. The makeself program takes a template HTML file and merges in the JSON file and a few other items at the right places. The `show_disk.html` file is the template. Doing this four times gives four different HTML files for display. The displayed HTML can be panned and zoomed to look at the timing details. Interface directions are in the comment at the first 30-odd lines of the HTML file.

5.8 Reading from Disk

On one of our sample servers, an overall disk-read display might look like Figure 5.7. The x-axis shows time after the asynchronous read, from 0 to about 800 msec. This is a bit longer than our initial estimate of 600 msec to read 40 MB at 65 MB/sec. But this is an old slow disk, so 800 msec is plausible. The y-axis is block number, 0 to 10,239.

The diagram looks a lot like 10,240 blocks coming in sequentially, but if you look closely, you will notice that the first block in, at the far left, is not block 0 but something more like block 200. On the far right, there is some hiccup at the top, and then the first ~200 blocks come in last, at the lower-right corner. What could be going on?

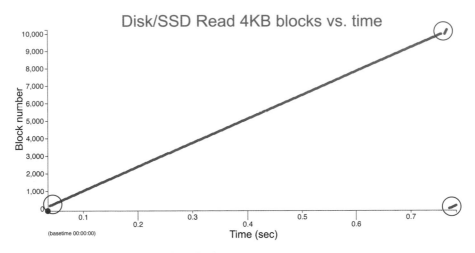

Figure 5.7   **Overall disk-read timing display**

Looking first at the beginning of the 40MB read, Figure 5.8 shows the first 100 msec. At this scale, we can see that the first block arrives about 39 msec after the asynchronous read is started. This is the time for the initial seek and rotate. It is somewhat longer than our estimated seek time of 20 msec. But this is an old, slow disk, so 39 msec is plausible.

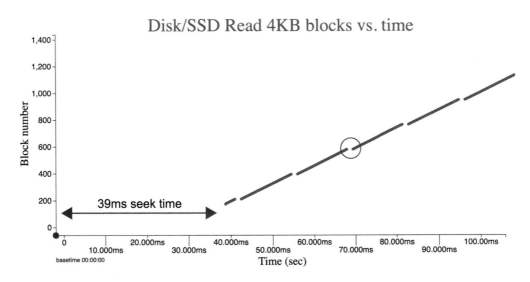

Figure 5.8   **Initial disk-read timing display, first 100 msec**

We can also see in Figure 5.8 little time gaps every 200 blocks or so. What are those?

Zooming in further, Figure 5.9 shows 5 msec across. Reading the details from the sorted JSON file, we see that the first block that arrives in our user-mode buffer is block 173 at 38.809 msec after the read starts. The first four blocks appear to arrive almost simultaneously, and then blocks arrive about every 65 usec for a while. This is about 60 MB/sec, which is what we expect. (The first four blocks arriving nearly simultaneously is a startup artifact of the slow scanning loop; see the earlier Section 5.5.)

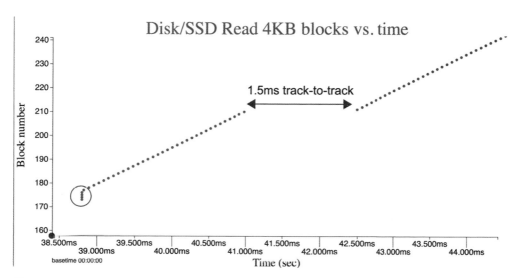

Figure 5.9   **Initial disk-read timing display, zoomed in on about 5 msec**

After block 210 at 41 msec, there is a 1.51 msec gap before block 211 arrives. This is a track to track head switch and re-servo time, taking about 1/7 of a revolution (11.11 msec / 7 = 1.59 msec). A similar-size gap happens after blocks 395, 579, 764, 948, etc. These mean a slightly varying track length of 184 or 185 4KB disk blocks. The variation may come from the fact that this is an old disk with 512-byte sectors and an actual physical track length that is not an exact multiple of 4KB. Or it may reflect one reserved block per cylinder for bad-block replacement.

Looking now at the end of the transfer in Figure 5.7, there are two odd sections: one at the upper right, Figure 5.10, and one at the lower right, Figure 5.11. At the upper right, a few tracks near the end of the transfer come into the user-mode buffer, up through 754 msec after the read starts. Then there is the expected 1.51 msec track-to-track gap followed by the transfer of a *single* 4KB block, a time gap of 6.46 msec, and then a transfer of exactly 256 blocks (1MB) at over 250 MB/sec, *much faster than the disk-surface* transfer rate. That megabyte transfer has some faint substructure of five transfers with tiny time gaps of 15–70 usec: 244KB, 140KB, 256KB, 192KB, and 192KB. What do we know about this?

Since it is faster than the disk-surface speed, the transfer must be coming from some sort of electronic buffer or cache. If the 1MB transfer were from a main-memory file-system cache, it should go at close to memory speed, on the order of 10 GB/sec and up. This is too fast for the observed transfer. If it were from the on-disk track buffer, the transfer rate could be up to the SATA III bus maximum transfer rate of 600 MB/sec, but would likely be slower. Since this is an old slow disk, it has only a SATA II connection with a design limit of 300 MB/sec. An on-disk track-buffer transfer rate of 250 MB/sec is thus quite plausible.

A good rule of thumb is that if a transfer size is a power of 2, it likely is determined by software, while if it is not a power of 2, it likely is determined by physical constraints. Since the transfer is exactly 1MB, it is not related to the size of the disk tracks. In this case, software or disk firmware likely dictated the transfer size. Note also that three of the five sub-pieces of this transfer, 256/192/192KB, are exact multiples of 64KB.

Other than identifying the disk buffer as the source of the transfer, I do not have a complete explanation for the Figure 5.10 dynamics.

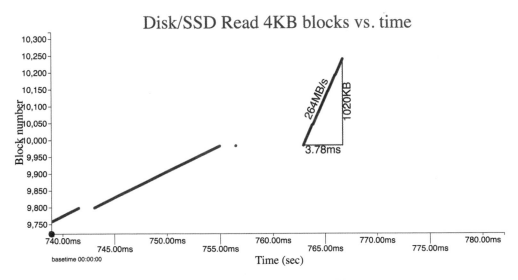

Figure 5.10   **Near-final disk-read timing display, 40 msec wide**

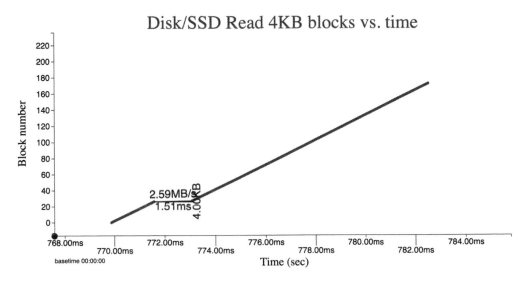

Figure 5.11   **Final disk-read timing display, 20 msec wide**

The final part of the read transfer is shown in Figure 5.11. The first 173 blocks of the file are transferred *last*, in two pieces. There is an unshown gap of 6.46 msec between the last block of Figure 5.10 and the first block of Figure 5.11. Then in Figure 5.11 block numbers 0–26 are transferred, there is a time gap of 1.51 msec, and then blocks 27–172 are transferred. Recall that block 173 was the first block transferred at the beginning of the read, so nothing is missing. What do we know about this behavior?

The 1.51 msec gap is a track-to-track seek, so the very front of the file started mid-track and continued for 27 blocks. After the gap, 146 blocks (27–172) were transferred. At the very front of the read, remember that 38 blocks (173–210) were transferred. These sum to 146 + 38 = 184 blocks, so in fact constitute a 184-block track. But why are the first 173 blocks of the file transferred last?

I don't know. Running the mystery3 program multiple times produces varying numbers of initial blocks transferred last. Running it on different disks can produce the much more obvious pattern of Figure 5.6a—transferring block 0 first, followed by the rest in order. One possible explanation for the observed dynamics: the file was written in two extents, a short one of 173 blocks, and then the rest. The 40 MB asynchronous read started at the front of the second extent (perhaps it was physically closer to the read/write head when the read started), read it entirely, and then went back to read the first extent.

The real point here, however, is that *we observed the true dynamics* of this 40MB disk read. They turned out to be much more complex than the simple picture in our head.

5.9 Writing to Disk

On our sample server, one overall disk write display looks like Figure 5.12. **What in the world has happened?** The x-axis shows the time after the asynchronous write, from 0 to about 800 msec. This is about the same elapsed time as our 40 MB read, *as it should be* since the disk rotates at exactly the same speed for reads and writes.

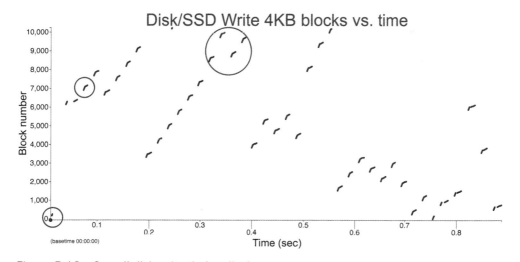

Figure 5.12 **Overall disk-write timing display**

If you count carefully, there are 40 different little transfers of exactly 1MB each, plus a couple of fragments. Running the program again, there will still be 1MB fragments, but they will land at different places in time. Clearly, some mechanism is breaking up our 40MB write into forty 1MB writes and then performing them out of order, with gaps of 10–12 msec in between. The visually dominant upslope shows 1MB writes with sequence gaps of 2MB in between. But gaps of -3MB, -5MB, 17MB, etc. also occur. We will revisit this in a little while.

Note the little fragment at the very far lower left, the first blocks written. Zooming in on the first 25 msec in Figure 5.13, we find a 13 msec delay from the beginning of the write until a block is copied out of the user-mode buffer. The first thing copied is block 173, just as in the 40 MB read. This suggests some common mechanism (not timing-dependent) shared by the read and the write. Perhaps the file system's data allocation strategy interacts oddly with this disk's driver. Perhaps a short first extent of up to 173 blocks is written last into the directory file. Tracking down the exact behavior is beyond the scope of this book. Again, the real point here is that *we observed the true dynamics* of this 40MB disk write. They turned out to be much more complex than the simple picture in our head.

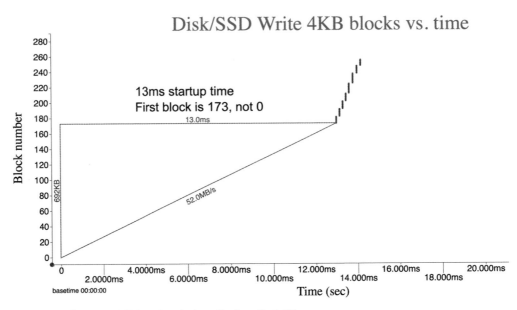

Figure 5.13   **Initial disk-write timing display, first 20 msec**

The initial 13 msec delay is the time to spawn the asynchronous write process, get the I/O path established, skip over 173 blocks for some reason, and start copying data to the disk, perhaps via an intermediate kernel buffer. The copying could start before the disk finishes seeking to the initial track. The overall slope of this initial transfer is about 250 MB/sec, again much faster than the surface speed. But for writes we expect the transfer to be to the on-disk write buffer at electronic speed followed by a later transfer from on-disk write buffer to the surface of the disk at the slower disk-surface transfer speed. Thus, 250 MB/sec is completely plausible.

In Figure 5.13 you will notice groups of several (9–12) blocks are given the same time. This is an artifact of the slow scanning loop as described in the earlier Section 5.5. These groups are spaced 150–180 usec apart, which is the initial actual time for one complete pass of the scanning loop, writing timestamps to 10K different block beginnings in memory (a little faster than our back-of-the-envelope estimate). After the first couple of transfers, this drops to 80–90 usec per pass and stays that way.

Figure 5.14 shows the detailed dynamics of a complete 1MB write about 50 msec later. The first 736KB is copied quickly at about 250 MB/sec, and then the copying slows down to about 60 MB/sec for the remaining 72MB. If we assume that copying into the on-disk write buffer at 250 MB/sec (electronic transfer speed) is overlapped with the disk copying out of it at 60 MB/sec (disk surface speed), the effective fill rate of the write buffer is about 250 - 60 = 190 MB/sec. During the 2.8 msec of the steep part of Figure 5.14, there is enough time to fill 532KB of buffer. This is suspiciously close to 512KB. So perhaps the dual-slope transfer is explained by filling and simultaneously emptying a 512KB on-disk write buffer, then when it is full only filling it at the emptying rate.

Alternately, the initial transfer in Figure 5.14 of 736KB is 184 blocks, the exact track size we observed while reading. So perhaps the dual-slope transfer is explained by the disk driver filling an on-disk write buffer for exactly one track's worth of data and then transferring the rest of 1MB more slowly. But other 1MB transfers later in the transfer have initial fill sizes of around 650KB when there is a closely following 1.5 msec delay for track-to-track seek, so I tend to favor the first explanation.

At the end of copying 1MB of data from memory to the disk buffer, the copying stops, but the buffer emptying to the disk surface must continue for another 2.8 msec, not visible here.

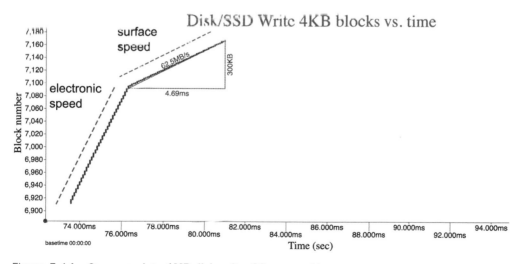

Figure 5.14   **One complete 1MB disk-write, 20 msec wide**

Each 1MB piece is longer than one track (256 blocks vs. 184-185 blocks), so every transfer must include a track-to-track seek, and some transfers must include two. Seeks are not visible in the timing data when they occur during the initial electronic-speed copying. But a seek is visible as a 1.51 msec gap when it occurs during the surface-speed copying. Figure 5.15 shows a group of four 1MB transfers, two of which have visible seek gaps at slightly different times in the surface-speed copying.

Figure 5.15   **Some 1MB disk writes; two on the left with track-to-track 1.51 msec gaps visible**

The figure also shows some variation in which fraction of each write is done at electronic speed and which at surface speed. This is consistent with the idea that the buffer filling is coupled to the emptying and not directly to the track size.

We switch now from measuring a rotating disk to measuring a solid-state SSD.

5.10   Reading from SSD

On our sample servers, one overall SSD read display looks like Figure 5.16. The x-axis shows time after the asynchronous read, from 0 to about 150 msec, i.e., about 5 times shorter than disk reads. Blocks arrive in the user-mode buffer in the simplest order, block 0 to block 10,239. There are in fact 40 separate 1MB transfers, not quite visible at this resolution.

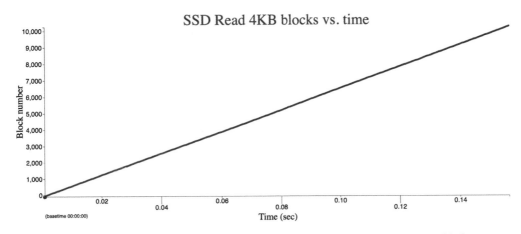

Figure 5.16   **Overall SSD-read timing display, five times faster than disk and with fewer anomalies**

Figure 5.17 shows the first 1MB read, starting with a delay of 1.14 msec before block 0 arrives. There are some scattered timing wrinkles in this first block that might be unrelated operating system activity, so we look instead at Figure 5.18, which shows a slightly later block.

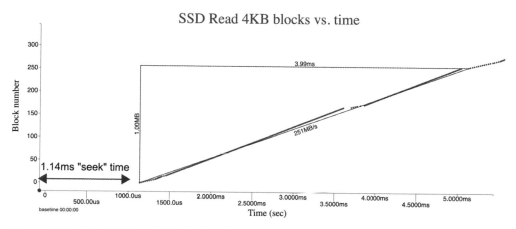

Figure 5.17   **First SSD-read block, showing initial 1.14 msec delay**

In Figure 5.18, there is a full 1MB transfer and parts of the following one. Each 1MB transfer takes 3.88 msec including the 94 usec gap between blocks. Including this gap, the average transfer rate is 258 MB/sec, again close to the SATA II bus limit on our cheap sample server.

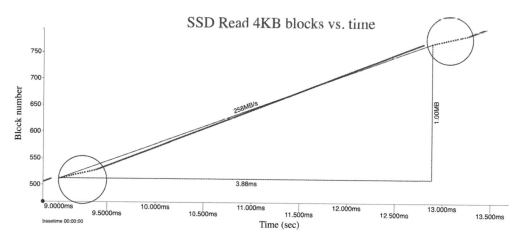

Figure 5.18   **Early SSD-read block, showing detailed timing**

Looking more closely at Figure 5.18, there are exactly 16 blocks at the beginning of each 1MB transfer that come in slowly, at a rate of about 164 MB/sec; then things speed up to 274 MB/sec for the rest (before the gap). It looks as though the 94 usec gap is the read access time and that there are 16 banks within the SSD. The first block from each bank arrives with some delay, so these are spread out in time, and then the rest arrive back to back about 1.6x more quickly, perhaps through bank interleaving and pipelining.

5.11   Writing to SSD

On our sample servers, one overall SSD write display looks like Figure 5.19. The x-axis shows time after the asynchronous read, from 0 to about 150 msec, about 5 times faster than the disk write. There are no surprises here. The initial delay for copying the first block out of our user-space buffer is 4.76 msec. There is no substructure whatsoever visible in the timing, indicating that the entire write is done at electronic speeds with perfect overlap between copying to the SSD write buffer and to the flash cells themselves. This implies that the flash cells are at least slightly faster than the SATA II bus speed.

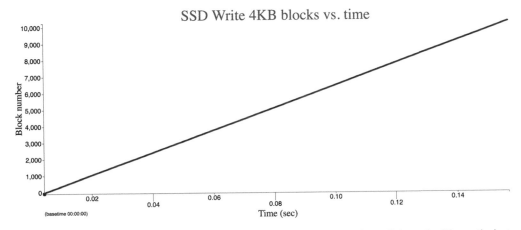

Figure 5.19   **Overall SSD-write timing display, five times faster than disk and with no timing anomalies**

5.12   Multiple Transfers

With 1MB transfers on both disk and SSD and for both reads and writes, we can tentatively conclude that breaking up 40MB read/write happens in some common file-system software design, not in the device itself. Why are there multiple 1MB transfers instead of a single 40MB transfer? *Because we are running on a virtual-memory CPU.*

How could that be related? Virtual memory means that our user-mode 40MB buffer is not necessarily contiguous in physical main memory but may be scattered across 10,240 different page frames, with the contiguous user-mode virtual addresses mapped to non-contiguous 4KB physical pages. How does I/O work in such an environment?

One possibility has to do direct memory access (DMA) I/O via user-space virtual addresses. This is rarely done. A related possibility has to do direct I/O via kernel-space virtual addresses. Doing so requires locking down all the pages involved and passing a piece of the kernel page tables to an input/output memory management unit (IOMMU) dedicated to I/O devices. The IOMMU fetches page table entries (PTEs) as needed and maps all the I/O transfer virtual addresses to corresponding physical memory addresses. The actual I/O devices know nothing about virtual memory. For fast devices such as SSDs and 10+ Gb/sec networks, IOMMUs have difficulty loading new PTEs with short enough latency.

Another possibility is to build in the processor's DMA I/O path (or in each I/O device) a modest-size scatter-gather table of physical page frame addresses and to pre-load this from the kernel PTEs before starting an I/O transfer. This is typically done, and the normal table size is 128 or 256 entries, each mapping 4KB. Our sample server appears to have a 256-entry hardware table that maps 1MB exactly. The table usage pattern is

1. Break each transfer into 1MB pieces.

2. Load the next (up to) 256 table entries.

3. Transfer (up to) 1MB.

4. At end of transfer, interrupt back to the operating system.

5. Loop back to load the next table entries.

Some part of the file system and/or device driver code is responsible for breaking up long transfers. Once a long transfer is broken up into several pieces, some device drivers may reorder these pieces as a function of some physical property of the I/O device, such as the current position of a disk's read/write heads.

5.13   Summary

This chapter is about measuring what the operating-system and device microcode layers of "automatic transmission" are deciding to do and when, compared to measuring simple user-mode "manual transmission" behavior.

We have examined disk and SSD transfer timing, not just aggregate MB/sec, but detailed timing of when each 4KB block enters or leaves a user-space buffer. The detailed timing reveals a large amount of substructure and some surprising dynamics. Most of the dynamics we can connect to known hardware and software designs, and we can usually advance plausible explanations for the remaining observations.

- There are many layers of software between a user-mode program and a storage device such as a disk or SSD.

- To measure activity at the device, defeat much of the caching, prefetching, and buffering.

- Recording the time that each 4KB block is transferred in or out of a user-mode buffer gives a detailed view of the actual hardware and software dynamics.

- From this detail, we can measure seek time, inter-track gaps, surface transfer rate, electronic transfer rate, and many similar items.

- The actual dynamics are much more complicated than the simple pictures in our heads.

- It is easy in datacenters and database systems to use storage devices inefficiently without realizing it. Being aware of their complex dynamics helps avoid this.

Exercises

Compile and run mystery3.cc, noting the critical g++ and −1rt command-line use and supplying the /datadisk/dserve/xxxxx disk filename to use. The program writes a file

    /datadisk/dserve/xxxxx_read_times.json

which has pairs of block number and time that block was transferred (to microsecond resolution) relative to the start time. Each run will get slightly different results, depending on which machine and which disk and where and how fragmented its free space is.

Use the makeself program described earlier to turn each JSON file into an HTML file so you can more easily see the patterns. Use the mouse to drag and mouse wheel to zoom. Clicking the lower-left red dot resets the view. Shift-click-drag-unshift-unclick measures time and bytes.

5.1 What causes groups of about 150–250 disk blocks with time gaps between? About what is the time between groups? What is causing this delay?

5.2 Extra credit: If some groups are one block shorter than others, why?

5.3 In the JSON file, find the smallest transfer time (which may not be at the front). What is the seek and rotate time to get to the very first block read, in milliseconds?

5.4 Find the largest transfer time, and divide it by the 40MB transferred. What is the overall transfer rate observed, in MB/sec? (This time includes the initial seek and all intermediate delays so is somewhat lower than any marketing number.)

5.5 Looking at a typical group of ~200 blocks with time gaps on both sides, what is the overall transfer rate within that group, in MB/sec? This should be the true transfer rate at the read/write head.

5.6 Look around for a group that has a **faster** transfer rate than the disk surface supports. What is the fast transfer rate, in MB/sec? What is going on when that happens?

5.7 Now run mystery3 on an SSD using /datassd/dserve. What is the seek time to read the soonest-delivered block? What is the overall transfer rate start to finish, in MB/sec?

5.8 The SSD timings probably have a different pattern than the disk timings, with perhaps very regular discontinuities or changes in rate. How many discontinuities are there? Comment briefly on what you think is happening.

5.9 Complete the missing part of `TimeDiskWrite()`. Mine is seven more lines, setting the block current times. This will be easy if you have followed what the strategy is, and a bit harder if you have been only skimming this text and the code. But when you are done, you will better understand what is going on.

5.10 Now re-run on disk and look at the disk write timings. Are you surprised? You might see a lot of discontinuities. How many discontinuities or big groups are there? Comment briefly on what you think is happening.

5.11 Finally, re-run on an SSD and look at the SSD write timings and comment briefly on what you think is happening. Use your order-of-magnitude knowledge to compare various time delays to possible causes. If the delay from a possible cause is a different order of magnitude than the observed delay, move on to another possibility.

Chapter 6

Measuring Networks

The fourth fundamental shared resource to measure is network activity—how long do real network transmissions take and what are their dynamics? In contrast to measurements of the internal dynamics of single operations in the previous chapters, we will look at multiple overlapping network requests. The environment for disk measurements (and for that matter CPU and memory measurements) is fairly simple, as shown in Figure 6.1. There is just the one program running on one CPU and accessing one disk with a single transfer at a time.

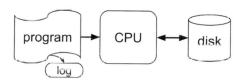

Figure 6.1 **Environment for disk measurements**

But the environment for network measurements is substantially more complicated, as shown in Figure 6.2. There are multiple client programs sending request messages to several server programs, which in turn send responses. These are all running on several different computers with network connections in between. Common server programs include database software.

In general, the different computers of Figure 6.2 could be located anywhere in the world, but we will concentrate in this chapter on computers that are physically close to each other, such as all inside a single datacenter room. The network connections could be Ethernet, Infiniband, Fibre Channel, or other choices, but we will concentrate on Ethernet connections. Various network protocols could be used, such as virtual channels, User Datagram Protocol (UDP), or Transmission Control Protocol/Internet Protocol (TCP/IP) software. We will concentrate on TCP/IP links, a common choice within datacenters.

The request messages and their responses could be structured in various ways; we will concentrate on *remote procedure call* (RPC) messages. Each RPC request message specifies a server computer to perform some work, the particular method (i.e., function or procedure name) to be called, and copies of all the method arguments. Each response message specifies the client computer to receive the response and the response data itself. The request and response messages can

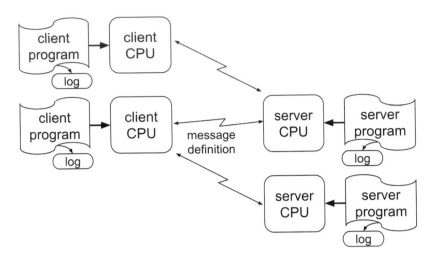

Figure 6.2   **More complicated environment for network measurements**

vary widely in size, from about 100 bytes to tens of megabytes. RPCs are usually *asynchronous*, meaning that the caller need not wait for the RPC response, but can instead continue executing and issuing other RPC requests in parallel, eventually waiting for responses that come back in arbitrary order. It is the highly parallel execution of many small pieces of work that allows datacenter software to respond quickly. Unlike TCP and other network protocols, RPC message formats are not standardized. This book uses a simple made-up format, described in Section 6.8.

In a large datacenter of 20,000 computers, with each computer running many different programs, an individual computer may have 10,000 network connections open at once, exchanging RPCs over all of them. While Figure 6.2 shows multiple point-to-point connections between client CPUs and server CPUs, these are just conceptual. The physical network may have just a single Ethernet link between each computer and a network router, with all the RPC traffic shared across these links. These underlying physical links and their associated kernel software are the shared network resource that we measure in this chapter.

> A note on notation. The word *server* is somewhat overloaded in the computer industry. It can refer to a box of hardware that is a computer, or it can refer to a program that performs some specific function on behalf of various client programs. To add to the confusion, a server program performing a specific function is often called a *service*. In this book, when the context is not clear we will refer to *server CPU* or *sample server* for a box of hardware and *server program* for a piece of software providing some service. The unqualified term *server* will generally mean a CPU.

As discussed in Chapter 1, datacenter software consists of layers and layers of subsystems, many running in parallel and often on hundreds or thousands of different servers. All this activity is tied together with some form of network message passing or RPCs. In this chapter we will observe and measure some simple RPCs, and then in the next chapter we will measure multiple overlapping RPCs. There are several layers of software involved, including user code, the operating system, and the TCP (transmission control protocol) stack on the client computer and the same three on the server computer. We will use RPCs from one user-mode program to another and back, measuring the behavior and delays between sample servers.

6.1 About Ethernet

Ethernet is the standard networking technology worldwide and is heavily used in datacenters. The original Ethernet at Xerox PARC in 1973 used a single coaxial cable (one wire inside a tube of a second wire with insulation in between), so it was a shared medium. Individual Alto computers connected to the wire with a *vampire tap* that poked an insulated spike through the outer wire to touch the inner wire, plus a second connection to the outer wire, as shown in Figure 6.3. (The vampire taps were shown to be unreliable and were soon superseded.) Just as polite people do when talking in a group, a computer desiring to transmit would listen to the coax (carrier-sense) waiting until it was idle and then try to transmit. During transmission, it continued to listen to determine whether the bits it transmitted were on the wire or whether they were garbled because some other computer was also starting to transmit. When that happened, both would stop transmitting, each wait a random amount of time, and then try again. Any node connected to the shared coax can observe all the packets, not just those addressed to that node. This is useful for monitoring network performance and debugging network problems, but it raises security issues.

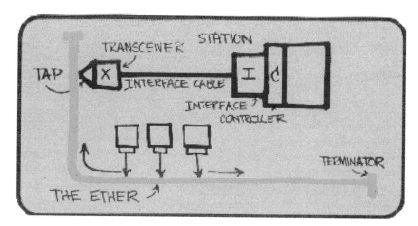

Figure 6.3   **Metcalfe's original Ethernet diagram, photographed by Boggs [Metcalfe 1976]**

Today, Ethernet data is transmitted as packets of up to 1,518 bytes (jumbo packets can be bigger) with gaps [Wikipedia 2021n] in between and a checksum at the end, as in Figure 6.4. Network software turns longer messages into sequences of packets. Individual packets are delivered with high probability, but are not 100% guaranteed to arrive. In particular, switches and routers that are overloaded are free to drop packets at any time. Packets with bad checksums are also discarded.

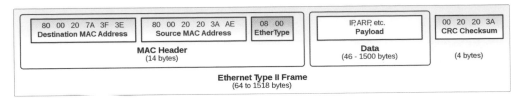

Figure 6.4   **Ethernet type II frame [Wikimedia 2020a]**

Each Ethernet packet starts with the 48-bit destination *Media Access Control* (MAC) address, followed by the 48-bit source MAC address, followed by a 16-bit *Ethertype* field and then the rest of the packet. The last 24 bits of a MAC address is an assigned Organizationally Unique Identifier (OUI) [IEEE 2021].

The remainder of a packet typically has several *headers* for layers of different switching protocols and then finally some user data. We will be using the TCP/IPv4 protocol pair, with a 20-byte IPv4 header giving the 4-byte IP addresses of the source and destination machines and a 20-byte TCP header giving the 2-byte port numbers on those machines plus data *sequence numbers* (SEQ) and *acknowledgment bits* (ACK) for accomplishing in-order guaranteed delivery.

We are using IP version 4 (IPv4) in our examples, but all the 32-bit IP numbers in this protocol are now used up worldwide, so the newer IPv6 is also being used in datacenters. IPv6 has 128-bit IP addresses, and an entire IPv6 header is 40 bytes instead of 20.

The MAC address is a unique 48-bit identifier assigned to each network interface controller in the world. (The original 3 Mb/sec Ethernet used 8-bit addresses.) The Ethertype field specifies how to interpret the following data bytes. For TCP/IP traffic, the MAC header Ethertype specifies IPv4, followed by a 20-byte IPv4 header in the first few data bytes of Figure 6.4. The IP header in turn specifies that it is followed immediately by a TCP header, which specifies that it is followed immediately by some number N of user message data or *payload* bytes.

> While the original 3 Mb/sec Ethernet used a single shared coax cable for connections, later implementations more often use twisted-pair copper wires or optical fibers running point-to-point from each computer to a hub or switch or router. These connections have progressively increased in speed from 10 Mb/sec to 100 Mb/sec, 1 Gb/sec, 10 Gb/sec, and now 100 Gb/sec with 400 Gb/sec on the horizon, *five orders of magnitude* faster than the original.

Note that network transmission rate is traditionally measured in bits per second while disk transfer rate is traditionally measured in bytes per second. Lower-case "Mb" is megabits while upper-case "MB" is megabytes. Marketing literature often confuses these, introducing factor-of-eight errors. Deliberately quoting disk transfers in Mb/sec is a cheap way to make your numbers 8x larger.

6.2   About Hubs, Switches, and Routers

Point-to-point Ethernet connections between more than two machines require some form of switching fabric. There are three different kinds that you may encounter.

A *hub* with N links is a very cheap and now rarely used design that just reproduces one incoming transmission on all inactive outgoing links. If two or more links have incoming transmissions at once, only one is copied, and the others are dropped. Since a hub can copy only one transmission at a time, it is a shared resource like the original coax.

Switches with N links store packets at each incoming port and immediately forward them to one or more outgoing ports. Smarter switches keep tables of which MAC address destinations are attached to which port and forward only to the right destination port. A switch may store as little as two packets per incoming port, forwarding one while a second arrives. If multiple packets on different incoming ports have the same outgoing port and there is not enough buffering for all of them, some of the packets are dropped. As mentioned, Ethernet does not guarantee packet delivery, just best-effort.

A *router* is a more complex form of switch, using not only the MAC address in each packet but also higher-level IP and other header address information to select the output port for each packet. Routers are often connected to other routers so that a packet may go from one end node through several routers to another end node:

$$A \to \text{Router1} \Rightarrow \text{Router2} \Rightarrow \text{Router3} \Rightarrow B$$

Typical use in a datacenter is to have 40–50 servers mounted in a vertical rack with a router at the top (or middle) each rack. Traffic between servers within that rack is delivered directly from the top-of-rack router, while traffic destined for other racks is sent from the source top-of-rack router to one of several intermediate routers that eventually send the packet to the destination top-of-rack router and on to the destination server. Often in this case, the cross-router links run at a higher speed than the individual server links: for example, 10 Gb/sec copper-wire server links within a rack and 100 Gb/sec fiber-optic cross-rack links. We will use the phrase *on the wire* to refer to bit transmission over any kind of link. Routers often have several packets of buffering per input port, so can handle a modest amount of network congestion with several input packets destined for the same output port.

Our sample servers each have a 1 Gb/sec Ethernet port, and several are connected via a five-port switch, four ports for up to four sample servers and the fifth port connected to the rest of the building, as shown in Appendix A.

6.3   About TCP/IP

The TCP/IP design allows packets to be routed not just within a single building but anywhere in the world that is connected to the global Internet. This routing sends packets across various media—not just Ethernet links, but also long-haul dedicated fibers, radio links to satellites, WiFi connections within houses, and many more kinds of sub-networks. The complex dynamics and delays of long-distance communication are beyond the scope of this book; we will concentrate just on the complex-enough dynamics and delays of Ethernet connections within a single building.

For a message from machine A to machine B, sending software on A for *guaranteed-delivery* protocols such as TCP keeps track of packets sent that do not arrive and retransmits them. Packets are therefore not guaranteed to arrive in the order originally sent, so receiving software further tracks them and reassembles messages in receive buffers. This tracking is done by the receiving TCP software on B sending back an ACK indication to A for one or more received packets. ACKs can be sent in short packets of their own but are usually piggybacked as part of other packets already going back B⇒A. Senders have a limited number of multiple *packets outstanding*—sent but not yet acknowledged. When this limit is reached, the sender must wait until some ACKs arrive. If a packet ACK does not arrive within some configured timeout period, the sender is responsible for retransmitting that packet.

We are using TCP/IPv4 to send RPC messages between servers, with each message possibly requiring many packets. Our remote procedure calls depend on the guaranteed delivery mechanism of TCP to deliver an entire message with the pieces in proper order.

It is unlikely in our little sample server cluster that we will see packets dropped and retransmitted because of hardware errors, but we will soon try to create enough network congestion to force some packet drops because of overloaded switch buffering. To try to protect the rest of any building network from also becoming overloaded when we do saturation experiments, it is best for our lab machines to connect directly with each other through their own local switch, as described earlier.

TCP establishes a reliable connection to carry a *pair* of byte streams between two programs on two machines, one stream in each direction. These are the bi-directional connections shown in Figure 6.2. Each machine is specified by its IP address and the specific program by its port number. Two-byte port numbers range from 0..65535, but ports below 1024 are restricted to specific uses. We will use ports 12345..12348 on our sample servers for RPC traffic. (Our lab machines may also have a software firewall that closes traffic on most other ports.)

Once a connection is established, there is a stream of data available in each direction between the two machines. A machine can send an (almost) arbitrary number of bytes at once, and the TCP software deals with breaking up long messages into multiple packets, or packing multiple short messages or fragments of longer messages into single packets. The communication model is just a stream of bytes, so a given RPC message may start and end in the middle of packets.

On the other end, a machine can request receiving an (almost) arbitrary number of bytes into a buffer, but the number actually delivered at once can be less than the buffer size. The receive calls normally return any data available, up to the requested amount, rather than waiting for receipt of the full amount requested. This design allows the receiving software some flexibility in managing buffers and in managing how long to wait for data (or what else to do in the meantime). The receiving logic thus must be prepared to do multiple receive calls to get all the pieces of a single complete message and must also be prepared to receive multiple messages and partial messages at each call.

6.4 About Packets

In addition to IP and TCP headers, datacenter packets may contain additional headers. For example, virtual local area networks (VLANs) can be implemented by having a 4-byte VLAN header before the IP header. Cooperating routers deliver packets based on their VLAN header, with the effect that packets from one virtual LAN can be prevented from reaching ports associated with other virtual LANs. This design allows multiple completely unrelated networks to use shared switching equipment. Packets without a VLAN header can be dropped by a router or sent to specific unsecured ports. Incoming packets with the wrong VLAN header for a particular port can be dropped. The goal is that each type of traffic is completely unable to observe any of the other traffic, even if some connected computers are spoofing their MAC and IP addresses to try to read, and even modify and forward, others' data. If the routers themselves operate correctly, this can give some level of security and privacy.

One use of VLANs is for a building-wide network with specific authorized machines (by MAC address) attached to specific router ports and using VLAN headers. An unauthorized machine connected to the network is not allowed to use any VLAN headers, and all it can see is a tiny default network consisting of itself and a gateway/authorization computer that may choose to stop all communication with the device, may convert it into an authorized node that can use VLANs, or may allow it to connect to an outside Internet port, thus supporting devices from guests visiting the building but otherwise allowing only limited access for those unauthorized machines.

Packets may also be encrypted. Enough initial information is left unencrypted to allow the packets to be routed, and then an encapsulation header is used to signal that the remaining bytes are to be passed on unchanged and uninterpreted by any routing mechanism. The encapsulated data can be encrypted in various ways by the sender and decrypted by the receiver. The encapsulation technique can also be used to carry byte streams that actually contain non-Internet bytes and use completely different routing protocols for some private network that connects different locations via encapsulated traffic sent over the regular Internet.

We will consider only unencapsulated packets for the rest of this book, since we are focusing on server-to-server network performance and not on all the possible ways to use the Internet.

6.5 About Remote Procedure Calls (RPCs)

Our lab experiments will use a form of remote procedure call. For a *local* procedure call, routine A calls some Method with arguments and gets back a return value, with all the code running on a single machine:

```
routine A {
    ...
    foo = Method(arguments);
    ...
}
```

For a *remote* procedure call, the idea is the same, but the Method (e.g., a C function) runs on a remote computer.

The Method name and arguments are passed to the remote server in a request message, and the return value is eventually passed back in a response message, as shown in Figure 6.5. The client and server programs are constructed with calls to an RPC library. Building, sending, and parsing the request and response messages is done by the library routines, implementing a particular RPC design. Non-blocking RPCs allow multiple RPC requests to be outstanding at once and allow responses to return out of order.

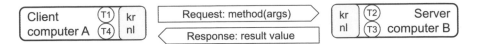

Figure 6.5   **A single RPC sending a request message and eventually receiving a response message; "krnl" is kernel code; T1-T4 are timestamps in user-mode code to send/receive RPC request and response messages.**

Each message is a network transmission. The request message goes from

- a user-mode client program on computer A at time T1 to

- kernel-mode code on A,

- over the network,

- to kernel-mode code on computer B,

- to a user-mode server program on B at time T2.

The response message travels in the opposite direction, at times T3 and T4. RPC latency is measured from the time T1 that the user-mode client program on A sends the request to the time T4 that the user-mode client program on A receives the response. When a response is delayed, the delay can be anywhere on the picture—request or response, user code or kernel code, machine A or machine B, send or receive network hardware. The four times T1..T4 help observe where the overall time went.

To examine the performance effects of network RPCs we will use timelines with events T1, T2, T3, and T4 indicating the RPC timing. We will draw individual RPCs as timelines with notches showing the times T1..T4, as shown in Figure 6.6. The notches do not take up much diagram space, but the human eye is quite good at picking them out, even when there are hundreds of RPC lines close together. The total RPC latency, as observed by the client user-mode program, is T4-T1. The total server time for the RPC is T3–T2.

Figure 6.6   **Diagram of one RPC, showing the four times. T1 to T2 is the time from client user-mode code sending an RPC request to server user-mode code receiving that request. T2 to T3 is the server time spent performing the request. T3 to T4 is the time from server user-mode code sending the RPC response to client user-mode code receiving that response. Times T1 and T4 are taken from the client CPU's time-of-day clock, while T2 and T3 are from the server CPU's time-of-day clock. The two clocks may be offset from each other by microseconds to milliseconds. We will deal with clock alignment in the next chapter. w1 is the time the client kernel-mode code sends the request to the network hardware ("w" for "wire"), and w3 is the time the server kernel-mode code sends the response to the network hardware.**

The return value from an RPC may be a single status number or may be thousands of bytes of data. It is convenient to always return both an overall status for the call (success, failure, specific error codes) and a possibly empty byte string of additional results.

Most datacenter software uses RPCs to send work between servers. For example, passing a paragraph of text to Google Translate via its web-page interface may send that paragraph to a load-balancing server that in turn forwards it to a least-busy translation server, which in turn may break the paragraph into sentences and send the individual sentences in parallel to a few dozen sentence servers that do sequences of multi-word phrase lookups in the source language and map into the best-score sequence out of many possible phrases in the target language. These results are then gathered back together by the translation server into a single translated paragraph.

6.6 Slop

The *slop*, or unidentified communication time, is (T4-T1) - (T3-T2) = (T2-T1) + (T4-T3). When the client RPC latency and the server time are nearly equal, the slop is small. When there are communication delays (usually in the kernel code on one machine or the other, not in the network hardware), the slop can be large. Figure 6.6 shows a large slop, with the overall RPC latency about 1.5x the server time. In Chapter 7, we will also subtract the estimated transmission time for request and response messages:

```
slop = (T4 - T1) - (T3 - T2) - requestTx - responseTx
```

When the slop is large, that means that there is significant delay somewhere between the two communicating user-mode programs. In Chapter 15 we will introduce recording the w1 and w3 times of RPC headers on the wire, shown in gray in Figure 6.6. They indicate here that request and response messages hit the wire almost immediately when sent, so the long delays are in kernel code on the receiving end.

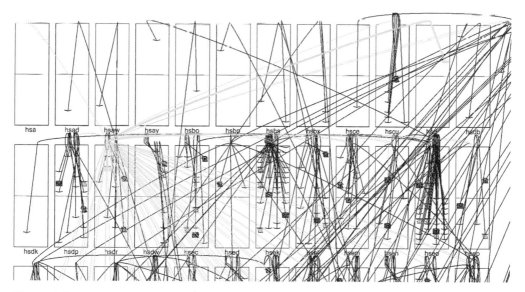

Figure 6.7 **Two-level RPC call tree for a single web search, farming out one search to about 2,000 partial searches of different parts of a web index. Each rectangle represents a rack of ~50 server machines. The light green arcs show about 100 top-level RPCs from one machine in rack "hsdr" to 100 others. The dark blue arcs show about 20 second-level RPCs from each of those 100 to a total of about 2000 servers.**

To complete the RPC picture, Figure 6.7 shows a two-level call tree of RPCs doing a single web search. The top-level ~100 light green RPC arcs coming from the top of the rack labeled "hsdr" are all done in parallel, and all the groups of second-level ~20 dark blue RPC arcs are also done in parallel, quickly spreading the work across about 2,000 servers. Each leaf in the call tree does a portion of the search, and those partial results are combined when all parallel RPCs in a group have returned.

6.7   Observing Network Traffic

In this chapter we will observe and measure some simple RPCs. In contrast to observing local CPU, memory, and disk activity, it takes two connected machines and two sets of software to observe network traffic. Rather than just observing isolated packets, we will observe an RPC system that has client software, server software, multi-packet RPC request and response messages, multiple server threads, and overlapped client calls. As usual, we wish to observe in enough detail to detect anomalous dynamics.

Figure 6.8 shows one example of such dynamics, captured by RPC logs and Dapper [Sigelman 2010]. Using the style of our single-RPC diagram from Figure 6.6, the notched lines in Figure 6.8 show the time layout of 93 parallel RPCs, similar to the top-level RPCs shown as timeless light green arcs in Figure 6.7.

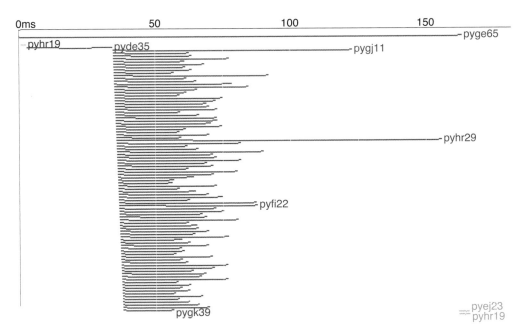

Figure 6.8   Diagram of ~100 RPCs at top level of a single web-search RPC. The "pyxxxx" notations to the right of each line are individual server names.

The very top notched blue line labeled pyge65 in Figure 6.8 shows an incoming single RPC requesting a single web search on server pyge65. It takes about 160 msec total. Underneath it are the outbound sub-RPCs that this initial call spawns, directed at other servers. You can see the sub-RPC transaction latency variation and can see that the 99th percentile slowest parallel RPC on pyhr29 determines the response time of the overall web-search RPC. You can also see that understanding and removing the sources of long latency can speed up this example by about a factor of 2, from 160 msec total to about 80 msec.

Look at the spawned RPCs. First, at the far upper left there is a short barely visible call to server pyhr19 (yellow line just under the "m" in "0ms") to check for a previously cached immediate answer. Using cached previous search answers noticeably speeds up identical searches. Then a blue call to pyde35 is a *canary request* [Dean 2010]. Only when that returns successfully, i.e., without crashing pyde35, are the other RPCs done. If you have a request that hits a code bug that crashes a server, *and you will*, the canary strategy results in crashing just one server instead of thousands. In Figure 6.8 the canary returns, so the 90-odd parallel calls to pygj11 .. pygk39 are started. Not shown are the 20-odd RPCs that each of these spawn in turn, about 2,000 in total, corresponding to the dark blue arcs in Figure 6.7.

Only when pyhr29 returns, the slowest of these parallel calls, does the initial web-search RPC complete. At the very lower right are two parallel calls to update duplicate cached results on pyej23 and on pyhr19 (yellow lines). These actually occur after the initial RPC completes. The vertical white line at 50 msec is just a time grid.

If you look carefully at the canary call to pyde35, you will notice that the request message takes over 10 msec to go from client user-mode code to server user-mode code, and the response message also takes over 10 msec to go from server to client. This slop is much longer than the slop time for most of the subsequent RPCs, so we have our first unexpected source of excess latency. For datacenter networks within a single building, the delay through the routers of the hardware switching fabric rarely exceeds 20 usec. So a delay that is 500x longer than that can only be a software, not hardware, delay, somewhere on the client or server in either user code or kernel code. We examine such delays in Part IV.

If you look carefully, the 93 parallel calls do not all start at exactly the same time—there is a slight tilt to the nearly vertical left edge. Their start times increment by about 6 usec each, reflecting the CPU time to create and send each RPC. The leftmost notch on each line shows that almost all the RPC requests arrive at their corresponding server program fairly quickly, except the calls to pyhr29 and pyfi22, which take over 20 msec to arrive. This is another latency mystery to be resolved.

The rightmost notch on each line shows that almost all the RPC responses are sent soon before they arrive at the client program, so there is no latency mystery for those.

Initially, however, we would be more interested in the exceptionally slow response times of pyhr29 and pygj11, since they delay the overall response time of the initial RPC by about 70 msec. Understanding those delays requires observing what is happening on each of those CPUs, applying our observation tools and thought to each in turn. The same kind of transaction log files that were used to create Figure 6.8 can be used on the logs from pyhr29 and pygj11 to see the dynamics of their delays. The general pattern is: observe to focus on the big issues and ignore the inconsequential artifacts, examine the important artifacts in more detail, resolve them, and then repeat.

The good news is that our picture of the RPC activity on just one machine has revealed two message-delivery latency mysteries and has pinpointed exactly the other two machines and time of day to the microsecond that contribute to overall slow response time for this one web search. Looking at multiple such web searches over a few tens of seconds will reveal whether pyhr29 and pygj11 are always slow or just happened to be slow for this one observation.

Our goal in this chapter is to capture enough information about each RPC to be able to draw diagrams like Figure 6.8 and then use those to track down root causes for delays. In later chapters, especially Chapter 26, we will add tools for observing the underlying reasons for delay(s) that our RPC diagrams reveal.

But before exploring the observation of network dynamics, we need to describe the sample "database" RPC system in a little more detail.

6.8   Sample RPC Message Definition

Local procedure calls have relatively simple dynamics—on a given CPU core, procedure A calls procedure B, and that CPU core then executes instructions in B; no further instructions in A execute until B returns. Local procedure calls may be nested, with A calling B, which in turn calls C. But these all execute sequentially on a single CPU core. We can observe a complete local call tree by capturing the entry and exit times of each procedure. Call nesting is implied by nested entry/exit times. In a multiple-core, multi-threaded-program environment, multiple local calls to B can occur simultaneously, but they are from different callers executing on different software threads possibly using different CPU cores.

Remote procedure calls are more complicated. Unlike a subroutine call, the transmission of the request message from client machine A to server machine B is not instantaneous, nor is the transmission of the response message back from B to A. Since these messages use shared network resources, other network traffic may delay them, so we at least want to capture send/receive times for each message.

As shown in Figure 6.8, an RPC may be *non-blocking*—the caller A may proceed with additional execution in parallel with B and issue additional parallel RPCs to C, D, E, etc. Eventual response messages from B, C, D, E, ... arrive at A asynchronously and not necessarily in order. To match up multiple request and response pairs in the RPC library code, each outstanding RPC is given a unique ID, and that is included in its request and response messages. To match up one RPC with any sub-RPCs that it does, each sub-RPC also includes the RPC ID of its parent; this allows us to reconstruct entire call trees.

A caller may wait for all its RPC responses before finishing, or it may finish early as in Figure 6.8 (pyge65 at the very top right returns before the calls to pyej23 and pyhr19 at the very bottom right). If a network link goes down or a server crashes, some responses may never arrive; the caller needs to detect and deal with this rather than waiting forever.

During the time that A is waiting for a response from B, other clients on the same or different machines may also be sending RPCs to B, and B may be working on those and not on A's. If that happens, a sub-RPC from B to some other server Z may be part of the work for A or for any other client of B. The parent ID shows the proper association.

> If A calls B with RPCID 1234 in the request message and B subsequently calls Z on behalf of A's request, the call to Z would have parent ID 1234 and its own RPCID of perhaps 5678.

All these complications happen fairly often in a large datacenter environment.

We can observe the dynamics of a complete remote call tree only by capturing the caller/callee pairs and send/receive times for each request and response message and explicitly recording the parent caller for all nested RPCs. Most of this information must be transmitted between machines in each of the request and response messages.

For our sample RPC system, each request or response message starts with an RPC marker followed by an RPC header followed optionally by a byte string that contains the argument values for a request or the result values for a response, as shown in Figure 6.9. Each complete message is broken up into the payload data carried in one or more TCP/IP packets. We will focus in the rest of this chapter on complete messages instead of individual packets.

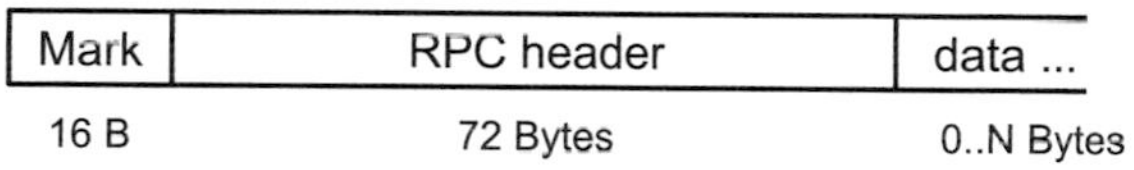

Mark	RPC header	data ...
16 B	72 Bytes	0..N Bytes

Figure 6.9   **Overall structure of a request or response message in our sample RPC design**

The 16-byte RPC marker, as shown in Figure 6.10, serves several purposes: delimiting messages, defining variable lengths, and sanity check.

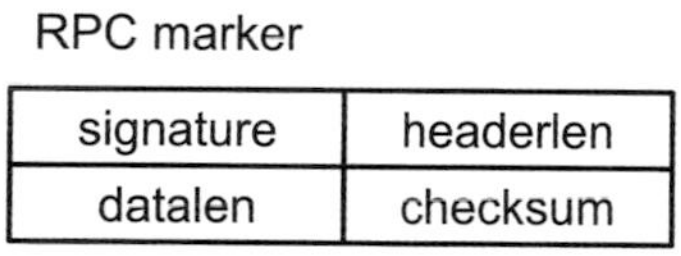

RPC marker

signature	headerlen
datalen	checksum

Figure 6.10   **RPC marker of 16 bytes**

The signature is a fixed 32-bit value. This allows a quick check that the subsequent bytes could begin an RPC message and are not something else. If somehow a TCP connection gets out of sync, it also allows scanning forward until a signature is found as a way to resynchronize. (This is not necessarily a good idea; it may be better to drop the connection and force a clean restart.) In Chapter 15, we use the signature field to filter packets that appear to be the beginning of an RPC message, recording KUtrace entries for each.

The 32-bit headerlen field gives the byte length of the following RPC header, whose size will likely vary over several months or years in a real datacenter as the RPC library is updated and expanded. To improve validity checking, headerlen values are required to be less than 2^{12}. For our sample RPC design, headerlen is always 72.

The 32-bit datalen field gives the byte length of the optional argument or result byte string that follows the RPC header. A length of 0 indicates no string. To improve validity checking and to make huge messages invalid, datalen values are required to be less than 2**24. The two length fields allow an RPC library to break a message into its variable-length pieces.

Finally, the 32-bit checksum field is a simple arithmetic function of the previous three fields, allowing a robust sanity check that the marker and subsequent bytes are highly likely to be the start of a valid RPC message.

The RPC marker is designed to be part of a complete network message but is not visible to the callers of the RPC library software. Those callers deal only with the RPC header and data string.

The RPC header, shown in Figure 6.11, has all the information to describe a single RPC request or response message. Fields are initialized to zero and are filled in incrementally by RPC library as an RPC is processed. For example, T1 and the first L are filled in by the RPC library when an RPC request message is about to be sent by a client program. The second L is filled in when an RPC response message is about to be sent by a server program, and T4 is not filled in until the RPC response message is received by the client program.

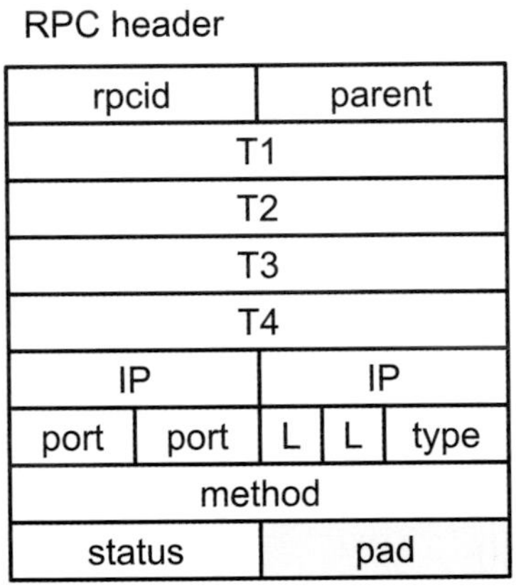

RPC header

rpcid		parent		
T1				
T2				
T3				
T4				
IP		IP		
port	port	L	L	type
method				
status		pad		

Figure 6.11   **RPC header of 72 bytes.**

Briefly, the naturally aligned fields are

- **RPCID** 32 bits, containing a unique ID number for each outstanding request.
- **Parent ID** 32 bits, containing the RPCID of the request that spawned the current request.
- **T1..T4** 64-bit wall-clock timestamps with microsecond resolution, giving respectively the request send time, request receive time, response send time, and response receive time; T1 and T4 are based on the client machine's time-of-day clock; T2 and T3 are based on the server machine's time-of-day clock.
- **IP** 32 bits and **port** 16 bits, giving the client and server machines' TCP/IP addresses,
- **L L** 8 bits each, giving the logarithm of the byte lengths of request and response messages.
- Message **type** 16 bits, to indicate request or response or other types of message.

- **Method** 64 bits (8 bytes), ASCII name of the routine being called, zero padded.

- **Status** 32 bits, return-value status indicating success, failure, or specific error number.

- **Padding** 32 bits, to make the header a multiple of eight bytes in total length.

The sizes of the RPC header fields are somewhat arbitrary; different sizes would work equally well. Reducing the byte lengths to logarithms is just an example of trading resolution (e.g., within 10%) for space.

This header format is somewhat less flexible than those used in real datacenters, but is sufficient for our sample RPC work.

6.9 Sample Logging Design

The client-server programs described in the coming text each write a log file of all the RPCs they process. This logging is our designed-in observability for the dynamics of the RPC system. As such, it is important that the logging is not so slow or bulky that it consumes significant resources or distorts the performance of the underlying service.

Our sample design target is to be able to process and therefore log up to 10,000 RPCs per second with little overhead. This is the right order of magnitude for a real datacenter service.

Back-of-the-envelope: If each log entry is 1,000 bytes, logging 10,000 RPC/sec would write 10MB/sec to a log file, or 864GB/day per service, with multiple services running on each server. This quickly gets bulky and can also consume significant bandwidth to a disk holding multiple log files. Each service would nearly fill up a 1TB disk every day, likely requiring multiple disk drives just for logging.

Instead, if each log entry is about 100 bytes, one service would log about 1MB/sec, and total about 86 GB/day. This is still a bit bulky, but several services writing 1MB/sec to a logging disk is an easily sustained rate, and those services would need just a single 1TB disk to hold a day's worth of log entries—a manageable amount.

For slower-rate services that handle only about 1,000 RPCs per second, we could roughly afford 1,000 bytes per log entry, although most logging does not need so much data per RPC. Do the back-of-the-envelope arithmetic at design time to document affordable limits on the logging overhead.

For our sample RPC design, the binary log format is just a copy of the current RPC header, with the full data length from the RPC mark moved to just in front of the data, and the data itself truncated or zero-extended to 24 bytes, as shown in Figure 6.12. Each log entry is thus exactly 96 bytes.

Log-system performance is a key consideration. Truncating the data keeps each log entry size bounded, and it also provides a bit of privacy for possible user-supplied data such as an email message. Including even a little of the data, though, helps identify what is going on when there is unusual latency. Recording log entries as binary fields instead of printed ASCII values saves file space and also saves CPU time for formatting all the numbers. This approach substantially reduces the logging overhead. Conversion to readable ASCII can be done by postprocessing binary log files as needed later.

Figure 6.12   **Sample log entry format, 96 bytes total**

Each server program will write a local binary file of these log entries as it runs, and each client program will write its own local binary file of log entries. For an overall service running on 2,000 machines, the server programs would write 2,000 local log files on those machines. Scattered clients would write local log files on their own machines.

In a large datacenter, all programs would periodically close their log files and open new ones. A background service would gather closed log files into a single place or into a distributed file system so that they could be postprocessed efficiently. To conserve space, most logs would be thrown away after a few days. There is little point keeping data if no one will ever read it again. For our sample environment, none of that log management is done: we just deal with multiple local log files written locally on individual servers.

6.10   Sample Client-Server System Using RPCs

The supplied `server4.cc` and `client4.cc` implement a sample RPC system with logging. In addition, the supplied `dumplogfile4.cc` turns binary logs into JSON-formatted ASCII so you can see what they contain and so that they can be displayed easily.

The service provided by these programs is an in-memory key-value store (a simple database). The server program accepts RPCs that read or write key-value pairs in RAM, while the client sends such requests. The server-implemented methods are

- **Ping**(data), returns a copy of data with no key-value action
- **Write**(key, value), remembers the pair
- **Read**(key), returns value
- **Chksum**(key), returns an eight-byte checksum of the value
- **Delete**(key), removes key and its value
- **Stats**(), returns some statistics on server usage
- **Reset**(), erases all key-value pairs
- **Quit**(), stops the server and all its threads

This pair of programs should allow you to get into trouble in myriad ways. Sending a burst of 100 values of 1MB each will saturate a sample server's 1Gb/sec Ethernet for at least a second. Doing two such actions independently between different machines should overload a sample four-port switch. Sending a burst of 100,000 one-byte values will saturate CPUs quite nicely and also clog up the logging system. Overlapping a heavy-duty burst with some more modest work will likely interfere with the modest work.

6.11   Sample Server Program

The server program shown in Figure 6.13 continuously accepts RPC request messages, processes them, and sends response messages. It usually runs with multiple threads handling independent RPCs applied to a single shared database.

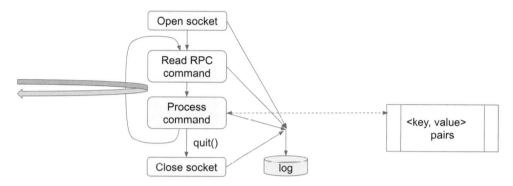

Figure 6.13   **Sample server program**

The program, server4.cc, takes two command-line arguments specifying the range of ports to listen on. For each port, it forks a dedicated listening thread. Each such thread opens a TCP/IP socket on its port and waits for RPCs, which it then executes sequentially as they arrive. The default behavior is use four sequential ports, 12345..12348, and to fork four corresponding threads.

As a safety move, each launch of server4 will self-destruct after four minutes, to protect against runaway or zombie programs, even if server4 is launched in the background via the command-line ampersand.

Multiple copies of server4 can be launched, so long as they use non-overlapping port numbers. Copies of server4 can run on multiple server machines. Nothing in the simple design except chance prevents multiple people from launching interfering runs at the same time.

Keys are byte strings restricted to less than 256 bytes, while values are byte strings restricted to less than 1.25MB (i.e., 5 * 256 * 1024 bytes). Total RAM storage space is restricted to be less than 200MB.

The database of key-value pairs is a C++ map of strings. It is shared across all server execution threads, so each operation that touches the database takes out a simple spinlock before accessing the data. By design, this is a somewhat flawed approach—everything works, but there can be severe blocking dynamics, which we will shortly observe.

6.12   Spinlocks

The spinlock protecting a software *critical section* is our fifth shared resource, along with the four hardware resources CPU, memory, disk, and network. There are many forms of software locks, with spinlock the simplest—whenever a thread cannot acquire the lock for a critical section of code, it simply loops (spins) trying over and over to acquire the lock, until eventually other threads free the lock and the subject thread successfully grabs it. Chapter 27 discusses locks in more detail.

The sample server code defines a C++ `SpinLock` class, which acquires a spinlock in its constructor and frees the lock in its destructor. Thus the code pattern

```
LockAndHist some_lock_name;

  ...

{
  SpinLock sp(some_lock_name);
  <critical section code here>

  ...

}
```

makes the inner block a critical section that can be executed by only one thread at a time. The C++ constructor/destructor mechanism for `SpinLock` guarantees to acquire the lock `some_lock_name` upon entry to the block and to release it upon exit from the block, even for an unexpected or exception exit. This design completely removes one source of programming error—processes that sometimes fail to release a lock.

The spinlock implementation also defines a small histogram to record lock acquisition times. This is another piece of designed-in observability. A common issue with software locks is that under some circumstances a program thread has to wait much too long to acquire a lock, resulting in long transaction latency on one thread whenever *another thread* holds a lock too long. A small histogram of lock-acquire times for each lock can tell you the normal time taken to acquire a contended lock and also can show how many much-longer times occur. If there are no long acquisition times for a given lock, then lock-waiting is not a cause for a long transaction latency, and you can look elsewhere.

The locking pseudocode looks like this:

```
start = __rdtsc()
  test-and-set loop to get lock
stop = __rdtsc()
elapsed_usec = (stop - start) / cyclesperusec
hist[Floorlg(elapsed_usec)]++
```

where `rdtsc` reads the x86 cycle counter and `Floorlg(x)` takes floor(log2(x)), returning 0..31 for a 32-bit unsigned int `x`. The variable `hist` is a small array of counts. Logarithm base 2 is sufficient resolution to put long and short acquisition delays into different count buckets. The `stats` command mentioned earlier returns this histogram array.

6.13   Sample Client Program

The client program, shown in Figure 6.14, takes command-line arguments and sends one or more RPCs to a specified server and port, repeated and spaced out in time in a stylized way.

Multiple instances of client4 can be launched in the background so that they overlap in time on a single machine, and of course multiple instances can be run from several different machines. Instances of server4 and client4 can also run on the same machine, but will not use the network for local communication; for this degenerate case, the kernel network code moves message bytes in RAM.

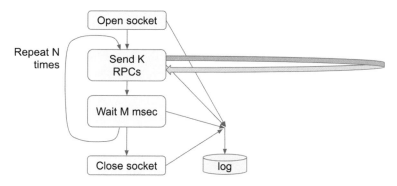

Figure 6.14   **Sample client program**

The command-line arguments to client4 allow specifying Rep repetitions of the pair of actions

<send K RPCs, wait M msec>

The first RPC of a burst of K is specified by its method and initial key/value data. Either field can be padded with pseudorandom data to a specified byte length. Subsequent RPCs in a burst keep the method and base strings but supply possibly incremented keys/values. Within a burst, each RPC is sent as soon as the previous one returns a response, but not before.

The client4 program takes a set of command-line parameters that form a little language:

```
./client4 server port
    [-rep number] [-k number] [-waitms number] [-seed1]
    [-verbose] command
    [-key "keybase" [+] [padlen]]
    [-value "valuebase" [+] [padlen]]
```

The write, read, and delete commands require a key, and the ping and write commands require a value.

-rep	Says to repeat the outer loop some number of times.
-k	Says to repeat the command some number of times (the inner loop) and then wait before continuing the outer loop.
-waitms	Says how long to wait (in milliseconds) after each burst of k commands.
-seed1	Says to seed the random number generator for padding bytes to exactly the value 1, allowing reproducible pseudorandom values.
-verbose	Prints a little about each request and response message.
-key "keybase" [+] [padlen]	Specifies a base character string that is optionally incremented and optionally padded with random characters. In the presence of -rep and -k repetitions, "+" indicates incrementing the base string, and padlen gives the padded length.
-value "valuebase" [+] [padlen]	Uses the same algorithm.

For example,

```
./client4 target_server 12345 -k 5 ping -value "vvvvv" + 10
```

sends five ping commands to target_server:port, with value strings such as

```
vvvvv_0u5j
vvvvw_trce
vvvvx_qxol
vvvvy_1bv3
vvvvz_dg1w
```

where the + specifies incrementing v w x y z in the base string, and the 10 specifies padding with random characters out to 10 characters total. Incrementing increases the low character of the base string by 1, wrapping 9 to 0, z to a, and Z to A, carrying into higher character places as needed (the next base value above would be **vvvwa**). Incrementing is most useful for keys and padding is most useful for values.

The individual commands are defined in a little more detail here.

ping [-value "valuebase" [+] [padlen]]

Sends an RPC request to the specified server:port containing RPC marker, RPC header, and optionally RPC data containing the specified value. The server responds with the same data.

write -key "keybase" [+] [padlen] -value "valuebase" [+] [padlen]

Sends an RPC request to the specified server:port containing RPC marker, RPC header, and RPC data containing the specified <key, value> pair. The server saves each <key, value> pair and responds with a status code, typically SUCCESS.

read -key "keybase" [+] [padlen]

Sends an RPC request to the specified server:port containing RPC marker, RPC header, and RPC data containing the specified key. The server responds with the matching value and a status code, typically SUCCESS.

delete -key "keybase" [+] [padlen]

Sends an RPC request to the specified server:port containing RPC marker, RPC header, and RPC data containing the specified key. The server deletes each matching <key, value> pair and responds with a status code, typically SUCCESS.

stats

Sends an RPC request to the specified server:port containing RPC marker, RPC header, with no RPC data. The server responds with an arbitrary status string and a status code, typically SUCCESS. For server4, the status string is a text version of the spinlock histogram described earlier—32 counts separated by single spaces.

reset

Sends an RPC request to the specified server:port containing RPC marker, RPC header, with no RPC data. The server removes all its <key, value> pairs and responds with a status code, typically SUCCESS.

quit

Sends an RPC request to the specified server:port containing RPC marker, RPC header, with no RPC data. The server responds with a status code, typically SUCCESS, and exits immediately afterward.

The client4 program prints the observed round-trip time for the first 20 RPCs it issues. At the end, it prints a log2 histogram of those times, plus total RPCs, total msec elapsed, total MB transmitted and received, and RPC messages transmitted and received per second. In a datacenter system, this is the kind of information that would be displayed on a dashboard web page.

6.14 Measuring One Sample Client-Server RPC

Recall our thought framework from Chapter 1. In thinking about performance issues, we will follow the programmer's discipline of first estimating how long some work should take, then observing how long it actually does take, and then reasoning about any differences. Figure 6.15 shows this framework again.

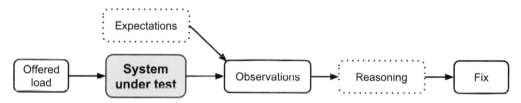

Figure 6.15   Framework for examining the performance of complex software

Consider the offered load of sending a single **write** RPC from client program to server program, with a 5-byte key and 1,000,000-byte value. What do we expect the timing to look like on our sample server configuration with a 1Gb/sec network?

Remember that 1 Gb/sec is roughly 100 MB/sec when we convert from bits to bytes and include some overhead, or about 100 bytes per microsecond. So sending ~1,000,000 bytes of RPC request should take about 10,000 usec (10 msec) across the wire. On the server side, creating a string of 1,000,000 bytes and putting it into a C++ map should take only about 100 usec or so if the main memory can transfer 10GB/sec. A short reply of 100 bytes should take about 1 usec on the wire plus some small software overhead. Overall, we might expect something like Figure 6.16 when we sketch out a timeline.

Figure 6.16   **Expected RPC timing sketch for Write() of 1MB of data**

This sketch is somewhat distorted, but you get the idea—a long time to transmit 1MB in the request message, 100x less time to put it into the key/value store, and 100x less time again to transmit the response message. Let's see what happens.

Compile server4.cc and run it with no arguments to get the default configuration of listening on four ports.

```
./server4
```

Compile client4.cc and run it on a different machine with these arguments:

```
./client4 target_server 12345 write -key "kkkkk" \
  -value "vvvvv" 1000000
./client4 target_server 12345 quit
```

Compile dumplogfile4.cc and run it on the client, pointing to the 1MB write log file written by client4.

```
./dumplogfile4 client4_20190420_145721_dclab-1_10479.log \
  "Write 1MB" \
   >client4_20190420_145721_dclab-1_10479.json
```

Compile makeself.cc and run it on the client, pointing to the previous JSON file.

```
./makeself client4_20190420_145721_dclab-1_10479.json \
  show_rpc_2019.html \
  > client4_20190420_145721_dclab-1_10479.html
```

Display the resulting HTML file.

```
google-chrome client4_20190420_145721_dclab-1_10479.html
```

6.15 Postprocessing RPC Logs

The programs `client4.cc` and `server4.cc` write binary log files of 96-byte records as described earlier.

The program `dumplogfile4.cc` reads these log files and turns them into JSON files with the timestamps and other information turned into ASCII text. The JSON file has a stylized header that contains among other things the start minute of the log records, the title from the second command-line argument ("Write 1MB" previously), and some axis labels. This header is followed by lines of text for the log records. By default, only log records for receipt of a response are included, i.e., just those records that describe a full round-trip transaction. The -all flag includes all records.

The program makeself.cc reads a JSON file and writes an HTML file based on a template, incorporating the JSON information. This is the same makeself.cc program we encountered in Chapter 5, but with a different template file, `show_rpc.html`.

The displayed HTML, such as Figure 6.17, can be panned and zoomed via mouse drag and mouse wheel, respectively. The lower-left red dot resets the display. The [Rel. 0] button at the top switches between showing multiple RPCs by wall-clock- time and showing them all starting at (relative to) time zero.

6.16   Observations

On a sample server pair of machines, I measured 9.972 msec to send the Write() request from client to server, 1.118 msec to process it on the server, and 10 usec to send the response back to the client. My estimates of the first and last times were pretty reasonable, but my processing time estimate was 10x too low (see Table 6.1).

Table 6.1   **Estimated RPC Elapsed Time vs. Measured**

Action	Estimate	Actual
Send 1MB request	10 msec	9.972 msec
Process request	100 usec	1118 usec
Send 100 byte response	2 usec	10 usec

Based on the client-side log, Figure 6.17 shows 10 such RPCs lined up on time across about 120 msec, using the style of Figure 6.8. The hollow part of the lines (more precisely, the white overlaid lines) show approximately the message transmission time for the 1MB client => server messages. Among other things, you can see the 1–2 msec gap on the client from the end of one RPC to the beginning of the next one (oval around the first gap).

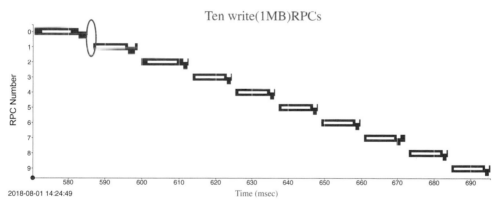

Figure 6.17   **Ten RPCs, each sending 1MB of data. The oval highlights the 1–2 msec gap between successive RPCs.**

Figure 6.18 shows the same 10 RPCs, but this time they are aligned to a common starting point, so the relative times of the different RPCs are easily compared. Now it is clearer that the first few RPCs take longer, and then the timing settles down a bit. It is also clearer that number seven has an extra delay in getting its response message back to the client.

The request time from client to server is about 9 msec, as we estimated, but the time processing on the server is about 1 msec, longer than the 100 usec per 1MB that we estimated. Why was our estimate off?

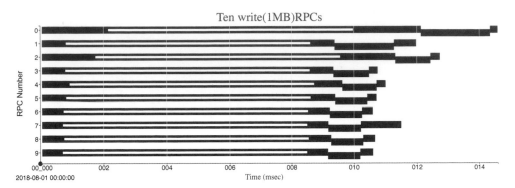

Figure 6.18   **The same 10 RPCs, but this time all with the same start time of zero**

Copying each 1MB message from network card to kernel buffer, then kernel buffer to user buffer, then user buffer to separate key and value strings, and then value string to map entry, each one MB in our sample server code is read or written to memory about eight times, not just once. This boosts our estimate to about 800 usec for all those copies, close to the observed 1 msec. To complete the picture, the response time from server to client is about 350 usec, a little longer than I would have expected but not terrible. Estimating ahead of time makes it easy to spot discrepancies.

6.17   Summary

In this chapter we introduced a sample remote procedure call database system and ran it on two networked computers, recording the times at which each RPC message is sent and received. The resulting notched-line diagrams show the measured time, the approximate transmission time for each message, the spacing between successive RPCs, and the relative timing of multiple similar RPCs. The underlying logging is sustainable at a rate of 10,000 RPCs per second per service.

In the next chapter, we will look in more detail at multiple overlapped RPCs on multiple clients and servers, at locking within transactions, and at time-aligning the clocks on multiple machines. We will expand the sample in-memory database to be an equally simple disk database. Later in the book we will examine the slow parts of these RPCs, including identifying the delays in message transmission and the delays in RPC processing.

- To understand the dynamics of multiple remote procedure calls, it is absolutely necessary to design in observation hooks, including at least RPC IDs, send and receive times, and byte lengths.

- These hooks must have low enough overhead to be useful under heavy live load.

- Creating RPC traffic requires at least one client and one server program running on different machines.

- A little stylized language lets us build a client to generate useful sequences of RPCs.

- Data structures for the RPC format across a network are part of the overall RPC design, and these must include observation metadata in the messages sent across a network, along with the actual operation and its data. This metadata information can fit in about 100 bytes.

- Logging to disk the timestamps and other metadata for every incoming and outgoing RPC message lets us observe a complete picture of where all the time went in an RPC call tree, and also a complete picture of all the *other* RPCs whose processing overlaps with and therefore possibly interferes with one of interest.

- Viewing the log data by wall-clock time lets us see delays within and between successive RPCs, and also lets us see overlapping of RPCs.

- Viewing the log data with all RPCs of a given kind starting at time zero lets us see differences among similar RPCs, and in particular lets us see what is different about slow ones vs. normal ones.

- Estimating what we expect to see makes it easy to spot discrepancies.

Exercises

Consider this work:

1. Send 10 ping messages of 100KB each.
2. Send 10 writes of 1MB of random data for keys kkkkk, kkkkl, kkkkm, ..., kkkkt.
3. Send 10 matching reads of 1MB from the same 10 keys.
4. Finally, send a quit command.

Draw yourself a little sketch of what you expect to see in the RPC timings.

Now run the `server4` program on one sample server and the `client4` program on another, sequentially sending commands for the previous sequences. Run the dumplogfile4 program and makeself program against the first three client log files and display the actual results.

You likely will find that the two servers' wall-clock times differ by a few milliseconds, which may be enough to make the HTML display look odd, if the send time for a message is timestamped after the receipt time. We will look at time alignment in the next chapter. In the meantime, you might consider hand-editing the JSON files to adjust T2 and T3 to be between T1 and T4. This is optional, but doing so will give you some insight about what your Chapter 7 program will need to do.

6.1 How long, in milliseconds, did you estimate for the ping requests and their response message transmissions? How long do they actually take? Briefly comment on the difference.

6.2 How long, in milliseconds, did you estimate for the write requests and their response message transmissions? How long do they actually take? Briefly comment on the difference.

6.3 How long, in milliseconds, did you estimate for the read requests and their response message transmissions? How long do they actually take? Briefly comment on the difference.

Chapter 7

Disk and Network Database Interaction

This chapter is a continuation of the RPC measurements in Chapter 6, introducing further complexity. Chapter 6 ended with a simple measurement of one client and one server with no overlap of RPCs. In this chapter we will learn how to time-align clocks on multiple CPUs. We will use multiple clients to send overlapping RPCs and will explore the resulting database and spinlock behavior on the server. We will change from the in-memory database to an on-disk one and then observe interactions between multiple overlapping RPCs accessing the shared disk. As usual, we will estimate the expected dynamics of each experiment, measure the real behavior, and then compare the two as we seek to understand the software dynamics, and in particular to understand the transaction latency variation.

7.1 Time Alignment

In the previous chapter, we skipped over one complication—aligning the time-of-day clocks on different computers. If those times differ by 100 usec or more (a *clock skew* of 100 usec), it becomes difficult to match up events on one machine with corresponding events on another, and as the difference increases it becomes progressively harder to make sense of a set of observations.

Each computer motherboard has a crystal oscillator, shown in Figure 7.1, that provides the base frequency for clocking the CPU chip and nearly everything else.

Figure 7.1   **Quartz crystal oscillator [Wikimedia 2021]**

The crystals on two different motherboards will not oscillate at precisely the same frequency. One might be 1–10 parts per million (ppm) faster than another, meaning that counting 3 billion clock pulses on a nominal 3.0 GHz machine (about one second) can be 1–10 usec faster on one board compared to the other. The time-of-day clock provided by the `gettimeofday()` C library routine on the two computers will therefore have *clock drift* (apart or closer together) by as much a 1–10 usec per second, or by 100-1000 usec over a 100-second performance measurement interval, as in Figure 7.2.

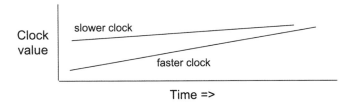

Figure 7.2   **Clocks on two different servers running at slightly different crystal frequencies**

Crystal frequencies also vary with temperature and input voltage, so the frequency difference between two clocks is not constant. Fortunately, the time for much change in crystal frequency is tens of minutes, and often two servers in the same room will see similar temperature and voltage changes, so will tend to track each other.

Even with access to a precise source of time and with software such as *Network Time Protocol* (NTP) [Wikipedia 2021o], clocks across many datacenter servers will be offset somewhat from each other, and those offsets will drift a little over the course of a minute or so. The upshot is that `gettimeofday()` can easily give results that differ by a few milliseconds between two computers. Software such as file systems may fail upon seeing time appear to go backwards, so it is important to pay attention to time offsets.

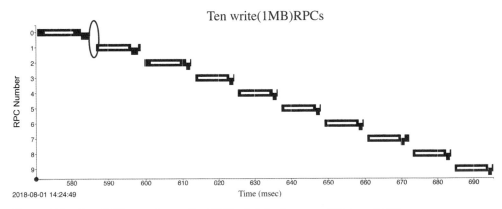

Figure 7.3   **Ten RPCs, each sending 1MB of data (a copy of Figure 6.17)**

The raw data for the first RPC in Figure 6.17, repeated here as Figure 7.3, has these times T1 through T4, in seconds from the start of a trace:

49.567609   T1 send request, client machine clock

49.582785   T2 receive request, server machine clock

49.585007   T3 send response, server machine clock

49.582178   T4 receive response, client machine clock

The T1 and T4 times are the *client* time-of-day clock, and the T2 and T3 times are the *server* time-of-day clock. Note the response message sent at time T3=49.585007 appears to be received at time T4=49.582178, i.e., about 3 msec *before* it was sent. The two computers' clocks were in fact offset by about 3.1 msec at the time of measurement, with the server running ahead, and I aligned the times to produce Figures 6.17 and 6.18 in Chapter 6. (A few days later, the two machines differed by about 0.1 msec in the other direction.)

Many efforts try to use various forms of hardware and software to synchronize time-of-day clocks across computers in a datacenter to within one microsecond or better, for example [Lee 2016]. But these efforts may not be cost-effective in big datacenters, may not work as well as expected over the course of several months or years, and may not be robust to equipment outages such as a single-point-of-failure GPS receiver. Recent work at Stanford and Google [Geng 2018] may improve on this.

It is simpler and cheaper and more reliable to just assume that the servers we observe have somewhat different clocks and to align the times in postprocessing software. We learn how to do that in this chapter.

Our four RPC timestamps come from two time-of-day sources, client and server. To align them, we wish to find a *delta time* such that

```
T2' = T2 + delta and
T3' = T3 + delta
```

will map T2 and T3 on the server machine into T2' and T3' in the client machine's time-of-day regime.

What do we know about delta from the four times shown previously? We know that a request message is sent before it is received, so that

```
T1=49.567609 must be less than T2'= 49.582785 + delta or
49.567609 - 49.582785 < delta or
-0.015176 < delta
```

We also know that the response message was sent before it was received, so that

```
T3'=49.585007 + delta must be less than T4=49.582178 or
delta < 49.582178 - 49.585007 or
delta < -0.002829
```

or roughly

```
-15.1 msec < delta < -2.8 msec
```

We in fact know something stronger. The estimated time to transmit a 1MB request message on an ideal 1 Gb/sec Ethernet is about 8,000,000 bits at 1,000,000,000 bits/sec = 0.008 seconds. If we assume that the data portion of packets has about 10% more bits added, including headers, checksums, and required gaps between Ethernet packets, then the best-possible real-world transmission time is more like 9 msec to send 1MB. This means that for the T1 => T2' transmission, a better calculation is

```
T1=49.567609 + 0.009000  < T2'=49.582785 + delta or
(49.567609 + 0.009000) - 49.582785 < delta or
-0.006176 < delta
```

A similar calculation for the short response message involves only about 1 usec of transmission time, so there is no real change to the arithmetic.

```
delta < -0.002829
```

From this one RPC, we can therefore bound delta to roughly

```
-6.1 msec < delta < -2.8 msec
```

With a few more RPCs, the bound can usually be tightened somewhat. Over hundreds or thousands of RPCs, there often will be some minimal-overhead messages that allow bounding delta to a range well under 100 usec.

But if we record RPC times over a minute or two, we must also account for clock drift—the value of delta at the beginning of an observation can differ by several hundred microseconds from the value of delta a minute or so later at the end of an observation, if the two machines' clocks drift from each other by as little as 2 usec per second, as shown in Figure 7.4. Fortunately, over the course of a minute or two we can assume the *rate* of drift is constant; time-varying effects such as datacenter room temperature changes are so gradual that they would take tens of minutes to affect clock frequencies. We are therefore justified in approximating the varying delta by a linear function over a time period of a minute or two.

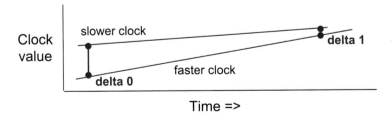

Figure 7.4 **Clocks on two different servers running at slightly different crystal frequencies, with drift in time difference highlighted**

The time alignment problem is simply stated as:

Given a set of RPC times T1-T4 between two machines, calculate an offset and slope for a linear approximation to the time-of-day difference, delta, between the machines.

We would like this calculation to be relatively insensitive to variations in software and hardware message transmission delays.

We introduced RPC *slop* in Chapter 6. We define it here as the total amount of RPC time not spent on the server and not spent in message transmission, i.e.,

```
slop = (T4 - T1) - (T3 - T2) - requestTx - responseTx
```

where requestTx and responseTx are the estimated times to transmit the request and response messages on an empty network. Messages with a small slop give us tight bounds on the time offset between two machines. To calculate a time-varying delta line, we would prefer to use RPCs with a small amount of slop. We really need only two good points, one near the beginning of a log or trace and one near the end of a log. But real RPC data can be a bit noisy and unpredictable, so RPCs with the smallest slop may not occur near the beginning and end of a log. It is more robust, then, to look for several relatively small slop events spread across an entire log and pick from those.

One simple way to pick off some small-slop events of an unknown-length RPC log while using a minimal amount of storage is to read an entire time-sorted log (sorted by T1), turning each RPC into a quadruple

```
slop, T1, mindelta, maxdelta
```

and record a useful subset of all these. That subset can be kept in a tiny number of array elements, such as eight, each containing the *smallest-slop* quadruple in a group of N consecutive RPCs, with N initially 1. Once the initial eight array elements are filled, we collapse them in pairs, keeping just the smallest-slop quadruple of each pair, freeing up half the buckets and then doubling N. Each of the thus-freed buckets is then filled with the smallest-slop quadruple of the next N RPCs. The collapsing is repeated as needed as an entire RPC log is processed.

At the end of this process, the entire log file is read, and five to eight buckets have useful smallest-slop quadruples spread across the entire log time, even though at the beginning we did not know how many entries to expect in the log file. We can then fit a standard

```
x' = m x + b
```

straight line to the two points in the first and last buckets, where x' is the client-machine time, x is the server-machine time, b is the initial offset, and m is the slope: the delta change per second. The first and last buckets contain the lowest-slop datapoints that are respectively near the front of the trace and near the end of the trace. These two points are good enough for fitting a useful clock-delta line.

Since the time values in microseconds may be large and the deltas small, the computation may be numerically more stable or accurate by first subtracting Toff, the smallest T1 value in the log and adjusting b to match:

```
x' = m (x - Toff) + b
```

The timealign.cc program does this time-varying delta fitting, using 16 buckets rather than the 8 in the example here. It takes as input the filenames of a *set* of our RPC log files, possibly two or more. It maps all the RPC times to a common time base, that of the lowest-numbered IP address in the logs, and then rewrites all the log files with "_align" added to the name, i.e., logfile_foo.log is rewritten as logfile_foo_align.log. The two-pass algorithm first reads all the log files and retains a small number of offset buckets between each pair of servers, then fits a time-varying line to those offsets, and then finally in the second pass rewrites all the log files with appropriate deltas applied.

In the first pass, after reading the first eight RPC times from Figure 7.3, the eight buckets look like this:

```
N = 1
      slop  T1  delta min..max   midpoint (all times in usec)
[0] 3452 49583896 -6281..-2829 = -4555
[1] 1184 49597153 -3573..-2389 = -2981
[2] 2696 49611677 -5520..-2824 = -4172
[3]  716 49623585 -3585..-2869 = -3227
[4] 1003 49635583 -3888..-2885 = -3386
[5]  789 49647344 -3686..-2897 = -3291
[6]  665 49658856 -3535..-2870 = -3202
[7] 1550 49670369 -3507..-1957 = -2732
```

At the ninth RPC, the buckets are collapsed by a factor of two, keeping just the smallest-slop entry in each pair. This gives

```
N = 2
      slop  T1  delta min..max   midpoint (all times in usec)
[0] 1184 49597153 -3573..-2389 = -2981
[1]  716 49623585 -3585..-2869 = -3227
[2]  789 49647344 -3686..-2897 = -3291
[3]  665 49658856 -3535..-2870 = -3202
```

We note in passing that the lower-slop entry in a pair often has a delta range whose absolute value is closer to zero than the higher-slop entry. I have seen this in production traces; large possible deltas between machine clocks are more often due to measurement issues than to actual time offset, so the lower-slop RPCs end up with more realistic estimates that have smaller offsets.

The remaining two RPCs fill up one more bucket:

```
[4]  669 49694473 -3541..-2872 = -3206
```

Fitting a line to the first and last points gives a slope of m = 0.001934065 (i.e., 1934 usec drift per second, fairly large) and a beginning offset of b = 3039 usec.

Depending on how many RPCs appear after the last 2x collapsing, anywhere from five to eight of the buckets will be filled at the end. In our example, five are filled. The first bucket will have the lowest-slop RPC in the first 1/5 to 1/8 of the trace, and the last bucket the lowest slop RPC in the last 1/5 to 1/8 of the trace if that bucket is mostly full. Worst case, the last bucket has only one big-slop RPC in it. In that case, a more careful line-fitting through all buckets might be in order.

In calculating the linear fit, the alignment we choose is the midpoint of the min..max range in the buckets. We could have chosen to use the end of the min..max range nearest to zero, to bias toward smaller clock offsets between machines. We also could have chosen to do a least-squares fit to all the filled buckets instead of just the first and last. Or we even could do a weighted least-squares fit based on the number of RPCs in each bucket, deemphasizing the last bucket if it is not very full. Even the simplest fit does pretty well, though.

The second pass of `timealign.cc` then applies the time-varying deltas shown and writes a new file:

```
Pass2: client4_20180801_142449_dclab11_14072.log
49567609 T1 += 3039,   T2 += 0,   T3 += 0,   T4 += 3067
49583744 T1 += 3070,   T2 += 0,   T3 += 0,   T4 += 3093
49596704 T1 += 3095,   T2 += 0,   T3 += 0,   T4 += 3120
49610541 T1 += 3122,   T2 += 0,   T3 += 0,   T4 += 3143
49622256 T1 += 3145,   T2 += 0,   T3 += 0,   T4 += 3166
49634255 T1 += 3168,   T2 += 0,   T3 += 0,   T4 += 3189
49645916 T1 += 3191,   T2 += 0,   T3 += 0,   T4 += 3211
49657450 T1 += 3213,   T2 += 0,   T3 += 0,   T4 += 3235
49669905 T1 += 3237,   T2 += 0,   T3 += 0,   T4 += 3258
49681525 T1 += 3259,   T2 += 0,   T3 += 0,   T4 += 3280
   client4_20180801_142449_dclab11_14072_align.log written
```

Note that the delta applied grows slowly as time advances, reflecting the non-zero slope of the time-varying delta line, about 200 usec over this example's 0.1 second span.

In Chapter 6, our postprocessing of logs did:

```
foo.log => foo.json => foo.html
```

We add in this chapter doing time alignment between machines:

```
foo.log => foo_align.log => foo_align.json => foo_align.html
```

7.2 Multiple Clients

We turn next to driving our simple server from multiple clients. The setup looks like Figure 7.5, with two client machines each running two client programs, for a total of four parallel RPC sources.

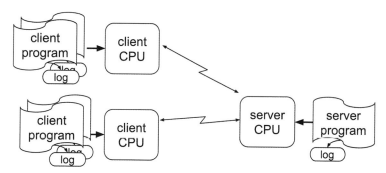

Figure 7.5 **Multiple client machines with multiple client programs each, accessing one server**

This setup allows enough client requests to create bottlenecks on the server network link, server CPU, database spinlock, and disk accesses.

7.3   Spinlocks

In Chapter 6 we introduced spinlocks to protect the database update code in the sample server program. We see them in action here in Chapter 7 and in more detail in Chapter 27. With only a single client program and at most one RPC outstanding at a time, the server program sees no contention for the spinlock. But with multiple clients and a server running multiple threads, two or more RPCs can overlap in time at the same server. When this happens, the server code must make sure that one RPC update of the database is done in its entirety without simultaneously trying to perform a conflicting update for another RPC. To manage this, the sample server has a single software lock for the entire database, acquiring and holding the lock for the entire time that an RPC is updating the database and then freeing the lock. Waiting to acquire the database lock can become a significant source of transaction delay. We will use RPC logs and some reasoning about delay times to observe and understand the dynamics of lock contention. A single lock for the entire database is likely a bad design, as we shall see.

7.4   Experiment 1

In our first experiment, we have each of four clients write 1MB values to a database in RAM on the server. Two clients start on one CPU writing 1,000 values and then about a second later two more start on the other CPU, writing just 200 values each. How long should we expect this to take?

For the Ethernet alone, we expect to see 1000 + 1000 + 200 + 200 = 2400 writes of 1MB at about 9 msec each, so a minimum of 2400 * 9 msec = 21.6 seconds just for the network traffic. If there were two servers and the traffic were split, we might expect transmissions to overlap and the total data transfers to take half this time, but in the sample server configuration shown, the single inbound network link to the one server will be the bottleneck.

For the server CPU and a nominal 10 GB/sec main memory bandwidth, we might expect each MB access to take about 1MB / 10 GB/sec = 100 usec. But as we saw in Chapter 6, this estimate is about 10x too low. So we expect the server time to be about 1 msec per write times 2,400 writes = 2.4 seconds. The server should only be about 10% busy over ~22 seconds.

Here is the setup for Experiment 1, using the programs from Chapter 6 and running on three different machines. Note the "&" between commands to allow the following command to start immediately.

```
server $    ./server4 &
client1 $   ./client4 server 12345 -k 1000 -seed1 write \
            -key "aaaa" + -value "valueaaa_0000" + 1000000 & \
            ./client4 server 12346 -k 1000 -seed1 write \
            -key "bbbb" + -value "valuebbb_0000" + 1000000
client2 $   ./client4 server 12347 -k 200 -seed1 write \
            -key "cccc" + -value "valueccc_0000" + 1000000 & \
            ./client4 server 12348 -k 200 -seed1 write
            -key "dddd" + -value "valueddd_0000" + 1000000
```

Figure 7.6a shows the actual measured time-aligned results, with four colors used to show RPCs from each of the four clients.

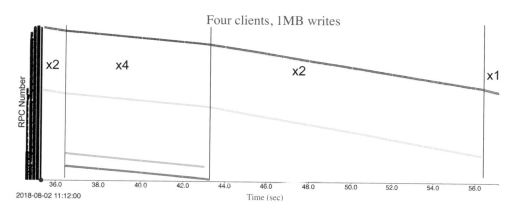

Figure 7.6a   **Diagram of 2400 write RPCs of 1MB each, from four different-color clients to a single server; absolute start times**

The top red line of Figure 7.6a shows 1,000 RPCs from one client program and the middle yellow line 1,000 RPCs from another. The green and blue lines at the bottom show 200 RPCs from the other two client programs. Each "line" actually consists of 1,000 or 200 notched RPC lines, as in Figure 7.3, but the scale is too small to resolve these.

At the far left of Figure 7.6a, there are just two clients writing for about one second, then over the next six seconds and 800 RPCs all four clients are writing, then back to two, and finally at the very right just one client is writing. The Figure 7.6a presentation is good for seeing the overall time flow, for showing overlapping RPCs, and for showing small changes in slope (throughput) in the different sections. Steeper slopes show more throughput.

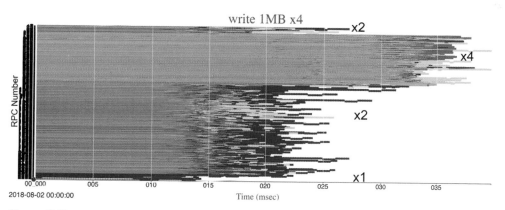

Figure 7.6b   **Diagram of 2400 write RPCs of 1MB each, from four different-color clients to a single server; relative to start time**

Figure 7.6b shows the same RPCs with the same colors, sorted by start time on the y-axis and using relative times with all RPCs starting at time zero on the x-axis. This presentation makes it clearer that the initial ~100 RPCs come from just the two red and yellow clients (labeled x2), then the next ~800 RPCs come from all four clients (x4), then back to two (x2), and at the very bottom back to one (x1). Why one? Because the two red and yellow clients ended up getting slightly different access to the network; the yellow one finished sooner, leaving just the red one finishing up at the end. You can also see in Figure 7.6b that with four clients, each RPC takes longer, due to the network bottleneck, and also at the very end that with one client each RPC is faster, due to lack of any network contention. In some cases, you can see the server-time notched line at the left end of an RPC. This shows that the large 1MB network transmission time is *before* the server code runs, as you would expect for a client writing data to the server. For 1MB reads from server to client, you would expect to see the large transmission time *after* the server code runs.

We look next at a few RPCs around these transitions as clients start and finish. Figure 7.7 shows the transition from two clients to four in Figure 7.6. With just two clients on the left, you can see that the estimated network time in white is approximately half of each transaction time, and with four on the right it is approximately one fourth. This synthetic white is just an estimate centered in the client-to-server time (the 100-byte server-to-client response time is there but too small to see). The actual network transmission may occur somewhat before or after the white bars, and with multiple overlapping transmissions the packets for different messages may be arbitrarily *intermixed*.

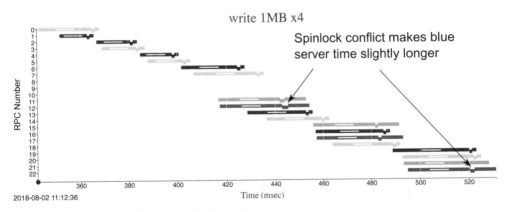

Figure 7.7   **Transition from two clients to four**

Even though the positions of the white are approximations, you can see that the total communication time for each RPC gets longer when there is an increase from two to four clients. You can also see occasional 2x longer server times with four clients (arrows to RPCs 12 and 22), when one server thread is waiting on the spinlock held by another thread.

Figure 7.8 shows the transition from two clients to one, at the very end of the run when the other three clients have all finished. With one client, the estimated network time in white is nearly the entire communication-time interval from client to server, as we would expect when running on an idle network.

Next, we will look at a similar client-server setup, but with database accesses to disk instead of RAM and with more processing time per transaction.

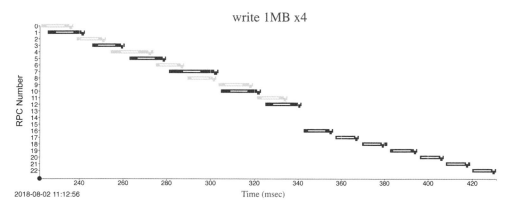

Figure 7.8 **Transition from two clients to one**

7.5 On-Disk Database

The server4 program keeps key-value pairs in RAM. The server_disk program is nearly identical, but it keeps key-value pairs on disk. Specifically, the key is used as a filename, and the value is the contents of the file. Using disk instead of RAM introduces seek and slow transfer times, causing longer server times. In contrast to the disk-measurement chapter, we use ordinary file I/O with no O_DIRECT or other changes.

7.6 Experiment 2

In our second experiment, we have three clients writing 1MB values to a database on disk. We also artificially extend the server processing time by 5 msec per RPC while holding the spinlock. One client starts on one CPU writing 1,000 values and then about two seconds later two more clients start on another CPU writing just 200 values each. How long should we expect this to take?

The network time is similar to Experiment 1 with 1,400 writes instead of 2,400: 1,400 * 9 msec = 12.6 seconds. The disk involved can transfer about 60 MB/sec, so writing 1400 MB should take about 23.3 seconds, longer than the network time. This is just disk data transfer time; seeks and directory accesses are additional. The 1,400 writes create 1,400 new files and their corresponding directory entries. Remember that disk I/O is usually buffered and cached in RAM, so we should expect that some or even all of the writes are buffered in RAM and that the disk writes happen later. This buffering will complicate the performance and our analysis of it.

Here is the setup for Experiment 2, using three different machines:

```
server$   ./server_disk&
client1$  ./client4 server 12345 -k 1000 -seed1 write \
             -key "aaaa" + -value "valueaaa_0000" + 1000000
client2$  ./client4 server 12347 -k 200 -seed1 write \
             -key "cccc" + -value "valueccc_0000" + 1000000 & \
          ./client4 server 12348 -k 200 -seed1 write
             -key "dddd" + -value "valueddd_0000" + 1000000
```

Figure 7.9 shows the actual measured result, with three colors used to show RPCs from each of the three clients. As in Figure 7.6a, each "line" actually consists of 1,000 or 200 notched RPC lines, but the scale is too small to resolve these. This 26-second diagram has several anomalies; look carefully.

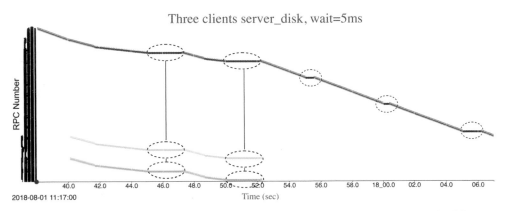

Figure 7.9   **Three clients writing 1MB values to disk server with extra 5 msec of RPC processing inside spinlock**

The total time of 26 seconds is longer than our estimate of network transmission time and a little longer than our disk transfer time estimate, but in the right ballpark. It suggests, however, that the writes cannot all be buffered up in RAM, since doing so would put our total time closer to that of a RAM-only server, as we saw in Experiment 1 (with 2,400 writes instead of 1,400 here).

There are five sets of horizontal lines indicated by ovals starting at about times 45, 50, 55, 60, and 65. These indicate that *no* RPCs completed during that time, implying large response times. Note that the first two at times 45 and 50 affect all three clients, not just one. That suggests that the cause is much more likely at the common server, not at the three individual clients. Also note that the even spacing at five-second intervals suggests that some piece of software is doing something odd every five seconds. A reasonable guess is that some part of the file system is flushing buffers to disk every five seconds. In later chapters we will revisit this when we have more observation tools.

The throughput slope changes slightly for all three clients at about time 42 and again at 49. In other words, something changes the performance of the RPCs during two stretches of identical three-client offered load. This does not happen at, for example, times 57 and 63 with just a single-client load.

We will zoom in and look at each of these anomalies in more detail. Figure 7.10 examines the transition at time 40.1 from a single client to three. Figure 7.11 examines the slope transition at time 41.7, as throughput slows down. Figure 7.12 examines the long 2.2-second delay at time 45.0, death for a user-facing real-time transaction system.

Figure 7.10 shows RPCs from a single client on the left and then from three clients on the right. The single-client RPCs all have client-to-server times that are entirely 8–9 msec of network time for sending 1MB, followed by 5 msec of server processing time, as we expected with no disk writes.

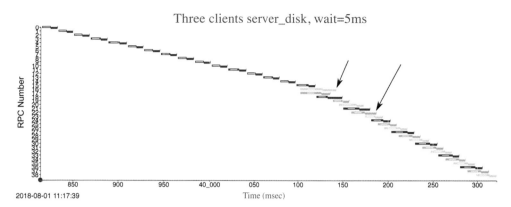

Figure 7.10   **Transition from one client to three**

After the other two clients start up, the pattern changes: longer client-to-server times as the transmission of 3 MB of parallel RPCs takes about 24 msec, some of it overlapped with the RPC processing time. You can also see processing times longer than 5 msec (arrows) when overlapping RPCs contend for the single database spinlock. This part of the picture is about what we estimated.

Figure 7.11 shows an unexpected change. On the left, the first ten RPCs from three clients are perking along as in Figure 7.10, with a repetition rate per client of about 24 msec. In other words, each red RPC starts about 24 msec after the previous red one started. This is consistent with spending about 3 * 8 msec sending three 1MB requests as the clients end up with round-robin access to the network.

Then there is a phase change (arrow) and requests start taking 55–100 msec to complete, with all the extra time spent on the server. With a repetition rate per server of 60–80 msec, the network is no longer very busy, so the client-to-server request time drops back to 8–9 msec. What can be causing the longer server times?

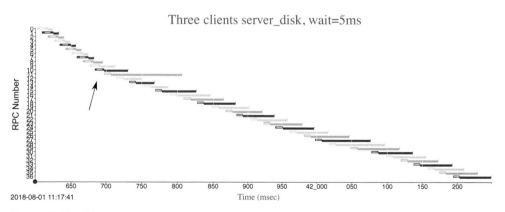

Figure 7.11   **Phase change from three-client RPCs running well to three-client RPCs running 30 msec longer**

A reasonable guess is that the phase transition reflects a change from buffering writes in RAM to sending them (or some buffered earlier write) to disk. The extra ~30 msec per RPC is about the right amount of time to do one disk seek and a 1MB transfer: ~13 msec seek time and ~17 msec transfer time for 1MB at 60 MB/sec on our slow disk. We will reexamine this behavior later in the book when we have more observation tools.

But in the meantime, consider how estimates of known CPU, memory, disk, and network behavior (from earlier chapters) can guide our interpretation of the actual values of various time delays. In particular, they guide our interpretation of what *cannot* be happening—for example, the fast 24 msec RPCs cannot be waiting 30 msec for a disk write for each one, so something must be buffering writes in RAM during those RPCs. These deferred writes must eventually be done, however, costing time when they do happen. "Pay me now or pay me later" is the technical term for deferred work [Fram 1972].

On to Figure 7.12, which shows a disconcerting 2.2 second delay, all on the server and for outstanding RPCs from all three clients. Our earlier guess about flushing buffers to disk is consistent with the detail we can now see.

Just before the long delay, the first three RPCs at the left of Figure 7.12 show the same pattern as Figure 7.11's slow RPCs—about 55 msec per RPC, assumed to be doing one disk write each. Just after the delay, the RPCs on the far right have switched back to the same pattern as Figure 7.11's fast RPCs—about 25 msec per RPC with not enough server time to do anything but buffer 1MB in RAM.

The most likely explanation for the long delay is that some file-system software flushed the accumulated write buffer data (it is too long to be an individual on-disk write buffer flush). We see from Figures 7.9 and 7.11 that the initial burst of fast RPCs lasted from time 38 to 41.7 seconds, doing about 180 RPCs of 1MB each, so buffering up to 180 MB of write data (we can't tell yet whether the buffer is also being copied to disk at a slower rate). The long pause in Figure 7.12 is long enough to write about 120 MB to disk, but not long enough to write 180 MB, so we might guess that the other 60 MB were written to disk overlapped with the slow 55 msec RPCs, helpful but not keeping up with the incoming rate.

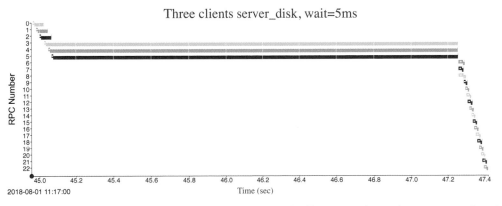

Figure 7.12   **Long 2.2 second delay, with RAM write buffer appearing to become emptier at far right**

At the left edge of the long pause, note that the three initial fast incoming RPCs are spaced out a little in time and that the next three that don't return for seconds also start spaced out in time with about the same spacing. So nothing looks amiss in starting the RPCs at the server. The story is different at the right end of the long pause—all three delayed RPCs return at nearly the same time (they differ by only about 0.8 millisecond). That behavior is consistent with one of the RPCs holding the spinlock and the other two waiting on it; then, when the first one finally releases the lock, the other two quickly do their short CPU-bound work and return.

The second long delay in Figure 7.9 at time 50 is also about 2 seconds. The remaining three delays in Figure 7.9 are shorter, about 0.5 seconds, but by then the offered load is three times smaller.

For user-facing datacenter software, delays like these are unacceptable. To avoid them, data-center software usually does I/O on separate threads, perhaps one per disk/SSD drive, so that the user-facing threads do not block. It also tightly controls the size of write buffers and prior-itizes reads ahead of writes to the same disk. Some large datacenter software companies write their own file system in order to gain even better control over I/O delays [Ghemawat 2003, Hildebrand 2021].

7.7   Experiment 3

In the first two experiments, we had an environment with the network bandwidth a bit larger than the disk bandwidth (either reading or writing), so we could not easily observe disk con-tention. In our third experiment, we introduce a new server operation to checksum an existing on-disk value. Like read, it reads a full file from disk, but it only sends an eight-byte checksum response over the network. It will thus allow us to create and examine disk and spinlock conten-tion without intermixed network contention. One client program starts on one client CPU ask-ing the server to read and sum 1,000 values of 1MB each and then about a second later two more clients start on another CPU asking the server to read and sum just 200 values each. The values are in disk files, but may be cached in RAM if accessed recently. How long should all this take?

If a file is in RAM, it should take only about 100 usec to read and checksum, based on memory bandwidth of 10 GB/sec. If it is on disk, it should be like Experiment 2: ~13 msec seek time and ~17 msec transfer time for 1MB at 60 MB/sec on our slow disk. We might hope that successive files are contiguous on disk so most after the first one will not need a seek.

Here is the setup for Experiment 3, using three machines:

```
server$    ./server_disk&
client1$   ./client4 server 12346 -k 1000 -seed1 chksum \
           -key "aaaa" +
client2$   ./client4 server 12347 -k 200 -seed1 chksum \
           -key "bbbb" + & \
           ./client4 server 12348 -k 200 -seed1 chksum \
           -key "bcaa"
```

Figure 7.13a shows three clients calculating checksums over 1,000 + 200 + 200 = 1,400 files, the files written in Figure 7.9. Even in this simple environment, the dynamics of the interactions between the three clients, the files, and the spinlock are quite complex. The total elapsed time is

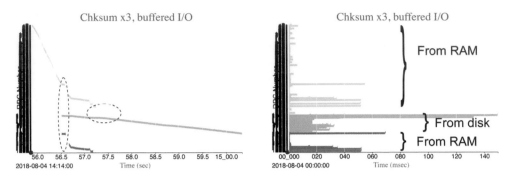

Figures 7.13ab   **Three clients checksumming 1MB values from disk server. Left 13a: absolute start times; right 13b: relative to start time = zero**

only 4 seconds: the first 1,000 files (top yellow line) and the last 200 (bottom blue line) were already buffered in RAM. Only the middle files (green line) are read from disk. In Figure 7.13b, we can see that most of the 1,000 files for `client1` in yellow take about 1 msec, which is too fast to be reading 1MB off disk. We also see that most of the next 200 files for `client2` in green take about 17 msec, which is about right for reading 1MB from disk if there is no seek time. We look next at just the leading and trailing edges shown in ovals.

The leading edge in Figure 7.14 shows just `client1` running initially, summing a file every 1 msec. Then the other two clients start up. Immediately, there is contention on the spinlock. Zooming in on the start time would reveal that the second client grabbed the lock first, but this is easier to see by looking at the staggered lock releases, marked by three arrows: second client releases, allowing first client to start, then first client releases allowing third client to start, then third releases.

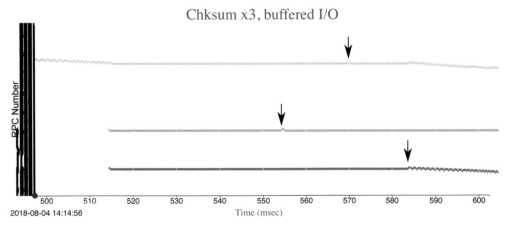

Figure 7.14   **Three clients checksumming 1MB values from disk server, expansion of client 2 and 3 startup from Figure 7.13**

The server thread for `client2` got the lock first and released it 40 msec later at the leftmost arrow, time 555. During this time, the server actually went to disk with roughly 15 msec of seek and 25 msec of transfer time, possibly with a directory access. Next, the server thread for `client1` got the spinlock and released it 15 msec later at time 570. Then the `client3` thread got the lock and released it 13 msec later at time 83. These times suggest that threads one and three also went to disk (and that even without the spinlock would have waited on disk contention). After this, at the right of the diagram threads for clients one and three do many back-to-back sums from files buffered in RAM. But the thread for `client2` remains *starved out*—it keeps failing to get the spinlock because the other two keep grabbing it first.

Starvation is a real issue with just three contenders for our simple spinlock. It only gets worse with a dozen or more contenders. This is why datacenter locking libraries put effort into avoiding starvation, typically by making a list of pending waiters and dispatching them one at a time and *in order of arrival* whenever a lock is freed up. More about starvation in Chapters 13 and 27.

Near the end of the work, Figure 7.15 shows threads for clients one and two winding down. Thread 1 is doing 1–2 RPCs per msec from files buffered in RAM. Thread 2 is continuing to read its files from disk, taking 20–40 msec each time.

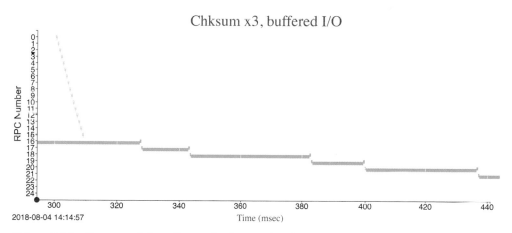

Figure 7.15   **Two remaining clients checksumming 1MB values from disk server, expansion of winding down from Figure 7.13**

This figure just confirms that the data for `client2` is all being served from disk, not RAM.

7.8 Logging

I hope you are beginning to appreciate the power of careful low-overhead logging of timestamps for all transactions in a datacenter. The figures in this chapter are drawn directly from the simple 96-byte RPC logs we introduced in Chapter 6. They reveal unexpected software dynamics, and they also reveal some strong clues in the *values* of delays, clues about what can and cannot be the cause of those delays. We will look more at logging in the next chapter.

7.9   Understanding Transaction Latency Variation

Recall from Chapter 1 that we defined software dynamics as "... the activity over time—what pieces of code run when, what they wait for, what memory space they take, and how different programs affect each other." We saw a little bit of unexpected dynamics in Chapter 5 on disks, but we see much more in this chapter.

CPU and memory contention reveal themselves when one program runs slowly just when some other program is running and consuming shared CPU or cache resources. Disk contention reveals itself in longer-than-expected delays accessing a shared storage device. Network contention reveals itself in longer-than-expected delays when sending RPC requests or responses over a shared network. Critical-section contention reveals itself when a server is delayed waiting to acquire a software lock. All of these contribute to variations in transaction latency. Recognizing them involves having some reasonable estimate of expected behavior, observing actual behavior, and comparing the two.

Recall also from Chapter 1 our framework of an offered load driving a system under test, a human estimate of the expected behavior, measured observations of the real system, reasoning about the observations and from that reasoning creating fixes for some performance issues. The observations in this chapter immediately suggest a problem with the combination of write buffering and synchronous disk I/O. Changing the I/O design to avoid blocking will substantially reduce the 99th percentile response time of our simple RPCs. Having multiple locks, such as one per distinct key or one per group of keys that hash to the same value, instead of a single database-wide one can also speed things up.

7.10   Summary

The interactions between network requests and disk accesses reveal a more complex performance environment. We learned several lessons that were not obvious in the disk-alone and network-alone chapters.

- Time alignment is needed across multiple servers. Doing this in postprocessing software is easy.

- Timestamping and logging all RPCs gives a baseline view of transaction latency. This can be done with minimal overhead.

- Including parent and child RPC IDs in each message allows reconstructing complete call trees. Call trees plus timestamping give a complete view of the dynamics of every RPC, including a view of unrelated RPCs that overlap in time.

- Viewing multiple RPCs by wall-clock time shows overlaps and gaps.

- Viewing multiple RPCs relative to their start time shows how slow ones differ from fast ones.

- Lock contention is a major source of datacenter delays, so look for it.

- Design in simple operations such as `ping` and `chksum` that allow you to separate different potential bottlenecks.

- First, sketch what you expect to see, and then measure actual behavior. All the learning is in the discrepancies.

In the rest of this book, we will look further at tools to observe and understand the root causes of such variations in transaction latency.

Exercises

7.1   From the client log files you created in the Chapter 6 exercises, run `timealign.cc` and `dumplogile4.cc` and `makeself.cc` to create original HTML pictures and time-aligned HTML pictures.

7.2   Build and run Experiment 1 yourself on whatever sample servers you have available. Reconstruct Figures 7.6a and 7.6b from your data. Comment briefly on the differences you observe.

7.3   Build and run Experiment 2. Reconstruct Figure 7.9 from your data. Comment briefly on the differences you observe.

7.4   Build and run Experiment 3. Reconstruct Figures 7.13a and 7.13b from your data. Comment briefly on the differences you observe.

7.5   Build and run Experiment 3, but this time specifying `O_DIRECT` (i.e., uncached and unbuffered disk accesses) and `O_NOATIME` using code fragments from `mystery3.cc`. Reconstruct Figures 7.13a and 7.13b from your data. Comment briefly on the differences you observe.

Part II

Observation

A man should look for what is, and not for what he thinks should be.

—Albert Einstein

As discussed in Part I, measurement is the act of ascertaining the size, amount, or degree of something.

Observation is a broader term than *measurement*. It refers to watching something carefully and attentively, but covers multiple aspects. A measurement determines a numerical value (with units) of a single aspect, while an observation encompasses many aspects at once, some of which may be unexpected. An observation may also encompass a time sequence of events—the dynamics.

This second part presents techniques for observing the behavior of time-constrained software. Good code logs the start and stop times of every transaction and sub-transaction, along with enough information to construct the timestamped call tree of many messages or remote procedure calls doing the work of each user-facing transaction across all servers. This log information shows which software piece was slow when an overall user-facing transaction time is long, and logging many transactions per second shows patterns of unexpected slowness. But alone it does not tell *why* some piece is slow; Parts III and IV cover that.

Part II also discusses dashboards that show key health metrics for complex software, it surveys existing observation tools, and it introduces and motivates the concept of low-overhead tracing to account for every nanosecond of elapsed time on every CPU. At the end of this part, the reader will have a grasp of techniques to observe the fundamental behavior of complex software interacting with an operating system and modern computer hardware.

Chapter 8

Logging

A log is a timestamped sequence of events in a software system. Logs are fundamental to understanding the offered requests and their responses for any software, along with useful internal details. Logs underpin recording simple counts, samples, or traces for later analysis and thought.

8.1 Observation Tools

Counters are observation tools that simply count events, such as instructions executed or cache misses or transactions performed or elapsed microseconds. *Profiles* are observation tools that quasi-periodically sample some value, such as program counter (PC), queue depth, or system load. Counters and profiles are low-overhead observation tools. They do not capture any time sequencing, and they do not distinguish unusual transactions from normal ones.

Traces are observation tools that record time-sequenced events such as disk seek addresses, transaction requests and responses, function entry/exit, execute/wait transitions, or kernel/user mode execution transitions. Traces are a way to understand the dynamic behavior of running programs, but unless carefully engineered, they can be high-overhead tools and hence produce distortion of the system under test. Such overhead can make them unsuitable for observing live time-constrained systems. Traces can distinguish unusual transactions from normal ones. They are the only approach that works well for understanding unpredictable unusually slow transactions.

8.2 Logging

In this chapter we cover log files for a datacenter-like program. A log file is one kind of trace, containing a sequence of timestamped text or binary entries describing the operations performed by a particular instance of a software service, such as the RPC logs discussed in Chapters 6 and 7.

Logging is a tool for observing the overall behavior of datacenter software. For high-rate operations, the logged data may be austere, while for lower-rate operations it may be quite elaborate. Log files may be binary-format data for compactness and quick generation or may be text-format for direct reading by people or other programs. Logs written in a binary format can be converted to text format offline, at time of use.

Why is logging discussed here as the first of many tools for observing interference?

If you can afford only *one* observation tool, it should be logging. Only with logs for a particular service can you see how many transactions it did over each time interval, which times of day had particularly light offered loads and which had particularly slow response times. When there are occasional slow transactions, timestamped logs can show what else was going on at about the same time and thus give some clue about possible sources of interference. Logs also show when a service is down/disabled/crashed, when it is starting or stopping, when it is so overloaded that it is refusing new requests, and when it is only limping along doing a minimal number of requests per second. When service A is running unexpectedly slowly at some time and service A depends on another service B which is limping along and responding slowly during that same time, correlating the two logs will quickly suggest looking first at B's problems.

8.3 Basic Logging

All good datacenter software should have a designed-in logging infrastructure: libraries to make logging easy and a documented style of use so that multiple services use logging in similar ways.

Logging involves writing a series of log entries about a service to a file, such that the file can later be read to see what happened and when it happened. Each log entry is timestamped with the date and time to a fraction of a second (often to the microsecond). Log entries may have a stylized type or importance, they may have the name of a function or process that created them, and they may have text or binary information fields.

The simplest log entry just has a timestamp and a text string. This form is especially useful for recording major service events such as startup and shutdown, configuration options, missing dependencies, inadequate resources, and other events that are outside the expected normal operation. Including a type or importance, either as an explicit field or as a stylized word at the front of each text string, makes it easy to filter out unimportant messages when there is a need to quickly find messages about critical error conditions. The Linux kernel `printk` routine, for example, has eight levels of importance for kernel log messages (those retrieved by the `dmesg` command-line program): emergency, alert, critical, error, warning, notice, info, and debug.

For a service driven by RPC requests, every request and response should be logged. One form of log entry has a timestamp and information about the request, while another form has a timestamp and information about the response. For services with a low rate of requests, these entries could just be formatted text, but for higher-rate services, binary logs containing fields copied directly from the RPC messages can be created with much lower overhead.

We saw a simple but not very robust example of RPC logging in Chapter 6. In particular, the simple code cannot easily accommodate any intermixed simple <timestamp, text> entries, and it cannot accommodate any expansion beyond its fixed format. But it contains the key information for each request and response: RPC ID and parent ID, timestamps for send/receive of request and response, IP:port pairs for the two servers involved, request and response message lengths, message (really log entry) type, RPC method, and return status. For a service with 10,000 RPCs per second (see Chapter 9's Figure 9.7, for example), recording this information in about 100 bytes of binary is as complicated as we can afford while maintaining low overhead.

8.4 Extended Logging

For lower-rate services, more extensive logging is possible and may be desirable. If a service usually has about 1,000 transactions per second per server and each transaction generates about two log entries (e.g., request and response), then for every 1 msec transaction using 5 usec to create and write/buffer each log entry would represent a 1% logging overhead. At 100 transactions per second, the time spent logging can be correspondingly longer.

Extended logging could include more information about queueing behavior at each request— for example, how much work is queued in front of an incoming request and how much data is queued for the network connection(s) ahead of each outgoing response.

Extended logging could give a breakdown of time spent within a transaction—major software pieces and how much time is spent in each.

Extended logging could record more of the parameters for an RPC request; for example, software that serves disk data could record each request's disk number, filename, operation, priority, starting byte offset, and byte length. For each response, additional data could record whether the request was an in-memory cache hit or miss to disk and whether the request was over or under its administratively set quota.

In some environments, it can make sense to have optional detailed logging that is usually turned off but can be enabled for debugging. For example, each request and all its parameters could optionally be expanded into a text format and added to the log. Or a process that develops and scores many answers and returns the best could log all the intermediate values.

8.5 Timestamps

Timestamps are a key part of logging. It is best for them to include the complete date, time to the second, and microsecond fraction within that. This is precisely the information that the C language `gettimeofday()` call provides. By including the complete date, saved logs from years ago still have their exact context. If some bug is postulated that occurs only on the first Saturday of each month, old logs can be combed to see if there is any evidence of it. By including microsecond resolution, events that occur very close together in time can be identified and put in proper sequence (A before B). Millisecond resolution is no good for transactions that take about

50 usec. Nanosecond resolution is possible but is probably overkill for the next 10 years, unless CPUs get suddenly 10x faster.

The `gettimeofday()` call returns a 32-bit second since January 1, 1970, and a 32-bit field containing 20 bits of usec within that second. These 64 bits could be recorded verbatim in a log entry, but it will often turn out to be more convenient to use a wrapper function that directly returns a 64-bit usec value: `(tv_sec * 1000000) + tv_usec`. Subtracting these values gives durations, and this is common enough in datacenter code to suggest doing the conversion just once at timestamp creation.

There is the question of time zones for timestamps. If a company has datacenters in multiple time zones and individual logs use local time, it is messy and error-prone to try to correlate events from logs at two different datacenters. Even the act of copying a log file from one datacenter to another has the potential to lose time zone information. A much better design uses the same time zone for all logs company-wide. The two viable choices are coordinated universal time (UTC, essentially Greenwich mean time) [Wikipedia 2021p] or the time zone of the company's Galactic Headquarters. If the latter is chosen, there is the additional complication of how to handle daylight saving time, especially events that occur near the twice-yearly transitions to/from standard time.

In any case, there is also the complication of leap seconds [NIST 2020, Scott 2015]. These are inserted just before midnight on the last day of June or December as UTC 23:59:60 about once every 1.5 years to compensate for the slowing rotation of the earth. Note that GPS time does *not* insert leap seconds so differs from UTC by an extra second every few years. The more perverse among you will enjoy reading about the intricacies of computer timekeeping in Babcock [2015]. Some companies smear their datacenter time for several hours before and after a leap second so that there is no sudden discontinuity but an extra second has transpired those hours. For the rest of us, just be aware of some discontinuities and try to build software that does not crash upon encountering one.

8.6   RPC IDs

In Chapter 6 we introduced the concept of RPC IDs—nearly unique integers used to identify individual RPCs. These are needed for matching up responses to requests when a client has multiple requests outstanding and responses arrive out of order. For observation tools they allow recording exactly which RPC any given CPU core is working on any nanosecond, and they allow correlating log files and event traces across multiple machines with slightly different clocks, as we saw in Chapter 7. To record call trees of RPCs, it is sufficient to record the parent RPC ID of each lower-level call. (This is not very robust for a multi-level call tree if data for an intermediate level is lost or spoiled, but it is the minimum sufficient information.)

The term *nearly unique* means that it is OK to use the same number for two different RPCs if they usually occur far enough apart in time. The thing we want to avoid is the ambiguity of having duplicate RPC IDs *frequently* reach the same machine at nearly the same time.

We address here the question of how to generate RPC IDs across thousands of computers in a few dozen datacenters scattered around the world. Each computer could start at boot time generating ID numbers 0, 1, 2, ..., but that turns out to create too many duplicates when lots of computers are using the same tiny subset of a large space of ID numbers. We would prefer a mechanism that starts each computer at a random place in a large space of eventually repeating ID numbers. In addition, it is convenient but by no means necessary to have subsets of the ID field change often. If the ID is a 64-bit number that starts at a random value and is incremented by 1 each time, seven of the eight bytes remain constant for 255 increments, and four of the eight remain constant for 4B increments.

A slightly more robust method of incrementing is to use a linear feedback shift register with several XOR taps. This is just a fancy way to say

```
rpcid = rpcid shifted left one bit
if the original high bit was 1,
  rpcid = rpcid XOR constant
```

where the constant is carefully chosen [Wikipedia 2021q] to have 1-bits in multiple bytes and to guarantee that the sequence of RPCID values has a maximum-size cycle (2^{64} -1 in the case of a 64-bit RPCID; the value 0 increments to itself and is therefore not used at all). In C, this can be done in branch-free code via four instructions, by using an arithmetic right shift to turn the high bit into either 0x0000000000000000 or 0xFFFFFFFFFFFFFFFF and using this to AND against the constant:

```
static const uint64 POLY64 = 0x42F0E1EBA9EA3693;
uint64 x;
// ... Increment x:
x = (x << 1) ^ (((int64)x >> 63) & POLY64);
```

Generating pseudorandom RPC IDs this way has the convenient property that any subset of the bytes will change value at every increment, so for example the low two bytes of an RPC ID can be used in a space-constrained tracing record to represent the entire ID number. But unlike incrementing by 1, these low two bytes have successive values that bounce around a lot based on the high bits of the RPC ID. If two sources of RPC IDs send a server IDs with matching low two bytes, it is highly unlikely that the next several values in sequence will also match.

We will take advantage of this property of pseudorandom RPC IDs in the KUtrace design in Part III of this book.

8.7 Log File Formats

As mentioned several times, log files may be binary-format data for compactness and quick generation or may be text-format for direct reading by people or other programs. Measurements on our sample server show that 20,000 calls per second to write binary 128-byte log records takes about 0.3 usec each, low enough to be only a small fraction of the time for transactions that arrive every 100 usec, with two log records per RPC.

On the same machine, 20,000 calls per second to construct and then write text 128-byte log records takes about 6 usec each, 20 times longer. The construction involves calls to `gettimeofday()` and `ctime()` for the timestamp, and `sprintf()` and `fwrite()` for the formatting and fixed-size write. Logging overhead of 12 usec every 100 usec is unacceptably high.

Binary log file records can be quite brittle, however. Adding a new field as a service evolves can invalidate all previously saved log files, or it can require careful use of version numbers. Deleting a field is even worse if some downstream log-processing software depends on finding that field. Over time, it is easy to lose track of the exact definition of old binary files [Rothenberg 1999].

Another disadvantage of binary log records is that they often have inflexible fixed-size fields for numbers and for text. Such fields can waste space but can also constrain text that with normal phrasing would be too long to fit into some field.

A third design choice is to use a mechanism like protocol buffers [Google 2021, Wikipedia 2021r]. These are a low-overhead variable-length binary format containing <key, value> pairs. Keys are all small integers, numeric values are stored in a minimal number of bytes, and text values are stored in a minimal number of bytes with a length on the front. Combined with a definition file, offline programs can turn the key numbers back into meaningful names.

Protocol buffers have no artificial constraints on field sizes or number of fields. Fields can be added at any time in a design by simply using a new key number. No-longer-used fields can be left out entirely. There is a minimal amount of formatting for numbers to remove unnecessary bytes and a minimal amount for text to add an explicit length. The transmitted or disk-written byte format is very compact with just 1–2 bytes per key and the rest all data. The performance is thus close to that of binary log entries, but the flexibility is close to that of arbitrary text. Highly recommended.

8.8   Managing Log Files

It is useful to make log file names self-identifying. For example, for the server4 program in Chapter 6 we used this form:

```
server4_20180422_183909_dclab5_22411.log
```

containing the program name that created the log file, its start date and time, the server it was created on, and the process ID of the program that created it (this protects against duplicate file-names for two instances of server4 being started in the same second). Such a naming convention avoids mistakes of looking at a log file from the wrong day or wrong server and makes it easier to find one from early December years ago: 20131201. The field order and date/time formatting is chosen so that vanilla sorting of filenames is useful; dates such as 01-12-2013 are harder to sort.

If log files are based on protocol buffers or a similar mechanism, the definition files are best kept with the creation program sources, with the log files themselves, or in a well-defined repository. The goal is to avoid losing the definitions over time; keeping logs and their definitions together is often safest.

Normally, log files are written to local disks on each server and then either thrown away after a few days or explicitly copied to some log repository for longer-term storage. In this environment, it is not helpful to open a log file for some low-rate service and write to it for months at a time, never closing it. Nor is it helpful to open a log file for some high-rate service and write 86 GB in the first 24 hours as one huge single file.

Part of a logging design therefore must include in the logging libraries simple mechanisms for closing log files and starting new ones based on time and size and for migrating selected files to a repository. Usually, some simple log-saver daemon program is needed to manage and perform the migrations. None of this is complicated, but it is most easily included early in the design.

8.9 Summary

If you can afford only a single observation tool, build a low-overhead logging system and use it in all your datacenter programs. The data in the logs will give you at least some insight to bottlenecks, offered loads, and unexpected software dynamics. Without even simple logs, you really have no idea what your software has been doing.

•

Chapter 9

Aggregate Measures

The performance analyst has an overall goal of understanding the dynamics of some software, understanding when and why it is slow, and understanding how to diminish the number and severity of slow transactions.

For a service processing 10,000 requests per second, there are nearly a billion requests per day (86,400 seconds per day). Just recording the arrival time of each request gives us ~1B data points, and recording anything else, such as latency or response size in bytes, gives us billions more. With a huge number of individual times or measurements, it will be useful to summarize them in several different ways, each with the purpose of revealing a different kind of performance problem. In this chapter, we will look at various ways to summarize simple event *counts* such as request arrivals and then ways to summarize per-event measured *values* such as request latency or bytes transmitted.

The purpose of some summaries is to show baseline normal/average behavior, while the purpose of others is to reveal not-normal behavior or possible performance issues. A powerful summary technique is to show high-density patterns of behavior, from which the exquisite human eye can ask "What is *that*?" when spotting an unexpected confluence of bad behavior.

Summaries are not designed to show the *reasons* for not-normal behavior, just to show that it is happening so that someone or some program can look at it in more detail to seek the reasons. Summaries are also useful for showing what is *not* a problem, reducing time wasted looking for latency in all the wrong places.

Dynamic behavior happens at many different time scales and has only a loose definition of what is normal and what is slow. The measurements we make are almost all time-sequences of counts or measured values, such as latency or bytes transferred,

    <time, event> pairs or

    <time, value> pairs

for thousands of transactions each with a starting time. We will want to summarize these by rate and by value and to gather multiple measurements over time. The next sections cover these topics in detail.

9.1   Uniform vs. Bursty Event Rates

Draw yourself a little five-second sketch of a service receiving "seven requests per second," using an "o" for each request.

Did it look a bit like Figure 9.1a?

o o o o o o o	o o o o o o o	o o o o o o o	o o o o o o o	o o o o o o o

Figure 9.1a   **Uniform arrivals**

It could equally well look a bit like Figure 9.1b.

oooooooooo	oooooooooo	oooooooooo	ooooo

Figure 9.1b   **One burst of arrivals**

Or like Figure 9.1c.

	oooooooo o ooooooo o	oooooo oooo o	o o	o ooo o

Figure 9.1c   **Multiple bursts of arrivals**

Transactions in a datacenter environment are extremely *unlikely* to be spread out evenly; their requests are much more likely to occur in bursts. In the third picture, Figure 9.1c, there are 0, 17, 11, 2, and 5 requests per second during the five one-second intervals. Almost always, the bursty nature of offered work causes or interacts badly with performance problems. When presented with an average rate for some set of events, it is helpful to get in the habit of imagining Figure 9.1c, not 9.1a.

If we are looking for a smooth calculation of requests per second, we could measure over the entire five-second interval and find 35 requests/5 seconds = 7 req/sec for any of the three Figure 9.1 pictures. If instead our purpose is to spot possibly destructive short bursts of requests or other unexpected patterns, we could measure over 1-second intervals in the third picture and think about how the "7 requests per second" service behaves with 17 requests in 1 second. Is 17 per second the worst case, or are there frequently 50 or more requests per second, or perhaps seven requests in 1/10 of a second = a rate of 70 req/sec? How could we find out?

9.2 Measurement Intervals

A rate is simply a count over some time interval, for example requests per second or errors per minute or restarts per month. A good start for measuring rates is to decide the minimum time interval that makes sense.

For the purpose of understanding the overall baseline load for service, we might be interested in a one-day measurement interval. For the purpose of understanding why a particular service has unusually long latencies around 6:01 p.m. every day, we might be interested in multiple one-second measurement intervals around that time. For the purpose of detecting terribly bunched-up requests, an extreme interval such as one millisecond might be useful.

As always, we are looking for summaries that give some insight to both desired and undesired performance. We often will not quite know what we are looking for so will need to look in different ways until we can spot unusual behavior. Starting with a series of short-interval measurements, we can derive longer intervals, and we can sort the measurements to remove the time sequencing to look at the distribution of measurements. But we cannot do the reverse—turn long-interval measurements into reasonable short-interval measurements. Thus, it is best to err a little on the side of shorter intervals than longer intervals when gathering initial measurements.

If a service is receiving thousands of requests per second, a one-second interval might be good. But if the service has a 200 msec deadline for responses, it will be useful to look at requests in 200 msec or even 100 msec intervals, to be able to observe the kind of bunching that could queue up enough work for "the last guy" response to be much over deadline. (If that happens frequently, one could raise the deadline, increase the compute power, or look at the callers and try to reduce or smooth out their requests.) On the other hand, if a service is receiving a few requests per minute, a one-second measurement interval will just show lots of seconds with zero requests and a few seconds with a request or two. In this case, a 10 second or 1-minute measurement interval might be more appropriate.

Calculating rate per measurement interval is our first method for summarizing lots of data, turning billions of arrival events into millions or thousands of intervals. We will want in turn to summarize those summaries.

9.3 Timelines

Assume we have a service with a few thousand measurement intervals per day. What are the various ways we could show and summarize those?

Since performance problems often come from interference between events or bursts of events that are close together in time, one useful presentation is just a timeline graph of all the measurements—a graph with time on the x-axis and count or rate on the y-axis.

The example timeline graph in Figure 9.2 shows how many marine species went extinct during ~3M year intervals stretching back 542M years [Wikipedia 2021s, Wikimedia 2008].

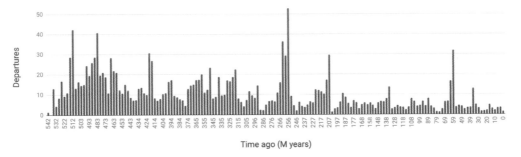

Figure 9.2   **Timeline of marine species departures (extinctions) per ~3M years**

A timeline is good for spotting peaks, "normal" behavior, and any periodically repeating patterns. It is also good for spotting phase changes in dynamic behavior—one kind of behavior before the change and a substantially different pattern after it. In Figure 9.2 we can see a baseline of about 5–10 species becoming extinct every 3 million years, with occasional peaks over 30 and a maximum of 53.

This Figure 9.2 graph has about 165 data points. If you have thousands or millions of data points and no specific subset of the time to focus on, timelines with that many points become unwieldy. Figure 9.3 shows the same data as Figure 9.2 but aggregated in groups that are five times wider, about every ~15 million years. There are just 34 bars instead of 165. The large peaks around time 256 in Figure 9.2 happened to get split across two groups so have shrunk in Figure 9.3, while the peak around time 483 and its nearby values got combined and emphasized in Figure 9.3. There is still a baseline of about 5–10 species becoming extinct every 3 million years, but it is shown in Figure 9.3 as 25–50 species becoming extinct every 15 million years, making it difficult to compare the graphs. These two graphs would be easily comparable if the y-axis were the same on both: in common units of, say, extinctions per 10M years. Do that in your designs.

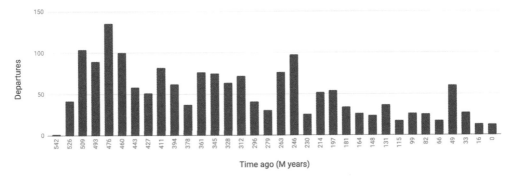

Figure 9.3   **Timeline of species departures, aggregated into one-fifth as many groups as Figure 9.2**

There is a trade-off between resolution and bulkiness in Figures 9.2 and 9.3. Err on the side of better resolution if your purpose is to spot the anomalies.

9.4   Further Summarizing of Timelines

Figure 9.4 shows the same data as Figure 9.2 sorted by rate, ignoring the time sequencing. This is the basis for percentile calculations. The median or 50th percentile is a value such that half (50%) of the data samples are below it and half above, in this case about 7.85 extinctions per 3 million years. The 99th percentile is a value such that 99% of the data samples are below it, in this case about 41.3 extinctions. The same idea applies to other percentiles.

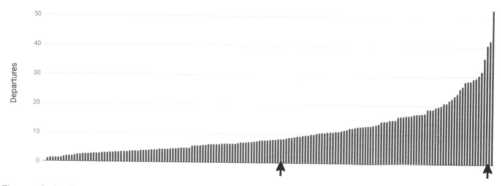

Figure 9.4   **Data in Figure 9.2 sorted by departures per 3M year interval; left arrow marks the median or 50th percentile value (7.85 departures per ~3M years), and right arrow marks the 99th percentile value (41.3 departures).**

Figure 9.5 shows a *histogram* of the intervals in Figure 9.2, using bins that are 1 extinction wide. There was one interval with 1 extinction, 7 with 2 extinctions, 13 with 3, etc. out to 1 interval with 53 extinctions. Just like histograms of datacenter measurements, we have a clump of lower values on the left followed on the right by a long tail of occasional larger values (Chapter 1, Figure 1.3).

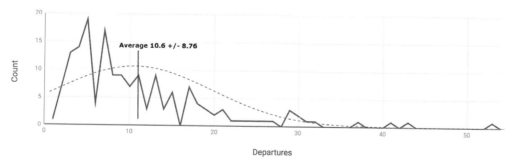

Figure 9.5   **Histogram of data in Figure 9.2, showing average and standard deviation for the best-fit Gaussian normal distribution. It is a bad fit to the skewed data. Don't use average to summarize long-tail distributions.**

The average value is 10.6, and the standard deviation is 8.76, giving the Gaussian hump (normal distribution) shown here as a dashed line. Since the normal distribution is symmetrical about the average, it is a poor approximation to long-tail data. In particular, it poorly represents the data below the average, it poorly represents the major peaks, and it poorly represents the small number of large values at the far right, the ones we are most likely interested in for understanding performance issues. Do not use average and standard deviation to summarize a non-Gaussian distribution.

Figure 9.6 shows that same data with 50th and 99th percentile values. Because the extreme values in the long tail raise the average but do not raise the median, the median will be lower than the average for a long-tail histogram. The median is closer to the center of the big hump on the left, and the 99th percentile shows how far out all but the last 1% of the long tail extends. Datacenter performance analysis is often about understanding that rightmost 1%.

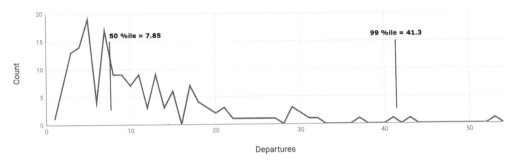

Figure 9.6   **Histogram of data in Figure 9.2, showing 50th and 99th percentile values. These are better summaries for long-tail distributions.**

The median and 99th percentile are good summaries for describing normal behavior and the extent of peaks; for long-tail distributions, use them in preference to average and standard deviation. Finding and fixing performance bugs that create the 1% long tail will reduce the 99th percentile value even if those changes do not materially affect the median.

Another common approach to describing (and responding to) bursty traffic is to count events in the busiest second, the busiest minute, the busiest hour of the day, and the busiest day of the year. These are also good summaries for describing normal behavior and the extent of peaks. The shorter time frames suggest the equipment needed to handle peak or near-peak loads, while the busiest day suggests the equipment needed for a heavy baseline load, and the ratios between suggest how extreme the peaks are. As early as 1896, telephone equipment in the United States was designed to handle the busiest hour of the day, and by 1904 statistics were being carefully gathered of calls per hour across different kinds of exchanges [Anonymous 1896, Anonymous 1905]. In the United States, Mother's Day has been the busiest day of the year for telephones [Goldsmith 2010].

Table 9.1 has the summary values for the data in Figure 9.2. Overall, we can summarize time-lines in a variety of simple ways. As we said, average and standard deviation are only rarely appropriate to describe datacenter latency distributions; median and 99th percentile are usually better for highlighting normal and peak values. Minimum and maximum are occasionally useful to describe a set of values, but they are easily distorted by a single extreme value over the course of a day or more. Busiest time periods are good for sizing equipment for expected loads and are also productive hunting grounds for performance problems.

Table 9.1 **Summary Values for Figure 9.1 Data**

Average	10.6 departures/~3Myears
Standard deviation	± 8.76 departures/~3Myears
Median (50th percentile)	7.85 departures/~3Myears
99th percentile	41.3 departures/~3Myears
Minimum	0 departures/~3Myears
Maximum	53 departures/~3Myears
Busiest ~3M years	53 departures/~3Myears
Busiest ~15M years	145 departures/~15Myears = 29 per ~3Myears

9.5 Histogram Time Scales

When displaying long tail latency distributions, it is not obvious how to manage the latency axis. Consider the disk-server latency histogram from Chapter 1, Figure 1.3, repeated here in Figure 9.7c, with a median of 26 msec at the left red line, a 99th percentile latency of 696 msec at the right red line, and an overall range of 0 to 1,500 msec. Normal transactions have latency measurements in the approximate range 0–100 msec, while slow performance-problem ones stretch out from 100 to 1,500 msec.

One traditional design for the x-axis is a linear scale 0–1500 msec, as shown in Figure 9.7a. The normal range is highly compressed into the first ~6% of the graph while the tail goes on for the remaining 94%. The humps in the normal part of the graph are barely distinguishable.

Another traditional choice is to use a logarithmic scale, as shown in Figure 9.7b. About one-third of the x-axis covers 0–10 msec (showing < 1 msec as 1 msec), one-third 10-100 msec, and one-third 100–1000 msec. This substantially distorts the graph for normal latency accesses under about 100 msec, and by expanding the 1–10 msec range so much it makes it difficult to visually compare the 1–10 msec range and the 11–20 msec range. It makes symmetrical (Gaussian-like) humps asymmetrical by expanding the left side and compressing the right side. It also severely compresses the graph for the more interesting part out to the 99th percentile.

A less traditional choice is the piecewise-linear graph in Figure 9.7c, changing the scale twice across the x-axis. The pieces I chose use half the x-axis for the normal range 0–100 msec, then 7/16 for the range 100–1000 msec, and the remaining 1/16 for 1000–1500 msec, each time changing the scale by about a factor of 10. This allows direct visual comparison within the normal range, while still capturing the performance-bug humps at 250, 500, 750, ... msec. The linear piece under 100 msec also more accurately shows half of the area under the curve up to the median, and half of the area above the median, with just a little area distortion for the last few percent.

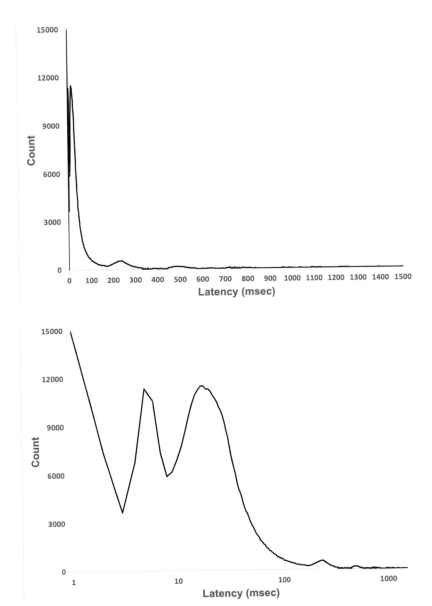

Figures 9.7ab   Histogram displays with linear and logarithmic x-axes, respectively. For long-tail distributions, linear at top contracts the normal range excessively; logarithmic at the bottom expands it excessively.

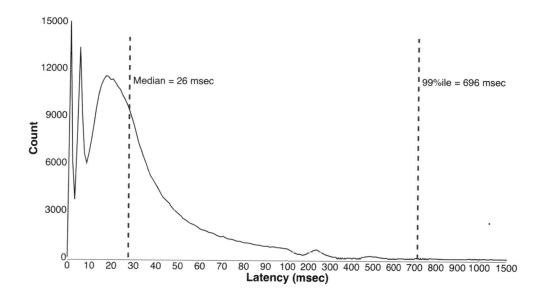

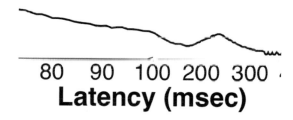

Figures 9.7cd   **Histogram displays piecewise-linear x-axis. Piecewise linear at the top shows the normal range undistorted and the long tail somewhat contracted but still visible. Figure 9.7d at the bottom shows the detail of a 10x scale change in Figure 9.7c.**

Figure 9.7d shows some detail of Figure 9.7c at the first piece transition. There is a slight discontinuity drawn in the axis line at 100 with the piece ends pried up and down, and the numeric labels change from incrementing by 10 to incrementing by 100. The hump centered at about 250 msec remains symmetrical since it is all in one linear piece (the design would still distort a hump exactly crossing the 100 msec scale change). Be careful with piecewise-linear: the casual user can easily misinterpret the result.

Other designs are possible. Just be sure to pick one that lets the user spot surprising data.

9.6   Aggregating Per-Event Measurements

RPC request arrival rates are simple counts per time interval. Usually, there are also many measured *values* associated with each counted request, the most important of which is duration (response time). If we have thousands of RPCs per second, how can we usefully summarize the associated measured values? What can we say about these across thousands of seconds (3,600 seconds per hour, for example)?

Figure 9.8 is a picture of some RPC arrivals and their durations with each RPC on a line by itself. For now, ignore the names and symbols and just glance at the horizontal lines showing CPU execution intervals for each RPC. There is usually in a single execution interval of about 50 usec, but occasionally an RPC has multiple execution intervals separated by waiting. The duration or response time for each RPC is measured from the request arrival at the left of its first execution interval to sending its response at the right of its last one. Because the RPCs overlap in time, they are drawn with some vertical offset so we can see the individual RPCs. Compare this figure to the simpler Figure 9.1, which just has some (unrelated) arrival times.

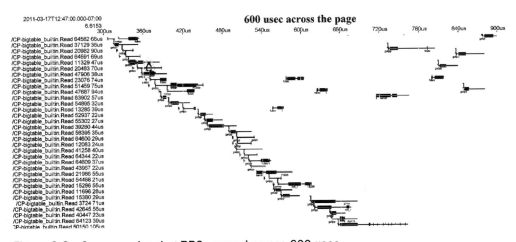

Figure 9.8   **Some overlapping RPCs spread across 600 usec**

The full timeline picture is important for understanding interference between overlapping RPCs, but that discussion will wait until after Chapter 14 on gathering the data that allowed the drawing of Figure 9.8.

How can we summarize the individual durations in Figure 9.8? Instead of just a count per measurement interval such as one second, we have a whole collection of different measured values. We can say that the arrival rate is 33 per 600 usec (55K per second), but what about the 33 durations? While most are about 50 usec, there are 5 of them that take over 500 usec. As performance analysts, we of course are more interested in these slow ones, and in summary information that tells us they exist.

To summarize the durations in the given 600 usec time interval, we can use some of the summary measures from Table 9.1, giving a median duration of about 50 usec and a 99th percentile of 600 usec. The same measures work well for longer intervals such as 1 second, 10 seconds, etc. It can also be useful to record median and 99th percentile values over multiple short time intervals such as 1 or 10 seconds and then construct two timelines, one for median and one for 99th percentile, with lines or sets of bars on a single graph. In particular, the variation of 99th percentile over time can sometimes highlight important patterns, such as the disk latency pattern in the following example.

We may also be interested in measures that describe the total CPU load, such as the sum of CPU time across one second, or in measures that describe overlap density, such as peak and 90th or 99th percentile queue depth for a work queue of started but not yet completed RPCs. Total CPU time per second for the busiest minute of the day might inform how much CPU time to reserve for this service.

If the 90th percentile queue depth is usually 2 on a particular server and the queue depth spikes to ~35 during 20 minutes when the response time is terrible, it will be important to understand whether the queue depth spiked because of a huge burst of arrivals or because of big delays in departures. The latter probably indicates a performance problem that needs fixing on this server while the former probably indicates issues on the RPC clients that caused them to send or bunch together too many requests. In addition to queue depth, it can be useful to track queue insertion and removal rates over appropriately small time intervals.

9.7   Patterns of Values Over Time

So far, we have summarized raw data into short time intervals to give a timeline and in turn aggregated or summarized those lines into just a few numbers. Timelines reveal useful and often unexpected patterns that the summary numbers do not. An even more powerful timeline technique is to display many different measured values in parallel, all aligned in time and possibly revealing correlations between nearby events.

One method to show such patterns is a heat map. Two dimensions on a screen or paper are used to spread out time intervals and parallel values, and color is used as a third dimension to show values for each time interval. Heat maps trade precision (we cannot easily distinguish hundreds of on-screen colors) for information density. Heat maps can be used to put nearly a million data points on a screen or sheet of paper. They are excellent for revealing time-based patterns that would not be apparent when reading large lists of numeric values or when looking only at summaries.

In Figure 9.9, the y-axis shows measurements from 13 disks, the x-axis shows an hour of time, and the color axis shows 99th percentile disk read latency. The red areas are much-too-slow read latencies of 200 msec or more. From this figure, we learn three important things about the slow

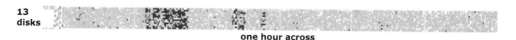

13 disks   **one hour across**

Figure 9.9   **Heat map of 99th percentile disk-read latency for 13 disks for an hour of time. Time resolution is 10-second intervals. Blue color indicates latency under 50 msec, and red color indicates latency over 200 msec (white is no activity). This is a subset of a one-page 24-hour picture.**

performance: (1) it lasts for six minutes in the first stretch and a few minutes each in the other two, not just for a few hundred milliseconds; (2) it occurs three times in an hour (and occurs occasionally in other not-shown hours) but not in any predictable pattern; and (3) it affects essentially all disks simultaneously, not just a single overloaded or slow disk.

Remember that summaries are not designed to show the *reasons* for not-normal behavior, just to show that it is happening so that someone or some program can look at it in more detail to seek the reasons. The original data in this case was logs with microsecond request/response time-stamps of *all* the RPCs to this disk server for 24 hours, so it was possible to zoom in on just the minute around the phase change at beginning of one of the red areas to see how the RPC behavior changed. That examination revealed the *why*—the disk server process was getting locked out by the Google-specific scheduler for exact multiples of 250 msec, because it was exceeding its too-low CPU quota! Fixing the underlying cause by increasing the disk-server CPU quotas across the fleet took about 20 minutes and saved millions of dollars by improving disk access times, reducing the 99th percentile time from 700 msec to 150 msec.

We have covered different ways to aggregate event counts and event values, and ways to use timelines and heat maps to reveal patterns of misbehavior. In the next few sections we will add a little more detail.

9.8   Update Intervals

When showing aggregate values on screen for people to watch, the values should be refreshed periodically. Separate from the choice of measurement or calculation interval, we can choose to provide a summary statistic every *update* interval, which can be longer or shorter than the measurement interval. If the update interval is longer than the measurement interval, it means that we are providing just a sample or aggregate of the calculated measurements, not all of them.

More commonly, the update interval is equal to or shorter than the measurement interval. For example, we might want to show the number of disk accesses per second measured/smoothed over 10 seconds but update that measurement every 2 seconds. To do so, we will employ a sliding window over the most recent five 2-second intervals, as described in the following text. If the summary is being viewed by a person, not just being logged to a file, an update interval in the 1–15 second range is usually best for people to glance at the values now and then or to watch them intently while changing/fixing something about the observed service.

In choosing an *update* interval, we really are choosing how much smoothing to do. Small values that bounce around a lot can be more distracting than informative, while values that are calculated over long times may obscure important short-term fluctuations. Calculation intervals can be structured in many different ways. Figure 9.10 shows some of the design choices for summarizing 34 requests arriving over a total of five minutes. You also see various forms of this process when watching progress bars for many-minute software downloads.

Figure 9.10a shows requests in *non-overlapping* full two-minute intervals, taken on exact two-minute boundaries; a complete two-minute interval is needed before the requests-per-minute calculation can be done, limiting the update rate to a rather long two minutes. Figure 9.10b shows the same requests in *overlapping* two-minute intervals; now only the next complete one-minute interval is needed to do the requests-per-minute calculation. A generalization of using overlapping intervals is to combine a new interval with an exponentially decaying average of all prior intervals, implemented as Xavg' = Xavg - (Xavg * k) + (X * k) for new interval X, where k is the decay constant. If k is 1/2, 1/4, etc., the calculation is a few shifts and adds.

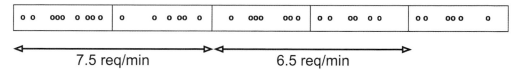

Figure 9.10a   **Requests in non-overlapping two-minute calculation intervals**

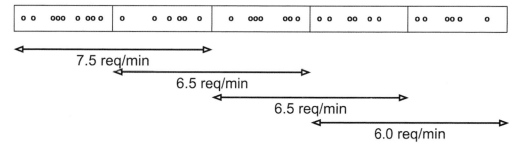

Figure 9.10b   **Requests in two-minute calculation intervals, overlapping pairs of aligned one-minute boundaries**

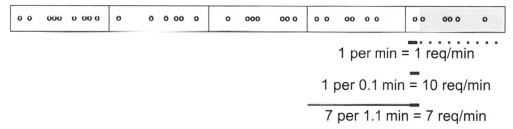

Figure 9.10c   **Single request in 1/10-minute calculation interval, top = assume interval is a full 1 minute; middle = assume interval is 0.1 minute; bottom = use previous full interval plus partial interval to total 1.1 minutes**

Figure 9.10c shows some detail of doing the calculation in a *partially full* interval, after just one request has arrived in the first six seconds (0.1 minute) of the last one-minute interval.

The calculation in Figure 9.10c at the top red line is one request in the pretend-it-is-full one-minute interval = one request per minute. This form of the calculation starts out low and bounces around a lot during the first part of an interval, depending on the exact timing of the first few requests in that interval.

Another possible calculation, the middle red line, is 1 request in the partial 0.1-minute interval = 10 requests per minute. This form of the calculation starts out high and also bounces around a lot during the first part of an interval.

A third possible calculation, the bottom red line, is to combine the *partial* interval with the previous *full* interval (or several of them), giving 6 requests in the previous full interval plus 1 request in the partial 0.1-minute interval = (6 + 1) requests / (1 + 0.1) min = 6.4 requests per minute. This third technique of combining a full interval with a partial one gives more accurate and more stable results, so is recommended.

9.9   Example Transactions

In addition to the various summaries discussed earlier, it can be useful to record and show to performance analysts some examples of complete recent transactions. How could we select some sample transactions with widely varying response times? If you know a tight bound on the possible range of measurements, perhaps 10–50 msec, you could save a few recent transactions in each of four equal-width bins of 10–20, 20–30, 30–40, and 40–50 msec response times, plus two more bins for <10 and >50 msec. That would make it possible to see if there is anything systematically different between the 10–20 msec and 40–50 msec transactions.

More often, we do not have a tight bound on response times or other measured values. In fact, we are looking at some service precisely because it has some unusually long times. In this environment, bin widths based on logarithms can be more useful. To cover a generous million-to-one range of values it is sufficient to have 22 bins:

< 1 usec

[1..2) usec

[2..4) usec

[4..8) usec

. . .

[512K .. 1024K) usec

> 1024K usec, i.e., 1.024 seconds

Figure 9.11 shows a few binned examples pulled out of Figure 9.8. The bins have RPCs with durations of 16–31 usec, 32–63, etc. Just the first two and the last bins are shown.

16-31us

32-63us

256+ us

Figure 9.11abc   **A few example RPCs from Figure 9.8, binned by log 2 RPC duration**

The RPCs in each bin are aligned so that they all start at the left edge. This makes it easy to spot that the main difference between the top bins and the bottom one is that the long-duration RPCs have two to three execution intervals separated by waiting. Understanding what they are waiting for likely will suggest what to change to make them almost 10x faster. Part IV discusses reasons for waiting.

With perhaps three recent example transactions remembered per bin, we can see from the empty bins the actual bounds on measurement values and can see live examples of the normal ones and non-normal ones. Keeping counts of how many transactions landed in each bin gives a quick low-resolution histogram of the values. Low-resolution histograms in power-of-2 or even power-of-10 buckets are a powerful technique. Chapter 27 uses this for tracking lock-acquire times. If slow times are related to the actual transactions, as earlier, a few examples in the larger bins will help reveal exactly what is making them slow.

On the other hand, if slow times are *not* related to the actual transactions, but instead related to surrounding interference, the examples will have no interesting patterns. They are just innocent bystanders. In this case, timelines, time-aligned parallel heatmaps, and complete traces (Part III) will be needed to identify the interference patterns.

9.10   Conclusion

Often, a large number of data points are needed to capture unexpected execution patterns that reveal performance issues, but we need simple ways to highlight areas of possible interest, separating out the chaff of uninteresting normal behavior. Various aggregation and summation strategies give us some of those highlights.

First and foremost, any kind of rate calculation involves a time interval, so individual events must at least be grouped together in such intervals, a first step of summarization. The minimum interval size chosen is a balance between being long enough to have a useful number of events and short enough to avoid smoothing away important spikes. Hundreds or thousands of intervals can be shown as timelines or heatmaps to give high-density patterns. Timelines of individual events or measurements can be further summarized as histograms, and these in turn can be summarized by measures such as median and 99th percentile values, or busiest second, minute, hour.

For looking at values in real time, updates can be calculated over one or more recent intervals. For focusing attention on differences, it is helpful to keep and display some recent transactions, binned or grouped by duration or another measure of interest. In the next chapter, we will discuss real-time displays of summary performance information.

Chapter 10

Dashboards

Dashboards are tools for observing the current and recent overall behavior of datacenter software. A dashboard is a collection of useful performance information for a particular service or instance of a service, a server, or some other system of interest. While logs give detailed historical information about datacenter software, dashboards give summaries of current real-time information. Dashboards are usually HTML pages that are updated frequently and served to the browser of anyone with the proper permissions. This makes it possible for anyone to observe the current performance of any service, observe any sub-services that it uses, or observe what else is happening on any computers that it uses. Dashboards tell us *what* the current performance is, but not *why* it is that way. But dashboards are vital for focusing attention on performance problems, triggering the use of more detailed tools as needed [Ousterhout 2018]. Every well-designed datacenter program has one or more dashboards as part of its design.

Good dashboard information is also designed to be read by computer programs, perhaps by scraping the HTML pages or more likely by having a separate interface that provides, for example, formatted JSON text. Such computer programs can implement more extensive monitoring scripts that look for common problem patterns across several dashboards.

To make the design of dashboards a bit more concrete, we will describe a simple made-up sample datacenter service and then suggest useful data to show on its dashboards.

10.1 Sample Service

The sample service for this chapter, BirthdayPic, shows each user a picture on their birthday. It is an internal service not directly called by users but called by other front-end user-facing services whenever a person logs in or otherwise sends a request to some front-end service. For example, a user doing a restaurant review search on her birthday might be shown a happy-birthday picture she previously provided.

The input to BirthdayPic is an RPC request containing the user ID of a person using some front-end service for the first time each day. Its output is an RPC response specifying it is not the person's birthday today or containing that user's designated picture. The calling services expect an answer within 100 msec; otherwise they ignore the result and show the user nothing. There are about 5 million total users of the front-end service(s), and each picture is about 100KB in size. Thus, the total data accessed by BirthdayPic is about 500GB. Since BirthdayPic is a low-budget sidelight to the main user-facing services, these pictures are stored on disk, not in more expensive SSD or RAM. The front-end services are so popular that nearly every user accesses at least one of the services every day.

Just from this simple description, what do we know about BirthdayPic's likely performance?

If there are 5M users, then each day we would expect 5M requests per day, but over 99% of these will not be the person's birthday. The response time for BirthdayPic will be bi-modal: the not-birthday requests will be handled quickly via a quick in-memory user ID lookup and response, while the birthday requests will require slower disk accesses and picture transmission.

Of the real birthday requests, there will be not exactly 5M_users/365.25 = 13689.3 such requests per day, but varying perhaps 3x either way = 4,000 .. 40,000 such requests per day, or about 3–30 requests per minute on average, if spread evenly across a 24-hour day. But more likely the requests are bunched up a bit, with some hours busier than others. Let's assume that most of the traffic is concentrated into 8 busy hours or ~500 minutes, so 5M requests/day would be about 10000 requests per minute, of which there are 10–100 slow birthday requests per minute, with some peaks above 100. This is a reasonable back-of-the-envelope estimate of the rate of requests.

How long should each request take? The fast requests need to look up a user ID in memory to see if today is that person's birthday. With 64-bit user IDs and 9-bit birth days (1–366 within a year), a full 5M-entry table is about 50MB and if kept sorted can be binary searched in about 23 comparisons. Even if each of these is a cache miss to main memory, it will be hard for the lookup to take more than about 5 usec, while the request rate is about one per 5 msec. An alternate design saves space by keeping just the smaller list of user IDs that *do* have a birthday today, changing that list every midnight. In either case, over 99% of the requests should take a tiny amount of time. We therefore concentrate on the slower real-birthday ones.

If we read 100KB from a random location on a rotating disk, we expect about 12–15 msec of seek and rotate time plus about 1 msec of disk transfer time and another 1 msec of network transfer time. But that estimate assumes we are reading from an already-open file. If each picture file is first opened, then read, and then closed, the time involved will be perhaps 3x longer, since the open and close operations read and write one (or more) directory files. We might expect roughly **50 msec** for one entire picture lookup and response, or about 20 lookups per second. This is a reasonable back-of-the-envelope estimate of the expected response time or latency of each request.

With the disk system able to supply 20 requests per second and the rate of requests estimated to peak at about 100 per minute (~2 per second), we don't expect any performance issues at all.

However, we might expect the service to be somewhat fragile if it runs a single instance on a single server, using a single local disk. If the disk holding the pictures crashes or if the computer running the service crashes, no birthday pictures are served. For redundancy, the service is run on three different machines and requests are load-balanced across all three, but we will base our performance design on having a single machine handle the entire load, in case two of three machines have crashed. In general, if one of the BirthdayPic machines crashes and does not reboot and return in about 15 minutes then a replacement instance might be started on some new machine and the database of pictures copied to it. But that copying will load down the machine that has a complete set of pictures, so could easily be the source of over-deadline delays on that machine if not carefully rate-controlled. Every robustness improvement has some non-zero secondary cost.

10.2 Sample Dashboards

How many different dashboards does this service need, and what information should they display? There are at least *seven* different dashboards that are relevant:

- A BirthdayPic *master* dashboard showing the overall service

- Three BirthdayPic *instance* dashboards showing it running on each of three machines

- Three *server* dashboards showing the health and performance of those machines

The overall master dashboard must at least show whether the BirthdayPic service is up and running at all. (Not up may be indicated by being unable to access the URL for the master dashboard.) More likely, the service has many possible states, including down, coming up, up, and going down. The coming up and going down states may persist for a few seconds or a few minutes or get stuck—all depending on the detailed design of the software. For example, the coming-up state may look for three running instances on different machines and choose to wait many minutes or forever if at least one of these is not found.

If BirthdayPic is up, the master dashboard should show something about the individual instances, at least how many should be up and how many are actually up. For a small number of instances, this could just be a list of one to three machines on which the service instances are running. For a large number of instances—hundreds or thousands—such a list becomes impractically long, so instead a count of the number expected and number running can be given, with perhaps some additional information about the missing ones or the 5–10 running but slowest ones. There might in this case be an option button to expand into a full list and contract back down. It is particularly useful to make each machine-name text in an instance list also be a link to the respective instance dashboard. Thus, if the master dashboard shows instances running on servers srvaa12, srvaa13, and srvcc04, those names could be three links to the corresponding instance dashboards. If BirthdayPic on srvaa13 is down, the link to its instance dashboard might be unresponsive or in a slightly better design might be responsive and show that the instance is stuck in some way.

10.3 Master Dashboard

For starters, we have a master dashboard with information like that shown in Figure 10.1.

This gives us the high-order bit that the service is up but does not yet tell us anything about its performance. What else would we like to know? It would be good to know how many requests are arriving, how many are going to each instance, and how long they are taking.

Summarizing request arrival rate. We could show requests per second, per minute, per hour, or some other unit. What would be best? We have three interacting design dimensions for rates:

- Display units

- Update interval

- Calculation interval

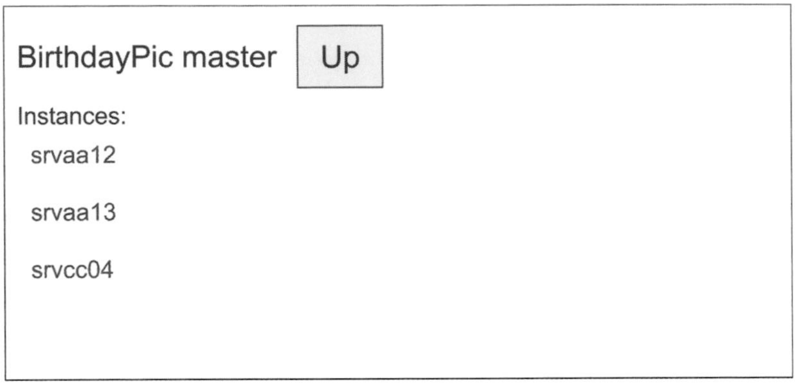

Figure 10.1   **Initial master dashboard sketch**

In designing dashboards, it helps to use the same set of *units* everywhere across all dashboards in a company and to pick units that are familiar human terms. In choosing display units, it also helps to show values that do not have a hard-to-digest excess of digits. Values and times larger than six digits or fractions with more than six decimal places are undesirable. On the other hand, values that are only single digits may be hiding useful information. Values that have 3–4 mostly integer digits are especially useful—big enough to show changes on the order of a few percent and small enough to be absorbed quickly. For data sizes, a judicious choice of bytes, kilobytes, megabytes, etc., for the units can result in 3–4 mostly integer meaningful digits.

For BirthdayPic, we choose to show both non-birthday and birthday requests separately, since these have such different performance characteristics. The non-birthday request rate can be shown as integer ~10,000 req/min, and the birthday rate can be shown with one decimal place: 10.0 to 100.0 req/min. Using birthday requests per second would give awkward numbers in the range of 0.167 to 1.667 req/sec, and using birthday requests per hour suggests a time frame that is far from current. The extra decimal digit gives us a hedge against our rate estimate being somewhat off: even if the actual rate turns out to be close to 1 request per minute, we can see displayed value changes that would be invisible if rounded to whole digits: 1.0, 0.9, 1.2 req/min instead of 1, 1, 1.

In choosing an *update* interval, something in the 1–15 second range is usually best if humans are to glance at the values now and then. Since the interesting slow-performance BirthdayPic requests are done at a low rate, we choose to update the dashboard display and numbers every 10 seconds.

In choosing a *calculation* interval, we would like enough individual birthday requests to give a somewhat-smoothed request rate. With only about 10–100 slow requests per minute, too short an interval could give highly fluctuating results. For BirthdayPic, we will therefore calculate the request rate over intervals of 1 minute but updated every 10 seconds, using a sliding window of six 10-second intervals, similar to Figure 9.9 in the previous chapter. The 10-second intervals match the chosen update rate, so we do not need to deal with partial intervals.

Summarizing request latency. Each request has a server response time or latency or duration, measured from RPC arrival at a BirthdayPic server to RPC response sent from that BirthdayPic server. These are times T2 and T3 as described in Chapter 6, Figure 6.6. Note that the *server* latency is all we can observe on the server, but the client necessarily sees a longer *client* latency T1..T4 that includes RPC creation and transmission time, which might be sources of performance problems even when the server latency is reasonable. Part of the point of a dashboard is to indicate whether server latency is reasonable or slower than expected (or slower than last month).

We estimated previously that the server latency should be about 5 usec or less for non-birthday requests and about 50 msec for birthday requests. What would be the best way to summarize many requests? Because the two kinds of requests perform substantially different amounts of work, we display their statistics separately. For fast requests, we choose to show average latency as usec with one decimal place as the unit and precision, and for slow requests we choose to show average latency as msec with one decimal place. This should give us two to three integer digits in both cases for showing server latency.

The average latency calculation interval also parallels that of rate calculations—pick an interval big enough to show a few percent change in the summarization statistic. In the case of BirthdayPic, we also choose intervals of one minute updated every 10 seconds.

Another way to define measurement intervals is by number of events. We could look at groups of 100 or 1,000 or . . . events. This has the advantage that there are more measurements during a busy time and fewer measurements during slack times. Just be careful not to stop measuring entirely if no requests arrive for a long time. For examining the performance of a given service, it will usually be obvious which choice(s) of measurement interval make sense.

> In the 1990s, I once had the experience of having my picture taken late in the day at the local Massachusetts driver's license office and then waiting and waiting for them to hand me the laminated picture license. It turned out that they used a Polaroid camera to take two half-frame pictures per piece of film (saving money), and they had been waiting for a second person to show up. Just at closing time they gave up and wasted the half-frame.

Multiple time groupings. You will often find it useful to summarize requests over a few *different* human-scale measurement intervals, with an emphasis on observing the busiest intervals. There is rarely much to be learned about performance during the less-busy intervals. In this context, "human-scale" means intervals that are common in everyday life and are spread apart by approximately a factor of ten: 1 second, 10 seconds, 1 minute, 10 minutes, etc. No one wants to try to make sense out of measurement intervals that, for example, are 4, 16, 64, 256, . . . seconds.

> One performance anomaly I have seen with less-busy loads occurred at Google several years ago. Some services would run more slowly and hence have noticeably longer response latencies under very light load than under normal or heavy load. The issue turned out to be CPUs on multiple servers that were so idle that they dropped into deep power-saving mode, and then it took a hundred microseconds or so to come back out and start executing instructions again when a request arrived. That request was initially serviced with empty CPU caches, so the request itself

ran slowly after the late start. Cascading a top-level request's remote procedure call tree across many subsystems could encounter this slowdown on each server touched. The performance was a mystery when the power-saving transitions were not observable, and completely obvious once they were. We will see another example in Chapter 23. The same phenomenon can occur when spinning up cascades of idle virtual machines.

In understanding the performance of a service, multiple time groupings allow us not only to see its current performance, but also to see its performance in the recent past and to see its intended or normal performance. For BirthdayPic, we choose one time grouping of req/min calculated over the most recent five minutes, and a second grouping of req/min calculated over the most recent hour. Other services might show three or four such time groupings.

What is missing? The time of last dashboard update is missing. Only when someone sees this value changing every 10 seconds and sees that the time of day is correct are they sure that the data is current. Also missing is the number of requests that got errors, including those exceeding the time deadline and those that were rejected for being abusive offered load.

We have now arrived at a master dashboard with information like that shown in Figure 10.2.

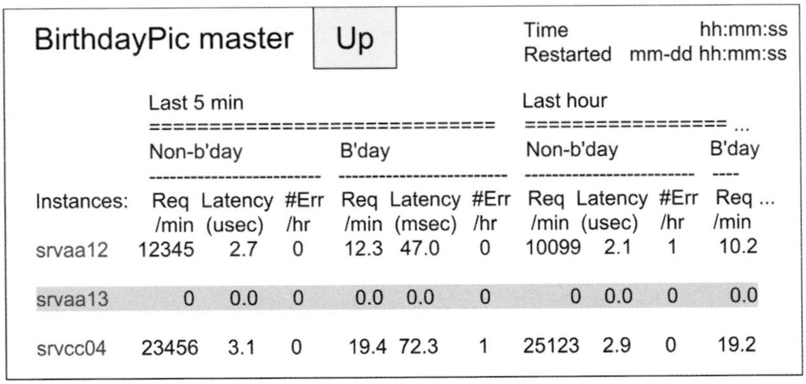

BirthdayPic master	Up	Time hh:mm:ss Restarted mm-dd hh:mm:ss

	Last 5 min						Last hour				
	=============================						================= ...				
	Non-b'day			B'day			Non-b'day			B'day	
	---------------------------			---------------------------			---------------------------			----	
Instances:	Req /min	Latency (usec)	#Err /hr	Req /min	Latency (msec)	#Err /hr	Req /min	Latency (usec)	#Err /hr	Req ... /min	
srvaa12	12345	2.7	0	12.3	47.0	0	10099	2.1	1	10.2	
srvaa13	0	0.0	0	0.0	0.0	0	0	0.0	0	0.0	
srvcc04	23456	3.1	0	19.4	72.3	1	25123	2.9	0	19.2	

Figure 10.2   **More-detailed master dashboard sketch**

What else is missing? The terse column headings such as "Req/min" could usefully be links that when clicked show more-detailed text spelling out the abbreviations and giving the calculation details. This is especially useful for people who do not use a particular dashboard every day.

Sorting is a powerful tool for finding patterns in large amounts of data. Make dashboards sortable by column wherever that makes sense.

It would be helpful to highlight the fact that srvaa13 is not doing any requests at all (the red highlight in Figure 10.2), and that srvcc04 is doing about 2/3 of the total load; percentage of total load per instance might be good, or just the ratio of expected load fraction to actual. It would be useful to state the total number of requests per minute and median response time for the entire service, summed over all three instances.

Along with median, it might be useful to give the 99th percentile response time seen in each update interval. It might be useful to indicate the expected or "normal" total load and expected overall response time and to state any limits or deadlines on that.

If the service has been down, it is useful to give the last time it went down, why it went down, and the time it successfully restarted (thus how long it was down), plus perhaps the number of restarts in the last month. If the last restart was weeks ago, all is good. If it was 9 a.m. today, the service bears more careful watching. If there were zero restarts in the last month, all is good. If there were 10, something is probably amiss. For some contracted services, total availability as a percentage over the last year (i.e., 315 seconds of unscheduled downtime per year = 99.999% availability) can be an important metric to display.

There might be controls on a dashboard for changing instances or updating the set of pictures or pausing/terminating the service, incorporated as buttons on the dashboard with appropriate double-checks for expensive actions such as terminating the service.

For BirthdayPic, if experience with the service suggests that requests sometimes arrive in bursts that are handled too slowly (perhaps just after midnight), it could be useful to state the busiest second, 10 seconds, and minute over the last 24 hours, giving the time they occurred and the corresponding 99th percentile response times over the same intervals.

The purpose of the master dashboard is to give a quick overview of the health of the entire service, while the purpose of the per-instance dashboards is to give more detail on how each contributes to handling the total load.

10.4   Per-Instance Dashboards

The three per-instance dashboards show their part of the information on the master dashboard, plus any additional detail that would be useful to help understand how that instance's performance varies or differs from the other instances. If the load is not well-balanced across the instances, their dashboards should show enough information to explain why, or at least show the information that the load-balancing algorithm uses, such as queue depth, response time, etc.

In addition to summary values such as median and 99th percentile, it would be reasonable on per-instance dashboards to show explicit histograms of requests and response times over the last several hours or a day. It might be useful to show the last seven days of requests and response times summarized by the hour, to give some context for baseline performance.

For total errors per time interval, a breakdown can be given by kind of error. When a person fixes some problem, the fixer wants to watch this dashboard to see that (1) the errors in the last few minutes quickly revert toward zero, and (2) the errors in the last hour or so drift down appropriately with time.

The last few errors or last of each type could be shown in more complete detail, giving the exact time of the request, which client machine the RPC came from, what user ID, what size picture, etc. The exact time of an error, given to the millisecond or microsecond, might correlate with the time of some other event on this server or on some other server. There may be other clues in the detailed information about the cause of the error.

For especially slow transactions, it is similarly useful to give the exact timestamp, which client machine the RPC came from, what user ID, what size picture, etc. This can be done across logarithmic bins of response time so there are automatically a few examples of fast transactions and a few of slow ones, and bin counts to give a rough histogram of overall response times. Figure 9.11 in Chapter 9 is one example.

Just as the master dashboard should have links to the per-instance dashboards, each of these should have a link to the master, and another to the corresponding per-server dashboard.

10.5   Per-Server Dashboards

The three per-server dashboards each show the overall health of that server and list all the programs that are running on it. Each listed program name could be a link back to the per-instance dashboard for that program.

If the server itself has just rebooted, is too hot and therefore throttling its clocks, or has some other problem, that information should be shown explicitly, making it easy to explain why some or all programs are slow. If the server has several disks attached but one is dead, that should be shown so it can explain some problems. If the server's network bandwidth is overloaded in one direction, that should be shown so it can explain other problems. These are just a few examples of the detail contributing to showing the overall server health.

Since the server is a shared resource across many programs, this server dashboard should show what faction of that resource each program is consuming—CPU time, memory space, disk time and space, network bandwidth, etc. Units might be seconds of CPU time, KB or MB of memory space, disk accesses per second, disk KB or MB per second transferred, network Tx and Rx MB (or Mb) per second. The update interval might be 1, 2, 5, or 10 seconds. The information might be grouped for the last minute, 10 minutes, hour, etc.

The goal here is to allow spotting gross interference—a program other than BirthdayPic that is taking up 95% of the disk accesses, for example, making all other programs that use that disk run slowly. Sometimes the pattern will be that BirthdayPic struggles to meet its deadline whenever program X happens to be running on the same server. Spotting that correlation will lead to examining what surprising behavior X has that interferes with BirthdayPic, or perhaps what normal behavior X has that BirthdayPic is surprisingly sensitive to.

10.6   Sanity Checks

Part of a good dashboard design is a set of sanity checks and corresponding messages to display when checks fail. After all, if the BirthdayPic service on srvaa13 has no directory full of 5M images, it cannot run usefully. A sanity check should flag this, rather than having the dashboard simply record 100% failures for incoming RPCs. Sanity checks should be run at service startup and possibly periodically thereafter. For important services, some sanity checks may page an on-call service engineer if they fail.

What can we sanity-check for the BirthdayPic service as a whole?

The number of running instances should be 1..3. (Zero is bad. 1 is OK but not robust.)

The number of requests per minute should usually be non-zero. Certainly, the number of requests per hour should be non-zero. The number of requests per minute should be less than 5 million. In fact, it probably should be less than 50,000. The number of errors per minute should be less than, say, 10. You can think of a few more sanity checks for the service as a whole.

What about the individual instances?

Each instance should have a directory of ~5M images, likely in some stylized set of sub-directories with stylized filenames. If the subdirectories are organized by birth date, today's sub-directory should exist and be populated by a plausible number of images. The image files should each be of a plausible size—10 bytes is too small and 10MB is too large. They should be valid or at least plausible images.

Each instance should have a file of user ID to birthday mappings. If the user IDs are not directly transformed to filenames, then the filename mapping could be here also. The number of user IDs should be about 5 million. If a new mapping file is supplied, its size should be within about 10% of the size of the previous mapping file. (This is a really important sanity check—lots of software mistakes can make the new file of length zero or half as big as it should be.) The user IDs, birthdays, and filenames should all pass validity or plausibility checks.

Some plausibility checks can be deferred until actual use so that startup checking takes only seconds, not tens of minutes.

10.7   Summary

If you can afford only two observation tools, build a logging system, and even if only one computer or service is involved, build dashboards.

A dashboard is a collection of performance data for a particular service, available remotely to people and software managing that service. For a service whose implementation is spread across multiple machines, it is useful to have both a master dashboard for the service as a whole and dashboards for the service on each machine.

At a minimum, use a dashboard to show whether a service is up, up but unhealthy, or down. Show something about the offered load of requests and something about the response time to these requests, and show those over a few human-meaningful time intervals. Show error rates and highlight them if excessive. If a service does any configuration sanity checks (and it should), show failures on dashboards to focus attention on possible root causes of poor behavior.

Plan to include additional information on dashboards as you learn more about a service's behavior in real use.

Exercises

10.1. What is wrong with 50 msec nominal and 100 msec deadline? What happens if three requests all arrive within the same 50 msec interval? Does the third request meet its deadline? What is the probability of that happening with 60 requests per minute? If we have 10,000 requests in a day, how many do you expect will miss the deadline?

Chapter 11

Other Existing Tools

There are myriad existing software performance observation tools [Saive 2015]. In fact, web searches for software packages

```
atrace, btrace, ctrace, ... ztrace
```

find thousands of hits on all 26 names. In this chapter, we will give an overview of a baker's dozen of commonly used Linux tools. For a deeper treatment, I highly recommend Brendan Gregg's excellent *Systems Performance* book [Gregg 2021].

11.1 Kinds of Observation Tools

We categorize observation tools by what they observe and how frequently. The three general categories are

- Counters
- Profiles
- Traces

Counting tools simply count events such as disk accesses (reads plus writes), interrupts, correctable memory errors, L1 cache misses; or sum quantities such as bytes of transmitted network data, milliseconds of wall-clock time, etc. Such counts are usually very fast to gather. They give an overview of the activity in a computer system without giving much detail. Ratios of various counts can be useful for understanding overall loads or rates—transmitted bytes per second, errors per million disk accesses, or context switches per second, for example. Unusually high or low counts, compared to recent averages, can signal various forms of trouble, such as a sudden increase in an error rate, or a sudden collapse of disk activity. Counters can cover not only CPU events, but also memory, disk, network, locks, and wait/idle time.

Most overview tools, such as the Linux `top` command or the pseudofiles `/proc/diskstats` and `/proc/meminfo`, use counts to give summaries of the total load on a server, typically updated every few seconds.

Some counting tools count events across all programs running on a server, while others allow selective counting of events just associated with a single program. The former tools are most useful for understanding overall server behavior, of interest to datacenter owners and engineers.

The latter are most useful for understanding the overall behavior of single programs, of interest to programmers responsible for individual programs. Both forms of counting are useful, but for different audiences.

Because they are low overhead, counting tools are useful for running continuously, to observe the average or normal behavior of a complete server or of individual programs.

Profiling tools quasi-periodically accumulate samples of some quantity. The most common quantity is the program counter value, PC, for a CPU core while it is running an individual program. With enough samples, a PC profile can give a reasonable indication of where a program spends most of its execution time. Depending on the sample rate, profile tools can be low-overhead and hence suitable for examining programs in live datacenters. I chose Georges Seurat's picture of the Eiffel Tower for the cover of this book as an example of sampling.

Some profilers use a periodic clock interrupt of 100 or 400 or 1,000 times per second to sample the PC. These profilers are blind to their own operation (since they are never running when the interrupt occurs), blind to the time spent in the clock-interrupt routine, and likely blind to all time spent in kernel code. Other profilers use a hardware performance counter to create sampling interrupts more quickly, perhaps every 64K CPU cycles, or about once every 20 usec with a 3.2GHz CPU clock rate. It is common for these to vary the cycle count between such interrupts so that the samples do not get in lockstep with some significant program repetition time or some program delay. We call these quasi-periodic interrupts.

Some kernel code is not interruptible, so sampling interrupts that occur during its execution are deferred until some interruptible code is reached, effectively distorting the samples by giving zero of them in the non-interruptible kernel code and extra ones in the just-following code (interruptible kernel or user). Sometimes all kernel mode samples are deferred to a following user-mode instruction, charging all kernel time to nearby user-mode routines. If half the time is spent in kernel mode, this contributes a 2x distortion to the measurement of some user-mode routines.

PC profiles are good for understanding the *average CPU-only* performance of programs, but they intermix normal execution paths with unusual ones, effectively hiding any unusual behavior. PC profiles are blind to waiting time, program startup/shutdown time, and as discussed earlier may be blind to or highly distort kernel time. They are thus unsatisfactory tools for understanding performance problems in any of these areas.

Tracing tools record the time sequence of some set of events, such as all the accesses on a disk drive or all the system calls in a program. They are the most powerful tools for understanding the *variance* in performance. The subsequent chapters will all focus on tracing tools.

Logging tools (Chapter 8) are a kind of tracing tool. The events they record are program-generated log messages, usually text strings but sometimes binary records that can later be postprocessed into text strings. After modest buffering, a logging library writes messages to ordinary disk files. The messages are timestamped, often to the microsecond. Each program running on a server has a separate active log file. The logging library may periodically rotate these files (old one closed and new one opened) and eventually either archive or delete older ones after a day or so. Log files are particularly useful for recording program startup/shutdown/restart events, detected errors, unusual situations, and for flagging slow transactions. For sufficiently low-rate services such as remote disk servers, logging may be used to record the begin and end times and limited parameters of every offered transaction. Binary logs with strictly limited information content may be able to keep up with higher-rate transaction services.

Locking tools (Chapter 27) are another kind of tracing tool. They record contention for software locks that guard code critical sections, such contention causing one thread to wait for a lock held by another thread. Many datacenter programs run with dozens to thousands of threads, and a substantial fraction of performance problems involve unexpected locking behavior.

11.2 Data to Observe

The following 12 tools observe the dynamic use of the 5 fundamental resources: CPU, memory, disk, network, and critical sections. In addition to these, some performance understanding is complete only by also observing the offered load to a service and observing its outbound calls to other services, discussed in Section 11.15. Any of these aspects can produce unexpected delays, resulting in long transactions. Table 11.1 shows the tools discussed, along with a few of their properties.

They are almost all free and common in Linux distributions. Many commercial tools are also available but are not discussed here. Using the free tools and looking to understand their limitations will make you a better-informed buyer of commercial tools, should you find a need to shop for one. Those marked as High overhead are not suitable for use in time-constrained environments.

Table 11.1 **Tools Discussed in This Chapter**

Name	Type	Single Program or All*	Main Resources	Overhead	Observed Data
top command	Counters	All	CPU	Low	CPU time, memory alloc
/proc and /sys	Counters	All	CPU	Low	Myriad software counters
time command	Counters	Single	CPU	Low	User/kernel/elapsed time
perf command	Counters	All	CPU	Low	Myriad hardware counters
oprofile	Profile	Single	CPU	Med.	Program counter
strace	Trace	Single	CPU	High	System calls
ltrace	Trace	Single	CPU	High	C runtime library functions
ftrace	Trace	All	CPU	Med.	Linux kernel functions
mtrace	Trace	Single	Memory	High	Memory dynamic alloc.
blktrace	Trace	All	Disk	Med.	Disk/SSD block accesses
tcpdump	Trace	All	Network	Med.	Network packets
lock trace	Trace	Single	Critical sections	Low	Software lock activity
Offered load, outbound calls	Trace	Single	CPU, net	Med.	Incoming RPCs

*Most programs marked "all" also have filters to observe just a subset.

This chapter is not a tutorial on those tools; it is instead a discussion of what information they can provide and thus when it is helpful to use them. The corresponding Linux man (manual) pages and discussions elsewhere give much more in-depth information about setting them up and using them.

You will notice a few common patterns in the design of these tools. Several take a subject command as a parameter and then run that command while measuring it. These tools generally observe just the single program, not the entire system. Observation tools may display their output as text on a screen or may use a *collector* program to write binary or text data to a file to be decoded and viewed by a second *analyzer* program later. Some collectors write binary information to in-memory buffers or data structures for a limited amount of time, to be analyzed a little later when no observation is underway. Some collectors run continuously in so-called *flight-recorder mode*, writing in wrap-around fashion to a RAM trace buffer until some software event stops the tracing.

These strategies are all driven by choices for the observation overhead, both in CPU time and in memory/disk space, and occasionally by choices for disk bandwidth when recording observations to files. Herewith are the 12 tools, all Linux-centric.

11.3   `top` Command

The `top` command (and the related `htop` with more graphical options) provides a dynamic real-time view of a running system. By default it shows the dozen or so top processes that are using the most CPU time, refreshing every few seconds. It also shows memory usage and total accumulated runtime for those processes. A summary section shows across the entire computer overall load, number of tasks, memory allocated, and CPU time spent executing user code, system (kernel) code, idle, and a few other variations. The Windows task manager, not further discussed here, is a similar program.

The `top` command uses software counters, so has very low overhead. It displays only average behavior and thus is not useful for discovering sources of latency (other than complete server overload). It gives no detail within kernel CPU time about which parts of the kernel are busy and no detail within user tasks about which pieces of code are busy.

The `top` command is suitable to run at any time on any datacenter server, giving a quick overview of how loaded that system is, how much idle time there is, and which processes are consuming the most CPU or memory resources. It does not show disk or network usage; nor does it show any detail about shared memory or cache behavior.

If a server's total CPU or memory is overloaded, `top` will tell you. If a runaway task is consuming 100% of some CPU core or a huge amount of virtual memory, `top` will tell you. If a task is not running but you think it should be, `top` will confirm that it is sleeping (but generally not why it is sleeping). If some kernel-management processes with low PID numbers are taking a lot of unexpected CPU time, `top` will tell you.

The `top` command is an ordinary program, so it shows up in the list of running processes. It thus shows itself so you can easily see how much overhead it is consuming—usually about 0.3% of the CPU time on our sample servers. It is one of the few tools discussed here that shows its own overhead.

11.4 /proc and /sys Pseudofiles

Linux has a number of pseudofiles—objects that appear to be disk files but are in fact purely software creations. They are used to communicate extensive information about a running system, and sometimes to change parameters by writing new values to some files. The filename /proc is the top of a software-faked directory of files about process information, while /sys is the top of a similar directory of files about various kernel subsystems. Within /proc, the numbered subdirectories describe each running task by PID number, and the other subdirectories generally give text or counter values that apply to the entire system.

If you are interested in performance and are not familiar with these files, take a while to browse through many of them to get an idea what information is available. The actual files and their contents vary across different Linux implementations, so exploring can be the best way to find out what is available on your system. Some files just give a list of numbers. Documentation on what these mean can be quite sketchy, but start with the proc man page and with web searches for something like

```
linux /proc/stat
```

Unless these files are accessed, they consume little or no overhead. When they are accessed, the underlying software that produces their text contents uses a little CPU time, but not much—perhaps 10% of one CPU for a few milliseconds. Listing individual pseudofiles is reasonable to do at any time on any datacenter server (but it is not reasonable to do so repeatedly at very short intervals).

If you suspect a performance problem related to some subsystem, examining related /proc or /sys files a few times several seconds apart can reveal a counter that is incrementing a lot more quickly or a lot less quickly than you expect. This won't necessarily explain exactly what is going on, but it can help whittle down the possibilities.

11.5 time Command

The time command, followed by a command line with arguments, runs that subject command and reports system resource usage. By default, it reports three times: real, user, and sys. Real is elapsed time in minutes, seconds, and fraction. User is user-mode CPU time, and sys is kernel-mode CPU time. The unstated difference real - (user + sys) is waiting time.

The time command is a handy way to get a quick reading of how much elapsed and CPU time a single program uses. It is more useful for batch programs than for long-running datacenter services. The time command uses simple counters so has almost no overhead.

11.6 perf Command

The perf tools for Linux give access to built-in hardware and software performance counters. The perf sub-commands are stat, top, record, report, and list. They are described in separate man pages named perf-stat, perf-top, perf-record, perf-report, and perf-list. The perf stat command is detailed next. The perf top command operates somewhat like top, except by default it displays cumulative percentages from when it was started, while top displays percentages over just the most recent update interval. The perf record command is like perf stat except that it writes its observations to a file, to be subsequently used by perf report. The perf list command shows the available counter names.

The command perf stat <COMMAND> runs the subject command, just as time <COMMAND> does. For example, the word count command, wc, applied to the convenient file /etc/hosts produces output like Code Snippet 11.1 on a sample machine.

Code Snippet 11.1 **Word count command and output**

```
$ wc /etc/hosts
   9   25  222 /etc/hosts
```

This shows 9 lines of text, 25 words, and 222 characters. Running under perf with default parameters, the output looks like Code Snippet 11.2.

Code Snippet 11.2 **Word count as sub-command to perf stat**

```
$ perf stat wc /etc/hosts
   9   25  222 /etc/hosts

 Performance counter stats for 'wc /etc/hosts':

     0.701717  task-clock (msec)       #  0.632 CPUs utilized
            0  context-switches        #  0.000 K/sec
            0  cpu-migrations          #  0.000 K/sec
           65  page-faults             #  0.093 M/sec
    1,065,926  cycles                  #  1.519 GHz
      192,609  stalled-cycles-frontend #  18.07% frontend cycles idle
      135,916  stalled-cycles-backend  #  12.75% backend cycles idle
      914,402  instructions            #  0.86 insn per cycle
                                       #  0.21 stalled cycles per insn
      180,917  branches                #  257.820 M/sec
 <not counted>  branch-misses             (0.00%)

     0.001109696 seconds time elapsed
```

The default performance counters are derived from a mixture of software and hardware. The first four, task-clock, context-switches, cpu-migrations, and page-faults, come from kernel-maintained clock and counters. The remaining ones come from x86 hardware performance counters [Intel 2021]. This degenerate use ran the wc command for only 1.1 msec. The CPU executed 914K instructions in 1066K cycles (rounded), so 0.86 instructions per cycle (IPC).

Of the 1066K cycles, 193K had no instructions available, frontend stall, meaning that the instruction decode hardware was waiting for the I-cache to deliver some instructions. An additional 136K cycles had instructions ready to issue, but they were not issued, backend stall, meaning that the execution unit(s) for those fetched and decoded instructions were busy and could not accept the new instructions (see the Chapter 2 discussion around Figure 2.3). In the remaining 737K cycles, 914K instructions were actually issued and executed. To reach an average execution rate of 0.86 instructions per cycle, the CPU actually issued 914K instructions/737K cycles, or

1.24 instructions per non-stall cycle. Multi-issue CPU designs thus help hide some of the underlying stall cycles.

Note that the 1,065,926 cycles over 0.001109696 seconds = 0.968 GHz, which does not equal 1.519 GHz in the comment on that line. The actual CPU chip for this example runs at a nominal 3.5 GHz, which also does not equal 1.519 GHz. It is good to get in the habit of doing these sanity-check calculations in your head when looking at new performance tool output.

The CPU chip was completely idle when I ran the perf command, so the measured times were taken across an interval during which the CPU was cranking up from some nominal idle clock rate of perhaps 800 MHz to full speed, averaging about half of full speed. It is likely that the elapsed time includes some perf program startup time, while the cycle count is only for the subject wc command. For such a short example, the slightly different timespans give quite inconsistent results. Over a longer time spent in the subject command there would be less difference.

If you suspect a performance problem related to some subsystem, examining related counters can reveal a counter that is incrementing a lot more quickly or a lot less quickly than you expect. This might explain exactly what is going on, but even if not, it can help whittle down the possibilities.

11.7   oprofile, CPU Profiler

oprofile is a PC profiling system for Linux. For generating sample interrupts, oprofile makes use of the hardware performance counters provided on x86, ARM, and other processors. It can profile a selected program or the whole system. There are four commands involved: the commands operf <COMMAND> and ocount <COMMAND> run the subject command and write a file of accumulated counts, while the opreport and opannotate commands merge a file of previously accumulated counts with the original program binary or source files to produce human-readable annotated output. These tools work best with C or C++ source code that has been compiled specifically for profiling—in particular, compiled with a debug symbol table that maps PC addresses back to function names or even line numbers.

Recall that a PC profiler is an observation tool that samples the program counter periodically and then shows what fraction of the samples landed in a particular function or line of code, with samples taken within kernel code typically assigned to the next-following user-mode instruction. Code Snippet 11.3 shows a piece of the output from oprofile run against the very old 1972 Whetstone benchmark (transliterated from Fortran to C). We will see Whetstone again in Chapter 22.

Code Snippet 11.3   A piece of oprofile output showing PC sample counts at the left, percentage of total counts, and then the corresponding line of source code

```
    :/*
    :C
    :C        Module 2: Array elements
    :C
    :*/
    :        E1[1] =  1.0;
    :        E1[2] = -1.0;
```

```
              :        E1[3] = -1.0;
              :        E1[4] = -1.0;
              :
 563  0.0608 :        for (I = 1; I <= N2; I++) {
 243  0.0263 :            E1[1] = ( E1[1] + E1[2] + E1[3] - E1[4]) * T;
1527  0.1650 :            E1[2] = ( E1[1] + E1[2] - E1[3] + E1[4]) * T;
1838  0.1986 :            E1[3] = ( E1[1] - E1[2] + E1[3] + E1[4]) * T;
1129  0.1220 :            E1[4] = (-E1[1] + E1[2] + E1[3] + E1[4]) * T;
              :        }
```

There are four initializing assignment statements that had zero samples and then a `for` loop that iterates N2=12 million times, containing four assignment statements. The loop-counting code was sampled 563 times, the assignment to E1[1] 243 times, to E1[2] 1527 times, etc.

This run of `oprofile` used a performance counter interrupt to generate a new sample about every 27 usec. The total run took 25 seconds and accumulated 925,000 PC samples.

Figure 11.1a shows all the benchmark main-program lines with non-zero sample counts, displayed so that the height of each line is proportional to its sample count and so that the entire picture totals 100% of the apparent main-program execution time, i.e., 100% of all the PC samples that landed in the main program. Such a visualization makes it trivial to see any hot spots that take up more than about half a percent of the total execution time.

A careful programmer can use such profiles to tune hot spots and improve algorithms and thus increase the average performance of a program. One usually starts with the lines of code or list of routines that take the most time, improving those that are easy to fix. Once a profile becomes relatively flat, with no obvious hot spots, simple tuning of average performance is over. If the average performance remains unacceptable, then deeper algorithm changes are needed (or a complete redesign).

Unfortunately, Figure 11.1a is a lie, with the times off by about a factor of three.

Figure 11.1b shows a more complete picture, containing at the top in red the samples that landed within the `oprofile` runtime itself, from source files named `mcount.c` and `_mcount.S`. The main program samples in blue are from Figure 11.1a. The black samples are from C runtime libraries. The sampling runtime itself takes about 47% of the total time, the main program only 30%, and the runtime libraries about 23%. We will find in the exercises that `oprofile` can be used with much smaller overhead.

From this last picture, we learn that the profiling overhead is about 1.5 times the main program time, and the library routines nearly 0.8 times the main program time. If you look carefully at the library routine names, they are `sin`, `cos`, `atan`, `exp`, `log`, etc. (There is no `sqrt` library routine, because `sqrt` turns out to be a CPU instruction.) These correspond to the calls in the first few lines of the main program and in fact take more total time than the corresponding calls. Be careful when profiling to include the library times and to understand the profiling overhead.

Notice that the oddly named `fenv_private.h` code is taking a substantial amount of time. This code messes around with the IEEE float rounding modes. It takes more time than any but the two largest main-program lines of code. This is the kind of code that a less-careful profiler would

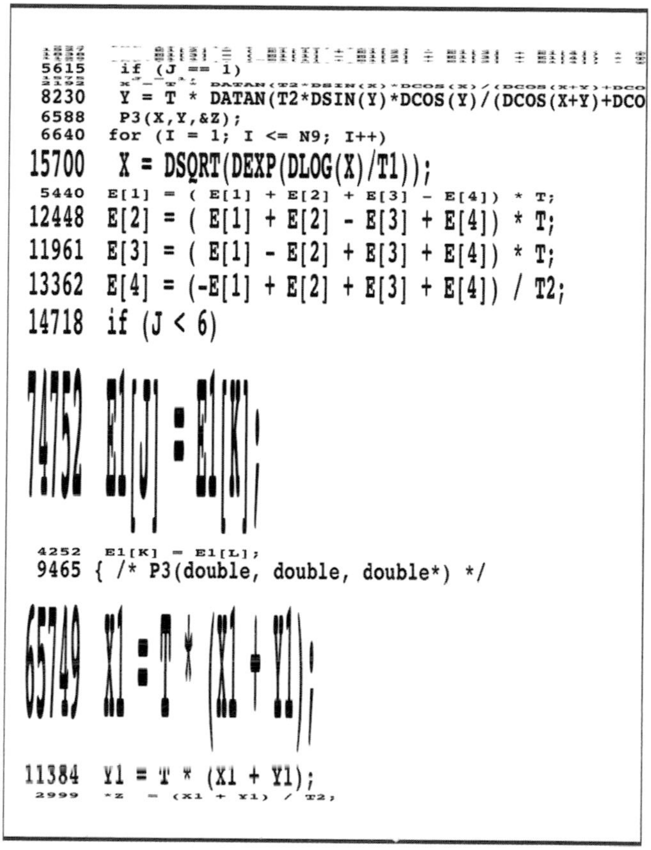

```
:::::       ...  ::::: : : ::::: :::::: : ::::: : ::::: : ::::: : :
5615        if (J == 1)
:::::        :.  .  ::::::::(::-::::::(::)-::::(::)-(::::(::::)-:::
8230        Y = T * DATAN(T2*DSIN(Y)*DCOS(Y)/(DCOS(X+Y)+DCO
6588        P3(X,Y,&Z);
6640        for (I = 1;  I <= N9;  I++)
15700       X = DSQRT(DEXP(DLOG(X)/T1));
5440        E[1] = ( E[1] + E[2] + E[3] - E[4]) * T;
12448       E[2] = ( E[1] + E[2] - E[3] + E[4]) * T;
11961       E[3] = ( E[1] - E[2] + E[3] + E[4]) * T;
13362       E[4] = (-E[1] + E[2] + E[3] + E[4]) / T2;
14718       if (J < 6)

74752       E[J] = E[K];

4252        E1[K] = E1[L];
9465        { /* P3(double, double, double*) */

65749       X1 = T * (X1 + Y1);

11384       Y1 = T * (X1 + Y1);
2999        *z   = (x1 + y1) / T2;
```

Figure 11.1a   **The main program non-zero PC samples displayed with text height proportional to sample count. The for-loop lines from Code Snippet 11.3 are barely visible at the top, just above the line with count 5615.**

miss entirely. Note that the entire benchmark (without the profiling overhead) would be more than 10% faster if the reason for this apparently useless code were understood and then avoided.

The good news about oprofile is that it shows us samples that land within itself. Without that, we would have to measure separately to realize that the observation tool is nearly doubling the benchmark run time, and therefore may be substantially distorting its behavior. Certainly, this 2x overhead is not acceptable for a tool used in live time-constrained code. The fundamental problem is that oprofile appears to use over 10 usec of kernel interrupt and signal handlers to record each sample, and there are almost 40,000 samples per second (corresponding to the default rate of one sample every ~100K CPU cycles, at 3.7 GHz). Dropping the sample rate by 10x would directly reduce the overhead by 10x. Dropping the code path per sample to 1 usec instead of 10 would also give a 10x reduction in overhead. Doing both would give a tool that is useful in time-constrained environments. We will look more carefully at oprofile overhead in the strace section next.

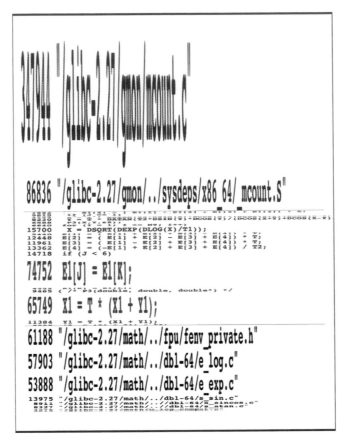

Figure 11.1b   The full set of samples from 25 seconds of running the profiled benchmark, showing only 30% of the time is in the benchmark code itself (middle,blue), with the rest in the profiler (top, red) and in the runtime math library (bottom, black)

Like all profilers, `oprofile` is helpful for understanding and tuning the average CPU-only behavior of a program. Normally, profilers take 100–1,000 PC samples per second so have very low overhead. This particular sample run of `oprofile` took almost 40,000 PC samples per second and had much higher overhead, for reasons yet to be fully determined.

We learned from Figure 11.1b to be aware about exactly what code is being profiled, so that you don't overlook something important—a little bit like using a magnifying tool to watch a spider build a web in the corner of your living room while being oblivious to the kitchen fire.

11.8   strace, System Calls

The command `strace <COMMAND>` runs the subject command, tracing all its system calls by writing text descriptions to `stderr` or a file. It traces only system calls, not any other kernel activity. It operates much like the previous five commands but can have somewhat higher overhead, depending on the density of system calls. If there are 100 system calls per second, the CPU overhead is perhaps 1% or less, but if there are 100,000 system calls per second (a reasonable datacenter value), the overhead can be 100% or more. This means that `strace` is more suitable for offline examination of a program than for use in a live datacenter.

Code Snippet 11.4 gives the `strace` output for a vanilla, non-profiling execution of Whetstone. The initial `execve` call loads the main program, ./whet. Three sequences then load files for the shared libraries and set up their memory protection: /etc/ld.so.cache, /lib/x86_64-linux-gnu/libm.so.6, and /lib/x86_64-linux-gnu/libc.so.6 (note libc vs. libm spelling). The next sequence sets up a 12KB (12288 byte) read/write area that I believe corresponds to the original Fortran `common` area. The last sequence prepares and then writes to `stdout`, file ID = 1. At the end is the `exit_group` call, which doesn't return.

These may be more system calls than you were expecting in getting the program started. There are a few repeated calls, but they are just small performance sins. The main information that is missing for performance purposes is the time spent in each system call and the time spent in user code between them. This vanilla version took 6 seconds to run.

Code Snippet 11.4   **Partial strace output from vanilla Whetstone**

```
execve("./whet", ["./whet", "1000000"], 0x7ffca1ef6fc8 /* 53 vars */)
    = 0
brk(NULL)                                         = 0x55f60dd0d000
access("/etc/ld.so.nohwcap", F_OK)  = -1 ENOENT (No such file or dir.)
access("/etc/ld.so.preload", R_OK)  = -1 ENOENT (No such file or dir.)
openat(AT_FDCWD, "/etc/ld.so.cache", O_RDONLY|O_CLOEXEC)   - 3
fstat(3, {st_mode=S_IFREG|0644, st_size-76093, ...})     = 0
mmap(NULL, 76093, PROT_READ, MAP_PRIVATE, 3, 0)     = 0x7fe0155c8000
close(3)                                          = 0
access("/etc/ld.so.nohwcap", F_OK)  = -1 ENOENT (No such file or dir.)
openat(AT_FDCWD, "/lib/x86_64-linux-gnu/libm.so.6", O_RDONLY|O_CLOEXEC)
    = 3
read(3, "\177ELF"..., 832)                        = 832
fstat(3, {st_mode=S_IFREG|0644, st_size=1700792, ...})  = 0
mmap(NULL, 8192, PROT_READ|PROT_WRITE, ...)       = 0x7fe0155c6000
mmap(NULL, 3789144, PROT_READ|PROT_EXEC, ...)     = 0x7fe015016000
mprotect(0x7fe0151b3000, 2093056, PROT_NONE)      = 0
mmap(0x7fe0153b2000, 8192, PROT_READ|PROT_WRITE, ...)  = 0x7fe0153b2000
close(3)                                          = 0
  ...
```

Now look at Code Snippet 11.5, the output for the instrumented profiling version used in the previous `oprofile` section. It was compiled with extra flags.

Here is the vanilla version:

```
g++ -O2  whetstone.c -o whet
```

And here's the oprofile version:

```
g++ -DPRINTOUT -fprofile-arcs -ftest-coverage -fno-inline \
  -pg -g -O2  whetstone.c -o whet_pggp
```

The `strace` output starts out the same; then it loads an extra runtime library `/lib/x86_64-linux-gnu/libgcc_s.so.1`, and a little bit later it calls `rt_sigaction` to field signals and calls `setitime` to interrupt 100 times per second (tv_usec=10000). These interrupts happen about 2500 times total, each delivering a `SIGPROF` signal that ends with `rt_sigreturn`. These 2,500 interrupts at 100 per second correspond to the Whetstone runtime of 25 seconds we saw in the earlier `oprofile` section. At the end, the profiling runtime writes its gathered data to the extra files `gmon.out` and `whetstone.gcda`, as we would expect.

Code Snippet 11.5   **strace output from instrumented Whetstone used for oprofile**

```
execve("./whet_pggp", ["./whet_pggp", "1000000"], 0x7ffcbb7a1cc8 /* 53 vars */) =
0
brk(NULL)                                              = 0x557b7c175000
  ...
access("/etc/ld.so.nohwcap", F_OK)     = -1 ENOENT (No such file or dir)
openat(AT_FDCWD, "/lib/x86_64-linux-gnu/libgcc_s.so.1", ...)  = 3
read(3, "\177ELF\2"..., 832)                          = 832
fstat(3, {st_mode=S_IFREG|0644, st_size=96616, ...})  = 0
mmap(NULL, 2192432, PROT_READ|PROT_EXEC, ...)         = 0x7fa7a22f9000
mprotect(0x7fa7a2310000, 2093056, PROT_NONE)          = 0
mmap(0x7fa7a250f000, 8192, PROT_READ|PROT_WRITE, ...) = 0x7fa7a250f000
close(3)                                              = 0
  ...
rt_sigaction(SIGPROF, {sa_handler=0x7fa7a202c240, sa_mask=~[], ...) = 0
setitimer(ITIMER_PROF, {it_interval={tv_sec=0, tv_usec=10000}, ...) = 0
fstat(1, {st_mode=S_IFCHR|0620, st_rdev=makedev(136, 1), ...})  = 0
write(1, "     0     0     0 1.0000"..., 76)          = 76
--- SIGPROF {si_signo=SIGPROF, si_code=SI_KERNEL} ---
rt_sigreturn({mask=[]})                               = 571659
--- SIGPROF {si_signo=SIGPROF, si_code=SI_KERNEL} ---
rt_sigreturn({mask=[]})                               = 1056338

    ... [about 2500 pairs]

--- SIGPROF {si_signo=SIGPROF, si_code=SI_KERNEL} ---
rt_sigreturn({mask=[]})                               = 4607182418800015908
--- SIGPROF {si_signo=SIGPROF, si_code=SI_KERNEL} ---
rt_sigreturn({mask=[]})                               = 1
--- SIGPROF {si_signo=SIGPROF, si_code=SI_KERNEL} ---
rt_sigreturn({mask=[]})                               = 1
write(1, "93000000      2      3   1.000"..., 77)     = 77
write(1, "\n", 1)                                     = 1
write(1, "Loops: 1000000, Iterations: 1, Duration: 25 sec", 49)     = 49
write(1, "C Converted Double Precision Whetstones: 4000.0 MIPS", 53)= 53
setitimer(ITIMER_PROF, {it_interval={tv_sec=0, tv_usec=0}, ...)     = 0
rt_sigaction(SIGPROF, {sa_handler=SIG_DFL, sa_mask=[], ...)         = 0

openat(AT_FDCWD, "gmon.out", O_WRONLY|O_CREAT|O_TRUNC| ...)     = 3
write(3, "gmon\1"..., 20)                             = 20
writev(3, [{iov_base="\0", iov_len=1}, {iov_base="@\36"...)     = 4601
```

```
close(3)                                                        = 0

getpid()                                                        = 9192
openat(AT_FDCWD, "/home/dsites/code/whetstone.gcda", O_RDWR| ...) = 3
fcntl(3, F_SETLKW, {l_type=F_WRLCK, l_whence=SEEK_SET, ...)      = 0
fcntl(3, F_GETFL)                        = 0x8002 (flags O_RDWR|O_LARGEFILE)
read(3, "adcg*37A"..., 4096)                                    = 880
read(3, "", 3216)                                               = 0
lseek(3, 0, SEEK_SET)                                           = 0
lseek(3, 12, SEEK_SET)                                          = 12
write(3, "\0\0\0\243W"..., 868)                                 = 868
close(3)                                                        = 0

exit_group(0)                                                   = ?
+++ exited with 0 +++
```

Did you notice the big discrepancy?

The completely vanilla version of the benchmark in Code Snippet 11.4 took 6 seconds to run. The instrumented-for-profiling version in Code Snippet 11.5 took four times longer, 25 seconds. Without timestamps, we cannot tell if the SIGPROF .. rt_sigreturn code is taking all the extra time or something else that does not involve system calls. But as we saw in the oprofile section, about half of the extra time comes from the ~40,000 hardware-driven PC samples, not visible at all in the system call trace.

The lesson here is to understand the *complete* overhead of your observation tools. The directions for oprofile suggested the previous compiler switches to use, but we did not initially compare the running time of the vanilla and the ready-to-profile versions, both executed without actually profiling. A little work compiling with 1, 2, ... of the extra flags will reveal which one(s) create the extra running time. The suggested preparation for profiling directly distorts the running time by a factor of four, so cannot be ignored. More about this in the exercises.

11.9 ltrace, CPU C Library Calls

The command ltrace <COMMAND> runs the subject command, intercepting and recording the dynamic library calls that are invoked by the executed process and the signals that are received by that process. It can also intercept and print the system calls executed by the program. Its use is similar to strace, but its overhead can be much higher, since there can be many more library calls than system calls.

As an extreme example, I reran the Whetstone program shown earlier under ltrace, sending the text output to the null file to cut down on overhead.

```
$ ltrace ./whet_pggp 1000000 2>/dev/null
```

Instead of 25 seconds, it took 11 hours!

```
Loops: 1000000, Iterations: 1, Duration: 39566 sec.
C Converted Double Precision Whetstones: 2.5 MIPS
```

Now, this is a synthetic benchmark consisting of loops that run millions of times each, with some of those loops containing calls to `sin`, `cos`, `atan`, `log`, etc. So the program does tens of millions of library calls. It is an extreme example, not representative of datacenter code. But you should be wary of trying to trace live datacenter code in so much detail unless you have a tool explicitly designed for low overhead when recording up to a million events per second.

11.10   `ftrace`, CPU Trace

`ftrace` is a facility to trace kernel functions. It is not designed for looking at user-mode programs and their interactions, but it can occasionally be useful for peering into the kernel activity. The primary purpose of `ftrace` is for kernel debugging, which is not the topic of this book.

The normal use of `ftrace` is to record a trace in RAM or in a binary file and then later decode it into text. Code Snippet 11.6 is a little example of tracing calls to the `__do_page_fault` function, run on an idle machine.

Code Snippet 11.6   **`ftrace` recording of `__do_page_fault` for a few seconds**

```
$ sudo trace-cmd record -p function -l __do_page_fault
  plugin 'function'
Hit Ctrl^C to stop recording
  ... wait a few seconds here ....
^C
CPU0 data recorded at offset=0x4f4000
    4096 bytes in size
CPU1 data recorded at offset=0x4f5000
    8192 bytes in size
CPU2 data recorded at offset=0x4f7000
    4096 bytes in size
CPU3 data recorded at offset=0x4f8000
    4096 bytes in size
```

The recorded information is in a kernel RAM buffer. Code Snippet 11.7 is the formatted output, showing one page fault within `gnome-shell` and 14 within `trace-cmd` itself. The second column gives the CPU number, and the third column is a timestamp to the microsecond.

Code Snippet 11.7   **`ftrace` report of the data gathered in Code Snippet 11.6**

```
$ sudo trace-cmd report
cpus=4
   trace-cmd-2940  [001]  1172.651718: function:  __do_page_fault
   trace-cmd-2940  [001]  1172.651723: function:  __do_page_fault
   trace-cmd-2940  [001]  1172.651740: function:  __do_page_fault
   trace-cmd-2941  [003]  1172.651997: function:  __do_page_fault
   trace-cmd-2941  [003]  1172.652003: function:  __do_page_fault
   trace-cmd-2942  [002]  1172.652015: function:  __do_page_fault
   trace-cmd-2942  [002]  1172.652019: function:  __do_page_fault
   trace-cmd-2943  [001]  1172.652024: function:  __do_page_fault
```

```
    trace-cmd-2943   [001]  1172.652026: function:  __do_page_fault
    trace-cmd-2944   [002]  1172.652044: function:  __do_page_fault
    trace-cmd-2944   [002]  1172.652046: function:  __do_page_fault
  gnome-shell-1531   [002]  1174.853922: function:  __do_page_fault
    trace-cmd-2944   [003]  1176.628836: function:  __do_page_fault
    trace-cmd-2942   [000]  1176.628839: function:  __do_page_fault
    trace-cmd-2943   [001]  1176.628869: function:  __do_page_fault
$
```

The ftrace facility is powerful and flexible. As usual, the cost of this power is a substantial slowdown of the entire system if very much data is being recorded. The few calls to __do_page_ fault earlier did not generate much trace data, just 20KB, much of which may be unused due to rounding up allocations to multiples of 4KB. But the fact that the six events on CPU 1 did not fit into 4KB tells us that each event takes over 600 bytes to record. This is too large for live data-center work. The only way ftrace is useful is to be *very* selective about what is traced. Whenever you come across a tool that touts its ability to trace subsets of all events, be wary of its performance with no subsetting.

As an extreme example, the short trace in Code Snippet 11.8 of *all* kernel functions for just *one second* generates much more trace data—about 366MB! During this time, about 2.3 million events were lost because the recording could not keep up and only about 500,000 events were kept. After hitting Ctrl^C, all that trace data is sitting in kernel buffers—and starting to cause the operating system to thrash, paging to disk on our little 4GB-of-RAM sample server.

Code Snippet 11.8   **ftrace recording of all kernel functions for a few seconds**

```
$ sudo trace-cmd record -p function
  plugin 'function'
Hit Ctrl^C to stop recording
^C
CPU 0: 704445 events lost
CPU 1: 252465 events lost
CPU 2: 977030 events lost
CPU 3: 404650 events lost
CPU0 data recorded at offset=0x4f4000
    94187520 bytes in size
CPU1 data recorded at offset=0x5ec7000
    85381120 bytes in size
CPU2 data recorded at offset=0xb034000
    68059136 bytes in size
CPU3 data recorded at offset=0xf11c000
    118435840 bytes in size
```

Code Snippet 11.9 has the decoded form of just a tiny bit of this data. There are sometimes four to five events traced per microsecond.

Code Snippet 11.9 **`ftrace` report of the data gathered in Code Snippet 11.8, showing a tiny subset**

```
$ sudo trace-cmd report |head -n34
cpus=4
   trace-cmd-1873  [001]   109.774175: function:      mutex_unlock
   trace-cmd-1873  [001]   109.774176: function: __mutex_unlock_slowpath.isra.11
   trace-cmd-1873  [001]   109.774177: function:     _raw_spin_lock
   trace-cmd-1873  [001]   109.774177: function:     wake_q_add
   trace-cmd-1873  [001]   109.774177: function:     wake_up_q
   trace-cmd-1873  [001]   109.774177: function:     try_to_wake_up
   trace-cmd-1873  [001]   109.774178: function:     _raw_spin_lock_irqsave
   trace-cmd-1873  [001]   109.774178: function:     select_task_rq_fair
   trace-cmd-1873  [001]   109.774178: function:     idle_cpu
   trace-cmd-1873  [001]   109.774178: function:     update_cfs_rq_h_load
   trace-cmd-1873  [001]   109.774179: function:     select_idle_sibling
   trace-cmd-1873  [001]   109.774179: function:     idle_cpu
   trace-cmd-1873  [001]   109.774180: function:     _raw_spin_lock
   trace-cmd-1873  [001]   109.774180: function:     update_rq_clock
   trace-cmd-1873  [001]   109.774180: function:     ttwu_do_activate
   trace-cmd-1873  [001]   109.774180: function:     activate_task
   trace-cmd-1873  [001]   109.774180: function:     enqueue_task_fair
   trace-cmd-1873  [001]   109.774181: function:     enqueue_entity
   trace-cmd-1873  [001]   109.774181: function:     update_curr
   trace-cmd-1873  [001]   109.774181: function: __update_load_avg_se.isra.38
   trace-cmd-1873  [001]   109.774181: function:     decay_load
   trace-cmd-1873  [001]   109.774182: function:     decay_load
   trace-cmd-1873  [001]   109.774182: function:     decay_load
   trace-cmd-1873  [001]   109.774182: function: __accumulate_pelt_segments
   trace-cmd-1873  [001]   109.774182: function:     decay_load
   trace-cmd-1873  [001]   109.774182: function:     decay_load
   trace-cmd-1873  [001]   109.774183: function:     decay_load
   trace-cmd-1873  [001]   109.774183: function: __accumulate_pelt_segments
   trace-cmd-1873  [001]   109.774183: function:     update_cfs_group
   trace-cmd-1873  [001]   109.774183: function:     account_entity_enqueue
   trace-cmd-1873  [001]   109.774184: function:     __enqueue_entity
   trace-cmd-1873  [001]   109.774184: function:     enqueue_entity
   trace-cmd-1873  [001]   109.774184: function:     update_curr
```

After tracing, be sure to free up the kernel memory used to hold a trace, as shown in Code Snippet 11.10.

Code Snippet 11.10 **`ftrace` cleanup**

```
$ sudo trace-cmd reset
```

Overall, ftrace is an extremely powerful tool but must be used with care in a live datacenter due to its potentially large CPU and memory overhead. It is better suited for finding kernel bugs in an offline environment.

11.11   mtrace, Memory Malloc/Free

The mtrace facility is a GNU extension for C and C++ code. It is not a command-line tool but instead is a runtime library tool. Use it by including in a C or C++ program

```
#include <mcheck.h>
mtrace();
muntrace();
```

and setting an environment variable

```
export MALLOC_TRACE=some_file_name
```

Compiling and running the program will trace every malloc/free between the mtrace and muntrace calls, writing a text description of each operation to some_file_name. For the little program snippet Code Snippet 11.11, the mtrace output file is shown in Code Snippet 11.12.

Code Snippet 11.11   **A little example program for mtrace**

```
const char* key1 =    "key1_678901234567890";        // 20 bytes
const char* value1 = "value1_89012345678901234";     // 24 bytes
const char* key2 =
  "key2_678901234567890key2_678901234567890";        // 40 bytes
const char* value2 =
  "value2_89012345678901234value2_89012345678901234"; // 48 bytes

typedef std::map<std::string, std::string> StrStrMap;
StrStrMap foo;

// Allocates 21 96 31 bytes
foo[key1] = value1;

// Allocates 41 96 49 bytes
foo[key2] = value2;
```

Note that since all the malloc calls are in C runtime library routines and there is no call-stack trace, we are hard-pressed to correlate the output with our original program. This is a common problem with observation tools that are supposed to be helping us but then drop the ball when we just want to know what source function or line of code is involved.

Code Snippet 11.12 **`mtrace` output running the program in Code Snippet 11.11**

```
= Start
@ /usr/lib/x86_64-linux-gnu/libstdc++.so.6:(_Znwm+0x1c)[0x7f23ce04a54c]
    + 0x561f579312b0 0x15
@ /usr/lib/x86_64-linux-gnu/libstdc++.so.6:(_Znwm+0x1c)[0x7f23ce04a54c]
    + 0x561f579312d0 0x60
@ /usr/lib/x86_64-linux-gnu/libstdc++.so.6:(_Znwm+0x1c)|0x7f23ce04a54c]
    + 0x561f57931340 0x1f

@ /usr/lib/x86_64-linux-gnu/libstdc++.so.6:(_Znwm+0x1c)[0x7f23ce04a54c]
    + 0x561f57931370 0x29
@ /usr/lib/x86_64-linux-gnu/libstdc++.so.6:(_Znwm+0x1c)[0x7f23ce04a54c]
    + 0x561f579313b0 0x60
@ /usr/lib/x86_64-linux-gnu/libstdc++.so.6:(_Znwm+0x1c)[0x7f23ce04a54c]
    + 0x561f57931420 0x31
= End
```

Converting the last column from hex to decimal, we find allocations of 21, 96, and 31 bytes for the insertion of key1, and 41, 96, and 49 bytes for key2; we will explain each of these weird values.

The first of each triple allocates a copy of the key string, including one extra byte for a trailing NUL so that `c_str()` is always a zero-cost operation. The third of each triple allocates a copy of the value string, including one extra byte for a trailing NUL. For some reason, short value strings are rounded up to a 31-byte allocation, instead of the expected 25 bytes for value1. Longer values are not rounded up, as you can see by the 49-byte allocation for value2.

The second of each triple allocates 96 bytes for a node in the internal balanced tree implementation of map<>, enough room for twelve pointers or twelve 64-bit integers. I presume that two of these point to the key and value and that two point to other tree nodes, with possibly also a pointer to each node's parent. Four hold allocated and in-use lengths for each string. The total space is enough to store short strings of <= 15 bytes (plus one for the NUL) directly in the 96-byte tree node instead of allocating a string copy and pointing to that. In fact, shortening value1 to 15 bytes removes the third allocation, while making it 16 bytes still allocates a 31-byte value.

Running a little program that inserts 100,000 map entries and hence does 300,000 allocations in a tight loop takes 0.54 seconds without `mtrace` and 6.657 seconds with it on a sample server, so using `mtrace` in this setting makes it about 12 times slower with an overhead of about (6.657 – 0.54) / 300000 = 22 usec per allocation. Even though this is an extreme example, it suggests that `mtrace` is unsuitable for live datacenter execution of programs with much dynamic memory allocation.

11.12 `blktrace`, Disk Trace

The `blktrace` command turns on a kernel facility to record all the activity on a given disk or SSD block-IO device. The data are accumulated in files with names like `sda.blktrace.0` for the CPU 0 accesses to disk tracked by

```
sudo blktrace -d /dev/sda
```

It has minimal overhead for disk devices so could be used occasionally in a live datacenter. Because of the higher number of accesses per second on an SSD, thousands vs. about 100, its overhead when tracing SSD accesses may be a bit too high for live datacenter use. As always, try it out over a known load, timing the CPU usage with and without blktrace running. Code Snippet 11.13 shows the two quick results from running mystery3 (with write timing added) from Chapter 5. The times vary by about 5%, some faster and some slower. This is about par for the course in reproducibility of rotating disk timings. There is no evidence here of much overhead for running blktrace. You could do longer more careful measurements.

Code Snippet 11.13   **The mystery3 disk read/write program run with and without blktrace**

Without blktrace	With blktrace
TimeDiskRead opening temp for write	TimeDiskRead opening temp for write
TimeDiskRead opening temp for read of	TimeDiskRead opening temp for read of
40960KB	40960KB
Async read startusec 1539971382967532,	Async read startusec 1539971397516114,
stopusec 1539971383675708, delta 708176	stopusec 1539971398200190, delta 684076
scancount 18611, changecount inside scan	scancount 16922, changecount inside scan
10240	10240
59.227MB/sec overall	61.313MB/sec overall
temp_read_times.txt and ... written	temp_read_times.txt and ... written
TimeDiskWrite to be completed	TimeDiskWrite to be completed
TimeDiskWrite opening temp for async	TimeDiskWrite opening temp for async
write...	write...
Async write startusec 1539971383837798,	Async write startusec 1539971398394019,
stopusec 1539971384671272, delta 833474	stopusec 1539971399281066, delta 887047
50.323MB/sec overall	47.284MB/sec overall
TimeDiskWrite opening temp for read	TimeDiskWrite opening temp for read
temp_write_times.txt and ... written	temp_write_times.txt and ... written
real 0m3.592s	**real 0m3.404s**
user 0m1.613s	**user 0m1.620s**
sys 0m0.041s	**sys 0m0.064s**

The corresponding output for the blktrace run in the second column of Code Snippet 11.13 has about 3.4 seconds of individual disk driver actions spread across 3700 lines of output and then a summary. Code Snippet 11.14 shows just the read actions that correspond to the asynchronous read of 40MB from thread number 14881.

Code Snippet 11.14   **blktrace output for queueing reads (Q R) of 40MB**

Device	CPU	Seq	Seconds	PID	Action	Sector + blocks
-----	---	----	-----------	-----	------	-------------------------------
8,0	0	2	0.882966608	14881	Q	R 19974144 + 4096 [mystery3w_opt]
8,0	0	12	0.883117924	14881	Q	R 19978240 + 4096 [mystery3w_opt]
8,0	0	25	0.883260472	14881	Q	R 19982336 + 4096 [mystery3w_opt]

```
8,0    0     38   0.883387790 14881  Q   R 19986432 + 4096 [mystery3w_opt]
8,0    0     51   0.883518405 14881  Q   R 19990528 + 4096 [mystery3w_opt]
8,0    0     64   0.883652768 14881  Q   R 19994624 + 4096 [mystery3w_opt]
8,0    0     77   0.883770568 14881  Q   R 19998720 + 4096 [mystery3w_opt]
8,0    0     90   0.883890361 14881  Q   R 20002816 + 4096 [mystery3w_opt]
8,0    0    103   0.884010065 14881  Q   R 20006912 + 4096 [mystery3w_opt]
8,0    0    116   0.884129328 14881  Q   R 20011008 + 4096 [mystery3w_opt]
8,0    0    129   0.884270433 14881  Q   R 20015104 + 4096 [mystery3w_opt]
8,0    0    142   0.884387582 14881  Q   R 20019200 + 4096 [mystery3w_opt]
8,0    0    155   0.884503548 14881  Q   R 20023296 + 4096 [mystery3w_opt]
8,0    0    168   0.884617310 14881  Q   R 20027392 + 4096 [mystery3w_opt]
8,0    0    181   0.884732154 14881  Q   R 20031488 + 4096 [mystery3w_opt]
8,0    0    194   0.884847049 14881  Q   R 20035584 + 4096 [mystery3w_opt]
8,0    0    207   0.884963356 14881  Q   R 20039680 + 4096 [mystery3w_opt]
8,0    0    219   0.885042450 14881  Q   R 20043776 + 4096 [mystery3w_opt]
8,0    0    230   0.885112126 14881  Q   R 20047872 + 4096 [mystery3w_opt]
8,0    0    241   0.885178125 14881  Q   R 20051968 + 4096 [mystery3w_opt]
```

Since 20 read actions read a total of 40MB, each one must be reading 2MB. This is described as reading 4,096 "blocks." Doing a little division in your head, $2**21 / 2**12 = 2** (21-12) = 2**9 = 512$, reveals that "block" in this context means 512 bytes—thanks to the long history of backward compatibly in our industry. This sector size first appeared in 1973 for the IBM 33FD eight-inch floppy disk and is still used today 45 years later even though physical disk sectors moved to 4KB circa 2011 [Wikipedia 2021t].

Code Snippet 11.15 shows the summary output for mystery3 with write timing. The program reads a total of 80MB, 40 for the read timing and 40 for the readback in the write timing. It also writes a little over 80MB, 40 before the read timing and 40 in the write timing. The remaining MB or so of writes are the mystery3 and `blktrace` output files.

Code Snippet 11.15   **`blktrace` summary output for mystery3**

```
CPU0 (sda):
  Reads Queued:      20,  40960KiB  Writes Queued:      28,  40992KiB
  Read Dispatches:   32,  32768KiB  Write Dispatches:   33,  32800KiB
  Reads Requeued:     0            Writes Requeued:     0
  Reads Completed:    0,     0KiB  Writes Completed:    0,     0KiB
  Read Merges:        0,     0KiB  Write Merges:        7,    28KiB
  Read depth:        32            Write depth:        32
  IO unplugs:        81            Timer unplugs:       0
CPU1 (sda):
  Reads Queued:       0,     0KiB  Writes Queued:       4,    16KiB
  Read Dispatches:    0,     0KiB  Write Dispatches:    1,     4KiB
  Reads Requeued:     0            Writes Requeued:     0
  Reads Completed:    0,     0KiB  Writes Completed:    0,     0KiB
  Read Merges:        0,     0KiB  Write Merges:        0,     0KiB
  Read depth:        32            Write depth:        32
  IO unplugs:         1            Timer unplugs:       0
```

```
CPU2 (sda):
  Reads Queued:         0,      0KiB  Writes Queued:         16,      304KiB
  Read Dispatches:      0,      0KiB  Write Dispatches:      11,       44KiB
  Reads Requeued:       0            Writes Requeued:        1
  Reads Completed:      0,      0KiB  Writes Completed:       0,        0KiB
  Read Merges:          0,      0KiB  Write Merges:           2,        8KiB
  Read depth:          32            Write depth:           32
  IO unplugs:           4            Timer unplugs:          0
CPU3 (sda):
  Reads Queued:        32,  40960KiB  Writes Queued:        104,    41664KiB
  Read Dispatches:     41,  49152KiB  Write Dispatches:     142,    50128KiB
  Reads Requeued:       0            Writes Requeued:       17
  Reads Completed:     73,  81920KiB  Writes Completed:     173,    82976KiB
  Read Merges:          1,    512KiB  Write Merges:          14,       56KiB
  Read depth:          32            Write depth:           32
  IO unplugs:          82            Timer unplugs:          1

Total (sda):
  Reads Queued:        52,  81920KiB  Writes Queued:        152,    82976KiB
  Read Dispatches:     73,  81920KiB  Write Dispatches:     187,    82976KiB
  Reads Requeued:       0            Writes Requeued:       18
  Reads Completed:     73,  81920KiB  Writes Completed:     173,    82976KiB
  Read Merges:          1,    512KiB  Write Merges:          23,       92KiB
  IO unplugs:         168            Timer unplugs:          1

Throughput (R/W): 24439KiB/s / 24754KiB/s
Events (sda): 3741 entries
```

The `blktrace` command is useful for observing overall disk activity and for identifying the sources of that activity by process ID number and name. It can add to your understanding of shared disk dynamics. Just be careful to track its overhead when used with higher-rate SSDs.

11.13   `tcpdump` and Wireshark, Network Trace

The `tcpdump` command turns on a kernel facility to record all the activity on a given network link. The data can be written to a binary file and parsed/printed later. By default, `tcpdump` looks up each IP address via DNS (domain name service) somewhere on your network. This can slow down `tcpdump` and create extra network traffic and can even overload a DNS server if there are thousands of different network nodes in use (as there might well be in a datacenter). To avoid doing these name lookups and therefore just recording nodes by numeric IP address, use the `-n` flag.

Also by default `tcpdump` saves/copies every byte of each packet. A busy 10 Gb/sec network link can transmit about 1GB/second. Saving all the bytes of every packet means writing 1GB/sec to the screen or output file, both of which have too little bandwidth to support this, so in the trace packets will be lost. To manage the overhead, ask `tcpdump` to just keep enough of the initial bytes of each packet that you can identify what it is and what node is the other end of the connection.

Often, 128 bytes is enough, as specified by the scarf flag, -s128. You may need to scarf a somewhat longer prefix in different environments.

Normally tcpdump writes its text output to the screen unless you specify a binary output file with the -w <filename> flag. That file can later be formatted into text via the -r <filename> flag. So to take a relatively low overhead network trace, use something like

```
$ sudo tcpdump -n -s128 -w tcpdump_out.bin
```

And later to look at this trace, use

```
$ tcpdump -r tcpdump_out.bin
```

The default text output has each packet timestamped to the microsecond, some decoding of the network protocols involved, and a hex dump of the initial packet bytes, as shown in Code Snippet 11.16.

Older versions of tcpdump delivered every packet to a second tracing process before forwarding to the intended target, causing about a 7% CPU overhead, too slow to be used in datacenters. Newer versions work within the kernel with lower overhead, so might be suitable in datacenters. But you should measure the overhead in your environment before using it with heavy live traffic.

Wireshark [Wireshark 2021] is a widely used and sophisticated network protocol analyzer. Like tcpdump, it can capture and dump packets, but it also can decode and meaningfully display a wide variety of network protocols and capture-file formats, do deep packet inspection, decrypt messages, and more. It supports a wide variety of wired and wireless network implementations, not just Ethernet. Its detailed use is beyond the scope of this book, but any networking professional should become familiar with it.

Code Snippet 11.16 **tcpdump trace of a few degenerate packets**

```
12:17:40.381706 STP 802.1d, Config, Flags [none], bridge-id
0fa0.18:9c:27:19:a4:b2.8001, length 43

12:17:40.471659 18:9c:27:19:a4:b2 (oui Unknown) > Broadcast, ethertype Unknown
(0x7373), length 118:
0x0000:  1211 0000 0040 a693 0ae6 a5fc 686f 548e  .....@......hoT.
0x0010:  834b 987c 164c c270 1009 3890 c0cb 9dc1  .K.|.L.p..8.....
0x0020:  c45b 9184 e201 0000 0201 8003 0618 9c27  .[.............'
0x0030:  19a4 b204 0104 0701 0108 0618 9c27 19a4  .............'..
0x0040:  b209 0102 0e18 0000 0000 0000 0000 0000  ...............
0x0050:  0000 0000 0000 0000 0000 0000 0000 1908  ...............
0x0060:  61ff 451c e24f b653                      a.E..O.S

12:17:40.471783 18:9c:27:19:a4:b2 (oui Unknown) > Broadcast, ethertype Unknown
(0x7373), length 118:
0x0000:  1211 0000 0040 a693 0ae6 a5fc 686f 548e  .....@......hoT.
0x0010:  834b 987c 164c c270 1009 3890 c0cb 9dc1  .K.|.L.p..8.....
0x0020:  c45b 9184 e201 0000 0201 8003 0618 9c27  .[.............'
0x0030:  19a4 b204 0104 0701 0108 0618 9c27 19a4  .............'..
0x0040:  b209 0102 0e18 0000 0000 0000 0000 0000  ...............
```

```
0x0050:  0000 0000 0000 0000 0000 0000 0000 1908   ...............
0x0060:  61ff 451c e24f b653                        a.E..O.S

12:17:43.877894 IP6 unknown b8975af85270.attlocal.net.37764 > qj-in-x8a.1e100
.net.https: Flags [.], ack 3939294343, win 334, options [nop,nop,TS val
1869126913 ecr 4116297880], length 0

12:17:43.968438 IP6 qj-in-x8a.1e100.net.https > unknown b8975af85270.attlocal
.net.37764: Flags [.], ack 1, win 248, options [nop,nop,TS val 4116344447 ecr
1869080288], length 0

12:17:44.263196 IP6 unknown b8975af85270.attlocal.net.50290 > dsldevice6.
attlocal.net.domain: 30562+ [1au] PTR? a.8.0.0.0.0.0.0.0.0.0.0.0.0.0.0.8.0.c.0.d
.0.0.4.0.b.8.f.7.0.6.2.ip6.arpa. (101)
```

11.14   `locktrace`, Critical Section Locks

Fake-out. This tool does not exist. There are several tools and tracepoints within the Linux kernel for kernel debugging of locks (see `ftrace` earlier), and there are several offline tools for detecting locking bugs in user code—deadlock, races, lack of locking entirely, etc. [Valgrind 2021], but no broad-brush low-overhead tools for understanding waiting times for contended locks by tracing user-mode code lock usage.

Critical-section locks are a software construct, so many datacenter programs use in-house locking libraries. The widely used POSIX threads library (`pthreads`) does not have a designed-in tracing facility for contended locks. Some specific implementations [IBM 2021] have tracing facilities, and some tools [Google 2012] use the Linux process trace facility `ptrace` to essentially attach to a running program as a debugger and trace locking behavior at various breakpoints. But these are too slow to be used for 100% of the locks in live datacenter code.

We looked at a simple spinlock in Chapters 6 and 7. Later in this book (Chapter 27) we will build a low-overhead mutex library that traces contended locks and tracks a small histogram of latency for acquiring each lock. This allows identifying the sources of unusually long locking.

11.15   Offered Load, Outbound Calls, and Transaction Latency

The Dapper tool [Sigelman 2010] mentioned in Chapter 6 timestamps and traces the four send/receive times of every RPC, along with identifying the endpoints, the message sizes, and the parent RPC. Similar tools include Zipkin [Aniszczyk 2012] and Money [Comcast 2018]. We specifically designed Dapper to have low enough overhead to record every single incoming and outgoing RPC for datacenter services that perform thousands of transactions per second. The resulting binary log files, when gathered across all the servers involved, allow reconstruction of RPC tree timelines such as the one shown in Figure 6.8 in Chapter 6. Complete, low-overhead RPC logs also allow examination of the offered load for any service.

Commitments on service response time, often called service level agreements or SLAs, are meaningless unless they *also* contain commitments limiting the offered load. A service designed for 2,000 rides per hour, such as Disney World Space Mountain [Williams 2019], is no fun at all when 20,000 people show up at once. Similarly, a service designed for 1,000 transactions per second with message sizes around 10KB fails miserably when the offered load is 5,000 per second with messages of 1MB. You can waste some stressful time tracking down a performance issue that is not a performance issue at all, but is instead an offered-load issue.

Consider these abusive offered loads from a single client to a disk server that nominally can do 100 transfers (read or write) of 256KB per disk per second across 12 disks, with network bandwidth of 300 MB/sec in each direction, and with several MB of RAM read/write buffering:

- 50,000 writes per second of about 243 bytes each
- 1,300 reads per second of the *identical* 1MB from a single file
- Random-location reads of about 2700 bytes each across a 35GB file, for 17 hours straight
- A 1GB write

The first offered load consumes all the available CPU time handling tens of thousands of RPCs per second, delaying all the other clients. The second load gets its data from RAM cache but saturates the outbound network link with an attempt to transfer 1.3 GB/sec over a 1.1 GB/sec link, delaying all the other clients. The third load keeps one disk continuously seeking 100 times per second for 17 hours and raises the question, over several months of this program running every day, of how many seeks a drive can do before the arm mechanism wears out; it also delays all other clients trying to use that disk. The fourth load ties up the inbound network for at least 3.3 seconds solid while delaying all the other clients, overflows any RAM buffering, and ties up one disk for at least 10 seconds solid (at 100 MB/sec on a single disk). These are all real datacenter loads I have encountered over the years. All were client design mistakes or oversights.

Lesson one: Before tackling a performance issue, look at the offered load. No tools? Add them.

Lesson two: Build your services with an offered-load agreement and do checks against that agreement in real time at every RPC arrival, throttling clients or rejecting requests that are out of specification. This is the only way to protect the other clients.

In many cases, a single incoming RPC to a service will trigger several or hundreds of outgoing RPCs to lower-level services. A tool such as Dapper allows you to see all of them (nothing missing) and to see when the inbound transaction is slow whether the cause is some slow lower-level RPC, and if so which one and on what server. Good logs from that server can show how busy it was at the time and perhaps why it was slow.

In all cases, timestamping each RPC request/response message directly records the server-side latency for every transaction, allowing you to see the long-tail transactions. Doing the same on the client side and subtracting the server time allows you to see transmission delays—not usually in the network hardware but instead in client or server software, or perhaps in queuing for an overloaded network link. Recording the message sizes for each RPC allows back-calculating how busy those links must be at any given time.

11.16   Summary

In this chapter, we have surveyed a few existing software performance observation tools and commented on their usefulness for understanding datacenter software dynamics. Some have low overhead but only report average behavior. Some can trace individual transactions to show specifically what is different about the slow ones but have too-high overhead to be useful in a live datacenter. Only a few are both specific and fast. In the next chapter we look more carefully at tracing tools.

Exercises

11.1   Pick a simple program of yours and run some of the existing tools to observe it. Did you find any surprises?

11.2   Pick two existing tools and use one to observe the overhead of the other while running one of your programs.

11.3   Run the Whetstone benchmark after compiling it with incrementally more of the suggested `oprofile` compilation flags, detailed just before Code Snippet 11.5. Which one(s) produce a substantially slower runtime?

Chapter 12

Traces

This chapter defines and motivates our interest in low-overhead tracing tools, in contrast to simpler counting and profiling tools.

As we discussed in the previous chapter, *counters* either count individual events such as packets sent or sum quantities such as bytes written to disk.

Profiles periodically count samples of some quantity. The most common quantity is the program counter value, PC, for a CPU core while it is running an individual program. With enough samples, the resulting profile shows approximately where all the CPU time was spent during the timespan being profiled. CPU profiles, however, are completely *blind* to the time a program spends waiting and not executing at all. They may also be blind to other threads in a multi-thread application, and they often are blind to operating system kernel time. And, by design, they are blind to other, possibly interfering, programs running on the same server.

Traces are records of time-sequenced events, such as all the accesses on a disk drive or all the system calls in a program. Usually, the individual events are timestamped to the microsecond or better.

12.1 Tracing Advantages

Tracing everything happening on a disk or CPU lets us see otherwise-hidden activity stemming from system libraries, file system metadata accesses, kernel code, and other non-program sources. A well-designed trace lets us see which events come from which programs and see which events overlap in time and hence might interfere with each other.

A well-designed trace also has *nothing missing*—every single event within the timespan of the trace is recorded, with no gaps or missing samples. The nothing-missing property lets us state definitively what did *not* happen—impossible if any kind of sampling or subsetting is used.

Traces let us distinguish unusual transaction behavior from normal behavior, even when we don't know ahead of time which transactions will be unusual. Event traces, or merged multiple event traces (e.g., CPU, disk, network) put together on a common timeline let us see and understand causes for a program to end up waiting instead of executing. They can show the difference in execution paths between unusual and normal transactions, the dynamics of code on one thread waiting for code on another thread, and the dynamics of interfering programs that are using shared resources.

Simpler counters and CPU profiles completely miss non-CPU waiting times, they completely miss time sequencing, and hence they completely miss cause-and-effect and other interactions between nearly simultaneous events.

Traces are thus a way to understand the dynamic behavior of running programs.

12.2   Tracing Disadvantages

As always, there is a trade-off between precision of observation and its effect on the underlying system being observed. Designing good tracing tools involves choosing a careful engineering balance between precision of observation and *distortion* of the system under test. In the next chapter, we discuss this topic in detail.

> . . . also je genauer der Ort bestimmt ist, desto ungenauer ist der Impuls bekannt und umgekehrt.
> — Werner Heisenberg
>
> [. . . so the more precisely the location is determined, the less precisely the impulse is known and vice versa.]

Unless carefully engineered, tracing can be a high-overhead tool. Such overhead makes it unsuitable for observing live user-facing datacenter systems. Traces, however, are the strongest tool for distinguishing unusual transactions from normal ones. Tracing is the only approach that works for understanding *unpredictable* unusual transactions. So we want to use or build tracing tools with sufficiently low overhead.

Keep in mind that any individual trace is just a large coherent sample of computing activity. Repeated traces will all be slightly different. A single trace may turn out to be unrepresentative of the performance problem you are trying to understand, so expect to take multiple traces and compare them for overall consistency.

12.3   The Three Starting Questions

When designing a tracing observation tool, there are three important questions:

1. What to trace?
2. How long to trace?
3. With how much overhead?

We will look at each of these in turn. Often, transaction latencies will suggest a performance problem, and counters or profiles will suggest which computer resource is related to a performance mystery, but not identify the underlying reason. These are the places to start in unravelling the problem. Include them on your dashboards.

What to trace? You can trace events for any of the five fundamental resources, always with the goal of understanding complex and unexpected sequences or patterns. Different levels of detail allow trading precision of observation against trace overhead. At a very fine level, a CPU trace tool could track every conditional branch and computed branch target in a single program but with about a 20x slowdown when done in software [Perl 1996] or microcode [Agarwal 1986]. At a slightly less granular level, a CPU trace tool could track and timestamp every function call and return in a single multi-threaded program with about 1.2 to 1.5x slowdown [Sites 2004]. At a less granular but more complete level, a CPU trace tool could track and timestamp every transition between kernel-mode and user-mode execution across all programs and all cores of a multi-core processor with less than 1% overhead (Part III). At the least granular, a CPU trace tool could track and timestamp just context switches across all programs and all cores of a multi-core processor, with much less than 1% overhead. All such tools will give you some insight into the true software dynamics in a complex server system.

A memory trace tool could record every dynamic allocation and free in a single program with small overhead. It is straightforward for such a tool to record the program location that does each operation, but it turns out to be insufficient for careful understanding of unexpected memory usage patterns when almost all the allocations occur within a single shared library, as we saw with mtrace in Chapter 11. A better tool records not just the location that does each operation but also the call path leading to that location. This makes it possible to distinguish expected allocations via one call path from unexpected allocations along a different call path (or missing frees for those allocations). However, it requires careful engineering to keep the overhead of such a tool low enough.

A disk trace tool could record and timestamp every read and write on every disk/SSD on a server with tiny overhead, since the rate of such events rarely exceeds 100 per second for a disk or a few thousand per second for an SSD. Such a tool running at the operating system level can capture all the traffic to all disks. Running at a single-program level, it can capture the behavior of that program but not capture any interference from other programs.

At a very detailed level, a network trace tool such as tcpdump in Chapters 11 and 26 could record every transmitted and received packet, capturing the time, size, and other network node (IP address and port, for example), but the overhead of doing this in software becomes impractical above about 10 Gb/sec network speeds—at 100 Gb/sec there can be a new minimum-length packet every 6.4 nsec, about 20 CPU cycles. At a less granular but more practical level, a network trace tool could record and timestamp every transmitted and received RPC *message*, capturing the time, size, and the other network node with low overhead if the average message size is a few thousand to a few million bytes, i.e., several to several thousand full-size packets per message [Sigelman 2010]. Even at 100 Gb/sec, a full 1,500-byte packet would take 1.25 usec on the wire, so it would be practical, with careful engineering, to trace messages of that size or bigger. The KUtrace design in Part III of this book has such a low-overhead facility.

At the finest level, a critical-section trace tool could trace every software lock acquisition and release. But from a performance point of view we rarely care about uncontended locks—only contended locks and the waiting imposed on losing threads. Assuming a good lock design in which there is usually little actual lock contention, a lower overhead and thus more practical trace tool could trace and timestamp just every *failed* attempt to acquire a contended lock (one already held by another thread) and the subsequent successful acquisition of that lock, along with identifying the thread that was holding it. See Chapter 27.

In summary, software can trace all five fundamental resources. Carefully chosen levels of granularity can give tools with low enough overhead to be useful in live datacenters. A few processor designs have modest hardware support for CPU tracing, which can extend the level of detail traced or reduce the tracing overhead. External hardware can also be used, usually attached to one-of-a-kind systems [Friedenberg 1964, Emer 1984].

In this chapter, we will look at an early external-hardware tracing system and also look at a software-only trace tool for function calls and returns. In subsequent chapters we will design and build a low-overhead software trace tool for kernel-user transitions across all programs on all CPU cores of a server.

Over the years, I have built or used tracing systems for nine different kinds of events: source statements [Knuth 1971], VAX PC addresses [Agarwal 1986], Windows NT for DEC Alpha instruction and data addresses [Perl 1996], C program function entry/exit [Sites 2004], remote procedure call request/response [Sigelman 2010], kernel-mode/user-mode transitions [Sites 2017], network packets [Chesson 2006], disk accesses [Google 2008], and malloc/free [Linux 2021a]. Each reveals a different aspect of program dynamics.

How long? How long to trace depends on the time scale of the performance problem you have. In general, you want to trace long enough to capture several complete examples of the problem. If the problem is unexpected transaction delays of about 8 seconds, a trace length of 16 seconds is the minimum needed to have some reasonable chance of capturing a complete slow transaction, instead of just a fragment of one. If such slow transactions only about occur once per minute across 10 servers, you will want to trace on all those servers for several minutes each.

If trace entries accumulate quickly enough, the only reasonable place to record them is in main memory. The product of

- trace entry size
- entries per second, and
- total duration in seconds

will determine how much trace-buffer RAM you will need. If this is larger than you have, you will need some compromise in at least one of the factors.

One compromise is to record very small trace entries of 1/2/4/8 bytes, keeping only the smallest amount of data that will give you some clue about unexpected dynamics, but having poor time resolution or poor location resolution.

Another compromise is to record events that occur less frequently than you really want, but that still give a complete picture of where all the time went. This might still be enough to guide you to an underlying problem.

Sometimes the compromise is to take multiple trace shots of limited duration, each recording for however long you can afford, followed by dumping the data to disk or by scanning it quickly to see if it is likely to contain an example of the performance problem. If not, throw the data away and start a new trace. If so, dump it to disk first and then start a new trace. This strategy fails if you cannot record long enough to contain at least one complete bad example.

A variation of this does continuous recording, so-called *flight-recorder mode*, wrapping around in the trace buffer, while also looking for excessive overall time delays or other indications of trouble. If one occurs, stop tracing, dump the buffer, and start up again. This approach is best combined with a strong emphasis on reducing the overhead of the continuous recording. Be sure to turn it off if no one is going to look immediately at the resulting data; I'm not a fan of gathering lots of trace data that then sits unused on disk for years.

Once you have a few examples of a problem, stop tracing and start looking at the data. Keep in mind that you don't really know what you are looking for, so it is better to have several examples instead of just one, and it is better to have some examples of normal behavior to compare against.

In all cases, start by scribbling down for yourself what you expect a trace to look like—which events, how frequently, and in what order. This makes it much easier to spot trace portions that differ from your expectations, and there is always learning in that difference.

With how much overhead? For live datacenter work, CPU or memory tracing overhead of more than 1% is rarely acceptable. For offline work, much larger overhead, even up to a factor of 20 times slower (2000% overhead) can be acceptable. Somewhere beyond a 20x slowdown, timing-dependent workloads or network protocols or operating systems may start breaking.

12.4   Example: Early Program Counter Trace

An early instruction counter trace came from an IBM 7010 Operating System Timing Report in 1964 [Friedenberg 1964]. The goal was to understand the performance of the manufacturer-supplied sort program.

The mystery. The IBM-supplied system sort routine ran more slowly than expected, but no one was sure why. A group of engineers built one-of-a-kind external hardware to record the program counter (PC) of a running machine.

Here are the answers to our three tracing questions:

1. **What?** Every program counter value PC, quantized into buckets of 100 characters (bytes in today's terminology).

2. **How long?** Five seconds, quantized into buckets of 20 msec.

3. **Overhead?** Zero. External hardware was attached to the PC address bus where it fetched instruction characters from main memory.

It appears that the trace entry size could have been just one bit, in an array of 250 by 250 bits (or maybe 256x256), with any program counter reference setting the corresponding bit for its 100-character instruction address bucket and the current 20 msec time bucket. These ~64K bits would have fit in 8K bytes (which was more than the main memory of the base model of the IBM 1401-1410-7010 computer line). The external hardware was possibly something like a 2 foot by 2 foot by 6 foot external rack with its own core memory stack(s). These numbers are all speculation on my part; a more likely implementation recorded more information, and the visible bucketing was done during postprocessing. Even with such minimal hardware by today's standards, the authors were able to observe and understand the dynamics of some important early software, leading to significant performance improvements.

In the Figure 12.1 diagrams, the instruction counter address is on the y-axis, running from 0 to 25,000 six-bit characters, and time is on the x-axis, running from 0.0 to 5.0 seconds. The trace is of the startup of the 7010 `sort` program. External hardware recorded the time and instruction-fetch addresses, which were subsequently displayed on a cathode ray tube (CRT), photographed, and eventually printed in the report. I scanned a paper copy of that report. The net result is the blurry image in Figures 12.1a and 12.1b, for which I reconstructed and re-typeset the axis labels.

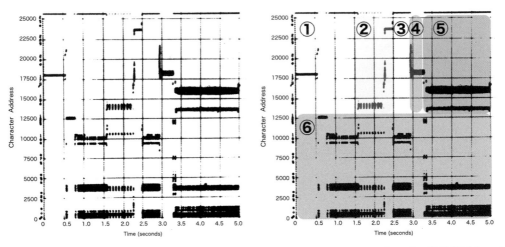

Figures 12.1a and 12.1b   **CRT output: trace of program counter vs. time for IBM 7010 sort routine startup**

The dynamics. Figure 12.1a gives the raw trace output. Figure 12.1b shows the activity parsed into major computation pieces, based on the description in the original report. The lower addresses from 0 to 12,599 contain the Resident Monitor, a rudimentary operating system that fit in 12.3KB. This is the bottom pink rectangle ⑥. The user-code sort program is in the upper addresses. The upper white area ① from 0.0 to 1.5 seconds is the Monitor load routine bootstrapping itself into memory, starting with a loop around address 18000 that loads the low memory region from disk or tape (I don't know which) and then branches to it about half a second in. During the time between 0.75 and 1.5 seconds the monitor loads the first part of the sort program into high memory and then branches to it. The sort program's yellow-rectangle ② Assignment routine runs from 1.5 to 2.5 seconds, reading control cards [Wikipedia 2021u , IBM 1959] describing the sort fields. After Assignment, during the white time ③ from 2.5 to 2.9 seconds, just the Monitor runs overlaying the high-memory Assignment code with the real sorting code.

Then the green ④ Initialize phase of the sort runs from 2.9 to 3.2 seconds, and finally the blue ⑤ Open and Get routines run to fill the Record Storage Area with the first few records to be sorted. In this blue region from 3.2 seconds on, the user-code comparison routine at 15,800 is the upper black band, and the user-code input routine at 13,700 is the lower black band. The input routine draws heavily on the Monitor's I/O routines near the bottom right of the diagram.

Looking again at the yellow region, you can see nine blips of user code starting at 1.5 seconds near address 13,700. It is reading 9 control cards, with each of these reads using operating system code at 10,500 and two lower ranges of addresses. A little under seven read-card blips occur in the first half-second, so 13–14 cards per second or 780–840 cards per minute. This trace timing exactly matches the card reader's rated speed of 800 cards per minute. Had the CPU code been a bit slower it would have missed a card-reader mechanical rotation point, and the rate would have dropped to 400 cards per minute, with the blips spread out accordingly. So this part of the picture confirms that the code was driving the card reader at full speed.

The mystery resolved. The performance group discovered from traces like this that the disk sort was losing a revolution at every full-track write because the CPU was not fast enough to get the next write out to the disk before it passed the beginning of the next track. This slowed the sort by a factor of two. They suggested writing less than a full track to gain some inter-track time and also suggested overlapping reading the next group of records to sort while sorting the current group. Such double-buffering was likely worth another factor of two in performance, for an overall factor of four performance improvement. Such was the state of the art in 1964.

This technical report is the earliest example I have encountered of performance engineers using real instruction traces to find root causes for slow performance.

12.5   Example: Per-Function Counts and Time

A programmer has a performance problem that suggests some functions in a large code base are taking too much time for each call or that there are unexpectedly large numbers of calls to some functions. A standard low-resolution sampling PC profile is fairly flat and by its nature is unable to provide estimates of call counts.

The programmer decides that he needs to observe a trace of the exact calls and elapsed time spent in every function in this large collection of C++ code. Observing for 5 minutes is sufficient, and a 1% CPU overhead is desired. Thus, the answers to our three starting questions are:

1. **What?** Exact call counts and total elapsed time spent in every function

2. **How long?** Every call, for 5 minutes

3. **Overhead?** 1% CPU time (goal)

How would you design the observation tool?

We will approach a possible design in two steps, first just counting calls and time in each function without keeping a time-sequenced trace and then in the following section expanding the design to do a full trace.

Counting. Assume that we have a way of instrumenting the code, perhaps though source-code rewriting, through compiler code insertion, or though binary code rewriting in the executable. An instrumented function looks something like this:

```
int foo(int x, const char* y) {
  INSTRUMENTED_ENTER();
   ... code that manipulates x and y and sets a return value
  INSTRUMENTED_EXIT();
  return retval;
}
```

where we want `INSTRUMENTED_ENTER()` to read the cycle counter or some other high-frequency consistent time base, and we want `INSTRUMENTED_EXIT()` to read again, subtract, add the difference to some running total time for that function, and increment the number of calls for that function. Assume that the time and call count are stored in a big array of 50,000 pairs for 50,000 different functions, with the subscript used for each a constant created by the code instrumentation process.

Back of the envelope. The performance of the observation design depends entirely on "How frequently" there is a call. If there is a call every 100 msec, any sort of reasonable design will have less than 1% overhead. On the other hand, if there is a call every 100 nsec, no design will deliver 1% (i.e., 1 nsec per call) overhead. Let us estimate how frequently there could be a call, assuming we are looking at some large datacenter code.

First estimate. We know from previous chapters that datacenter code does about 200K system calls or returns per second (per CPU core), or about one system call/return pair every 10 usec. These system calls are triggered by user-mode code that typically involves a few levels of function calls to get from some processing code to a system call. Order of magnitude, we might be looking at about three function calls per 10 usec, or about one every 3.3 usec. For a 3 GHz CPU executing about 1 instruction per cycle, that is about one function call per 10,000 cycles. To meet our 1% overhead goal, that gives us a budget of 100 cycles per function call for recording an observation.

The instrumentation code inserted into each function looks something like this, where each line is 1–3 instructions, for a total of about 10 instructions:

```
INSTRUMENTED_ENTER():
  temp = __rdtsc()

INSTRUMENTED_EXIT():
  temp = __rdtsc() - temp
  array[12345].time += temp
  array[12345].calls += 1
```

If our budget is 100 cycles of CPU overhead per function call, these 10 instructions should easily fit, right? Maybe not. How fast is the `rdtsc` instruction when doing many of them back to back? A little program like this, doing 100M `rdtsc` instructions,

```
gettimeofday()
for (int i = 0; i < 10000000; ++i) {
  sum += __rdtsc();
  sum += __rdtsc();
  sum += __rdtsc();
  sum += __rdtsc();
  sum += __rdtsc();
  sum += __rdtsc();
  sum += __rdtsc();
  sum += __rdtsc();
  sum +- __rdtsc();
  sum += __rdtsc();
}
gettimeofday(), subtract, divide, print
```

reveals that `__rdtsc()` takes about 6.5 nsec at each use on one of our sample servers, or about 20 cycles at 3GHz. Our 10 instrumentation instructions then will take about 50 cycles, not 10 cycles. This is within our budget, but not by a lot.

> For performance instrumentation, the slow `rdtsc` is a disaster. In contrast, the Cray-1 in 1975 had a one-cycle `rdtsc` instruction, as did the DEC Alpha starting in 1992. Current ARM64 implementations also have faster 2–10 cycle reads of a time counter.

There is another potential source of observation overhead to consider. How about cache misses in the counter array? If most the accesses to array[12345] take a cache miss to main memory, figure another 100 cycles each time. If they miss to L3 or L2 cache, figure another 40 or 10 cycles, respectively. If most of our function calls occur in loops, we can estimate that almost all accesses to array[12345] will be L1 cache hits, so not much of a problem. That turns out to be the case in real datacenter code, even though theoretically every call could be to a different function and the entire array of 50,000 entries of 2 x 8 bytes each would only fit into an L3 cache, with about 40-cycle access time. Here, we will estimate that cache misses do not add to the observation overhead, but will keep an eye out for evidence to the contrary.

Second estimate. What happens if there is a completely different function-call pattern with lots of calls to trivial very short (5–10 instruction) functions taking perhaps 10 cycles each to execute? Remember, we have a performance problem that suggests "some functions … are taking too much time for each call or … large numbers of calls to some functions." Much C++ code lends itself to writing lots of short functions and invoking many layers of such short routines. If we instrument all the trivial functions and they are heavily used, we would add a 50-cycle overhead to each 10-cycle function, distorting the system under test. What can we do?

Reducing overhead. One viable strategy is to revisit your answers to the three starting questions, perhaps relaxing the constraints. Another is to look for some more-easily measured information that is a proxy for the desired information. Another strategy is to refine the measurement to reduce its overhead. We will look at this last strategy first.

It might be possible to run an appropriate load against the software while it suffers high observation overhead, perhaps by cloning the load presented to a live datacenter version of the code, sending the same requests to a parallel version running the instrumented code but not replying to live users. From the high-overhead data gathered, identify functions that have lots of calls but accumulate very little total time (after subtracting the distorting observation overhead). Then re-instrument the code *without instrumenting* these functions. Or perhaps instrument them just to count calls but not count time using the slow `rdtsc` instruction. This partially instrumented version might have low enough overhead to meet the original constraints. By continuing to count calls, you can confirm that the partially instrumented code has about the same call behavior when run live as the fully instrumented version did when run in parallel.

For the proxy-measurement strategy, you could arrange to execute the instrumentation code, or at least the slow `rdtsc` part, less often. One approach is to do something like running a global counter and use its low few bits to execute the instrumentation code only one time out of 8 or some other convenient frequency, e.g.,

```
if ((counter++ & 7) == 0) {
  instrumentation
}
```

This trades a little observation precision for lower overhead. Keep in mind that a single global counter is a disaster if multiple threads are using it simultaneously from multiple CPU cores, thus inducing cache thrashing on the cache line containing the counter. If that could be a problem, use per-CPU counters, or perhaps use the per-function call counters themselves to condition running the slow instrumentation code, e.g.,

```
array[12345].calls++;
if ((array[12345].calls & 7) == 0) {
  slower rdtsc instrumentation, 1 time out of 8
}
```

Yet another approach is to try to get any short high-frequency functions inlined (which is generally a good idea anyway) and not instrument them. This adds their time to the containing function, which can distort the results if the inlined functions do in fact take a lot of time. But this design at least guarantees no loss of total time.

In the next section, we will find excessive observation overhead and use the third method of refining the measurement to reduce its overhead by identifying and then minimally instrumenting the trivial functions.

Counting function calls and time gives a higher-resolution picture of execution time than a sampling profile, but it does not have any time sequencing. It gives an average picture but does not separate unusual slow transactions from frequent normal ones. For this you need traces, described next.

12.6   Case Study: Per-Function Trace of Gmail

A per-function trace facility explained one performance mystery in Gmail, circa 2006, separating unusual slow transactions from normal ones. The problem occurred when delivering a number of messages during an offline test. The performance mystery was an unexpected 10x variation in the per-message response time, with an average transaction latency of about 50 msec, but a 99th percentile transaction latency of over 500 msec.

A CPU-time *profile* of Gmail running the offline test showed the per-function distribution of Figure 12.2a.

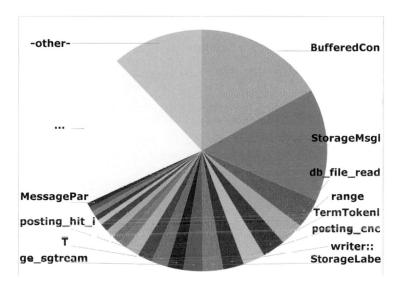

Figure 12.2a   **CPU-time function profile of early Gmail offline test**

As we have discussed, profiles average together normal and unusual transactions, making it impossible to see what is different about the unusual ones. *Profiling is the wrong tool for understanding variation.* To emphasize this, Figure 12.2b highlights three of the functions we discover through tracing that are *called only* in slow transactions.

The profile has another major flaw—it covers only CPU *execution* time, not *wait* time. The sum of these two is elapsed time (we are dealing with only one thread here). Figure 12.2c shows the true profile of *elapsed* time, including the two dominant routines on the right that are missing from Figures 12.2a and 12.2b. They wait for critical section locks (`semaphore::`) and wait for new work (`SelectServer`), accounting for over half of the elapsed time. In particular, waiting for locks takes over 40% of the elapsed time.

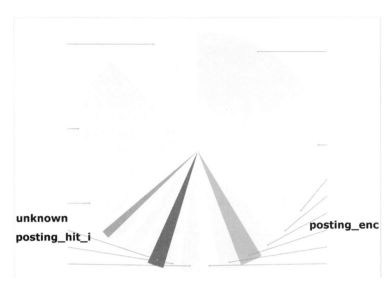

Figure 12.2b   **Three functions used only in slow transactions**

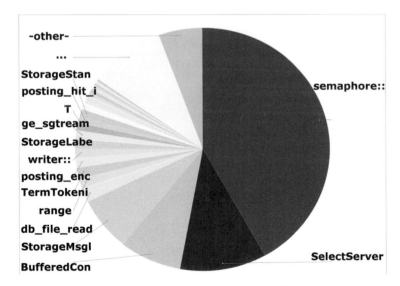

Figure 12.2c   **Elapsed-time function profile of early Gmail offline test, including the two routines that wait instead of using CPU time**

A Google internally built function trace tool called Thoth [Sites 2004] instrumented every dynamic function call to record its entry and exit times, the CPU it executed on, and the thread ID. Writing the trace entries across multiple CPUs was slower than just counting, as earlier, and the information recorded was a little more elaborate. In particular, capturing the thread ID initially involved a system call to `getpid()` at every function entry. This was much too slow even for offline testing. A useful proxy turns out to be the value of the stack pointer register truncated to a multiple of 4KB, since every thread executes with a different run-time stack of at least one page. Thus, a little side table of <SP-value, thread-ID> pairs avoided doing the slow `getpid()` call almost all the time.

Before we go into the specifics of what the trace revealed about Gmail, we will look a bit more carefully at some tracing implementation details.

Controlling trace size/overhead. As usual, the size of trace records dictates how practical it is to gather large traces, and our goal is five minutes of function calls totaling millions of entries. To keep the entry size small, we pack 4–5 bytes of timestamp, plus routine number, entry/exit bit, and perhaps the CPU number into an 8-byte aligned trace entry. We arrange that each CPU or thread writes its trace to a separate buffer to avoid cache thrashing. This mechanism is a little more elaborate than just counting, but once you have it in place, you can use it for many different software systems.

For trace data generated at the rate of millions of events per second, we can record it only in a large RAM trace buffer. If the trace entries are eight bytes and the trace has 100M entries, then 800MB of RAM will be needed to record the trace, or it will need to be written to a file in real time without creating much interference. One way to end up with 100M entries is to create an entry every microsecond for 100 seconds, short of our duration goal. We might not know ahead of time how many entries to expect per second, but the very first one-second run will tell us. A buffer of 800MB might well be more than a target 1% memory-space overhead, so it is likely that trace-buffer space is an issue. How could we reduce it?

We don't have a tight upper bound on how long may elapse between enter/exit trace entries, so will want to err on the side of too many bits of timestamp. With at least two bytes to hold 30,000 different function numbers, this makes a four-byte-per-entry design unlikely. So we are stuck at eight bytes. Perhaps we can reduce the number of entries recorded instead.

A starting place is to decide the minimum timestamp resolution we need. We are mostly interested in the sequence of function calls and in any large time consumers. For this purpose, a time resolution of a single cycle is overkill. A perfectly adequate resolution might be increments of 256 CPU cycles, about 80 nsec at 3 GHz. At this resolution all non-trivial functions will see multiple timestamp increments. But the problematic high-frequency 10-instruction functions will often see increments of zero with occasional increments of one. We can take advantage of this. One way to shorten the trace is to *delete* all adjacent entry pairs of the form

```
call to function 12345, time T1
return from function 12345, time T2
```

where the two timestamps T1 and T2 are *equal*. We lose no total time when deleting a zero-elapsed-time pair, preserving our nothing-missing design tenet for elapsed time. But we lose some call counts for those fast functions. If this looks like a problem (it might well not matter in the overall scheme of understanding a performance mystery), a little engineering thought might suggest keeping a side table of a few pairs <function number, count>, incrementing the count whenever we delete an enter/exit pair, and putting the old extra counts into the trace as a distinct trace item whenever a new pair replaces an old one in the side table. We then lose no call counts but just slightly delay recording them, completely preserving our nothing-missing design tenet.

The Gmail function trace. In contrast to the Figure 12.2 profile, Figure 12.3 is one page of a multi-page full function trace diagram. It shows the exact time sequencing, with 500 msec across the page. Each new mail message starts a new line, making understanding of the dynamics much easier than in a run-together presentation. The large red, yellow, green, and cyan (light blue) grouping backgrounds delimit four major pieces of the processing code, with many function calls within each piece. Most function executions are too small to distinguish well at this resolution, but you can see the long-duration ones and see the overall patterns. The original had small numbers marking some function durations, corresponding to the numbers in a legend, but these are deleted here for clarity. Most messages take 50–60 msec, but four near the bottom take much longer (the third-to-last takes over 500 msec so covers two lines).

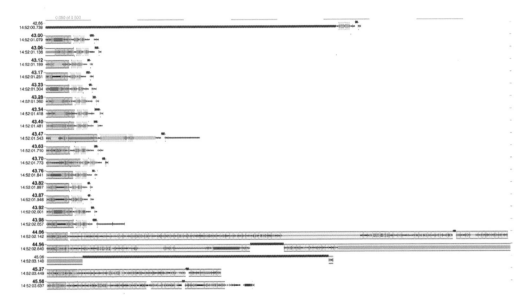

Figure 12.3   **Function call/return elapsed-time trace of very early Gmail code uploading messages. Each message starts on a new line. Half a second across the page.**

The not-shown legend has the individual functions sorted into decreasing order of total time and numbered, with the first function `semaphore::dec` taking 42% of all the elapsed time in the entire trace, only part of which is shown in Figure 12.3. Two numbers in the legend for each function give total execution time and total number of calls. Suffixes indicate routines with high and very high call counts but very little accumulated time, i.e., exactly those for which the measurement shortcuts we discussed earlier would be appropriate.

The prominent red lines in Figure 12.3 are the function that waits for new work, `SelectServer::RegularPoll`, i.e., waiting for the next transaction. It does not loop executing CPU instructions; it blocks and yields its CPU core for other programs. You see it near the end of each transaction unless a subsequent transaction has already arrived. Timestamping and tracing function entry/exit allows us to see functions that wait, not just CPU-bound ones. This is the advantage of tools that account for *all* elapsed wall-clock time instead of just active CPU execution time. Only tracing is good enough to observe this.

Show your overhead. The complete tracing display also gives the back-calculated tracing overhead of 31.4%, leaving 68.6% of the time for the execution that would have occurred in the absence of tracing. The ratio 100/68.6 gives the slowdown due to tracing overhead, nearly 1.5x slower than a normal run. This is slow because of the previously discussed trace-writing, thread ID, CPU ID, and `rdtsc` overheads. Turning off the tracing for just the first five functions marked as high call counts with tiny time (i.e., starting with the 2M calls of `TermTokenizer::get`) would noticeably reduce the tracing overhead.

We can estimate the total trace time from the first few legend entries—`semaphore::` takes 15.0 seconds, which is about 42% of the total time; `SelectServer` takes 3.91 seconds, which is about 10% of the total time. Thus, the total trace time is about 38–40 seconds. Roughly summing up the larger call counts (including `-other-`) in the legend gives 25–30M calls. This trace therefore has about 30M/40sec = 750K calls per second or a call every 1.3 usec. At 3GHz, this is about 4,000 cycles, so our 1% budget should be about 40 cycles, but the actual function trace overhead is closer to 1,200 cycles. This is not great but is OK for an offline test, especially since it gives enough information to determine which trivial functions not to trace when running in a live datacenter environment.

More nothing-missing. The last legend entry is the all-important `-other-` category, taking 1.97 seconds and 10M calls. This nothing-missing presentation of the data allows us to see that the tracing of the low-accumulated-time functions accounts for 5% of the total time, but more importantly has a high number of calls and hence contributes materially to the tracing overhead.

Mystery resolved. Returning to the red, yellow, green, and cyan backgrounds that show four major pieces of the processing code, we can now easily see what is different about the four slow transactions at the bottom—they all spend a lot of extra time in the cyan-background code, which is all inside the top-level function named `layered_store::merge_run`. This is the root cause of the performance mystery.

Until I printed this page, the unexpected dynamic for this datacenter software was unknown. The incoming-mail code sometimes called `merge_run` to index all the words in the just-arrived mail messages and merge them into the overall text index for each given user—so that the just-arrived mail text would be searchable. The performance bug was doing this indexing and merging on the main execution thread, *blocking* all other incoming-mail processing until the index update finished. Moving the index/merge code to a separate thread reduced the 99th percentile transaction latency quite substantially. A simple fix once you can see the true software dynamics.

12.7 Summary

This chapter defined and motivated our interest in low-overhead tracing tools, in contrast to simpler counting and profiling tools. We covered the advantages and disadvantages of tracing, especially the advantage of a "nothing missing" design, and discussed techniques to keep the overhead of such tools small enough to be practical in live datacenters.

We looked at several trade-offs among what level of detail to trace, for how long and with what overhead. We looked at two extended tracing examples, one of PC values from 1964 and one of function calls from about 40 years later. We contrasted the Gmail function call trace with the corresponding function profile, highlighting the inability of the simpler profile tool to reveal the root cause of long-latency transactions and emphasizing how easily the trace revealed the problem.

To be useful, tracing requires careful engineering, with attention to data structures, CPU time, and trace entry size. We discussed a few techniques for reducing trace space and time overhead.

Turning trace data into understanding of software dynamics requires thoughtfully designed presentations of the data—pictures that reveal the unexpected behavior(s) and their root causes. For the main picture in each example, we explored the myriad information available upon close examination.

In the next chapter we will explore some of the underlying design principles for good observation tools.

Chapter 13

Observation Tool Design Principles

In the first part of this book, we learned how to do careful measurements of four of the five fundamental shared computer resources: CPU, memory, disk/SSD, and network (we defer discussion of critical section locks to Chapter 27). We learned about displaying measurement results in useful ways. We observed variations in transaction latency in Chapter 7, and unexpected software dynamics in Chapters 5 and 7. We touched on transaction delays on one machine stemming from waiting on RPCs to other machines, from interference by other programs and the operating system on the one machine, and from unreasonable offered loads.

In this second part, we have looked at tools for observing software dynamics —logs, dashboards, other existing tools, and traces. This chapter discusses design principles for good observation tools.

In trying to understand performance problems, the starting place for choosing or designing observation tools is to answer three fundamental questions:

- What do you need to observe?
- How frequently and for how long?
- With how much overhead?

13.1 What to Observe

The question "What do I need to observe?" is not the same as the question "What can my current tools observe?" The first is aspirational—something that one hopes or intends to accomplish, while the second is more based on inertia. Knowing where you want to go is the basis for discussing how to get there. Similarly, knowing what you need to observe is the basis for discussing how to observe that or how to observe something similar if direct observation is not possible within other constraints.

For example, if a particular transaction is repeatedly slow, we would like to observe where all the time goes during that transaction, with emphasis on the word "all"—observing some of the time and being blind to the rest is no good if the slowness is in the missing part. But if unpredictably only some transactions are slow and we therefore don't know ahead of time which ones will be slow, we need to observe much more. We need to observe where all the time goes during many transactions, and we need to observe any surrounding transactions or programs or shared-resource users (CPU, memory, disk, network, critical section) whose interference could result in a slow transaction. This is the motivation for our discussions of logging and tracing in the previous chapters.

If there is an offered-load agreement (or even if there is not), we need to be able to observe the offered load and fix the clients or increase the servers if the load is too high. If there is an agreement or target maximum load, it is important to check against that at runtime and clearly call out the unreasonable load if it is too high. This can save a lot of time tracking down non-existent performance problems on a server when the real problem is on clients offering too much load.

13.2   How Frequently and For How Long?

Armed with an explicit statement of what we need to observe, the next question is how frequently and for how long we need to make those observations in order to understand a performance problem. For example, if we have a problem that appears related to bursts of excessive disk activity, looking at total disk reads and writes over five-minute intervals won't tell us much about three-second bursts of disk saturation. A one-second or shorter interval would be more appropriate in that case. My friend Michael once passed on an observation about dealing with a bureaucrat unable to give a reasonable answer to a question: "You are dealing with an automaton. If the automaton is unable to answer your question, you must deal with a different automaton." If the only tool you have just observes five-minute intervals, then you need a different tool.

For understanding unpredictable performance issues, there is also the question of how long to do a continuous observation in order to have an excellent chance of observing several bad cases. If unexpectedly slow transactions happen several times per second during the busiest hour of the day and each transaction (including the slow ones) takes under a second, then a several-second observation window may be sufficient. If unexpectedly slow transactions happen only every 10 seconds or so and the slow ones take 8–12 seconds each instead of half a second, then we need an observation window of 30–60 seconds to catch several such slow transactions in their entirety.

If you need to observe all memory allocations and deallocations to find some extremely subtle memory leak and the leak is only noticeable after several hours of running, then you need to observe for several hours.

In a different context, if it appears that code execution violates a software lock due to an *extremely* rare hardware glitch that fails to enforce a memory-barrier instruction, then it may be necessary to build a small program that just does the corresponding locking and memory barrier sequence as often as possible, and then observe that program for 24 hours or more until the glitch occurs. Only then is a chip manufacturer likely to buy back the broken chips of a particular CPU stepping ID and replace them with fixed ones. In the meantime, you can test software workarounds that might make the sequence reliable, using the same standalone program testing over 24 hours or more. This is an old real-world example circa 2005, but the issue is now back [Dixit 2021, Hochschild 2021].

13.3   How Much Overhead?

Once we know what to observe, how frequently, and for how long, we must deal with the question of how much overhead we are willing to afford for the observations. This overhead has two components—the extra CPU time used, and the extra storage space used.

At one extreme, consider a CPU chip designer who wants a long stream (trace) of actual memory addresses from complex running code in order to design a next-generation cache subsystem [Borg 1990]. If she gathers this via software simulation of a complex instruction set, the slow-down might be 1000x (and likely tracing only user-mode accesses in simple C benchmarks). If she gathers this via code rewriting or via microcode, the slowdown might be 20x, which is still much too slow for running any live datacenter load. If she gathers it via a CPU chip with hardware memory-address trace support, the slowdown might be 2x, and it might be feasible to gather real traces for a few seconds at a time during slow datacenter hours.

How big is such a trace? A main memory system with 20 GB/sec bandwidth and 64-byte cache lines might service about 300M cache-line transfers per second, recording 40-64 bits (5-8 bytes) of address for each one, plus a few bits to record read vs. write, data vs. instruction, speculative vs. architecturally required, prefetch vs. demand access, etc. The corresponding trace will produce about 300M * 8 bytes = 2.4 GB/sec.

At the other extreme, consider a hard-disk designer who wants a long stream (trace) of actual seek addresses from complex running code in order to design a next-generation disk drive. With seek times that average about 10 msec, only 100 seeks per second can happen. He can create this trace with essentially zero overhead, recording at most 8 bytes every 10 msec. The corresponding trace will produce about 100 * 8 bytes = 800 bytes/second.

For observing time-constrained software dynamics, a good rule of thumb is to budget no more than 1% CPU and memory overhead. Rarely will this be too much of a burden, even for observing the most complex live software during its busiest time. Sometimes a higher CPU overhead of 2–10% might be tolerable, but it is rare that an observation tool with 20% CPU overhead would be acceptable. The problem with a 20% CPU overhead is that it can easily cause *exponential* increases in transaction delay, completely distorting the system under test while also ruining the customer experience. Avoid this highly non-linear slowdown.

Some systems can easily handle a 20% memory overhead because they are running on computers with substantial excess RAM. Others, though, may be closer to the edge and would start encountering out-of-memory operating system errors if you effectively remove 20% of the RAM. The same consideration applies to disk space that is nearly 100% utilized before you attempt to use 20% of it to record observations. In a datacenter, generating almost a megabyte of trace data per CPU per second might be manageable with 1% overhead, while in dedicated controller environment much less trace data might be acceptable.

Overall, we will stick with the 1% overhead rule of thumb and see what the consequences are.

13.4   Design Consequences

The answers to our three questions determine much of the design of observation tools. If the observations you need are simple accounting information, counters, profiles, or other sampled values, then the CPU and space overhead of gathering them will usually be low and do not impose any design constraints.

In contrast, if the observations you need are some form of logging or tracing, do the back-of-the-envelope calculation of how much CPU time and memory space/bandwidth they take and compare that to your overhead time and space budget. Being over budget must force a simpler, faster observation design.

Don't make the mistake of first building some observation software and then working backwards to measure its overhead. Start with the budget and work forward; then measure to confirm that your design meets the budget.

13.5   Case Study: Histogram Buckets

A programmer wants to create and observe a histogram of response times for several services. He expects response times of 10 usec for the fastest services, but 1 second for the slowest ones, a 100K:1 ratio. The programmer would like to be able to measure a 1% improvement in average response time across several proposed software changes. He reasons that with a 100,000:1 range of response times, logarithmic-width buckets are better than linear-width ones. To be able to see a 1% change in (average) response time across hundreds of thousands of transactions, he assumes the bucket sizes should increase by no more than 1%. He quickly calculates that 70 buckets each 1.01 times larger than the previous will cover a range of 2:1 ($1.01^{**}70 = 2.00676$), so with an overall range of 100K or about $2^{**}17$, he will need about 70 * 17 buckets = 1190 buckets to cover the full range with 1% geometric increments in bucket size. Call it 1,200 buckets.

For each response-time measurement, he takes its logarithm and divides by the appropriate scaling factor to give a bucket subscript 0..1199 and then updates that bucket. As the design grows, he adds to the count field several more fields per bucket recording such context as CPU load average, bytes read and written on disk, bytes received and transmitted on the network, and total memory allocated. To handle multiple kinds of transaction requests within each service, he implements arrays of multiple histograms, each with 1200 buckets.

To be able to observe the histograms, he adds an interface to the existing web-served dashboard, displaying for any one histogram all 1,200 bucket values (or at least the non-zero ones) as a list of numbers and horizontal lines whose length is proportional to the value. To allow a person to watch for changes in behavior in real time, he adds a dashboard function to allow updating and re-displaying the histogram as fast as every second. Finally, to be sure that each displayed histogram is self-consistent, he locks all the histogram data while extracting and displaying its values, blocking any updates that would change the counts.

His users are happy for a while, but they do notice that the observed software services are running more slowly than expected. To understand this, they set up continuous histogram refreshing every few seconds. Multiple users do this, refreshing the histogram on each of their desktop computers. The software services seem to run even more slowly, but the histograms do not explain why.

Do you see any problems here? Maybe a few...

- If you only want the average, just count the total time and number of transactions and divide; you do not need a histogram.

- A 1% change in response time may be the same order of magnitude as the noise in minute-to-minute measurement variation, so would likely be undetectable. The measurement premise is suspect.

- 1,200 buckets are overkill. Using the tiny design of just 20 power-of-two buckets allows us to cover a million-to-one range. If we count latency measurements for a large number (100K+) of transactions, that would mean more than 5,000 counts in some buckets. If the latency times are at all reasonably dispersed, easily 50 of the measurements in each such bucket would move to a lower bucket if the code became 1% faster. This movement is enough to detect a 1% change, using 20 buckets instead of 1200.

- Calculating the bucket index slowly via a real logarithm calculation is bad. Better to use leading-zero-count (or 6 tests against masks) to get the right power of two within a 64-bit latency number and hence quickly have floor(log base 2(latency)) and then do a table lookup on the next few bits of the value to get any needed fractional log base 2. It is better (faster) to multiply, not divide, this by a scale factor to get the right subscript.

- Showing all 1200 values with proportional lines in HTML is bulky and requires non-trivial processing time for presenting the data.

- Allowing the design to grow too much will put it outside its original design target for CPU or memory overhead. At that point, the programmer should revisit the entire design. This revisiting is rarely done in practice.

- Allowing arrays of multiple histograms increases the processing time by a multiplicative factor, which can also put the use outside its original design target.

- Automatically updating dashboard data every few seconds increases the processing time by another multiplicative factor.

- Multiple users increase the processing time by a third multiplicative factor.

- Locking the histogram while extracting *and displaying* values is a deal-breaker; such designs are much too intrusive, blocking real work just for the sake of too-bulky and too-precise observation. Instead, just export the data with no lock and allow a little inconsistency. Or (as we will see in Chapter 27) lock, quickly copy the data, unlock, and then more slowly format the data without blocking other processing.

- Failure to record and display the overhead of the observation tool itself hides the cumulative effect of all the previous problems.

Just a few design problems to deal with. I have seen all of these in real production code, usually all at once in a single subsystem. Observation tools need careful and *modest* design.

> One performance mystery I encountered at Google involved code to lock a large sta-tistics data structure, malloc a text buffer in memory, read and format the statistics into the buffer, free the buffer, and then unlock the lock. The formatted buffer was never used! But the code locked out multiple threads and delayed real work quite substantially under heavy load. This was some debug code that had been left in by mistake, but since it did not display anything, no one noticed until we traced the dynamic locking behavior. One-line fix to do the debug test first.

13.6 Designing Data Display

Whenever possible, display measured data in both numeric and graphical forms. Unexpected patterns are much easier to spot in a well-chosen graphical display [Tufte 2001], but the under-lying numeric values are better for comparison to normal or previously observed values. For performance mysteries, *the important information is in the patterns*.

For dashboards, the goal is to display the overall health of some service or server. Summary values and a little time history are sufficient.

For finding root causes of performance mysteries, the goal is different. In this context, we want to show as much measured data as possible in a concise way, so that any unusual patterns reveal themselves. I often try to put a million data points on a single page of paper or a single high-resolution display.

For example, the heat map of Figure 9.9 in Chapter 9 is one hour of a single-page display that shows 24 hours of disk activity on 13 disks on a single slow server. The observed data came from a 24-hour log giving among other things the transaction latency for over 10 million disk read transactions (the buffered writes presented no performance problem). To represent a full hour of disk activity across one line, I chose a 10-second time interval and calculated the 99th percentile transaction latency in milliseconds for each interval. I then used colors running from blue to red to show these latency values, with white to explicitly show zero activity. The effect is to show normal disk activity in blue and very slow reads in red, with a few gradations in between. There are 360 measurements across a line, and I stacked lines for the 13 disks together in 1/3 of an inch. Twenty-four of these groups fit comfortably on a page, one for each hour. There are 360 * 13 * 24 = 112,320 total measurements on the page, usefully summarizing 10M observations.

This presentation immediately revealed multi-minute clusters of long-latency disk reads across all 13 disks at once, with a cluster every few hours. Although the data had been available for months, no one had drawn a revealing picture. The correlation across all disks removed indi-vidual disk behavior as a root cause, leaving the common CPU and network links as candidates. Cluster widths of many minutes instead of seconds removed simple offered-load bursts as a root cause. From this picture, we quickly identified the problem as CPU throttling. After an easy fix, long delays disappeared from multiple services across the company, including an ad-auction service that failed to produce corporate income whenever it ran late. The problem had been going on for three years.

Several techniques are important for building high-density displays of data. First and foremost, label the data and axes, carefully including units—counts, thousands, millions, usec, msec, seconds, etc. Include date and time of the original observations, so when you look back six months or six years later you know what you are looking at. Color is helpful for showing an additional dimension of the data. Line slopes convey rate information quickly to the human eye. Notches convey subinterval times while taking hardly any display space. Curved arcs can be useful to convey dependencies or reasons for waiting; curves stand out in otherwise-rectangular presentations. Sorting the data in multiple ways is particularly powerful; it can reveal correlations along one dimension that are not noticeable along other dimensions. Showing multiple transactions aligned by actual start time reveals behavior related to their juxtaposition. Showing transactions with all the start times aligned at zero reveals differences between normal ones and slow ones.

In searching for root causes, it is helpful to have (offline) interactive displays of large amounts of measured data. Interactive displays can allow a wide time-interval overview and then panning and zooming to look in detail at small time intervals that stand out as unusual. Dragging a cursor over time intervals or between events can give quick measurements of elapsed time or transferred bytes or bandwidth or other useful quantities. Be careful to engineer your display code so that it runs quickly enough to be useful even with millions of measurements to present. Finally, to make it easy to present your findings to other people, design-in simple ways to mark individual events or transactions that are part of the explanation of a performance problem root cause.

13.7 Summary

- Either pre-measure the overhead of an observation tool and re-measure it whenever someone changes or "improves" the tool, or measure the overhead whenever it is running. In either case, display to users any non-trivial overhead so they can understand how much the observation tool is distorting the system under test.

- Do your back-of-the-envelope estimates: calculate how many bytes you can afford per observation based on bandwidth; calculate how many bytes you can afford per observation based on total size over time.

- Pick your time resolution deliberately. Time resolution affects range and bytes per entry, and hence trace size.

- Show the offered load, at least as number of offered transactions per second. Show bursts of offered load, at least as busiest second or millisecond, etc.

- Show error counts, including offered transactions that a service refuses due to overload or abuse.

- Show examples of normal and slow behavior.

- Look for effective ways to summarize and to group, compare, and contrast transactions.

- Use the *nothing missing* design principle, at least showing an "other" category.

- Remember that often the important information is in the patterns, not in individual measurements or numbers.

This chapter completes the introductory material of the book. In Part III we will design and build a complete Linux tracing system.

Part III

Kernel-User Trace

In Part I, we learned how to do careful measurements of the four fundamental shared computer hardware resources: CPU, memory, disk/SSD, and network. In Part II, we looked at existing tools and techniques for observing the behavior of time-constrained software.

Part III teaches the reader how to build the low-overhead KUtrace tool to record for any server what kernel or user code is executing on each CPU core every nanosecond—all programs, all operating system code, all interrupt handling, all idle loops, etc. Such a trace not only captures where all the execution time went in processing a transaction, but also captures all the reasons for *not* executing: what the transaction is waiting for while not executing. A total trace also captures *all possible* sources of interference between simultaneously executing programs on a given server. It shows the page faults, kernel threads, unrelated interrupts, machine-health programs, and everything else happening on a server that programmers tend not even to think about but that can contribute to long-tail latencies. The KUtrace design is thus incredibly powerful in capturing *why* a transaction is slow.

Part III also walks the reader through building post-processing software to turn raw traces into human-meaningful dynamic HTML pictures of all the CPU activity, with the ability to pan and zoom from seconds of activity to nanoseconds. This allows the reader to see and internalize the dynamics of interference and other slowdowns as they actually happened. By the end of this part, readers will be able to use kernel/user tracing to examine their own programs. Readers with modest operating-system build skills will be able to port the tool to other environments.

"For Heaven's sake, why don't you go outdoors and trace something?"

Chapter 14

KUtrace: Goals, Design, Implementation

KUtrace is a Linux-based software facility that captures and timestamps every transition between user-mode and kernel-mode execution—every system call and return, interrupt and return, trap and return, and context switch. The CPU overhead is under 0.5% when doing 200,000 events per second per CPU core, so it is about 10x faster than a tool such as `ftrace`. Recording is into a pre-reserved kernel trace buffer of several megabytes.

14.1 Overview

To achieve its speed, KUtrace records only 4 bytes per event—20 bits of timestamp and 12 bits of event number. In reality, *pairs* of events are recorded in 8-byte entries. Everything else to turn traces into meaningful insight is done via postprocessing, which turns transition events (edges) into a complete set of timespans (levels) for each CPU core, showing what that core was doing every nanosecond, with no time missing. In addition to all the kernel-user transition events, there are events to record *names* for each event number and for each newly encountered process ID (PID). Markers can be manually added to kernel- or user-mode code to further annotate traces.

A small user-mode library linked directly into a program or used via a standalone control program controls tracing. When tracing is stopped, the accumulated raw binary trace is written to a disk file. Postprocessing this file turns the timestamped kernel/user transition events into execution timespans on each CPU core. The eventual result of the postprocessing is a JSON file with one line per timespan. A final postprocessing step loads the JSON into an HTML/SVG wrapper that provides a user interface for displaying timelines for each CPU, as shown in Figure 14.1.

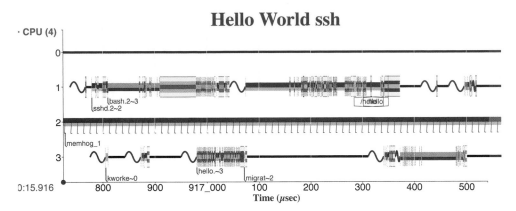

Figure 14.1   **Sample postprocessed trace on four CPU cores**

There are a few control buttons and a search box at the top of the HTML and then timelines for the CPU cores—in this picture, four cores and a trace timespan covering just a few hundred microseconds. Thin black lines are the idle job. Half-height multi-colored lines are user-mode execution, and full-height ones are kernel-mode execution. In the live HTML, you can pan and zoom the display to focus on any timespan of interest, click on individual timespans to show their names, and drag across multiple timespans to see their total elapsed time.

14.2   Goals

The goals of KUtrace are very simple:

- Show what each CPU core is doing every nanosecond, nothing missing
- With less than 1% overhead (CPU and memory) in time-constrained environments
- For 30–120 seconds at a time
- Including human-meaningful names

There are also several important *non-goals*:

- Not for debugging the kernel
- Not for debugging user programs
- Not for understanding simple reproducible single-program CPU performance
- Not for directly understanding interpreted languages
- Not for directly understanding dynamic memory usage
- Not for directly understanding virtual machine performance
- Not for directly understanding GPU performance

The choice of tracing transitions between kernel and user code is deliberate, the Goldilocks design. As we saw in Chapter 11, it is difficult to trace at a finer level of detail—such as function entry/exit, library routine entry/exit, or individual lines of source code—without incurring substantially larger tracing overhead. It is difficult to trace at a coarser level of detail and still observe the causes of interactions between programs or the interactions between threads of a single program. By tracing just transitions, we can account for every nanosecond of CPU time—nothing can be missing.

Tracing all the time spent in kernel code is the only way to understand whether that time itself is substantial, and capturing the time sequence of kernel events captures all the possible ways one process or external device can stop or restart another process. In traditional computer systems, protected kernel code mediates all of these interactions.

Tracing transitions between kernel and user code is thus both sufficiently fast and sufficiently useful, giving a broad-brush picture of everything happening inside a computer and its time-constrained software.

14.3   Design

As you would expect by now, the overhead goal entirely drives the design of KUtrace. At Google during the busiest hour of the day, we observed about 200,000 kernel/user transitions per second per CPU core. The 1% CPU overhead goal thus translates to 50 nsec per event, which is less than one cache-miss time to main memory. Thus, each trace entry must be less than one cache line in size. As we saw in Chapter 3, a common cache line size is 64 bytes. Because CPUs are slower at storing to unaligned addresses than to aligned ones, we want trace entries (or at least each of their fields if written separately) to be naturally aligned. As a practical matter, these constraints mean trace entries should be 4, 8, or 16 bytes each. The underlying design for KUtrace has 4-byte entries, but the final design has 8-byte entries that contain pairs of events 90–95% of the time.

At 200,000 events per second and 4 bytes per event, a trace records 800KB per second per CPU core. With 24 cores, this means almost 20 MB/second of recording bandwidth. To record at that rate for 120 seconds means about 2.4GB of trace buffer. For a datacenter server with 256GB of main memory, the trace buffer would happily just fit into our 1% memory-space overhead budget. For more modest processing on fewer cores and for only 30 seconds, a buffer of 20–40MB will be sufficient, again under 1% space overhead for a server with 4GB or more of main memory.

For some rare performance problems, it is helpful to be able to record continuously in flight-recorder mode (see Chapter 12), stopping and freezing the trace buffer when some software detects a likely instance of a problem. This technique captures 30–120 seconds of all the events leading up to the problem.

In all cases, a trace-controlling program starts and stops tracing and extracts the trace buffer, writing it to a disk file after tracing stops. The underlying control library can also be linked into arbitrary user C/C++ programs to make them self-tracing.

To give human-meaningful names to each execution interval, the trace design includes entries that give a name for each event: each system call, interrupt, fault, and user-mode process ID. To allow experiments in understanding occasional finer detail within kernel or user code, the trace design includes entries that mark a time instant by a name or a number. Calls to create these trace entries can be manually inserted in source code to record exactly when execution reaches the marked point.

There are two fundamental causes of long-tail transactions:

1. Processing that executes but *more slowly* than normal
2. Processing that ends up not executing but instead *waiting* for something

To allow observation of power-saving states and their associated clock slowdowns and subsequent restart time, the trace design includes entries to mark the CPU instructions that change the power state.

To allow observation of hardware interference between CPU cores, the trace design allows capturing at each kernel/user transition, not just the elapsed CPU cycle count, but also the number of instructions retired since the previous transition. This allows calculating for each microsecond-scale execution timespan the instructions executed per cycle (IPC). Doing so does not directly measure hardware interference for access to shared resources such as instruction execution units, caches, or main memory, but it allows substantial visibility to timespans that run unusually slowly compared to the same code running at other times. The IPC values thus give a slightly indirect indication of the most common execution slowdown mechanism: cache interference from some other thread or program (or the operating system itself). Sandhya Dwarkadas asked the original question that led to tracking IPC in KUtrace.

For a slow timespan on one CPU core, the only possible hardware interference comes from the processes executing on other CPU cores over the same timespan, or possibly executing on the one core just before that timespan. The IPC data per timespan thus reveals the existence of executing more slowly than normal and strongly suggests the underlying source of the interference that can create long-tail transactions.

To allow correlation of execution effort with user-mode RPC requests, the trace design includes entries that mark the RPCID that is being processed. These are inserted via an RPC library so that every request and response message is timestamped and recorded. The same entries can record all outbound RPCs, and thus allow observation of one RPC waiting for results from sub-RPCs. There are also trace entries to record hashes of filtered packets processed in the kernel very close to the time they touch the network hardware—the missing w1 and w3 times described in Chapter 6. These largely remove the ambiguity of whether an RPC message is delayed on the sending or receiving machine. This packet-hash recording explicitly reveals a possible root cause for transaction tail latency.

To allow observation of the waiting time to enter software critical sections, the fifth fundamental shared computer resource, the trace design includes entries that mark the failure to acquire a software lock, subsequent success in acquiring it, and the release by one thread of a lock that some second thread is waiting for. These are inserted via a user-mode locking library so that every locking delay is recorded, along with the reason for the delay: the previous thread(s) holding the lock. This lock recording explicitly shows another common root cause for transaction tail latency.

To allow observation of one thread making another runnable, but that second thread's dispatch is delayed for some reason, the trace design includes entries to mark the *make-runnable* change. The delay from that change to actual dispatch is time waiting for a CPU core to become available to run the second thread, yet another common root cause for transaction tail latency on busy machines.

The previous extra trace entries cover all the common reasons for the waiting that can create long-tail transactions. The other source of transaction tail latency is a program that is executing the request, but executing more slowly than normal, caused by some form of hardware interference in competing for shared hardware resources.

KUtrace is thus a low-overhead tool that allows fine-grained observation of datacenter software dynamics across multiple programs, multiple threads, and multiple execution cores; it is designed to reveal the root causes of almost all long-tail transactions.

14.4   Implementation

As shown in Figure 14.2, the KUtrace implementation consists of

- Linux kernel patches and a kernel-mode module to record trace entries
- A control program or linkable library to turn tracing on/off and save traces to a file
- A set of postprocessing programs to produce HTML/SVG as displayed in Figure 14.1

Trace recording is done into a pre-allocated kernel buffer of perhaps 20–2000MB. Tracing can either run until the buffer fills or run continuously wrapping around in the buffer until stopped. For a very busy machine, tracing consumes perhaps 2–20MB per second, so the size of the buffer determines how many seconds of trace can be kept.

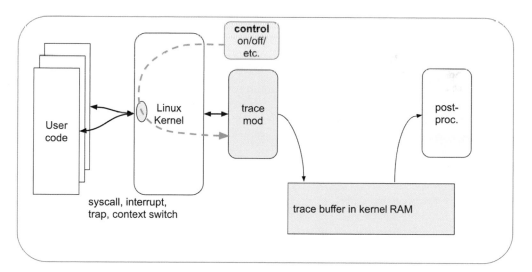

Figure 14.2   **Overview of the KUtrace implementation**

This chapter briefly describes the pieces and how they fit together, and subsequent chapters go into detail about building each piece from scratch.

14.5   Kernel Patches and Module

The files to be patched vary a somewhat across CPU architectures. For the ARM 64-bit architecture, seven Linux kernel files are patched, and two files are added. For x86-64 several more files are patched. These are all described in detail in Chapter 15.

A Linux loadable module is a separately compiled executable that can be dynamically loaded into the kernel. It is the standard mechanism for implementing device drivers and other kernel extensions. The KUtrace loadable module implements reading and writing trace entries and controlling the tracing. It is described in Chapter 16.

The individual patches are small and quite fast. Here is the interrupt-entry patch in `kernel/irq/irq.c`, recording the 8-bit interrupt number:

```
/* dsites 2019.03.05 */
kutrace1(KUTRACE_IRQ + (vector & 0xFF), 0);
```

The macro `kutrace1` expands into

```
if (kutrace_tracing) { \
    (*kutrace_global_ops.kutrace_trace_1)(event, arg); \
}
```

where `kutrace_tracing` is a Boolean compiled into the kernel and the implementation code for `kutrace_global_ops.kutrace_trace_1` is in the loadable module. Putting a timestamped trace entry into the buffer takes about 50 CPU cycles.

14.6   Control Program

Control of KUtrace is provided by user-mode code linked with a small runtime library or by a standalone control program that wraps the library, both described in Chapter 17.

The library also allows adding markers to the trace. Here is hello_world with two markers added. This is the exact code that produced Figure 14.1, with the `hello` and `/hello` markers at about 300 usec in that figure.

```
#include "kutrace_lib.h"
int main (int argc, const char** argv) {
  kutrace_trace::mark_a("hello");
  printf("hello world\n");
  kutrace_trace::mark_a("/hello");
  return 0;
}
```

The library implements control via an unused system call (the last in the range of syscall numbers and well above the last legal one). An alternate implementation could do this with an `ioctl` call, but that would be complicated by tracing of the `ioctl` itself.

14.7 Postprocessing

Once a raw binary trace file has been created, it can be postprocessed into an HTML file that can be displayed and dynamically panned and zoomed and annotated. There are five programs involved, two of which are optional, as shown in Figure 14.3.

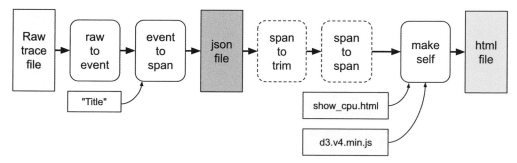

Figure 14.3 **Overview of trace postprocessing**

Chapter 18 further describes these programs. Chapter 19 describes the display HTML file and its user-interface actions.

14.8 A Note on Security

KUtrace by design records all CPU activity on a server, across all programs. Its intended use is by the owners of such servers or by the owners of programs running on dedicated servers. But one user can maliciously use it to examine the behavior of other users' programs. The only real control over this is the need to have proper administrative privileges to insert the KUtrace loadable module. Once that is loaded, the existence of the module also opens up a possible security issue due to the controlling `syscall(...)` implementation. With out-of-bounds subscripts and Spectre-like effort [CVE 2017, Kocher 2019, Lipp 2018], the underlying call for dumping trace buffer data can be used by a malicious user-mode program to read all of the kernel-mapped memory.

14.9 Summary

KUtrace is a software facility that captures and timestamps every transition between user-mode and kernel-mode execution. It gives extremely high-resolution traces of everything happening on all CPU cores with nothing missing and with tiny overhead. In addition to directly viewing the output HTML diagrams, we can learn about system anomalies by running search scripts over the intermediate JSON files.

The facility is not intended for kernel debugging nor for user-code debugging—it is intended to observe the (possibly unexpected) true execution dynamics of complex software.

Chapter 15

KUtrace: Linux Kernel Patches

The KUtrace software to capture and timestamp every transition between user-mode and kernel-mode execution is built from a set of Linux kernel patches, a runtime loadable kernel module, a user-mode control library, and various postprocessing programs. In this chapter, we look at the overall tracing design and the kernel patches. In the next chapter, we will look at the companion loadable module code that the patches call. The implementation mechanism is all isolated in this module; just the hooks are in patched kernel files.

The tracing code fills an in-memory reserved kernel buffer organized as multiple fixed-size blocks, each containing multiple individual trace entries. The entire buffer is allocated once (via vmalloc) in dynamic kernel memory space—a space that uses page tables to map contiguous virtual pages into discontiguous physical pages. KUtrace does not use the 1:1 kernel memory space, which requires contiguous physical memory (via kmalloc); the trace buffer can be too big to reasonably allocate in the 1:1 space.

The buffer is organized internally as multiple 64KB traceblocks, with each CPU core writing to its own currently active block and then occasionally switching to a new block. No multi-word trace entry may cross a traceblock boundary. The all-zeros entry is used as a NOP filler. Having the CPU cores all writing to different blocks accomplishes two things: there is no cache-line thrashing as there would be with multiple cores writing to the same line, and there is no need to store the CPU number in each trace entry; recording the CPU number once per traceblock is sufficient. Both of these contribute to making KUtrace low-overhead, the former reducing CPU overhead and the latter reducing memory overhead. The choice of 64KB is somewhat arbitrary: it is a power of two; it is small enough that are several traceblocks available per CPU core even with a modest trace buffer size, and it is big enough that the averaged overhead for switching to new blocks is small.

The first sections of this chapter describe the data structures used, including the individual trace entries, and the later sections describe the code patches that record individual entries.

15.1   Trace Buffer Data Structures

Figure 15.1 shows an example trace buffer layout, with some filled trace blocks, some empty, and four different CPUs actively writing to four blocks. CPU 3 and CPU 1 have only partly filled their active blocks with individual trace entries. CPU 2 is about to fill its traceblock and switch to the one pointed to by `next_free_block`, incrementing that pointer by 64KB. When `next_free_block` reaches `limit`, either tracing stops or (in flight-recorder mode) it wraps around to the front of the buffer and continues, overwriting older blocks. The optional wrap-around leaves traceblock[0] intact and starts overwriting traceblock[1], thus preserving the trace start time and the initial names of all the fault, interrupt, and syscall event numbers in traceblock[0].

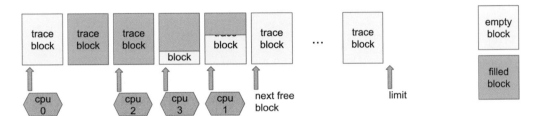

Figure 15.1a   **Trace buffer layout**

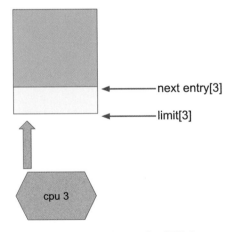

Figure 15.1b   **Active-block next and limit pointers for CPU 3**

Each CPU has a small per-CPU data structure describing its active block, containing a pointer to the next 8-byte trace entry to write in that block and a pointer to the end of that block, as shown in Figure 15.1b. When a CPU's `next_entry` pointer reaches the active block's `limit`, the tracing code switches to a new block.

When the optional instructions per cycle (IPC) recording is active, 7/8 of the trace buffer is used for traceblocks, as shown in Figure 15.1, and the remaining 1/8 is used to record four bits of IPC corresponding to each trace event. The next section describes individual trace entries. Most are fixed-length, but entries for names are variable-length.

15.2   Raw Traceblock Format

The raw traceblocks consist of 64KB blocks, each organized as 8,192 words of 8 bytes each. The first few words of each block have some metadata, followed by trace entries. Each traceblock is padded out with all-zero NOP words as needed. The raw trace entries have timestamps based on some free-running hardware time counter, but we would like to map these into wall-clock time. The mapping is enabled by recording <time counter, gettimeofday> pairs in each traceblock and the overall trace start/stop pairs in the first traceblock. By recording the full time counter in every block, this design also allows reconstructing the high-order timestamp bits for each event from the truncated 20-bit value in every entry.

As shown in Figure 15.2b, each traceblock has six words of metadata about it at the front, and the very first block has an additional six words of metadata about the entire trace, shown in Figure 15.2a. The remaining words contain trace entries, with an entry of 0 always indicating a NOP. There typically will be 0–8 NOPs at the end of a traceblock, but there may be a lot more, especially in the last-written traceblock for each CPU. No multi-word trace entry crosses a block boundary. This makes entry creation and later decoding simpler and slightly faster.

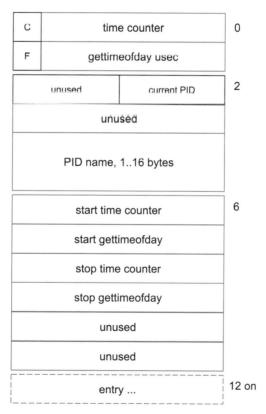

Figure 15.2a   **Very first 64KB traceblock layout**

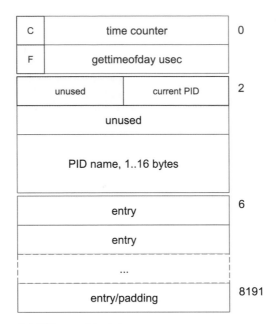

Figure 15.2b   **General 64KB traceblock layout**

The first word contains in its low 56 bits a time counter value at the time the block was assigned to a CPU, and the second word contains the corresponding `gettimeofday()` value in usec since the epoch. The high 8 bits of the first word contain the CPU number for all the entries in the traceblock. The high 8 bits of the second word contain some flags, detailed later. The next four words contain the current process ID and process name for the given CPU. This information is slightly redundant, but it makes the reconstruction of wraparound traces more robust. The unused fields allow future additions of per-traceblock metadata.

The very first traceblock has an additional six words of trace metadata, giving the overall trace start and stop time pairs, plus two unused words for future additions. In the case of wraparound traces, the start and stop times may be hours apart.

15.3   Trace Entries

As we mentioned in Chapter 14, the underlying design for trace entries is to consume just 4 bytes each, containing a 20-bit timestamp and 12-bit event number. However, system calls and returns are usually the majority of trace entries, and Ross Biro observed in 2006 that there is great benefit in recording a little bit about system call arguments and return values if we can. About 94% of the time in a trace, a matching return entry immediately follows a system call or interrupt or fault entry (Figure 15.3, top).

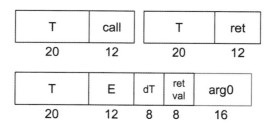

Figure 15.3   **Underlying idea of two 4-byte trace entries (top) and actual 8-byte trace entry (bottom) with argument and return values**

KUtrace takes advantage of this by packing matched call/return pairs into a single 8-byte entry (Figure 15.3 bottom) and using three freed-up bytes to record the low 16 bits of the first syscall argument and the low 8 bits of its return value. As an added bonus, creating this single 8-byte entry is somewhat faster than creating two 4-byte entries, largely because there is only a single atomic update to the next_entry pointer. For simplicity and alignment and speed, all trace entries are 8 bytes, even if they contain a single unmatched event. Some single-event entries waste 4 bytes while others use the space to record a 32-bit argument.

The five fields in an 8-byte syscall trace entry are

- T: 20-bit timestamp for the syscall, incrementing once every 10–40 nsec and wrapping every million counts, 10–40 msec

- E: 12-bit event number: syscall number, interrupt number, fault number, other

- dT: 8-bit delta-time for an optimized call/return pair; the return time is T+dT; zero indicates a not-optimized syscall/interrupt/fault

- retval: low 8 bits of the syscall return value, signed -128..+127; large enough to hold all normal Linux error codes -1..-126

- arg0: low 16 bits of the first parameter to the syscall, often containing a file ID or byte count or something else useful

If dT or retval does not fit into 8 bits or other entries separate the syscall and sysreturn, two non-optimized entries are used, one for the syscall and its arg0 value, and one for the sysreturn and the low 16 bits of its return value (in the arg0 field). This happens only about 6% of the time.

Matched fault/return and interrupt/return pairs use the same optimized design, with nonzero dT indicating the optimized pair. Faults and interrupts do not use the ret and arg0 fields. The remaining much-less-common entries are also all 8 bytes or multiples thereof, preserving natural alignment (and hence speed and simplicity of creation) for all entries in all traceblocks.

Some trace entries contain names for the various events. These entries are variable-size, composed of two to eight 8-byte words. The first word is the format shown in Figure 15.3, and the rest of the words contain 1..56 bytes of the name (truncated if necessary), with the last word zero filled. For these entries, the event number specifies the entry size and the type of item being named, and arg0 specifies which specific syscall number, etc., is being named.

Appendix B gives further detail on trace entries.

15.4   IPC Trace Entries

When the optional IPC recording is active, each raw event has an additional 4 bits of IPC. With a pair of events packed into the actual 8-byte trace entries, the corresponding IPC pair is packed into 1 byte. The trace buffer is split into a trace entry array of N * 64KB and an IPC entry array of N * 8KB. The subscript used to address an 8-byte trace entry array item is also used to address a 1-byte IPC entry array item. Whenever an 8-byte entry records an optimized enter/return pair, the corresponding IPC byte contains a pair of 4-bit quantized IPC values. The net effect is that the underlying 32-bit entries become 36-bit entries, but the extra 4 bits are stored separately to keep everything aligned on good memory boundaries.

To calculate IPC, the trace implementation code records at each event the timestamp T and the running instructions-retired count R for the CPU core. At the next event, tracing records timestamp T2 and instructions-retired count R2 and then calculates IPC = (R2 - R) * C / (T2 - T) where the constant C maps timestamps to CPU cycles. This IPC value is quantized into just four bits and stored in the location corresponding to the T2 event. Each event thus has a corresponding IPC for the time interval leading up to it. For a trace entry that marks a transition into kernel code, the IPC describes the execution within the just-preceding user code. For a return entry that marks a transition back to user code, the IPC describes the execution within the just-preceding syscall/fault/interrupt kernel-mode code.

Instead of dividing, it would be possible to record the raw R2 value along with T2, but that would make trace entries at least twice as big, cutting the length of a trace in half or doubling the needed size of a trace buffer. By doing the division each time and quantizing to just 4 bits, the design trades a modest CPU time hit instead of a much larger memory-space hit.

The CPU overhead for reading the instructions-retired counter is nonetheless unfortunately large. On current Intel chips, the counter read is unnecessarily slow at about 35 cycles, and the division is also unnecessarily slow at about 30 cycles for producing just four quotient bits. In addition, reading the instructions-retired counter requires some per-CPU metadata setup to specify what to count and for a hyperthreaded x86 whether to count per physical core (two hyperthreads' counts combined) or per-thread. The kernel code to do this setup runs once per CPU thread at the beginning of each trace run, overwriting any previous setup. This means that IPC tracing is incompatible with anything else on the machine trying to use a different counter setup.

> It would be better if chip implementations provided, without any global metadata setup, one-cycle access to a free-running fixed-rate time counter and one-cycle access to a dedicated instructions-retired-per-hyperthread counter, plus an integer divide that took no more than a few cycles of startup plus 1 cycle per actual quotient bit (determined by the difference in number of leading zeros/signbits in dividend and divisor).

15.5   Timestamps

The 20-bit timestamp is derived from a computer's free-running high-resolution time counter that increments every 10–40 nsec. That resolution is consistent with the 10–20 nsec CPU overhead of creating a trace entry. Finer resolution is unnecessary because for short durations the trace overhead will overwhelm it; a coarser resolution becomes problematic as it begins to obscure actual time intervals. On x86 systems, the constant-rate cycle counter returned by the rdtsc instruction is used, shifted right by 6 bits—for a 3.2 GHz CPU clock, the shifted value runs at 50 MHz, so increments once every 20 nsec. On ARM systems, the physical timer count register, cntpct_el0, is used, running at 1/64 of the CPU clock: for a 2GHz CPU clock, cntpct_el0 runs at 31.25 MHz, incrementing every 32 nsec.

The low 20 bits of the time counter go into every trace entry. The 20-bit field wraps around every million (actually every 1,048,576) counts, or approximately every 20 msec for a timer incrementing every 20 nsec. A finer-resolution counter shortens this wraparound time, while a coarser resolution lengthens it. To later reconstruct the high-order bits of the timer counter, it is only necessary to have at least one trace event per CPU core per wraparound interval. But if no events at all occur on a CPU core for over 20 msec, the reconstruction fails. Timer interrupts suffice. The current KUtrace implementation thus depends on a timer interrupt to each core at least once every 10 msec.

15.6   Event Numbers

The KUtrace 12-bit event numbers consist of a few high bits indicating the type of entry and the remaining low bits giving a specific number for that type, as shown in Appendix B.

15.7   Nested Trace Entries

One of the complications of creating trace entries is that the modern Linux kernel is interruptable so that kernel code working on one thing can be preempted in order to work on something more important. In particular, processing a syscall can get preempted by an I/O interrupt. When this happens, KUtrace will record the sequence as

```
syscall number 1234
  interrupt number 56
  interrupt_return 56     (possible exit through scheduler
                             and context switch)
sysreturn 1234
```

In general, traced items can be nested several levels deep. Upon eventual return from a system call that blocked, the continuation may execute on and return from a different CPU than the one that started the call. Worse, interrupts may occur in the midst of the code that is creating a trace entry. This makes the trace implementation details fairly subtle. The next chapter expands on this topic.

In the meantime, just remember that syscalls, interrupts, and faults may nest and that a system call that starts on CPU A may be running on CPU B when it executes the matching sysreturn to user code.

15.8   Code

The kernel patches consist of a small amount of data plus typically one-line patches in several selected places. The Boolean kernel global `kutrace_tracing` is initially false, but is set true when tracing is enabled. Most patches just test this Boolean and do a single call to the tracing implementation in the loadable module. The pattern looks like this for a system call entry, where `kutrace_global_ops` is a small array of four procedure pointers, all going to implementation code in the loadable module:

```
if (kutrace_tracing) {
  (*kutrace_global_ops.trace_1)(KUTRACE_SYSCALL64 +
                                number, arg0);
}
```

Rather than inserting this code directly at each patch point, it is wrapped in a kernel macro. If the kernel is compiled without CONFIG_KUTRACE, the macro expands to no code; otherwise to the previous code. Most of the patches then consist of single lines of code:

```
KUTRACE1(event_number, argument);
```

Here, for example, is the entire two lines of patch (in bold) for recording timer interrupt and return in `arch/x86/kernel/apic/apic.c`, where IRQ is shorthand for *interrupt request*:

```
  ...
KUTRACE1(KUTRACE_IRQ + kTimer, 0);
local_apic_timer_interrupt();
KUTRACE1(KUTRACE_IRQRET + kTimer, 0);
exiting_irq();
set_irq_regs(old_regs);
  ...
```

Most trace entries are created by kernel-mode patches, but some are created instead by explicit user-mode code. Kernel-mode patches create syscall/irq/fault/scheduler entry and exit events, plus interprocessor-interrupt, set-runnable, sleep-state, packet-hash, context-switch, and PID-name events. User-mode code can create syscall/irq/fault *name* events, RPCID events, locking events, queueing events, and explicit human-meaningful marker labels and numbers.

15.9   Packet Tracing

In Chapter 6, we discussed the issue of a large unexpected delay in sending an RPC request message from user code on client machine A to user code on server machine B (or a similar delay in returning the result message). Without some idea of when messages actually travel over the network, it is difficult to understand whether the delay happened in client kernel code, in the network hardware, in server kernel code, or in server user code failing to ask for the message. Without knowing where the delay occurred, we don't know whether to fix client code or server code or network hardware.

KUtrace has a simple facility for recording when packets are seen in kernel TCP and UDP networking code. By timestamping the first packet of an RPC request or response message in the kernel and correlating that timestamp with user-code processing of that message on both client and server machines, we can identify where large message delays occur.

The patches for this are in the `net/ipv4` TCP and UDP code; similar patches could be added for ipv6. Just after *each* incoming RX packet has its TCP or UDP header parsed, a KUtrace entry can be created; just before each outgoing TX packet is queued for the NIC hardware, a KUtrace entry can be created. These points in the code are as close as practical to the hardware NIC receipt/transmission instant. They provide the missing `w1` and `w3` timestamps discussed in Chapter 6.

It is undesirable to have the kernel patches directly incorporate detailed knowledge of the specific RPC message format used in this book. It is also undesirable to create KUtrace entries for every single packet with 10 GB/sec networks and above because the KUtrace time can exceed the inter-packet arrival time. We thus need to filter which packets to trace and to do so quickly. The simple implemented mechanism ANDs the first 24 payload bytes of each packet against 24 bytes of mask, XORs these down to 4 bytes, and compares to an arbitrary 4-byte match-value. Packets that match create KUtrace entries. The mask bytes and match value are parameters to the KUtrace module when it is loaded, so are not compiled into the kernel at all.

The filter comparison has three 8-byte ANDs, four XORs, and a branch; it takes less than 10 nsec. The choice of 24 bytes is driven by the desire to be fast, while still having enough bytes to do useful filtering. An all-zero mask and zero match-value will trace all packets. An all-zero mask and nonzero match-value will trace no packets. A mask that passes just the 4-byte RPC marker signature field described in Chapter 6, and a match-value equal to that constant will pick off just those packets that start an RPC message as used in this book, plus occasional false matches. Fast identification of message beginnings was the motivation for having this constant signature field. Note that for TCP connections, some messages may start in the middle of a packet and thus not be seen by this design (for example the TCP code can combine two parallel 300-byte request messages into a single packet). You can't have everything if you need to be fast.

Once a packet is selected for tracing, it is undesirable to have kernel code parse it to find an RPCID or other high-level information as used in this book. Instead, the KUtrace entry records a packet-hash over the first 32 bytes of the packet payload—the data that follows the TCP or UDP header. Tiny packets with less than 32 bytes of payload are not traced. This hash is taken over the data that a user-mode program sees.

The final part of this packet-tracing design is code in the user-mode RPC library to also record and timestamp a hash over the same 32 bytes for each message sent or received, just before or after the system call to transfer that message. Postprocessing then has enough information to display the correct responsibility for any delayed RPC message. Alas, we did not have this packet tracing information when Figure 6.8 of Chapter 6 was created, so we never resolved where the transmission delays were. The upcoming Chapter 26 makes use of the packet tracing described here.

An alternate way to achieve a similar result is to use `tcpdump` or `wireshark` to capture the first 100-odd bytes of every packet and then identify the RPC message beginnings. This can work but it is 5–10x slower and also runs into a *time-base problem*. The kernel-mode time-of-day values recorded by `tcpdump` are not the same as user-mode `gettimeofday()` values, and the difference between them is not constant and not necessarily small. I have observed offsets of 200–400 usec with drift of 40 usec per second. This requires time-aligning `tcpdump` timestamps with KUtrace timestamps in order to understand message delays. I did this for some of the Chapter 26 diagrams. Recording packets directly in KUtrace is faster and gives consistent timestamps.

15.10   AMD/Intel x86-64 Patches

For the x86-64 architecture and Linux kernel version 4.19, a total of 16 kernel code files have patches. (There would be fewer files if x86 interrupt processing and idle power-saving were not so scattered.) The main patches trace system calls, interrupts, page faults, and the scheduler. The patched code runs on multiple CPU cores simultaneously, and as noted earlier nested interrupts/ faults may occur within some of the patched paths.

Whenever the scheduler decides to do a context switch, a patch creates a context-switch entry with the new about-to-run process ID. The implementation of this may also create a name entry for that PID.

The scheduler also participates when a blocked process is set runnable again, since that process may have a high-enough priority to run immediately. There are several hundred places in the Linux kernel source pool that set a task runnable, most of them in various device drivers, but none of these has any effect until the scheduler runs. We catch the most common `set_current_state(TASK_RUNNING)` transitions inside the wakeup code in the scheduler itself.

All the real implementation mechanism for KUtrace is in the loadable module, on the other side of the patching interface. The loadable module can be altered and rebuilt without changing or recompiling the patched kernel itself.

The build-time kernel `.config` file needs an additional `CONFIG_KUTRACE=y` line added at the end to create a kernel that includes KUtrace. Otherwise, the build will generate no KUtrace code at all.

The patched source files listed in Code Snippet 15.1 are in the `linux-4.19.19/` directory.

Code Snippet 15.1   **KUtrace x86 kernel patches**

```
Syscall kernel/user transitions:
    arch/x86/entry/common.c.patched  Also the trace_control hook

Interrupt kernel/user transitions:
    arch/x86/kernel/irq.c.patched      Most hard interrupts/top half
    kernel/softirq.c.patched           Most soft interrupts/bottom half
    arch/x86/kernel/apic/apic.c.patched   Timer interrupt
                                          also PC samples, CPU
                                          frequency samples
    arch/x86/kernel/smp.c.patched      Interprocessor interrupt
                                       send/receive
    arch/x86/kernel/irq_work.c.patched   Interprocessor interrupts
                                         more work

Fault kernel/user transitions:
    arch/x86/mm/fault.c.patched            Page faults

Scheduler:
    kernel/sched/core.c.patched        Scheduler itself, context switches
                                       also make-runnable, PID names
```

```
Idle loop:
    drivers/idle/intel_idle.c.patched        Intel-specific idle loop,
                                             power saving
    drivers/acpi/processor_idle.c.patched  Generic idle loop, power saving
    drivers/acpi/acpi_pad.c.patched          power saving
    arch/x86/kernel/acpi/cstate.c.patched  power saving
Other:
    fs/exec.c                                New-process PID names
    net/ipv4/tcp_input.c                     RX filtered packet hash
    net/ipv4/tcp_output.c                    TX filtered packet hash
    net/ipv4/udp.c                           RX/TX filtered packet hash
Build files:
    .config                                  Adds CONFIG_KUTRACE=y
    kernel/Makefile
    arch/x86/Kconfig
Added files:
    include/linux/kutrace.h                  kutrace definitions
    kernel/kutrace/kutrace.c                 kutrace variables
    kernel/kutrace/Makefile
```

A similar set of patches for ARM-64 implements KUtrace on a Raspberry Pi-4B board. Machine-specific patches are in arch/arm64 instead of arch/x86. The other patches are shared unchanged for both architectures. The loadable module contains all KUtrace accesses to machine-specific registers (MSRs), and these are conditionally compiled to match the respective architecture.

15.11 Summary

The KUtrace software, capturing every transition between user-mode and kernel-mode execution, is built from a set of Linux kernel patches, a runtime loadable kernel module, a user-mode control library, and various postprocessing programs. The patches affect fewer than 20 kernel source files and are just small hooks. All the real implementation mechanism is isolated in a loadable module, described in Chapter 16.

The tracing code fills an in-memory reserved kernel buffer organized as multiple fixed-size blocks, each containing multiple individual trace entries. Each CPU core writes to a different block, minimizing cache-line sharing.

Putting a timestamped trace entry into the buffer takes about 50 CPU cycles or less, so is well under 1% CPU overhead for 200K events per second per CPU core. The next chapter describes the loadable module implementation that delivers this astonishingly low overhead.

Exercises

15.1   Given an array of 20-bit timestamps and a starting full 64-bit timestamp, build a small routine to extend the 20-bit timestamps to 64 bits.

Chapter 16

KUtrace: Linux Loadable Module

A Linux loadable module is a separately compiled executable that can be dynamically loaded to link against the kernel and add new kernel code. It is the standard mechanism for implementing device drivers and other kernel extensions. One advantage of loadable modules is that they can be changed and rebuilt without recompiling the kernel and without rebooting. The KUtrace loadable module implements reading and writing trace entries and controlling the tracing.

16.1   Kernel Interface Data Structures

There is only a small interface between the kernel patches and the loadable module, consisting of two kernel-exported global variables, shown in Figure 16.1.

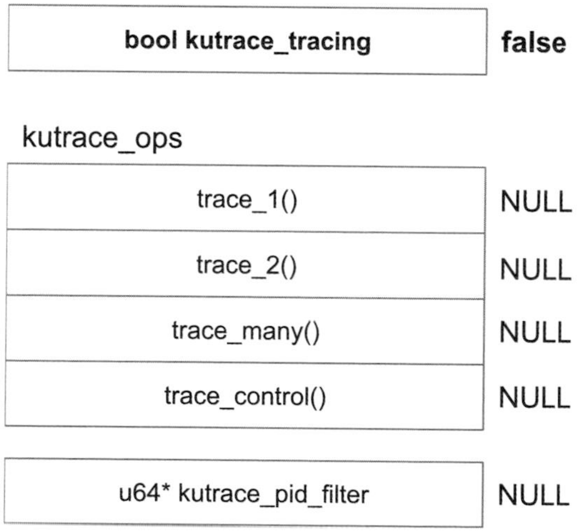

bool kutrace_tracing	false

kutrace_ops

trace_1()	NULL
trace_2()	NULL
trace_many()	NULL
trace_control()	NULL

u64* kutrace_pid_filter	NULL

Figure 16.1   **Kernel-exported interface to loadable module**

At boot time, the all-important `kutrace_tracing` Boolean is set to `false`, and the other fields are all `NULL`. When the kutrace loadable module is loaded and initialized, it allocates the trace buffer and sets the four `kutrace_global_ops` pointers to the addresses of the corresponding code routines within the module, as shown in Figure 16.2. When the loadable module is unloaded, it again sets `kutrace_tracing = false` and the other fields to `NULL`.

With tracing off, the kernel patches do nothing at all, and do so as quickly as possible: a single test and well-predicted branch. The overhead of the patches with tracing off is unmeasurably small. With tracing on, the kernel patches simply call out to one of the four procedures. Everything else about the tracing implementation is done in the loadable module, the subject of this chapter.

The loadable module has three groups of routines, one group for module load/unload, one for initializing and controlling tracing, and one group for implementing the trace calls in the kernel patches.

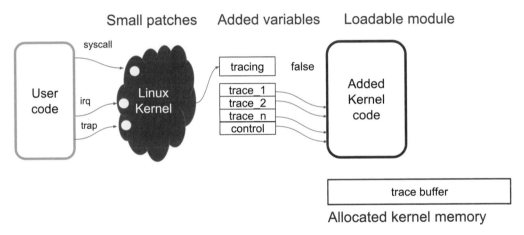

Figure 16.2   **Code and interfaces after module is loaded and initialized**

16.2   Module Load/Unload

The `kutrace_mod_init` routine is called when the module is loaded. It allocates the trace buffer, whose size is specified by a parameter on the module-loading `insmod` command line, and allocates a PID filter array of 8KB. It then sets up the initial tracing state of off with an empty trace buffer, and only after that it sets the four procedure addresses, prints a kernel message visible via the `dmesg` command, and finishes.

The `kutrace_mod_exit` routine is called when the module is unloaded. It ensures tracing is off, waits a few milliseconds for any in-progress trace entries to be completed on other CPU cores, sets all the trace buffer pointers to NULL, and then deallocates the trace buffer and PID filter arrays. Last, it resets the four procedure addresses to NULL, prints a kernel message, and finishes.

16.3   Initializing and Controlling Tracing

A user-space syscall to a dummy syscall number reaches the main trace-control routine. This call may be in the standalone kutrace_control program, or it may be compiled into any program that is designed to be self-tracing. This syscall goes to the normal kernel syscall handler in entry/ common.c or entry.S, fails the test for being a valid syscall number (less than syscall_max), and then on the seldom-used error path an explicit test for our dummy value sends it off to the trace_control entry point in the loadable module. If the module is not loaded, this last test instead falls though to return the standard ENOSYS error code for illegal system calls.

The controlling system call has two uint64 parameters, command and arg. The command is a small integer specifying 1 of about 10 different controlling actions, including KUTRACE_ON and KUTRACE_OFF. The argument is either an integer or a pointer to some larger data. Chapter 17 fully describes the controlling commands.

16.4   Implementing Trace Calls

The two main trace implementation routines are Insert1 for normal one-word trace entries and InsertN for variable-length name entries. These have one interface if called directly from kernel code and a slightly different one if called via the controlling syscall from user code. We will first describe the mechanism for kernel-mode Insert1 and then describe the small differences for InsertN and user-mode calls.

16.5   Insert1

Insert1 takes a single argument, a filled-in uint64 trace entry with T=0. Along the most-common path, it allocates space for an 8-byte trace entry via get_claim(1), reads the time counter, inserts the low 20 bits into the T field, stores that word, and returns the number of trace words used, 1. The get_claim routine checks that the length requested is reasonable, picks up the address of the current CPU's traceblock pointers, *atomically* increments the next pointer, compares to the limit pointer, and returns if the new entry fits in the current block. The code structure carefully allows for nested interrupts that add entries to the same traceblock, overflow it, and allocate a new traceblock. The common path is lock-free and is done while preventing kernel preemption that could move the running code to a different CPU core and hence a different traceblock and a different <next, limit> pair. All this takes less than 50 CPU cycles on our sample servers (about 15 nsec).

Several things can take the code off the normal fast path. Claiming the space for a trace entry is centered on the atomic increment of the next pointer. If this increment stays within the current traceblock, all is good, and no other trace entry can use the same space, even if the Insert1 code is interrupted and the interrupt handling creates additional trace entries before returning (see Code Snippet 16.1).

Code Snippet 16.1   **Interrupted get_claim, but after limit2 is read**

```
Insert1(syscall 123):
  T1 = time_counter
  get_claim(1)
  Get limit1 = limit[cpu]
  Atomic increment next[cpu], reserving address A
  Get limit2 = limit[cpu] again
    ---> interrupt occurs
    Insert1(interrupt 45), at A+1 with T2 = time_counter
    Insert1(interrupt_return 45), A+2 with T3 = time_counter
      BUT A+2 doesn't fit in current traceblock, so switch to a
      new one and change next[cpu] and limit[cpu] to match
    <--- interrupt returns
  Compare limit1 to limit2. If equal, all is good
  Compare A to limit2[cpu], the old one. All is good; return A
  Finish Insert1(syscall 123), with T1
```

What can happen in this case is that one of the nested interrupt's `Insert1` calls switches to a new traceblock just before the compare to `limit[cpu]`. To deal with this, the code reads `limit[cpu]` a second time just after the increment that reserves A. This read-twice approach follows ideas from [Lamport 1977] and his later papers. In Code Snippet 16.1 the interrupt happens after the second read, so `limit1 == limit2` and comparing `next` to `limit` validly tells us whether A fit into the original traceblock. Normally it does, and `get_claim` returns A. See Code Snippet 16.2.

Code Snippet 16.2   **Interrupted get_claim, but BEFORE limit2 is read**

```
Insert1(syscall 123):
  T1 = time_counter
  get_claim (1)
  Get limit1 = limit[cpu]
  Atomic increment next[cpu], reserving address A
    ---> interrupt occurs
    Insert1(interrupt 45), at A+1 with T2 = time_counter
    Insert1(interrupt_return 45), A+2 with T3 = time_counter
      BUT A+2 doesn't fit in current traceblock, so switch to a
      new one and change next[cpu] and limit[cpu] to match
    <--- interrupt returns
  Get limit2 = limit[cpu] again
  Compare limit1 to limit2. NOT equal, go back to the top of
    get_claim to allocate a new A
```

However, if the nested interrupt occurs before `limit2` is read, then the fact that `limit1 != limit2` indicates the change in traceblock, as shown in Code Snippet 16.2. When this happens, we cannot easily tell if A fit within the original traceblock. So instead, we do something simple— we abandon A and restart the `get_claim` for syscall 123. This new allocation will be at the beginning of the new traceblock so will always fit (barring starvation from ~4100 back-to-back interrupts that fill up the new traceblock; if this happens, there are worse problems than tracing progress).

What about the abandoned original trace entry slot A—won't some old bogus data show through if we never write A? This can be in only one of the last eight words of a traceblock, since the maximum get_claim size is 8 words. To avoid something showing though, we initialize the last eight words of a traceblock to NOPs every time we allocate a traceblock. Doing so also covers the case of a multiword allocation not entirely fitting in a traceblock—the last few words are abandoned, and the multiword item is allocated at the beginning of a new traceblock.

The sequence in Code Snippet 16.2 just leaves A as a NOP, followed by Insert1(interrupt 45) at the end of the original traceblock and then Insert1(interrupt_ret 45) followed by the retried Insert1(syscall 123) at the beginning of the new traceblock. After this rare sequence of events, the timestamps of the first two entries in the new traceblock, ts3 and then ts1, can be out of order, since ts1 was captured first. The reconstruction programs compensate by allowing timestamps to be slightly out of order. The postprocessing will sort them back into place.

However, there are three additional complications with Insert1: names, IPC, and optimized returns. If the item being inserted is a context switch to process ID P and P has not been seen before in the trace, the name associated with P is inserted into the trace first. It would be possible but wasteful to insert the name for P at every context switch; instead, the tracing code maintains a pid_filter array of 64K bits (8KB), subscripted by the low-order 16 bits of P. These array bits are initially zero. Whenever there is a context switch to P and the corresponding array bit is 0, the name for P is put in the trace and the bit set to 1, thus putting P's name into the trace just once. Well, almost. In flight-recorder mode, the code that wraps around also clears the pid_filter array so that after a wraparound context-switch names are again inserted into the trace. This compensates for eventually overwriting the older names after wrapping around.

If IPC recording is active, the get_claim return value is used to locate and update the corresponding byte of the IPC array. IPC recording is done only for one-word trace entries; for multiword ones, it is skipped entirely. To save overhead, the IPC array for each traceblock is not pre-zeroed. Instead, the design depends on the postprocessing code to ignore any unwritten bytes.

If the item being inserted is a return from event E, it should be combined with the prior entry if that was exactly the matching call to event E and if the delta-T and return values fit. This testing is done in two pieces for speed, first that the item is a return and that the return value fits in a byte, and second that the prior item is a call to E and that the delta time fits in a byte. If all the tests pass, the return value and delta-T are inserted into the prior entry, the unused high four bits of the prior IPC byte get the call-to-return IPC value, and Insert1 exits without ever calling get_claim. If any of the tests fail, the normal unoptimized Insert1 is used.

Finally, if get_claim runs off the end of the trace buffer and flight-recorder wraparound is not active, get_claim turns off tracing and returns NULL to indicate that there is no more space.

16.6 InsertN

The InsertN code is simpler than Insert1. After checking that N<=8, InsertN allocates space for an N-word trace entry via get_claim(N), reads the time counter, inserts the low 20 bits into the T field, stores that word, and returns the number of trace words used, N. There is no process name, IPC, nor optimized return processing for InsertN. As mentioned, get_claim handles the case of fewer than N words left in the current traceblock, leaving up to N-1 NOPs at the end of the original block and switching to a new one.

The only complication with `InsertN` is that the trace-entry data comes from main memory instead of being passed in a single register. When `InsertN` is called directly from kernel code, kernel `memcpy()` is used to copy those bytes. But when it is called from user code, the kernel-specific `copy_from_user()` routine is used to first move the data from user address space to a temporary within the kernel address space, handling any possible user-space page faults or access violations or blocking waiting for a disk page-in. If the copy fails, the pre-zeroed first word of the temporary is left zero, which specifies an illegal length N, so no entry is made, and tracing stops.

16.7   Switching to a New Traceblock

Whenever `get_claim()` finds that the requested number of words will not fit in the current traceblock, it switches to a new traceblock. Multiple CPU cores can end up switching simultaneously, but with 64KB trace blocks, there are 8K eight-byte entries per block, so switching is relatively infrequent. If a given CPU creates new trace entries at the rate of 200K per second, then switching would occur about 25 times per second, or once every 40 msec. With block-switching time under 1 usec, we don't expect much interference between CPU cores.

Switching traceblocks involves incrementing the global `next_traceblock` pointer and checking against the global `limit_traceblock` pointer. We don't want another CPU to interfere with this sequence, and we also don't want to have any interrupts delivered and traced in the midst of this, nor do we want the updating code to be preempted and moved to a different CPU. For simplicity, `get_slow_claim()` does the update in a critical section protected by a kernel spinlock.

Once the new traceblock is claimed, `really_get_slow_claim()` initializes that traceblock, including the metadata at the beginning and the eight words of NOP at the end, and only then does it set the per-CPU `next` and `limit` pointers to that traceblock.

16.8   Summary

The KUtrace loadable module implements all the tracing mechanism, minimizing the actual kernel patches to just a line or two at the small number of places that do transitions between kernel and user code. The interface between these kernel patches and the implementation module is just a single Boolean and an array of four procedure pointers for the patches to call.

Trace events are recorded in per-CPU traceblocks that are dynamically allocated as the various CPU cores fill up blocks at varying rates. The basic event recording reserves space for the event via an atomic add, stores the trace entry, and returns. A full traceblock triggers switching to a new block under protection of a global trace buffer spinlock. The code is carefully designed to be robust in the presence of multiple CPU cores, nested events, kernel preemption, process migration, etc.

For speed, the design avoids locks entirely on the frequent path. To avoid unnecessarily delaying interrupt delivery and any cascading waiting, the infrequent switch-traceblocks path is also carefully designed to do a minimal amount of work while holding the spinlock.

Chapter 17

KUtrace: User-Mode Runtime Control

The standalone kutrace_control program provides user-mode control of tracing. It uses the small kutrace_lib.cc runtime library, which in turn uses a system call to reach the kutrace_control entry point in the loadable module, as shown in Figure 17.1. The underlying implementation of all the controlling functionality thus resides in the loadable module.

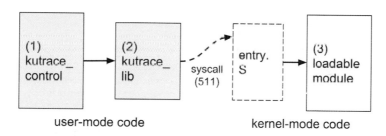

Figure 17.1   **Runtime control of KUtrace**

Self-tracing programs can call the library code directly for finer-grained or specialized tracing control. The user-mode library also allows adding human-meaningful markers to the trace, as we saw in Chapter 14 and as detailed in Appendix B.

17.1   Controlling Tracing

The library calls the loadable module implementation via an additional system call, above the range of valid syscall numbers. (An alternate implementation could do this with something like an ioctl syscall, but that would be complicated by tracing of the ioctl itself.) If the running kernel does not implement KUtrace or if the loadable module is not loaded, the controlling syscall returns the usual ENOSYS to indicate "function not implemented." To avoid any ambiguity, successful controlling calls never return this value.

The next three sections describe the kutrace_control program's command-line choices, the kutrace_lib entry points, and then the loadable module's controlling syscall commands.

17.2   Standalone kutrace_control Program

The user-mode kutrace_control command-line program has a simple terminal interface that types a prompt and reads one-line commands until the user enters the quit command. It implements several commands, but the simplest are

```
> go
> stop
```

The go command resets the tracing buffer to empty and starts tracing. Variants

```
> goipc,
> gowrap, and
> goipcwrap
```

set a couple of flag bits to enable tracking instructions per cycle (IPC) over each traced interval and/or enable flight-recorder wraparound tracing.

The stop command stops tracing (if it hasn't already been stopped) and writes the resulting raw binary trace to a file named by default with the current date, time, hostname, and process ID of the kutrace_control program, something like

```
ku_20180606_121314_dclab-2_3456.trace
```

The stop command takes an optional argument, which replaces the default filename.

```
> stop my_filename.trace
```

The wait command

```
> wait n
```

waits n seconds before executing the next command. With command input from a file containing go/wait/stop, this can be used to run kutrace_control to capture an *n*-second trace.

The raw trace file is self-contained, with human-readable names as embedded trace entries. Chapter 18 describes the postprocessing of raw trace files into JSON files, and Chapter 19 describes the HTML/SVG wrapper that displays JSON files. The names of all the system calls, interrupts, and faults are compiled into kutrace_control from the header file kutrace_control_names.h, which can be customized particularly for names for interrupt numbers used on a particular computer.

17.3   The Underlying kutrace_lib Library

The user-mode kutrace_lib library can be linked into any C program to include human-meaningful markers or to build a self-tracing version of the program. The library has routines named go, goipc, ..., stop that directly implement the controlling commands, plus several more low-level routines.

A few routines in kutrace_lib are particularly useful for user-mode code to insert KUtrace entries whenever tracing is active. Four routines insert user-chosen markers into the trace, as shown in the hello_world example in Chapter 14, and one general-purpose routine inserts an arbitrary trace entry, helpful for RPC and locking libraries to record which RPCID is being serviced or which lock is being held.

kutrace::mark_a(const char* label) inserts the one- to six-character label into the trace. The label is stored in 32 bits using base40 encoding, which allows 26 letters, 10 digits, and periods, slashes, and hyphens. These labels are drawn in red hexagons below a CPU timeline, as in Figure 14.1, for CPU 1. By convention, names starting with slash are drawn to the left and others to the right, so that "foo" and "/foo" can visually bracket a stretch of code. The mark_b routine does the same thing but drawn lower in a blue hexagon. The mark_c routine centers its label in a green hexagon. The mark_d routine takes a number as an argument and displays it below a CPU timeline.

Any user code can link in the library and directly call these routines, so alternate control programs or self-tracing programs are easy to build.

17.4   The Control Interface to the Loadable Module

The kernel-mode loadable library routine's kutrace_control() entry point is reached via

```
u64 syscall(__NR_kutrace_control, u64 command,
            u64 argument)
```

where __NR_kutrace_control is our dummy syscall number, the command is a small integer, and the argument is a single 64-bit parameter for the command. Each call has a 64-bit result. There are 12 control commands defined in kutrace_lib.h. If the kernel is not built with KUtrace code or if the loadable module is not loaded, this syscall returns ENOSYS for all commands. For an out-of-range command number, the call does nothing and returns ~0L, i.e., all ones.

17.5   Summary

Runtime control of tracing has three levels of interface:

- kutrace_control.cc is a standalone program that takes simple text commands.
- kutrace_lib.cc is a small library that can be used by any user-mode program to provide trace control or to insert extra trace entries such as markers or RPC IDs or lock acquire/release events.
- syscall(__NR_kutrace_control, ...) accesses the kernel-mode loadable library's kutrace_control() entry point to implement the other two interfaces.

The next chapter describes the programs that postprocess raw binary traces into JSON text and then dynamic HTML.

Chapter 18

KUtrace: Postprocessing

Once a raw trace file is created, it can be postprocessed into an HTML file that can be displayed and dynamically panned and zoomed and annotated. There are five programs involved, two of which are optional, as shown in Figure 18.1, taken from Chapter 14's Figure 14.3.

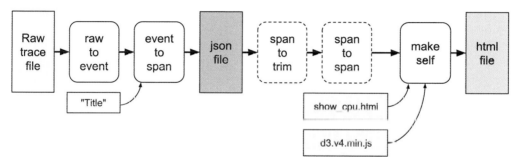

Figure 18.1   **Overview of trace postprocessing**

18.1   Postprocessing Details

A raw trace file consists of packed binary 8-byte trace entries. These entries largely record call-return pairs for system calls, interrupts, and faults, but they also include context switches, names of routines, and markers. The rawtoevent program reads a trace file and produces a text list of the events. The eventtospan program reads this list and turns them into timespans, producing a JSON file. The optional spantotrim program reads a JSON file and produces a smaller one with just the spans in a specified start..stop time range. The optional spantospan program reads a json file and produces a smaller one with more granular timespans no shorter than a specified number of microseconds. The makeself program reads an HTML template, the data-driven documents JavaScript library called d3 [Bostock 2020], and an input JSON file and then produces a self-contained HTML file with all the trace data and a dynamic user interface (UI). The output HTML file can reasonably support 100K to 1M timespans, but starts to run out of memory space in the browser around 2M timespans.

18.2   The rawtoevent Program

This program is a standard Unix filter, reading a raw trace file from `stdin` and writing a text form of each event to `stdout`. It reads each 64KB block in a trace file, and if the file contains optional IPC (instructions per cycle) information, it reads the additional 8KB of IPC per trace block.

```
Usage: rawtoevent [filename] [-v]
```

Normally rawtoevent reads from `stdin` and writes to `stdout`, but it optionally can take a file-name parameter to read from. The `-v` parameter produces verbose output showing each 8-byte trace entry in hex, plus its timestamp, event number, call argument, delta time between call and return, and return value. This is just a debugging aid; with `-v`, the output is not suitable for reading by eventtospan.

The beginning of each trace file block has a full timestamp and corresponding `gettimeofday()` value in microseconds. The remaining trace file entries have 20-bit timestamps that wrap around every 15..30 milliseconds. It is the responsibility of rawtoevent to expand these short timestamps to full ones by prepending the high-order bits and incrementing this value at every wraparound. The very first trace file block also has two pairs of *<timestamp, gettimeofday>* values taken at the start of a trace and taken at the end. These are used by rawtoevent to linearly map raw 20-bit timestamp counts to seconds of wall-clock time. The resulting times are relative to the starting minute of the trace, so normally are in the range of 0.0 to about 150.0 seconds, depending on the trace size. The output values are given in integer increments of 10 nano-seconds, so there is an implied decimal point before the last eight digits of each timestamp.

Flight-recorder-mode traces continuously wrap around in the trace buffer for many minutes before some program or manual event stops the trace, which then contains the last several seconds before the stop. In this case, the start time of the trace may be many minutes or a good fraction of an hour before the earliest retained trace entry. Since the earliest retained trace entry may not be known until the last block of the raw trace file is read, rawtoevent produces seconds of wall-clock time that may be quite large. The next program, eventtospan, adjusts the start time to make the earliest second of wall-clock time be in the range 0..59.

When tracing wraps around, the very first trace block is not overwritten; instead, the overwriting begins at the second trace block. This enables retention of the syscall/interrupt/fault names recorded in the first block and also the start/stop pairs of *<timestamp, gettimeofday>* values recorded there. The remaining entries in the very first trace block may describe events that are many minutes before the rest of the trace. To avoid a big gap in the final timespans, rawtoevent drops these orphan first-block non-name entries for wraparound traces.

The rawtoevent program is also responsible for extracting the names of every event and user-mode program, extracting the CPU number from the front of each trace block, extracting the current process ID at each instant, and extracting any identifier of the transaction (RPCID or otherwise) that each user-mode program is working on at each instant. It records these in each output event.

The output of rawtoevent must be sorted to put everything into time order. This is normally done by piping the output through the system sort, specifying a numeric sort:

```
cat foo.trace |./rawtoevent |sort -n |...
```

This sorted output is then piped into the next program, eventospan.

Some names appear physically in the raw trace file after the first mention in the trace file of the event being named. This can occur when the first use, and hence the name recording is on CPU A and a later use is on CPU B, but it turns out that B's traceblock was allocated earlier in the trace buffer than A's and hence is written to the trace file first. When this happens, some of the event output from rawtoevent will be missing names. To compensate, all the names are put into the event output in duplicate, at their original time and also at time -1. This lets them be sorted to the front so that eventtospan can add the missing names to all entries.

The main output of rawtoevent is a text file with one event per line. Each line contains the reconstructed full timestamp, duration, event, and propagated CPU number, PID number, RPC number, etc. Name definitions have the same timestamp, duration, and event fields as transition events, but they then have just an argument number and a name. The timestamp for a name is unused except to position the names in the input file. The duration for a name is completely unused. The event number specifies the kind of item to be named—PID, RPC method, trap, interrupt, lock, syscall, source file. The argument number specifies which particular PID, RPC etc., is being named.

The rawtoevent program writes a few summary lines to stderr as it finishes. These give the number of events and the timespan covered from the base minute. This last information is useful to guide spantotrim, described in Section 18.4.

18.3 The eventtospan Program

This program is also a standard Unix filter, reading text events from stdin and writing to JSON timespans to stdout. It reads the sorted events from rawtoevent and matches these kernel-user transitions into timespans. It is also responsible for producing the final start time and matching seconds, as mentioned earlier.

```
Usage: eventtospan ["Title"] [-v]
```

The first parameter is a string used as the title in the resulting HTML display. The -v parameter produces verbose output showing each line of event input. This is just a debugging aid; with -v, the JSON output is not suitable for reading by later programs.

There are a few trace parameters passed along from rawtoevent in event file comments (beginning with #), in a rather ad hoc way. These include the original trace-start date and time, trace version number and flags, and wraparound-trace actual minimum/maximum times. Other than that, the input consists of name definitions and transition events.

The rawtoevent program has already filled in all the names except some missing PID, RPC, and lock names, so eventtospan just remembers and fills them in.

In long traces, it is possible that the process PID numbers are reused or redefined via execv( ) or such. In that case, updating the names based on sorted time will have the effect of tracking those changes.

Within eventtospan, the main work of turning kernel-user transitions into timespans is done in ProcessEvent. For each CPU, there is an existing timespan that is being constructed, arbitrarily initialized to the idle process before the start of the trace. Transition events stop the existing timespan and start a new timespan. Call events stop the existing timespan and start a timespan for the target of the call—a specific system call or interrupt or fault. But return events need to stop the existing called timespan and return to—what? To reconstruct the what, `ProcessEvent` maintains a small stack of pending spans for each CPU. Each call pushes this stack and each return pops it. So if user-mode process 1234 is running and does a call to `syswrite()`, the matching return from `syswrite()` will start a new span of process 1234. Syscalls, faults, and interrupts can nest. In particular, interrupts can be delivered while in a syscall or in a fault handler. Including the user-mode program and the operating system scheduler, the maximum stack depth is five.

Each CPU has its own reconstruction stack. In addition, processes can migrate from one CPU to another. So at each context switch event, the stack for the old PID is saved under that PID number and the stack for the new PID is restored. If a PID has no saved stack, a new one is created on the fly.

Events can be mismatched in various ways. At the very beginning of a trace, there may be a return with no matching call. At other times, there may be a system call with no matching return because the call exited in a non-standard way through the scheduler (which is treated as a dummy syscall routine). An interrupt routine that causes a context switch can exit directly to the new user mode process instead of returning to an in-progress system call or fault handler, which will be resumed at some later time. So at each push and pop of the reconstruction stack, there are little routines called that create dummy pushes and pops as needed to keep things matched. The `PreProcessEvent` routine handles these little fixups and several others.

The final output from eventtospan is a JSON file that includes some header lines, some trailer lines, and a large number of timespan lines. Since each span is created when the ending transition is encountered but the eventual display depends on them being in order by start time, the output from eventtospan is sent again through the system sort routine, this time doing a byte-by-byte sort, not a numeric sort. In order to make sure the JSON header and trailer lines appear in the proper places after sorting, the lines have carefully inserted initial spaces and punctuation to make them sort to the front or back respectively when sorted by byte-value.

Unfortunately, the default Linux sort collation sequence is to sort *alphabetically* ignoring spaces and punctuation. When this happens, the sorted json is ill-formed and nothing displays properly. So it is important to set the collation sequence to use bare byte values via

```
export LC_ALL=C
```

before doing the sort after eventtospan. (It might be possible to use `LC_COLLATE=C`, but this fails if `LC_ALL` is set to something else.)

The eventtospan program writes a few summary lines to `stderr` as it finishes. These give the trace date and time, number of spans, and a short breakdown by span type. The sorted output of eventtospan is a JSON file that can be fed directly into makeself, but for large traces it can be useful to use the optional spanto* filters, described next.

The JSON file is all text, so it is suitable for *ad hoc* searching via `grep` or other tools to find execution patterns. Information from other performance tools such as `tcpdump` can be added to the JSON file to create additional correlated events or timespans.

18.4   The spantotrim Program

This program is a standard Unix filter, reading from stdin and writing to stdout. It reads a JSON file and writes a smaller one that contains only a subset of the full timespan of the incoming trace.

```
Usage: spantotrim start_sec [stop_sec]
Usage: spantotrim "string"
```

The start_sec parameter specifies a start time in seconds and fraction from the start minute of the trace. If the stop_sec time is also given, spantotrim keeps just timespans that begin or end in the [start .. stop] interval.

If just start_sec is given and it is zero, spantotrim is a NOP, keeping everything. If it is a positive number of seconds and fraction, spantotrim keeps that many seconds from the beginning of the trace. This can be handy because it does not require copying over the start time from the rawtoevent summary. If start_sec is negative, it keeps that many seconds from the end of the trace.

An alternate form of spantotrim takes a non-numeric string as its only argument. In that case, it keeps only timespans that contain that string, which might be a comma-space-PID-number or some kind of name. This form is of limited use; it differs from grep only in keeping the JSON header and trailer lines.

18.5   The spantospan Program

This program is another standard Unix filter, reading from stdin and writing to stdout. It reads a JSON file and writes a smaller one that contains more granular time resolution than the incoming trace.

```
Usage: spantospan resolution_usec
```

The resolution_usec parameter specifies the smallest timespan size in microseconds. If it is zero, spantospan is a NOP, keeping everything unchanged. Otherwise, for each CPU, spantospan accumulates smaller timespans while the total time deferred is less than resolution_usec. When that amount of time is reached or exceeded, the accumulated time is assigned to the most recent event and placed in the output file. This distorts the fine-grain timing of a trace, but places a tight bound on how many timespans per second are in the resulting output file. Such a file can be useful for getting a quick overview of the activity in a very large trace, followed by selective use of spantotrim to look at the more interesting portions.

Because spantospan produces its output at the end, not the beginning, of each span the resulting JSON must be sorted byte-by-byte once again.

18.6   The samptoname_k and samptoname_u Programs

The PC samples taken by KUtrace at each timer interrupt are just bare binary addresses, shown as PC=hex in the JSON name field. To turn these into meaningful names is finicky but possible. The optional samptoname_k program takes the JSON output of eventtospan and rewrites the

kernel-mode PC addresses based on a routine-name map from /proc/kallsyms provided by
the command

```
$ sudo cat /proc/kallsyms |sort >somefile.txt
```

The optional samptoname_u program does the same for user-mode PC addresses based on an
image-name map from /proc/*/maps provided by the command

```
$ sudo ls /proc/*/maps |xargs -I % sh -c 'echo "\n====" %; \
  sudo cat %' >someotherfile.txt
```

The net effect is to turn each PC sample into a subroutine name in the respective executable
image. Chapter 19 has more details about using these programs.

18.7   The makeself Program

This program is partly a Unix filter, reading from stdin and writing to stdout. It reads a JSON
file and writes a self-contained HTML file that displays that JSON along with user interface
controls for dynamically panning, zooming, and annotating the timespans. To do this, makeself
reads a specified template HTML file and also reads a copy of the d3 JavaScript library, which
must be in the current directory.

```
Usage: makeself template_filename
```

The template_filename parameter specifies an HTML file containing the user interface HTML
and JavaScript. This file must have several stylized selfcontained* comments that delimit
where to put the d3 library and where to put the JSON file from stdin. (With different tem-
plates, this program can be used to make other kinds of self-contained traces, such as the disk-
block displays in Chapter 5.) There is nothing fancy here. Everything is read into large buffers,
so an extremely large JSON file will fail. Use spantotrim or spantospan in that case.

18.8   KUtrace JSON Format

The JSON file has some metadata at the front and then a long series of events/spans sorted by
starting time, ending with an end marker event at time 999, the only event with no trailing
comma in order to produce valid JSON syntax. The design does not anticipate traces longer than
1,000 seconds (about 16 minutes). This file is carefully formatted with leading spaces and quotes
and brackets so that a byte-by-byte sort will maintain valid JSON syntax. The initial JSON opening brace "{" has two leading spaces to place it at the front after sorting.

JSON Metadata

The metadata fields label a diagram. They each have a leading space to place them after the
opening brace and before the events. Then they sort in alphabetical order.

> **Comment:** Random comment, not displayed. May be useful for tracking versions. The
> capital-C places this at the front of the metadata.

> **axisLabelX:** The x-axis label; no longer used because the x-axis units are dynamically
> changed within the JavaScript.

axisLabelY: The y-axis label; no longer used because the y-axis now also includes PID and RPC groups.

cpuModelName: The model name of the traced processor, taken by kutrace_control from `/proc/cpuinfo`.

flags: Value from the raw trace, not displayed. See `kutrace.h` for the bits. Lack of IPC bit grays out the IPC UI button. Otherwise ignored.

kernelVersion: The kernel version of the traced processor, taken by kutrace_control from `$ uname -a`.

mbit_sec: The network link speed of the traced processor, taken by kutrace_control from the maximum value in `$ cat /sys/class/net/*/speed`.

randomid: A random 32-bit integer inserted by eventtospan to allow save/restore of display state across browser reloads.

shortMulX: Multiplier for scaling X values, usually 1.

shortUnitsX: Suffix for short unit labels, i.e., "s" for seconds.

thousandsX: Multiplier for short units, either 1,000 or 1,024. Used to create prefix "ns," etc., when showing short values (similar triple for Y—multiplier for example can be used to convert 4KB disk block counts to bytes; not used for CPU numbers).

title: Placed at the head of the diagram.

tracebase: Original time of trace creation, for identification months later. Displayed at lower right in the HTML output.

version: Currently version 3, which includes an IPC field. Not displayed.

JSON Events

A long series of timespans follows the metadata. These are a big array mis-named "events", where the leading quote sorts before all the actual events, each of which starts with a leading "[". Each event line has 10 fields [ts, dur, cpu, pid, rpc, event, arg0, ret, ipc, name].

timestamp: Start time for a span in seconds and fraction. For easy correlation with logs and other files, the seconds part is offset from an exact multiple of one minute in the `gettimeofday()` time domain, rather than arbitrarily starting at zero at the beginning of a trace.

duration: Duration of a span in seconds and fraction.

cpu: CPU number as a small integer. The UI display groups all CPUs together on the y-axis.

pid: Process ID (actually thread ID; the kernel calls this "pid"), low 16 bits. The UI display groups all PIDs together on the y-axis.

rpcid: RPC ID for most work, but could be used for any additional value in other work. The UI display groups all RPCs together on the y-axis.

event: Event number that starts the timespan. Values less than 512 are names, markers, and other specials. Values 512–4096 are kernel events such as system call, interrupt, and fault.

These are drawn as full-height rectangles. Values 64K+pid are user-mode threads. These are drawn as half-height rectangles. Value 65536 is the user-mode idle thread, pid=0, drawn as a thin black line. The full list of event numbers is in `kutrace_lib.h`.

arg0: The low 16 bits of the first argument to a syscall, else 0.

retval: For a call/return span, the low 16 bits of the return value, else zero. Byte counts, etc., can be considered unsigned. Return codes can be considered signed. If a single system call is split into multiple spans because of nested interrupts or faults, the first span has the actual arg0, and the last span has the actual retval.

ipc: Instructions per cycle, quantized via truncation into 4 bits. Values 0–7 are multiples of 1/8 IPC, i.e., less than one instruction per cycle. Values 8–11 are 1.0, 1.25, 1.5, and 1.75 IPC, respectively. Values 12–15 are 2.0, 2.5, 3.0, and 3.5+ IPC.

name: Name of the kernel routine or user PID (originally from the kernel 16-byte `command` field per PID), etc., for this timespan. These names come from naming entries in the raw trace itself.

18.9 Summary

The postprocessing programs turn a raw trace into an HTML file with an embedded user interface for panning and zooming the timeline and controls for selecting what elements to display. The next chapter describes the user interface.

Chapter 19

KUtrace: Display of Software Dynamics

At last, we get back to the title of the book. It does no good to gather traces unless the information is presented in an understandable way—a way that allows a performance engineer to quickly understand *why* a collection of software is intermittently slow. The previous chapters of Part III cover gathering a trace of kernel-user execution transitions and postprocessing those into timespans that cover every nanosecond of elapsed time on every CPU core of a traced machine. This chapter covers turning those timespans into a meaningful visible display.

19.1   Overview

The self-contained HTML file created by makeself, described in Chapter 18, initially shows per-CPU timelines for the entire trace range. These timelines show exactly what happened during the trace, the dynamic interactions between different software threads, the interactions with and interference from the operating system, and also what did *not* happen. Because no nanosecond is missing from a KUtrace, a stretch of time showing no disk interrupts, for example, means that there was *no disk activity* slowing down the software. This is a powerful tool for focusing your attention on what *did* happen rather than what might have happened but in fact did not.

The `show_cpu.html` file used by makeself is a template that contains an HTML/SVG dynamic browser user interface for showing postprocessed traces from KUtrace. The overall layout has six regions, as shown in Figure 19.1.

Region 1 at the top has a number of HTML control buttons and text boxes, explained next.

Region 2 is the y-axis showing the various CPUs and optionally expanded PIDs and RPCs. The sample in Figure 19.1 shows four CPU timelines and an expandable group of 5 processes IDs.

Region 3 is the main timeline display showing what is running on each CPU every nanosecond. You can pan and zoom all around it, and Shift-click on any item to see its name. This is where you can see the actual software dynamics of a complete running live system.

Region 4 is the optional IPC legend; it appears only when the IPC button in Region 1 is active. The space also allows the timeline and labels to spill over a little.

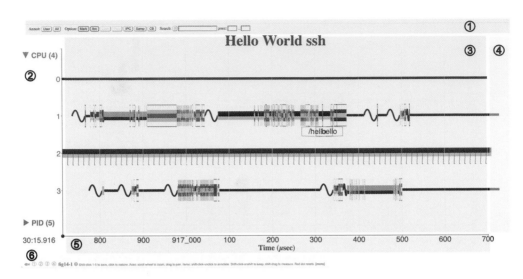

Figure 19.1   **show_cpu.html browser layout**

Region 5 is the x-axis showing time across the screen. The time scale changes as you zoom.

Region 6 at the bottom has save/restore controls and a brief text summary about the UI control actions.

19.2   Region 1, Controls

Within Region 1 there are three groups of buttons and text fields that select what data to display in the main timeline. At the far right is a text area that is usually empty but shows the results from active searches. Just after opening or resetting an HTML file, it shows the kernel version and CPU model name of the computer used for creating the trace.

The `Annot` group has three buttons. The `User` button annotates the first occurrence of a time-span for each process ID. It gives a quick overview of which programs are in the on-screen part of a trace. The annotations are short versions of the process name shown just below the timespan, with a vertical line down to the x-axis and a dotted line up to the top of Region 3. These lines allow you to visually see how events align in time across multiple CPUs. The `All` button annotates everything in Region 3, both timespans and point events. It is most useful when zoomed in to just a handful of spans. The blue label `Annot` is also an active button even though it is not drawn as one: it toggles shift-click annotations (described below) to a simplified form, indicated by lowercase `annot`.

The `Option` group has seven buttons, some of which are grayed out when none of the corresponding data is in the trace. The `Mark` button controls whether user-inserted marks, such as `hello` in Figure 19.1, are displayed. It cycles through four states: all marks, just alphabetic ones (mark_a, mark_b, mark_c), just numeric ones (mark_d), or none. The `Arc` button cycles through three states: showing cross-process wakeup arcs, showing them bold (mostly for presentations), or not showing them. The `Lock` button similarly cycles through showing contended lock waiting/holding lines. Since lock holding is process-specific and not CPU-specific, these lines are displayed above PID and RPC timelines, but not above the CPU timelines. The `Freq` button toggles showing a slow clock frequency overlay for each CPU. Full-speed CPU clocks have faint green overlay, medium-speed have three densities of yellow, and slow-speed red. Searching (next group, below) for `freq` will show the individual CPU-frequency changes in MHz. The `IPC` button cycles through four states: all IPC triangles, kernel-only, user-only, and none. The triangles are little speedometer indicators, swinging from pointing left for 0 to pointing almost right for 3.5+ instructions per cycle, as detailed in the Region 4 legend. The `Samp` button toggles showing PC samples that are taken at each timer interrupt. Non-idle samples are shown as two-color slightly slanted dashed lines above each CPU timeline, with bolder dashes for kernel-mode PC samples. To avoid clutter, idle samples are not shown. The lines extend between timer interrupts, with each sample instant at the top (right) end. Shift-click on any sample line or search for `PC=` to see the actual sample values. The `CB` button toggles the colors used in Region 3 as a weak aid for color-blind users. It simply rotates the RGB color channels to BRG. If there is no underlying information in the trace for a particular button, it is grayed out.

The `Search` group has a button, a text box, and a numeric range. Text typed into the text box is matched against the name fields of all events shown in Region 3, and each matching item is annotated with a short name and vertical lines. The match is case-sensitive. It is a generic JavaScript match, so for example the string `rx|tx` will match either "rx" or "tx" anywhere in an event's name. Use backslash escapes before punctuation characters such as period or parentheses. To avoid clutter, a few names such as `-idle-` start with a minus sign, and matches for them are normally suppressed. Explicitly type the leading minus sign to see them. The [!] button before the text box inverts the match, like the `-v` flag for `grep`. The numeric range limits all matches to spans whose duration is in the range. The first box takes an integer lower bound and the second an integer upper bound. The units word, shown in blue just before the lower-bound box, is an active button even though it is not drawn as one: it cycles through three states: `nsec`, `usec`, `msec`. At the far right, each search shows the number of matching items, the sum of the durations of those items, and the minimum and maximum matching durations. The last two can inform values to use for the bounds boxes to select especially interesting durations.

Initially, `Mark`, `Arc`, and `Freq` are on if available, and the other choices are off. In general, items that are too small to see (smaller than a few pixels horizontally or vertically) are not shown, so you might not see wakeup arcs or the frequency overlay until you zoom the x-axis horizontally—about a second full-scale for `Freq` and about 5 msec full-scale for `Arc`.

19.3   Region 2, Y-axis

Within Region 2, there are up to three groups of timeline labels. The CPU group is expanded by default, while the PID group and RPC groups are collapsed by default. Each group has an expand/contract triangle to click, group name, and a count of timelines in parentheses. If the count is zero, the group is suppressed. If the number of readable labels is less than the number of items to show, only some labels are shown. But in that case every item has a little tick mark on the y-axis, so you can see if there are unlabeled items. The timespans shown for each group are all the same—they are just sorted into different timelines based on CPU number, PID number, or RPC number, respectively.

The CPU group shows one timeline for each CPU in the trace, numbered from zero and vertically sorted in ascending order.

The PID group shows one timeline for each process in the trace, if there are any events from that process on-screen. Each label is the process name followed by the PID number. They are vertically sorted in ascending order by PID number. The idle process, PID 0, is never shown in this group.

The RPC group shows one timeline for each remote procedure call, if there are any. Each label is the RPC method name followed by the RPCID number truncated to 16 bits. They are vertically sorted by start time. In general, multiple unrelated RPCs can overlap in time, and this overlap can be an important root cause of slow completion. RPC 0 is considered no-RPC-executing and is never shown in this group.

With the mouse over the right 3/4 of Region 2, click-drag scrolls vertically, and the mouse wheel zooms vertically. Shift-click on a label toggles highlighting it, while Shift-right-click on a label toggles highlighting all with the same initial string (a-z0-9_-). If any labels in a group are highlighted, the expand/contract triangle for that group changes to cycle through three states: show all, show just highlighted, and show none. This allows you to focus on just a subset of the timelines. When any label in any group is highlighted, only the timespans in highlighted lines are shown in color, with all other timespans faded to gray. This enables you to focus, for example, on just the execution spans of two particular PIDs and one particular RPC on the CPU timelines. The scheduler spans on the timelines belong to the PID that was executing then the scheduler was entered. So in a sequence of process A and then process B executing, the scheduler span that does the A=>B context switch is part of A, and the scheduler span that switches away from B to something else is part of B.

19.4   Region 3, Timelines

Region 3 is the main timeline display. The initial view shows the entire KUtrace time on the x-axis and all CPUs on the y-axis. Processes and RPC groups are collapsed. The Mark, Arc, and Freq buttons are enabled. Clicking the red dot where the axes cross always restores this view.

For longer traces, this initial view may be mostly blank-looking except for idle lines, or it may be nearly solid timer interrupts. Zoom in a little and it will fill in more meaningful detail. Or click the User button in Region 1 to see the names of all the programs running and then pan and zoom toward the ones you care about.

For each CPU timeline, thin black lines show the idle process timespans, half-height multi-colored lines show user-mode execution, and full-high multi-colored lines show kernel-mode execution. The 255 different color pairs for each span vary by process ID or by syscall/interrupt/fault numbers.

Marks are enabled by default because they are user-inserted labels or numbers at various interesting points in some software. Arcs are enabled because the act of one process waking up another is usually an important part of the dynamic behavior of complex software. The frequency overlay is enabled because it can save the user a lot of fruitless time tracking down an apparent slow-execution problem when in reality a mostly idle CPU just is running at a 5x lower clock rate to save power. When they are unneeded, all of these display elements can be toggled off to reduce clutter.

The design center for this UI is to be able to display over a million timespans with fast response to any mouse input. Naïve use of current browsers fails to meet this goal with more than about 15,000 timespans on screen, so the JavaScript for display implements an important optimization. Based on the current x-axis zoom, it calculates the timespan, `Tpix`, that one screen pixel represents. Trace timespans shorter than `Tpix` are not displayed, but instead their time is accumulated on the fly in a side table for each CPU timeline, and the accumulated time is displayed in abbreviated form whenever it exceeds `Tpix`. If there are 2,000 pixels across the screen and 4 CPUs, this strictly bounds the number of displayed timespans to 8,000. Displaying just these is about 100 times faster than displaying a million timespans. As the user zooms in on part of the trace, `Tpix` shrinks and accordingly fewer timespans are set aside, while simultaneously more timespans move offscreen entirely. The bound on maximum displayed timespans remains constant but more and more detail is revealed for the portion of the trace that is onscreen. A similar mechanism operates in the vertical dimension as the y-axis is zoomed.

In such a scheme, there is a design question of what placeholder to display for the abbreviation that represents a number of tiny spans. The choice of displaying nothing is a disaster for the user—lots of uninformative white space. Another simple choice is to display a gray line whose length matches the accumulated time, but that is also uninformative. Instead, the KUtrace UI keeps in the per-CPU side list three sums: accumulated idle time, accumulated user-mode time, and accumulated kernel-mode time; plus the most recent event for these last two—PID number or syscall/interrupt/fault number. The abbreviated display picks the largest of the three times and displays a single line of the matching height and a single number-based color. The effect is to draw the abbreviation as an idle line if most of the time was idle, a single-color user-mode line if it had most of the time, and a single-color kernel line if it had most of the time. By distinguishing the three categories, the display is more informative, and by restricting the abbreviations to single colors, their display is somewhat faster than the full multi-color scheme used for complete unabbreviated timespans. As you zoom in, more and more detail is revealed. Any line that is drawn with more than one stacked color means it is full-form, not elided. This helps distinguish placeholders from exact timespans.

Annotations. Individual timespans can be annotated with their names, using either long or short annotations. Short ones just have the name elided to no more than eight characters, using the first six characters, tilde, and the last character. Long names have the start time, the full name, the duration (elapsed time), and the IPC if available. For user-mode spans, the full name is command-name and PID; for system calls it is `name(arg0)=retval`. For interrupts and faults, it is just the name. Each annotation has a single vertical line from the bottom of the display to the start point of the subject timespan and a dashed vertical line continuing from there to the top of the display. The line makes it easy to see how events on different CPUs line up in time. The dashed part makes it easier to distinguish which line belongs to which timespan. For each CPU timeline, the names rotate through several vertical positions, reducing the frequency of closely spaced names overwriting each other.

Shift-click on any span to display its long name. Shift-click-unshift multiple times puts multiple labels onscreen. Shift-click-unclick to remove them all. Shift-click-drag across multiple spans to get the endpoint names and elapsed time between the two. Shift-right-click shows all the same-item spans (e.g., all page_faults) in color and fades everything else to gray. In addition to picking out repeated uses, this can be a weak aid for color-blind users.

When there are any annotations displayed, panning or zooming will retain the vertical line and long form name of the *one* annotation nearest to the mouse cursor. This can make it easier to keep track of where you were while changing the display.

Point events (RPC start/stop, lock acquire/release, packets, mwait, etc.) have an artificial duration of 10 nsec, which makes them hard to click unless you zoom in to less than a few microseconds across the screen, at which time they show up as thin vertical bars sticking out a little above a timeline. They are best found via the search box.

Internally, the drawing JavaScript has a large array of timespans from the input JSON. Any pan or zoom or reset action triggers a redraw, which clears Regions 2, 3, and 5, and then repopulates them based on the new x- and y-axis values, quickly discarding any timespans from the array that are not on-screen, abbreviating multiple short timespans, and drawing the rest in full. The drawing converts individual timespans into stroked SVG lines or curves. Annotations are drawn or removed as described earlier, using magenta lines and black text.

There is a lot going on in the main display. Refer to the summary chart of Region 3 notations at the end of this book.

Idle display. For some processors, there are two forms of idle—normal idle and low-power idle. In the x86 family of processors, the idle loop uses the mwait CPU instruction to suggest to the hardware that it could drop into a power-saving mode, so-called C1, C2, ... C6 and higher states. The power-saving states reduce the CPU clock temporarily or may even turn it off entirely for one core and power down that core. Leaving a low-power state and returning to normal execution may take a substantial amount of time. To capture this dynamic behavior, KUtrace records context switches into and out of idle and also records any mwait instruction executed in the idle loop. The HTML display shows normal idle as a solid black line, low-power idle as a thinner dashed black line, and the approximate time switching out of low-power as a red sine wave. As usual, these details are suppressed if they are less than one pixel wide. However, if you zoom in to just a few microseconds after entering the idle loop on a CPU, you can see the transition from normal idle to low-power idle. If you zoom in to the microseconds leaving the idle loop, you can see any correspond low-power-exit sine wave.

Process wakeup. The wakeup arcs go from the instant that some thread or interrupt handler makes a blocked process runnable to the instant that it next starts executing. If your process A is blocked, the event or thread that wakes it up tells you what A was waiting for. Since not executing at all can be a significant source of unexplained software delays, the starting point of a wakeup arc is valuable information. And since there can be a substantial delay between waking up a process and having it actually execute on some CPU, the length of the wakeup arc is also valuable information.

The eventtospan program uses wakeup events to assign reasons for not executing, based on what routine did the wakeup. It turns the blocked delays for a given process or RPC into *non-execution spans*, shown on a PID or RPC timeline. These cover the five fundamental resources, CPU, memory, disk, network, and software lock, plus waiting on a software pipe and waiting on a timer. For example, if the disk soft interrupt handler, called BH:block, wakes up process A, it is deemed to have been waiting on disk. Between that wakeup and A actually executing again, it is waiting on

CPU, i.e., waiting for a CPU to be assigned and for the scheduler to finish context switching to A. In addition to color differences, the displayed thin non-execution lines end with Morse code characters: C for CPU wait, D for disk wait, etc.

Network packets. As described in Chapter 15, KUtrace by default records events for RPC message-header packets when seen by the kernel network code, and also the RPC library described in Chapter 6 records events for message-header packets as seen by user code in that library. Large delays between sending an RPC on one machine and receiving it on another can be subdivided by these event timestamps into kernel and user time on each machine, helping identify the root cause of the delay. To aid the user, the eventtospan program uses RPCID numbers, kernel and user packet timestamps, RPC request/response message lengths, and the network link speed to synthesize a naïve approximate picture of when the packets for each RPC were transmitted across the network hardware. The 32-byte packet hashes described in Chapter 15 are used to correlate kernel packet times with user RPCID and message length. Processing in eventtospan turns message length plus link speed into time duration, length into packet count, and then creates json entries for each message. Incoming request/response messages are shown on the link just before the TCP/UDP kernel code records them, and outgoing ones just after the kernel records them. This is naïve because it does not account for apparently overlapping messages whose packets in reality are sequenced and possibly intermixed on the network link; nor does it precisely track incoming packets after the message header or outgoing packets delayed in the network interface hardware. Nonetheless, it lets you see a useful approximation of the RPC network activity near a delay that you are studying. An example using this information is in the upcoming Chapter 26.

Because network traffic is for an entire processor, the synthetic RPC message information is drawn in Region 3 just above CPU 0. Incoming messages are drawn as downward-slanting lines with gaps at approximate packet boundaries and with RPC number below, and outgoing ones as upward-slanting lines with RPC number above. The slanting not only identifies transmission direction but also allows you to see multiple apparently overlapping messages.

Software locks. The locking library described in the upcoming Chapter 27 records KUtrace events for each failed attempt to acquire a contended software lock, each subsequent success-ful attempt, and each release of a contended lock. The eventtospan program uses these events to create json entries for lock waiting and lock holding. The lock information is displayed as dotted/solid lines above the corresponding PID timeline. Lock waiting may involve a short CPU-bound spin loop, or it may involve context switches to other processes. With multiple con-tenders for a single lock, waiting within a single process may involve multiple failed attempts to acquire the lock. All of these dynamics are revealed by the combination of KUtrace, the locking library, and the HTML display.

PC samples. At every timer interrupt, KUtrace records the program counter (PC) address of the instruction that was about to be executed when the interrupt was delivered. This is similar to pro-filers that collect PC samples at every timer interrupt, but it is *much more powerful* because it shows each and every sample in context, not just total sample counts over many seconds or minutes. The PC addresses help understand how the time is subdivided in long CPU-bound execution.

Raw hex PC values are pretty meaningless, so two postprocessing programs, samptoname_k and samptoname_u, can turn kernel and user PC addresses respectively into meaningful subroutine names.

Capturing names is finicky. The kernel map of addresses to routine names is in /proc/kallsyms, but this is accessible only with privileges:

```
$ sudo cat /proc/kallsyms |sort >somefile.txt
```

You need to do this after any loadable modules have been inserted into the kernel, including the kutrace_mod module. To further complicate matters, a common malware defense is to randomly start the kernel image at a different memory address for each reboot, called *address space layout randomization* (ASLR) [PaX 2003]. This means that you need to capture the kallsyms map after each boot.

The map of user addresses is even harder to get, particularly for processes that start up during a tracing run. The basic information starts with an address-to-image-name map in /proc/1234/ maps for process ID 1234. The maps include items such as dynamically loaded shared libraries. If you have 30 different programs running, there are 30 different maps to capture. If PID 1234 spawns multiple threads, they might be PIDs 1235, 1236, etc., or there might be gaps if other unrelated processes start up at the same time. In either case, there will be a map file only for the base process and none for the spawned threads. And of course if you want to make sense of all the programs running during a tracing run, you want maps for *all* of them, including ones that are not yours. This is accessible only with privileges:

```
$ sudo ls /proc/*/maps |xargs -I % sh -c 'echo "\n====" %; \
    sudo cat %' >someotherfile.txt
```

ASLR moves these addresses around each time a program starts or each time a shared library dynamically loads. This means that you may need to capture /proc/*/maps just before or just after or *during* a tracing run.

In any case, the image maps are just a first step. They tell for each process which images are loaded where but very little about the insides of those images. Step 2 is to call the Linux addr2line program to look up user-mode addresses to get routine names or line numbers within each image. And of course the addresses needed by addr2line are offsets within the image, not the raw PC addresses that KUtrace captures. The samptoname_u program handles all these details.

With all that in mind, samptoname_k and samptoname_u are filters that take an input JSON file and rewrite any PC sample hex addresses that they can. Piping the output of eventtospan through these two can result in meaningful subroutine names for most PC samples. You can see them in the HTML display by doing a search for PC= or by shift-clicking on a dashed PC sample line (not on the main timeline but just above it). The colors of the dashed lines vary according to a hash of the routine name (or hash of the hex address ignoring its low eight bits).

Non-execution. If a CPU is idle, the CPU timeline will show a thin black line. If a process is waiting for something (CPU, disk, etc.), the PID timeline will show a thin colored line during the wait, with up to three Morse code letters at the right end to identify what it is waiting for. Shift-click will show the wait reason. If the work for an RPC is partially completed and then put on a queue for another process to do additional work, the RPC timeline will show a dotted line during the queued wait. Shift-click will show the queue name.

KUtrace overhead. It is important to understand the overhead of observation tools and to determine when the overhead is high enough to distort what is being measured. To help with this, I have used a simple strategy of timing 100,000 getpid shortest system calls with no tracing, with KUtrace `go`, and with KUtrace `goipc`. Subtracting and dividing in the usual way gives an approximate average overhead in nanoseconds per trace entry and per IPC trace entry. The HTML display communicates this information by adding a diagonal white-line overlay to the beginning of timespans when you zoom in enough to see a 10–50 nsec overhead. For spans in the 50 nsec range, the overhead is significant or possibly dominant. For spans in the 5 usec range, the overhead is less than 1%. A second way to observe the overhead of KUtrace itself is via PC sampling. Occasionally, a timer interrupt will occur in the *middle* of KUtrace patches recording an event. When this happens, the sampled PC address is in KUtrace itself, usually the routine named `trace_1`. The frequency of this happening tells you (some of) the KUtrace overhead.

19.5   Region 4, IPC Legend

Region 4 simply gives a legend for instructions per cycle, IPC, when those are displayed. To help the eye distinguish values, the lowest four values are shown as black triangles, the middle eight as blue, and the top four as red. To further distinguish adjacent values, alternating triangles have a little notch in their short side.

19.6   Region 5, X-axis

Region 5 is the x-axis, showing wall-clock time left to right. There are approximately 10 labels (usually varying from 8 to 15), and each label has a faint vertical gray gridline. To avoid clutter, only a few digits of time are given in each label, all relative to the full date and time shown just to the left of Region 5, the base time. Within Regions 3 and 5, click-drag pans horizontally and the mouse wheel zooms. As you zoom, the base time and the axis units will change. You can zoom in to sub-nanosecond intervals and out to hours and minutes, but the practical intervals range from about 100 nsec to about 2 minutes, 9 orders of magnitude.

19.7   Region 6, Save/Restore

Region 6 has a few controls at the left and a cryptic description of the main mouse gestures. The circled numbers can be used to save and then restore specific views of the Region 3 data. Shift-click on a circled number saves the current view, blinks the display, and highlights that number as active. Clicking on an active number restores its view. (Clicking on an inactive number does nothing.) Each time the view is changed, the previous view is saved. The left back-arrow next to circle 1 goes back exactly one view. This facility can be particularly handy when preparing to give live presentations.

19.8   Secondary Controls

Shift-clicking on the red dot toggles bringing up an experimental set of secondary controls. These are largely intended to give better control over formatting for presentations (and book diagrams). The controls consist of five text boxes, two buttons, and at the far right a text area that shows the x- and y-axis domains.

The text fields control overall display aspect ratio, label width and font size, and timeline proportions devoted to spans and text.

The `Aspect` box specifies the aspect ratio for the Regions 2/3/4/5 display, given as single-digit `h:v` for horizontal and vertical. For example, 3:1 specifies a display area that is three times wider than it is high, 4:3 matches old TV displays, and 9:5 matches newer TV displays. If either value is zero, no constraints are imposed. When the aspect ratio constraint is active, the HTML code quantizes the pixel size of the browser window devoted to Regions 2/3/4/5 by forcing the height to be a multiple of 100 pixels. The pixel `width x height` is displayed briefly in the text area of Region 1 while you are resizing the browser window. This allows creating consistent-size pictures or screenshots.

The `Ychars` box specifies the number of characters for y-axis labels, while the `Ypx` box specifies the font size in pixels. These adjust the whitespace and readability of Region 2.

The `txt` and `spn` boxes specify how much vertical space in Region 3 to devote to drawing annotation text and how much for timespans. The units are lines of text, so for example `txt=5` `spn=2` specifies five lines of annotation text and two lines for drawing spans, i.e., 5/7 of the vertical space per row for text and 2/7 for spans.

The two buttons give additional control over the display. The `Legend` button displays the legend page on the inside back cover. It cycles through three states: normal timeline display, horizontal-layout legend, and vertical-layout legend. The `Fade` button turns all timespans light gray, allowing one to focus on just the annotations and time-aligned data while still having a little context of the underlying spans.

To the right of the secondary menu, the text field shows x-axis and y-axis domains. Each is of the form `start+width` where start is the leftmost x-axis time in seconds or topmost y-axis track number, and width is the x-axis full-scale time in microseconds or y-axis full-scale height in tracks. There are 20 tracks per timeline row. These values allow creating consistent matching alignments for pictures or screenshots.

19.9   Summary

The HTML display of KUtrace data is the key to visually understanding where all the elapsed time went—when each process was executing, why it blocked, and why it restarted. Without a dynamic display that can be panned and zoomed to any portion of a trace, it would be difficult to interpret the data captured in millions of little timespans.

That's it. The next part has several case studies of using KUtrace observations to determine why some software is occasionally slow. Have fun sleuthing!

Part IV

Reasoning

Do not read so much, look about you and think of what you see there.

—Richard P. Feynman

In Part I of this book, we learned how to do careful measurements of four of the fundamental shared computer resources: CPU, memory, disk/SSD, and network. In Part II, we looked at existing tools and techniques for observing the behavior of complex software: logs, counters, profiles, and traces. In Part III, we learned how to build and use the KUtrace tool. By simply recording every transition between kernel-mode execution and user-mode execution, users of KUtrace can observe all the execution and non-execution that occurs across all programs and all transactions running on all CPU cores.

This Part IV explores *reasoning* from the observations made by the tools of the first three parts. Chapter 20 discusses what to look for, while each of the Chapters 21–29 is a case study of one source of slow performance. Chapter 30 suggests topics for continuing study.

Part IV pulls all the previous material together to give the reader practice in spotting and understanding each of the common sources of long-tail latency in transactions: shared CPU, memory, disk, network, software locks, timers, and queues. At the end of this part, readers will be able to find, understand, and fix unexpectedly bad software dynamics within complex code.

Chapter 20

What to Look For

Given a program or set of programs exhibiting performance problems, how do we approach an understanding of the program dynamics that will lead to an understanding of why some operations are slow—and hence will lead to program changes that speed things up?

20.1   Overview

The hard part of performance analysis is observing what programs are actually doing rather than the simpler imagined picture in the reader's (or original designer's) head of what the programs are expected to be doing. At the end of this Part IV, readers will be able to find, understand, and fix unexpectedly bad software dynamics within complex code.

Figure 20.1 shows a framework for thinking about slow transactions. Within the elapsed time from start to end of a transaction, the computer server performing the work can be (1) running, working on the transaction at normal speed; (2) running slowly for some reason; or (3) not running at all, waiting for something. There are only three choices.

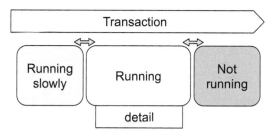

Figure 20.1   **Framework for transaction execution**

Long CPU-bound execution may also need some helpful detail about where the code is spending its time, the bottom box in the diagram.

Figure 20.2 shows a simple transaction execution timeline—just a single-threaded program that is completely CPU-bound doing the work of the transaction. It also shows three forms of slower execution: executing more code than the normal case (Chapter 21), executing the same code but more slowly as indicated by the instructions-per-cycle (IPC) speedometer triangles (Chapter 22), and sometimes not executing at all (Chapters 23–29).

Normal: expected
Slow: executing more code
Slow: executing slowly
Slow: waiting sometimes

Figure 20.2   **Normal execution of a single transaction vs. slower executions**

Figure 20.3a shows a slightly more complex transaction that normally runs on two parallel CPU-bound threads. Figure 20.3b shows a slow version with the two threads running sequentially—not the intended design and not the picture in the designer's head.

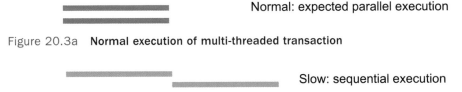

Normal: expected parallel execution

Figure 20.3a   **Normal execution of multi-threaded transaction**

Slow: sequential execution

Figure 20.3b   **Unexpected slow execution of multi-threaded transaction**

The way to think of the slow version is that the two threads are in fact running in parallel, but the second one is waiting for something during the entire time that the first one is running. Chapters 23–29 explore the various reasons that the second thread might be waiting.

We want to observe where the elapsed time went and observe the differences between normal-peed transactions and slow ones. We will look for and reason about CPU execution speed changes, interfering programs, and all sources of waiting.

KUtrace has facilities to cover these cases:

- Transaction start/end events (inserted by a software RPC library)
- Normal running: Showing all user processes and all system calls, interrupts, faults, and idle loop on all CPUs
- Running slowly: Tracking of CPU clock frequency, instructions per cycle, slow idle exits
- Not running: Context switches when each process starts or stops, wakeup event that makes a process runnable again; lock IDs (inserted by a software locking library); queued RPC work (inserted by a software queueing library)
- Detail: PC samples at timer interrupts; software labels/marks (inserted manually into user-mode source code)

In the subsequent chapters, we will use all of these facilities to tease out the root causes of example delayed transactions. In many cases, traditional observation tools cannot identify these root causes, or at least not when they occur only in live production environments.

Chapter 21

Executing Too Much

This chapter is a short case study of a transaction-server program whose intermittent performance problem is too much CPU-bound user-mode execution.

21.1   Overview

We will discover that the slow transactions execute too much code, i.e., that the slow instances involve a different longer and/or slower code path than the fast instances. In all these case studies, what we "know" about a program's behavior is the picture in our head. That differs, sometimes substantially, from reality. Treat the word *know* as a yellow flag that unsupported assumptions follow. In contrast, the word *measurement* refers to real-world behavior as observed by low-distortion tools. Treat these measurements as more reliable than the picture in your head.

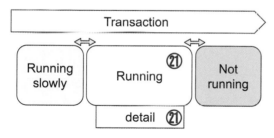

From our Chapter 20 framework, this chapter is about running but executing too much code. We use IPC to distinguish this from the case of running but executing too slowly—which is the subject of the next chapter. We use the detail provided by PC samples and manually added labels to identify the extra code paths.

21.2   The Program

Program mystery21 is a transaction server; in the source code you will find that for each RPC request, it does something like this:

```
if (SomeComplexBusinessLogic()) {
    // The case we are testing
    if (OtherBusinessLogic()) {
        DoProcessRpc(data);
    } else {
        DecryptingRpc(data);
    }
} else {
 ...
}
```

21.3   The Mystery

Recently, the performance of this server code has too much variability after a few software updates, often exceeding its time constraint target. We examine its performance via a client sending 200 *identical* RPCs. We expect the first RPC to be different from the others as it accesses data on disk, but we expect the other 199 to use the same data cached in main memory. Instead, we observe a 30x difference in transaction latency. *Why?*

When run with these identical transactions, the RPC logging (Chapter 8) mysteriously shows substantial variation in total elapsed server time, as shown in Figure 21.1. The 200 RPCs are sorted vertically by elapsed time, similar to Figure 9.4 in Chapter 9, but rotated 90 degrees. Previously, there had been some variation, but only by about a factor of 2. Simple counters such as the top command show that the program has elapsed time almost equal to user-mode CPU time. There can thus be no disk or network delays involved. The program is nearly 100% CPU-bound in user-mode code.

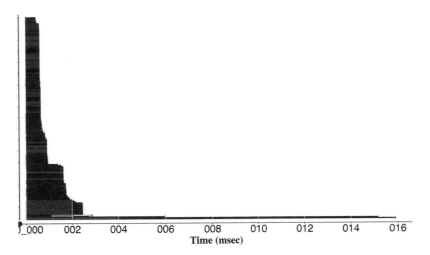

Figure 21.1   Graph of server log times for 200 RPCs in program mystery21, sorted vertically by elapsed time

In the 200 RPCs, most take about 0.5 msec, some take about 1.5–2.5 msec, and a few take about 15 msec. Based on previous behavior and initial estimates of execution time, we expect transactions to take about 1 msec. We "know" that DoProcessRpc and DecryptingRpc take similar amounts of processing time for each request. So we are hard-pressed to explain the wide variation in response times. Rather than guessing, we look for tools to observe the behavior of the program over all 200 transactions. In this chapter, we will focus on three groups of RPCs in Figure 21.1: the group of ~145 short 0.5 msec RPCs, the ~50 longer 1.5 msec ones, and the four very slow transactions.

21.4 Exploring and Reasoning

A simplistic non-idle PC-sampling *profile* of the program (Table 21.1) shows 4x more time in routines DoProcessRpc than DecryptingRpc, and also significant time in memcpy. This isn't quite what we expected. In particular, the profile doesn't explain the measurements in the server log.

The problem with the profile is that it intermixes the fast transactions with the slow ones, so all we see is the average behavior, with no clue about how fast and slow behave differently. This is never good enough. Instead, we want to separate the behavior of the fast and slow cases so we can see explicitly what is different.

Table 21.1 **Simple PC-Sampling Profile of Program mystery21; Indented Items Are Kernel Code**

Routine	Percent
PC=DoProcessRpc	50.8
PC=memcpy	33.3
PC=DecryptingChecksum	12.2
PC=FreeRPC	1.7
PC=__tls_get_addr	1.7
PC=finish_task_switch	1.7
PC=get_page_from_freelist	1.7

Running KUtrace on mystery21 reveals a lot of time in user-mode execution with very few kernel-user transitions. This is consistent with the counter measurements showing nearly 100% user-mode CPU time. The trace data does not tell us much about the fast-slow differences when sorted by CPU number. But the RPC begin-end markers let us sort the trace data by RPC ID, as in Figure 21.2.

Aha! Consistent with the RPC log data, we can now see that most individual transactions are fast, some are slower, and two at around times 200 and 340 are very slow. The full trace confirms that almost nothing is going on except user-mode CPU-bound execution on a single CPU core, with small gaps waiting for the next request from a client, so we can definitely rule out waiting for CPU, disk, system calls, etc. But we don't yet know why some transactions are slower than others.

Looking first at a few of the early RPCs, as shown in Figure 21.3, we see them executing on CPU 0 at the top and the same timespans sorted by RPC ID at the bottom. There are four fast ones and two slow ones. Within each RPC, the elapsed time is 100% CPU bound, so we can exclude the possibility of the longer ones waiting on something. Nothing is executing on the other three CPUs except short timer interrupts and some short network interrupts on CPU 3, so there is no obvious execution interference. The one non-idle PC sample, taken at time 985 (arrow), is in memcpy, consistent with the CPU profile in Figure 21.3.

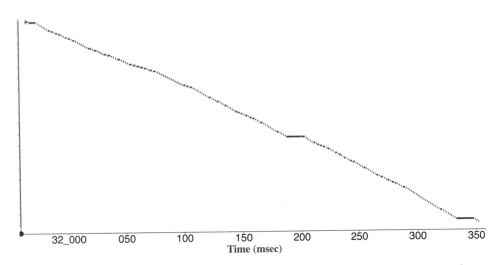

Figure 21.2   **KUtrace of program mystery21 on 200 nominally identical RPCs, sorted vertically by RPC start time**

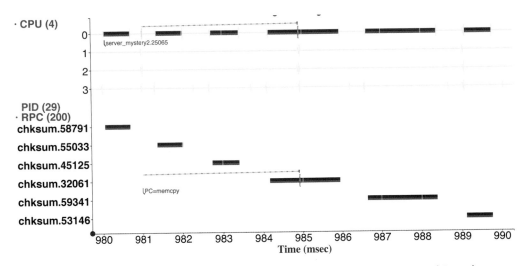

Figure 21.3   **Six of the nominally identical RPCs expanded: four fast ones and two slow ones; arrow at right end of the dashed line marks PC sample point in `memcpy`**

For similar or identical executable code, either the slow transactions are executing more instructions or they are executing the same instructions more slowly—there are only two choices.

With no obvious source of interference, we expect all the transactions to be executing instructions at about the same rate. Turning on the instructions-per-cycle display, as shown in Figure 21.4, indeed shows almost the same rate of execution across all six transactions, so we can now reliably conclude that the slow transactions are executing more instructions, about 2.5x to 3x more. Now all we need to know is *where* the extra instructions are coming from.

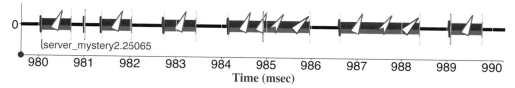

Figure 21.4 **The six RPCs of Figure 21.3, with IPC triangles shown**

The PC-sample profiles generated by KUtrace are embedded in the full trace of kernel-user transitions along with RPC ID begin-end markers. Turning on the PC-sample display shows scattered non-idle PC samples in many but not all transactions. Figure 21.5 covers several dozen of the early transactions. The PC samples here have been mapped back to function names (Chapter 19), with a few of them displayed.

Samples are sparse in these transactions, so there are not enough to form reliable conclusions about any single transaction, at least not the short ones. However, if we aggregate the samples across many normal transactions and separately across groups of slower ones, we can begin to see reliable differences. Beige samples are in Checksum, blue ones in memcpy.

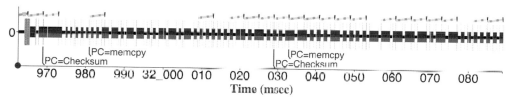

Figure 21.5 **KUtrace of program mystery21, showing about 50 RPCs with non-idle PC samples every 4 msec**

An automated way to do this grouping is to put RPCs into power-of-2 buckets by total elapsed server time (i.e., response time), displaying the average behavior of all the RPCs within each bucket. Without knowing ahead of time for any particular program how long fast and slow transactions might take, this simple bucketing will spread them out in a useful way. Other bucket sizes could be used, but we tend not to care so much about transactions whose performance varies by less than a factor of 2—we are more interested in the 5x or 100x much-too-slow ones. The very slow transactions will reliably fall into different power-of-2 buckets than the normal ones. Understanding those will likely also reveal a little about the only slightly slow ones.

Figure 21.6 shows six buckets for our 200 RPCs. Five RPCs are in the first [250..500) usec bucket, and 140 in the second [500..1000) usec bucket. The **average** behavior across all buckets and all 200 RPCs is next, followed by the [1..2) msec bucket, etc. We have accumulated the PC samples across all the transactions in each bucket, sorted from most frequent to least frequent PCs on each line. Because the PC sample durations are all multiples of the 4 msec timer interrupt interval, they may total somewhat more or less than the sum of the fine-grained execution durations. Our faster transactions are in the 250 usec and 500 usec buckets, and the ~3x slower ones are in the 1 msec and 2 msec buckets. The two extremely slow RPCs are in the [8..16) msec bucket. In most buckets, the samples are almost all Checksum and memcpy, but in the last bucket most of the PC samples are in DecryptingChecksum.

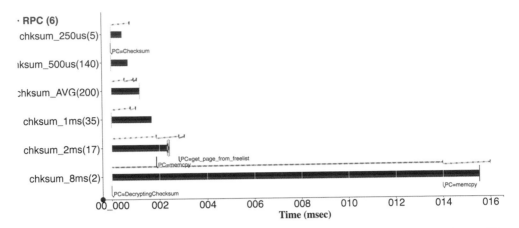

Figure 21.6   **KUtrace of program mystery21 bucketed by individual RPC elapsed times with aggregated PC samples per power-of-2 bucket**

Using the search box in the KUtrace display UI, we confirm that *all* the DecryptingChecksum PC samples are in the two slowest RPCs. So now we have measured that contrary to what we "know," the DecryptingChecksum routine is not the same speed as Checksum but is in fact about 30x slower. This explains the two extremely slow RPCs. Fixing them will require rewriting the DecryptingChecksum routine.

What about the other buckets? The PC samples are similar, with roughly 3/5 of the time in Checksum and 2/5 in memcpy. It is not yet clear what extra code is being executed in the slower group. Fortunately, we manually instrumented the mystery21 code slightly to include a mark_a label giving the RPC method name, "chksum" in this case, at the beginning of each transaction and a mark_b label "chk" at each call to the Checksum routine. Figure 21.7 shows these labels, making it obvious that in the longer transactions the Checksum routine is being erroneously called three times ("chk") instead of once.

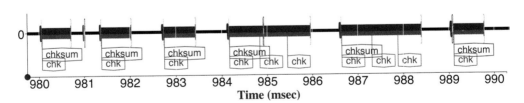

Figure 21.7   **The six RPCs of Figure 21.3, with labels shown**

21.5   Mystery Understood

Now we can see what is going on. The short elapsed-time buckets have all the normal transactions. They execute for about 0.5 msec in `DoProcessRpc`, but no time in `DecryptingRpc`. The medium buckets of about 1.5 msec are exactly the RPCs that erroneously call `Checksum` three times. The last bucket has the two DecryptingChecksum RPCs. Overall, the *real* code looks like this:

```
if (OtherBusinessLogic(x)) {
    // 1 of N, slower processing
    retval = DecryptingChecksum(s, chksumbuf);
} else {
    // Normal processing
    retval = DoProcessRpc (s, chksumbuf);
    if (WrongBusinessLogic(x)) {
        // about 1 of 5, extraneous processing BUG
        retval = DoProcessRpc (s, chksumbuf);
        retval = DoProcessRpc (s, chksumbuf);
    }
}
```

Looking now at the code and its change history, we quickly find that `WrongBusinessLogic()` is a latent bug that was introduced over two years ago, but no one noticed. It was unnoticed because the extra work's results were thrown away (rather than producing an overall wrong result) and the extra time didn't show up separately in a profile—it just increased the average time in `DoProcessRpc` over many transactions by about 40%. The change history for `DecryptingRpc` reveals a change in algorithm two weeks ago; before that, `DecryptingRpc` and `DoProcessRpc` in fact took about equal time, but `DecryptingRpc` was not doing the calculation it was supposed to do.

Removing the `WrongBusinessLogic()` takes about 10 minutes now that you have identified the bug. Improving `DecryptingRpc` looks difficult, so after a little discussion you and your peers decide to simply live with the slowdown until a proper faster implementation can be built and performance-tested.

Then you go back and measure the new version, looking at `top`, looking at the server RPC logs, and looking at KUtrace. You confirm that the changes produce the performance improvement you intended, that no other old problem is still lurking, and that the fixes introduced no new problem.

21.6   Summary

Here are the steps we took and the tools we used:

- Decline to guess.
- Look at `top`.
- Look at server logs, sorted by elapsed time.

- Look at a simplistic PC-sampling profile.
- Run KUtrace and sort by RPC ID instead of CPU number.
- Look at KUtrace output with IPC displayed.
- Look at KUtrace output with individual PC samples displayed.
- Bucket the RPCs by powers-of-2 elapsed time.
- Reason about the differences between fast, medium, and slow requests.
- Look at KUtrace output with manually inserted labels displayed.
- Look at the code and find simple changes.
- Measure the new code after making those changes.

Chapter 22

Executing Slowly

This chapter is a short case study of a program whose intermittent performance problem is executing the identical code multiple times, but sometimes more slowly than normal in the presence of other programs. We are interested just in CPU and memory interference, not disk or network or lock delays, which are the subject of later chapters.

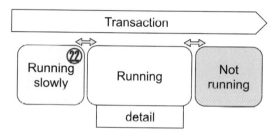

From our Chapter 20 framework, this chapter is about running but too slowly. We use IPC to distinguish this from the case of executing too much code. This chapter covers only one of the three reasons for running slowly—interference from other programs. Later chapters will touch on slow exits from idle and slow CPU clocks.

22.1 Overview

Interference that slows CPU-bound program performance stems from overuse of some hardware resource. For a hyperthreaded CPU in a multicore chip, the main resources are instruction fetch and decode units, instruction execution units (functional units), shared caches, and shared main memory. For a single-threaded CPU in a multicore chip, only cross-core shared caches and memory can be bottleneck resources. We will explore the interference issue by running a single program in conjunction with various other programs and see what happens.

Remember that what we "know" about a program's behavior is the picture in our head. That differs, sometimes substantially, from reality. In contrast, the word *measurement* refers to real-world behavior as observed by low-distortion tools. Treat these measurements as more reliable than the picture in your head.

22.2 The Program

The program here is not transaction-based. Instead, it is a synthetic floating-point benchmark program. The Whetstone benchmark [Longbottom 2014] was created in the early 1970s to mimic the operation distribution (a "mix") of some code at UK's National Physical Laboratory on an English Electric KDF9 computer. It was originally written in Algol60, then ported to FORTRAN, and much later ported to C. We "know" that it measures CPU floating-point performance. It inspired a later integer-only benchmark program called Dhrystone. Both are obsolete.

Benchmarking is difficult; it is surprisingly easy to build a program that does not measure what it claims to measure. One significant example is the matrix300 benchmark in the SPEC89 suite, mentioned in Chapter 4. It was a simple matrix multiply program that nominally measured floating-point performance. Rearranging the loops for better cache access made the benchmark run about 10x and showed that the program was in fact measuring memory access time, not floating-point performance.

In general, users of benchmarks are trying to show off their software's superior performance. This can lead to gaming the benchmark. It is surprisingly difficult to design a benchmark that resists gaming.

22.3 The Mystery

Does Whetstone measure floating-point performance or memory performance or something else? We shall soon see. We postulate that Whetstone uses floating-point operations extensively and hence is sensitive to interference from other programs that also do heavy floating-point work. We further postulate that it does not use memory operations extensively and hence is insensitive to interference from other programs that use memory heavily. We saw profiles of this program in Chapter 11.

The benchmark [Painter 1998] consists of eight loops, listed here using the original names and numbering with three loops (1, 5, and 10) dropped over the years:

>   module 2 Array elements
>
>   module 3 Array as parameter
>
>   module 4 Conditional jumps
>
>   module 6 Integer arithmetic
>
>   module 7 Trigonometric functions
>
>   module 8 Procedure calls
>
>   module 9 Array references
>
>   module 11 Standard functions

To see what sort of interference it is sensitive to, we will run Whetstone in conjunction with some antagonist programs—a floating-point hog and a memory hog. We start, however, by running the program against itself.

If a program completely saturates some hardware resource, running two copies will cause each copy to take twice as much elapsed time per transaction or other unit of work, giving no net increase in total work accomplished per unit time. On the other hand, if a program never uses more than half of each available hardware resource, running two copies will let each copy still take the original elapsed time per unit of work, and thus the pair will accomplish twice as much total work per unit time. Most programs land between these two extremes. Perhaps these mid-performance programs use 2/3 of a shared resource 100% of the time, or perhaps they use 100% of a shared resource 2/3 of the time. In this latter case, the net slowdown for two copies will vary depending on the phase overlap of the 100% use—1.33x slowdown with minimal overlap and 1.67x slowdown with perfect (but unfortunate) overlap.

To examine Whetstone, we will first run one and two copies on a single hyperthreaded Intel i3-7100 core and then will run against each of the hog programs, again on a single hyperthreaded core. In all cases, we will use KUtrace with IPC to observe what is happening.

Figure 22.1 shows a standalone execution of Whetstone. I added markers for each module. (I also added code to make all the variables live on loop exit so the loops would not get optimized away entirely, as we saw in Chapter 2.) Different loops/modules have different IPC, ranging from 3/8 (3 instructions every 8 cycles, left-pointing black triangles) in modules 2 and 3 to IPCs of 3.0, 2.5, and 3.5 in modules 7, 8, and 9, respectively (right-pointing red triangles).

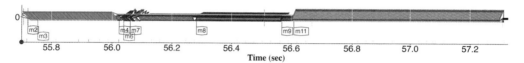

Figure 22.1   **The Whetstone benchmark executing by itself for about 1.6 seconds with IPC shown for each loop (module)**

Figure 22.2 shows the same binary executing twice on a hyperthread pair, CPUs 0 and 2. The IPC of modules 2, 3, and 11 are essentially unchanged, so these loops are not stressing any shared resource. On the other hand, modules 6, 7, and 9 slow down by a factor of about 2 and module 8 by a factor of about 1.5. Each of these four heavily uses some shared resource.

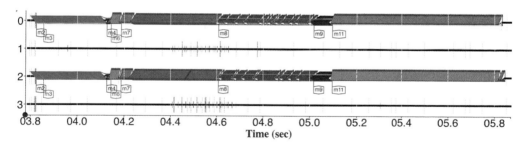

Figure 22.2   **Two copies of Whetstone executing on two hyperthreads of a single physical core for about 2.0 seconds with IPC shown for each loop (module)**

Table 22.1 summarizes the data so far. About 2/3 of this benchmark by elapsed time is not stressing the CPU, while about 1/3 (shown in bold) is. But we don't yet know which shared CPU resources are the source of interference in each of the modules 6–9.

Note that with 2/3 of the original runtime spent in loops that do not slow down, the parts that slow down by a factor of 2 are substantially diluted in the overall full-benchmark slowdown of 1.27x. This dilution is sometimes overlooked in benchmarking.

Table 22.1   **IPC and Execution Time of Each Whetstone Module Running One (1x) and Two (2x) Copies**

	IPC at 1x	IPC at 2x	Fraction of 1x time	msec at 1x	msec at 2x	msec ratio	
Module 2	0.375	0.375	2.1%	33.5	32.0	0.96	Array elements
Module 3	0.375	0.375	16.9%	268.0	269.6	1.01	Array as parameter
Module 4	3.0	2.5	1.0%	15.4	17.7	1.15	Conditional jumps
Module 6	**2.0**	**1.0**	**1.4%**	**21.7**	**42.5**	**1.96**	**Integer arithmetic**
Module 7	**3.0**	**1.5**	**14.0%**	**221.5**	**419.7**	**1.89**	**Trigonometric functions**
Module 8	**2.5**	**1.5**	**18.1%**	**286.7**	**420.9**	**1.47**	**Procedure calls**
Module 9	**3.5**	**2.0**	**2.5%**	**39.6**	**78.8**	**1.99**	**Array references**
Module 11	1.25	1.25	44.1%	698.9	726.1	1.04	Standard functions
Total			100%	1585.3	2007.3	1.27	

22.4   Floating-Point Antagonist

The first of our two antagonists, the flt_hog program, alternately executes a CPU-bound loop and sleeps doing nothing. While running, it periodically inserts a loop iteration count into the trace (for clarity, only some of the numeric values are displayed). It claims to heavily use the floating-point execution hardware. We confirm this by running two copies of the antagonist on a single hyperthreaded core and look at the KUtrace IPC results, as shown in Figure 22.3. I deliberately set the waiting times of the two copies to be slightly different at 20 and 21 msec each so that the two execution bursts would overlap differently over time, and then I picked a point of partial overlap to look at.

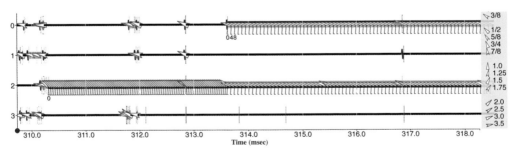

Figure 22.3   **Two copies of `flt_hog` running partially overlapped on a single hyperthreaded core, with IPC=3/8 standalone and 1/8 overlapped. Note that the IPC resolution is fairly coarse, at multiples of 1/8.**

On the left, just one copy is running, with an IPC of about 3/8. On the right, both copies are running, each with an IPC of about 1/8. The IPC values in Figure 22.3 are pushing the fairly coarse resolution KUtrace uses to fit those values into four bits per timespan. We see better resolution looking at the elapsed time between iteration-count markers: 33.8 usec standalone vs. 67.4 usec overlapped, a slowdown of 1.99x. So we can safely conclude that whatever `flt_hog` does, it is using 100% of some CPU resource.

Here is the inner loop, with variables that are all double-precision floats. When running full speed, each iteration is about 33 CPU cycles, consistent with issuing four add/sub, two multiplies and two divides each time around, plus the looping overhead. There are no memory references in the optimized gcc code. We conclude that the program indeed heavily uses the floating-point units.

```
for (int i = 0; i < n; ++i) {
  // Mark every 4096 iterations, so we can see how time changes
  if ((i & 0x0fff) == 0) {
    kutrace::mark_d(i >> 10);
  }
  sum1 += prod1;
  sum2 += divd1;
  prod1 *= 1.000000001;
  divd1 /= 1.000000001;
  sum1 -= prod2;
  sum2 -= divd2;
  prod2 *= 0.999999999;
  divd2 /= 0.999999999;
}
```

When we run Whetstone against flt_hog, we get Figure 22.4, showing that Whetstone modules 7–11 on CPU 0 all slow down significantly whenever flt_hog runs on CPU 2. Module 6 (not shown) IPC drops slightly from 2.0 to 1.75. Module 7 on the left drops from 3.0 to 5/8, module 8 from 2.5 to 3/8, module 9 from 3.5 to 2.5, and module 11 from 1.25 to 3/8. Interference from flt_hog severely impacts modules 7, 8, and 11, while module 6 Integer Arithmetic and 9 Array References are only moderately impacted. So we can conclude that just modules 7, 8, and 11 are actually measuring floating-point performance.

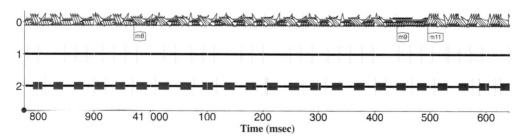

Figure 22.4   **Whetstone on CPU 0 and `flt_hog` on CPU 2, showing just the more interesting modules: 7 (partial), 8, 9, and `11` (partial)**

As an aside, we look more closely at interference in modules 6 and 11. Module 6 does zero floating-point arithmetic, and flt_hog does zero memory accesses in its inner loop. In fact, the generated code for module 6 does *no* integer arithmetic at all, other than the loop counter. The only remaining available interference effect for module 6 is instruction fetch/decode when both module 6 and flt_hog are both running—intermixing instructions from both programs on a single hyperthreaded core has the effect of defeating the loop optimization hardware that makes module 6 run fast standalone.

The gcc compiler did some quite sophisticated optimization to remove nearly everything in the inner loop of module 6, a level of optimization never contemplated when the benchmark was first created. This optimization makes the module meaningless.

Here is the module 6 source:

```
J = 1;
K = 2;
L = 3;
for (I = 1; I <= N6; I++) {
    J = J * (K-J) * (L-K);
    K = L * K - (L-J) * K;
    L = (L-K) * (K+J);
    E1[L-1] = J + K + L;
    E1[K-1] = J * K * L;
}
```

And here is the entire gcc-generated loop (with my comments):

```
.L30:
        addq    $1, %rax            // I++
        movsd   %xmm0, 16+E1(%rip)  // E1[L-1] = 6
        cmpq    %rax, %rdx          // I ? N6
        movsd   %xmm0, 8+E1(%rip)   // E1[K-1] = 6
        jge     .L30                // I <= N6
```

The gcc compiler did constant-folding to discover that the arithmetic for J, K, and L kept their values unchanged at 1, 2, and 3, respectively, every time around the loop, and so eliminated those calculations entirely! Benchmarking is difficult. *O quam cito transit gloria mundi.*

Module 11 does not slow down when run against itself but does by a factor of 3 when run against flt_hog. How can that be? The Whetstone loop,

```
for (I = 1; I <= N11; I++)
    X = DSQRT(DEXP(DLOG(X)/T1));
```

does `sqrt` and `div` instructions in a single non-pipelined functional unit on the i3-7100 (Kaby Lake), and the flt_hog loop also has divide instructions (two). As we measured in Chapter 2, the divide unit has an issue spacing of 15 cycles or so, meaning that a second divide cannot start until the previous one almost finishes. The `exp` and `log` library routines use multiply/add for polynomial evaluation, and the flt_hog loop has six of these, but the multiply and add units are fully pipelined so can start several new instructions every cycle. Thus, the divide unit is the only shared functional-unit resource that can cause more than a 2x slowdown of module 11 when flt_hog interferes. We conclude it is the source of the 3x slowdown.

So far, we have confirmed that modules 7, 8, and 11 in fact measure floating-point arithmetic, and module 6 does not measure integer arithmetic at all. What about memory?

22.5 Memory Antagonist

The second of our two antagonists, the memhog_ram program, alternately executes a memory-bound loop scanning a 20MB array (much bigger than the i3-7100 L3 cache, so every cache line misses to main memory) and sleeps doing nothing. We confirm this by running two copies, again with delays of 20 and 21 msec, on a single hyperthreaded core and look at the KUtrace result, as shown in Figure 22.5. Full-speed IPC is 2.0, and overlapped IPC is 1.25. Since the slowdown is not fully a factor of 2, we know that memhog_ram does not completely saturate the memory system, but it does use about 80% of the available bandwidth.

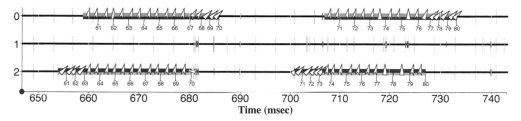

Figure 22.5 Two copies of **memhog_ram** running partially overlapped on a single hyperthreaded core, with IPC=2.0 standalone and 1.25 overlapped

When we run Whetstone against memhog_ram, we get Figure 22.6, showing that Whetstone modules 6–9 all slow down whenever memhog_ram runs, but module 11 is unaffected. Module 6 (not shown) drops from 2.0 to 1.25 IPC. Module 7 drops from 3.0 to 1.5, module 8 from 2.5 to 1.75, and module 9 from 3.5 to 2.0. The slowdowns are not as dramatic as those caused by flt_hog, and they affect the modules differently.

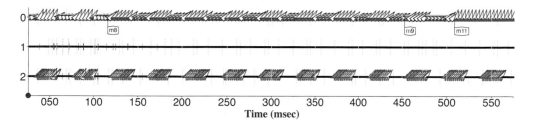

Figure 22.6 Whetstone on CPU 0 and **memhog_ram** on CPU 2, showing just the more interesting modules: 7 (partial), 8, 9, and 11 (partial)

We have confirmed that modules 6–9 are also sensitive to memory interference, but not as strongly as the floating-point interference shown earlier. So the benchmark also loosely measures memory performance. Especially with modern compilers and modern hardware, it is difficult to build a benchmark program that measures just one thing.

22.6   Mystery Understood

By running against CPU antagonists, we have teased apart which CPU resources are used by each piece of the program under study and hence have identified the individual interference mechanisms that can slow down its execution. Table 22.2 summarizes the measured results. Bold modules actually stress the CPU. Slowdowns of 2x or more are also in bold.

Table 22.2   Execution Time Slowdown of Each Whetstone Module Against Various Antagonists

	Fraction of total 1x time	Self slowdown	flt_hog slowdown	memhog_ram slowdown	
Module 2	2.1%				Array elements
Module 3	16.9%				Array as parameter
Module 4	1.0%				Conditional jumps
Module 6	**1.4%**	**2x**		**1.6x**	**Integer arithmetic**
Module 7	**14.0%**	**2x**	**5x**	**2x**	**Trigonometric functions**
Module 8	**18.1%**	**1.5x**	**7x**	**1.4x**	**Procedure calls**
Module 9	**2.5%**	**2x**	**1.4x**	**1.7x**	**Array references**
Module 11	44.1%		**3x**		Standard functions

We postulated that Whetstone uses floating-point operations extensively and hence is sensitive to interference from other programs that also do heavy floating-point work. We further postulated that it does not use memory operations extensively and hence is insensitive to interference from other programs that use memory heavily. Both turn out to be only partially true.

22.7   Summary

Looking at fine-grained IPC reveals detailed reasons for interference between programs. Antagonist programs are a simple way of creating that interference. Once you understand the overloaded resource causing interference, it may turn out that straightforward program changes can reduce the use of that shared resource, or it may turn out that some global processor assignment avoids putting interfering programs together, or it may turn out that your performance expectations are too high—they can be met only on unshared hardware.

The obsolete Whetstone benchmark was "known" to evaluate CPU-bound floating-point performance. Our measurements show that not to be fully true. Four of the eight loops use less than half of each CPU resource but contribute to 2/3 of the total benchmark runtime, thus diluting any observed overall performance difference. The other third of the runtime is in four loops that nearly saturate some CPU resource, as shown by running two copies on a single shared physical core. The saturated resource varies from floating-point hardware to memory hardware to instruction fetch/decode hardware. The compiler entirely optimized away one loop. On balance, this benchmark should not be used to evaluate floating-point performance.

In a production environment, you might have a collection of perhaps 30 programs some of which appear to interfere with each other when run concurrently on a single CPU. To determine which programs to keep away from each other, you *could* test all 30 * 30 combinations. But it is much simpler and faster to take a different approach first—test each of the 30 programs against a second copy of itself. Those that slow down substantially are using more than half of some shared resource. Mixing two such programs that bottleneck on the same resource will likely encounter interference. Mixing programs that run well against themselves likely will encounter little if any interference.

- Fine-grained IPC reveals detailed reasons for interference between programs and between programs and the operating system.

- It specifically shows contended hardware resources.

- Intermittent low IPC correlates with the source of interference running on other CPUs.

- Comparing IPC when running one copy of a program vs. running two copies simultaneously reveals parts that use more than half of any hardware resource.

- This can guide consideration of which combinations of programs may run well or badly together on a single server.

- Whetstone should not be used to evaluate floating-point performance.

Chapter 23

Waiting for CPU

This chapter is a short case study of a multi-threaded program whose intermittent performance problem is waiting to have a CPU assigned to some threads. We look at a parent thread that launches five child threads and waits for them to complete. Two problems occur: (i) using the default Linux Completely Fair Scheduler (CFS), we find that the child threads do not get a fair share of the CPU time, and (ii) when starting up, there are idle delays when runnable threads do not in fact execute.

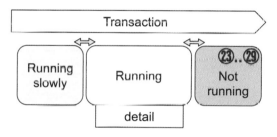

From our framework, this chapter is about not running while waiting for a CPU. A runnable process can wait for a CPU because (1) all the cores are busy, (2) an assigned core is delayed waking up from idle, or (3) the OS scheduler decides not to run the process on an available idle core. We look at all three in this chapter.

23.1　The Program

Program mystery23 is a synthetic scheduler test, based on an idea from Lars Nyland. It has a parent main program that launches a group of child threads, each of which repeatedly checksums a 240KB array that fits into an L2 cache. Each child thread runs for about 1.5 seconds. We look in detail at the case of five child threads when running on a four-CPU processor—musical chairs.

23.2　The Mystery

With five threads and four logical CPU cores on an Intel i3-7100 chip (two physical cores hyper-threaded), the default CFS scheduler [Linux 2021b] is supposed to "run each task at equal speed," meaning that each thread should get 4/5 of the total available CPU time over the four cores. We expect the scheduler to assign time slices to the five threads so that all five complete at nearly the same time. We find that is not completely true.

In addition, we expect all five threads to start at about the same time and all the CPUs to be busy as soon as the first four start. There should never be times when a thread is ready to run and a CPU core is idle, but the scheduler fails to run the ready thread. This property is sometimes called *work conserving* [Wikipedia 2020g]. This also turns out not to be completely true.

23.3   Exploring and Reasoning

As usual, we use KUtrace to examine the dynamic interactions between the threads when mystery23 runs. The full program launches groups of 1..12 child threads, but with four CPU cores, the scheduler has nothing interesting to do until there are at least five threads. We look here at just the group of five child threads, where we expect to see the threads getting equal time slices in a quasi-round-robin manner.

Figure 23.1 shows what happens when the parent thread `bash.3562` launches child threads `schedtest.3573,3574,3575,3576,3577` and then waits for all of them to complete before launching the next group of six threads at the far right of the diagram. Based on the number of active threads and the number of CPU cores, the CFS scheduler chooses a time slice of 12 msec, the squarish dots in Figure 23.1. But it does not assign time slices round-robin. Some threads alternately get one time slice and then wait for one time slice, while others get more than a dozen time slices in a row before they wait. The pattern of execution has no obvious symmetry and is different each time this program runs.

We expected the five child threads to all finish at nearly the same time (within 12 msec of each other for the chosen time slice). Instead, we see that the earliest thread finishes 13% sooner than the latest one, a difference of about 200 msec instead of 12 msec.

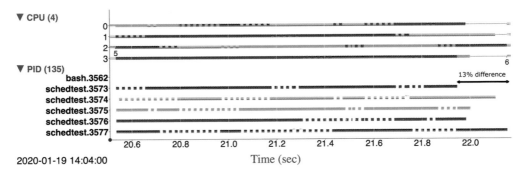

Figure 23.1   **Scheduling five processes onto four CPUs. Not completely fair: 13% difference in elapsed time. 1.6 seconds across.**

This is not an IPC issue as we saw in the previous chapter; all five threads execute at 1.75 IPC (not shown), except at the very end when there are only two threads remaining to complete: those two run at 2.0 IPC starting at about time 22.0 seconds (finally having exclusive access to the L2 caches that are otherwise shared across hyperthreads).

It is also not the case that the scheduler uses unequal idle times for the different threads. The expanded view in Figure 23.2 shows that the initial wait_cpu times are 12.0 msec, and that is consistent across the entire trace. The CFS scheduler simply assigns fewer active time slices to threads 3573, 3575, and 3576, creating the 13% difference in completion times, 207 msec out of 1617 msec.

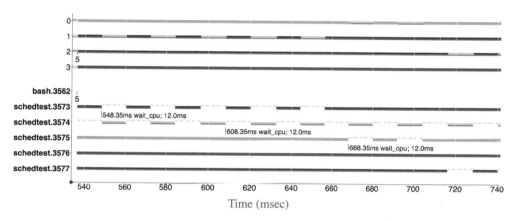

Figure 23.2 Scheduling five processes onto four CPUs showing tasks waiting 12 msec for CPU availability. 200 msec across.

Figure 23.3 shows that a perfect time-slice allocation exists for this particular scheduling problem, finishing all tasks within one time slice of each other, keeping all CPUs 100% busy, and minimizing task switches per CPU. But doing this would require perfect knowledge of upcoming compute demands of each thread.

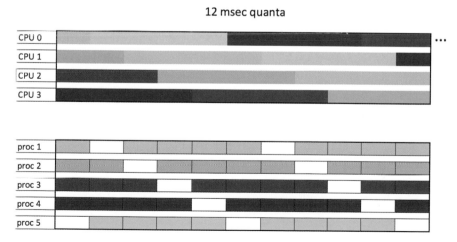

Figure 23.3 A perfect scheduling of five processes onto four CPUs

It is very difficult to build schedulers that perform well over a wide range of circumstances, but "completely fair" in the name is a bit misleading here. There is no obvious fix for this user program, but there may be improvements available in the operating system scheduler. The take-away idea is that scheduling choices can be less perfect than the picture in your head.

23.4   Mystery 2

The second problem in this trace occurs when starting up. The five child threads do not all start at once, and during the startup phase there is an excess of idle CPU time, as shown in Figure 23.4. The excess time is caused by CPU cores taking a long time to exit from idle, which can be considered either a not-running problem or an executing-slowly problem. Either way, it slows down programs. The diagram highlights the steps launching the first child thread, schedtest.3573.

The parent program, bash.3562, does five clone() calls to start the five child processes, but these five are separated in time. The first four clone calls are done sequentially on CPU 2 at step ①, but then the parent process is preempted by the fourth-launched process. The parent only does the fifth clone call on CPU 2 at about time 465. Oh, of course, we expected that . . . .

Now that we have seen this happen, we can adjust the picture in our heads to expect delayed clone calls for this group of five and for all later groups. If we wanted nearly equal startup times for 100 threads on 20 CPUs, we might want to restructure the parent to launch the first 10 and then have each of those launch 9 more. This might do what we expect, or it might have some other unexpected dynamic interactions between threads. The lesson is to observe what really happens rather than assuming a simple picture.

But back to the main point of Figure 23.4. It takes 120 usec from the clone call at step ① to the child process fully running at step ④. During this time, the four CPUs have substantial idle time. What is going on?

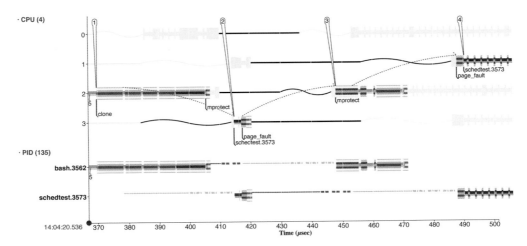

Figure 23.4   **Startup of scheduling five processes onto four CPUs, showing three consecutive 30 usec delays getting process 3573 going. 130 usec across.**

23.5 Mystery 2 Understood

In detail, starting the first child goes through four steps. Step ① is the parent thread cloning itself inside `pthread_create` to make a child thread. The child thread initially shares its address space with the parent thread. Via copy-on-write (CoW), each thread will get a separate copy of modified pages in this address space whenever either one does a write. But to do so, all the shared pages must first be marked as read-only.

When it executes, each child thread allocates a 240KB array on the stack, initializes it, and then enters an approximately 1.5-second loop repeatedly checksumming the array. The very first write of the array initialization in thread 3573 takes a page fault on CPU 3 at step ② to invoke copy-on-write. But that page fault *blocks* because the parent thread has not yet finished setting up the shared-address-space page tables. Instead, it wakes up the previously preempted parent thread. Not until the parent finishes its `mprotect` call at step ③ can *any* of the child processes continue. Our first child `schedtest.3573` finally resumes at step ④, where it starts taking about 60 more CoW page faults. This song and dance is repeated for all the other child threads. Strictly speaking, thread 3573 is partly waiting for memory (next chapter) between steps ② and ③, but the delay is long because CPU 2 takes a while to respond.

Now look at the waiting-for-CPU delays for individual threads in the bottom part of Figure 23.4, indicated by the thin orange lines (the brown lines we will discuss in the next chapter). Step ① wakes up the newly cloned thread, but that does not actually run until step ② some 36 usec later. Step ② wakes up the parent, but it doesn't run until step ③ some 30 usec later. Step ③ wakes up the child again, but it doesn't run until step ④ another 35 usec later. In all three cases, the wakeup is directed to an idle CPU core. Much too soon after it went idle, each of those cores issued an `mwait` instruction that had the effect of putting that core into an Intel C6 deep sleep state to save power. This is a Linux Intel-specific idle loop software performance bug.

Exiting the C6 state takes 30 usec on this chip, shown as the red sine waves in Figure 23.4, and the three wakeups do this *sequentially*, accounting for 90 usec of the total 108 usec delay from `clone` waking up the child to it actually running productively. The bug is that the code in `linux-4.19.19/drivers/idle/intel_idle.c` issues the `mwait` instruction *much too soon*, committing to C6 sleep after 250–500 nsec and then taking 30 usec to exit C6 sleep.

This behavior is a violation of the *Half-Optimal Principle* [Sites 2020].

> **Half-Optimal Principle**
> When waiting for a future event E, if it takes time T to exit a waiting state, spin for time T before entering that state—to take no more than twice the optimal time.

If event E occurs while spinning, i.e., before time T, the result is optimal: spinning until E with no wait state enter or exit. If E occurs just epsilon after spinning for time T, the result is half-optimal because we do a spin for time T, wait, and then immediately spend another time T to exit the wait, thus using up the CPU for 2 * T when T plus epsilon would have sufficed had we spun slightly longer. If E occurs further in the future, we never use up the CPU (and its electrical power) for more than 2 * T even if E is 100 times longer.

If the `mwait` transition to C6 deep sleep were held off by T=30 usec of spinning, the wakeups would occur first, and there would be no context switch to idle and no `mwait` into deep sleep. All the idle time in Figure 23.4 would disappear, and the first child would have started running productively about 80 usec sooner.

There is another, more subtle, scheduler problem in Figure 23.4. When awakened at time 454.35 in step ③, thread 3574 has to wait 11.9 milliseconds (!) before it runs—far off the right of this diagram—because thread 3577 gets cloned by bash just after step ③, and it starts running at about time 470 on the remaining available CPU 3 before 3574 gets a chance to resume.

Bumping 3574 this way reflects a subtlety in the Linux scheduler's *CPU affinity* behavior. It attempts to resume a thread A on the same CPU core that it was previously running on, waiting until that CPU core is available. In simple cases, this restarts thread A with warm caches after being blocked for a short time. But with another thread B running on the target CPU core while A is blocked, thread A likely restarts with cold caches. If different CPU core is idle while A is waiting, a more aggressive work-conserving scheduler would move A to run there instead.

Thread 3574 has affinity to CPU 0, where it runs at the upper left of Figure 23.4. Thread 3577 is assigned affinity to CPU 3 when it is cloned at time 460 because the `clone` call runs on CPU 3. Thus, when bash awakens thread 3574, the scheduler makes it wait until CPU 0 becomes available. When bash then blocks at time 470, thread 3577 is immediately started on CPU 3 and runs continuously until its time slice runs out about 11 msec later. This is much too long to make 3574 wait for a CPU core.

The arithmetic goes like this: moving a thread A from its previous CPU core X to another idle core Y in general will cause A to take extra cache misses. How much extra time would those take? If X and Y share an L1 cache (e.g., hyperthreads), moving thread A to run on core Y is *free* and should always be done immediately. See Table 23.1.

Table 23.1 **Approximate Costs of Process Migration for a Typical Hyperthreaded Chip**

Moving Process to a *Different* CPU Core	Arithmetic	Approximate Cold-Cache Refill Time
Sharing L1 cache (hyperthreads)	0	0
Sharing L2 cache	256 lines * 10 cycles L1_d 256 lines * 10 cycles L1_i	1.7 usec
Sharing L3 cache	4096 lines * 40 cycles L2	55 usec
Sharing DRAM	40960 lines * 200 cycles L3	2700 usec

Assumptions:

L1_d, L1_i size 32KB each, L2 size 512KB, L3 size 2.5MB/core, Line size all 64 bytes

Per-thread occupancy = half of L1 and L2, 2.5MB for L3

Fill L1 from L2 = 10 cycles/line, L2 from L3 = 40cy, L3 from DRAM = 200cy, ~3 cycles per nanosecond

No overlap of fill requests. Other threads immediately start filling what for them are cold caches.

If X and Y do not share an L1 cache but share an L2 cache, assume some plausible number for the size of A's L1 working set, say half of the L1 cache size, or 256 cache lines in our Intel i3 sample server. Moving A to core Y would then take 256 extra L1 cache misses that will hit in the shared L2 cache at a cost of about 10 cycles (Chapter 3) each or *very roughly* 2560 cycles total for L1_data and the same for L1_instructions. The Half-Optimal Principle suggests that the scheduler should make A wait no more than 2 usec before moving it to CPU Y. Since 2 usec is likely less than the context-switch time to start A, the move should always be done immediately.

If X and Y do not share an L2 cache but share an L3 cache, similar arithmetic suggests that the scheduler should wait roughly 50 usec before moving A to CPU core Y. If Y is on a completely different chip and shares no L3 caches with X, the break-even time might be more like 2–3 milliseconds. Even in this case, an 11 msec wait is unwarranted.

Keep in mind that any savings from affinity to the previously used core *decreases over time* as *other* (non-idle) threads use that core and disappears entirely after about 50 usec on-chip and 2–3 msec cross-chip.

23.6 Bonus Mystery

This mystery comes from a trace of software locks in Chapter 27, but the issue belongs here because the wait involved is for a CPU, not a lock. Figure 23.5 shows three worker threads running on the left and then a fourth dashboard thread running on CPU 3 while holding a lock, causing the other three threads to block for 600 usec. When the fourth thread completes, only two of the three waiting worker threads start up again; the remaining thread is delayed for over 1.7 milliseconds. But it is not waiting for a lock. It is waiting to be scheduled onto a CPU even though two CPUs are nearly 100% idle during those 1.7 msec. *This is a scheduler failure, not a locking issue.*

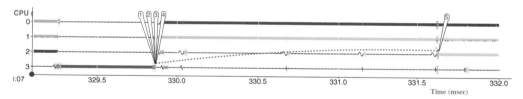

Figure 23.5 **Three threads wait for a lock held by a fourth thread, but only two of them restart in a timely manner.**

Notice in Figure 23.5 that the worker threads on the left are running on CPUs 0, 1, and 2, while on the right two have been migrated and the threads are running on CPUs 2, 1, and 0 respectively. Figure 23.6a shows the detail of the start of the long wakeup delay. There are four wakeups, not three.

The dashboard thread finishes by doing a `write` system call, which wakes up (1) an I/O thread that runs on CPU 2. Only then does it do the `futex` system call that wakes up the three worker threads. Wakeup (2) resumes the worker thread originally on CPU 1 and the scheduler puts it back on CPU 1. Wakeup (3) resumes the worker originally running on CPU 2, *but CPU 2 is in the middle of starting the I/O thread*. So the scheduler instead moves that worker thread to CPU 0. Wakeup (4) makes the worker originally running on CPU 0 runnable, *but CPU 0 is in the middle of starting the other worker thread*. At that instant, all four CPUs are busy (two coming out of premature deep sleep), including CPU 3, which is in the middle of the `futex` wakeup code itself. So the scheduler punts and does not assign a CPU for the third worker thread.

Just 3.5 usec later, the dashboard thread finishes and CPU 3 goes idle. *The remaining worker thread could have started here.* But instead, the scheduler has queued it to wait until a timer interrupt to try again to find a CPU for it.

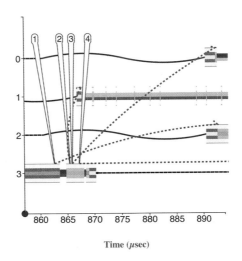

Time (μsec)

Figure 23.6a   **When the dashboard thread of Figure 23.5 finishes, it wakes up four threads, only three of which run.**

Figure 23.6b shows the timer interrupts 1.7 msec later. The `timer` hard interrupt handler on CPU 2 runs the `BH:sched` soft interrupt code to finally resume (5) the remaining worker thread on otherwise-idle CPU 2. Note that the thread was not waiting for a software lock, and it was not waiting (directly) for a timer interrupt. It was waiting for the scheduler to assign it a CPU.

This long delay is perhaps a consequence of the scheduler's affinity mechanism to preferentially resume a thread on the CPU core that it last ran on. Note, however, the other worker thread that was promptly moved from CPU 2 to CPU 0 back at wakeup (3). One difference between the two wakeups is that CPUs 0 and 2 are hyperthreads for the same physical core (and 1 and 3 for the other physical core) , so there is no cold-cache cost moving a thread between them. When CPU 3 went idle, moving the remaining worker thread then from CPU 0 to CPU 3 would have encountered some cold-cache cost. But waiting 1700 microseconds to save ~50 microseconds of cache-refill time from shared L3 is a bad choice in a time-constrained environment.

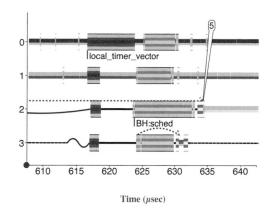

Figure 23.6b   **The fourth thread runs only 1.7 msec later after a timer interrupt invokes the scheduler soft interrupt handler (BH).**

23.7   Summary

- Observing the actual scheduler behavior reveals how wrong the picture in our head is.

- The Linux 4.19 CFS scheduler is not completely fair.

- Bouncing back and forth between threads can encounter unnecessary idle-loop delays when processors are not busy and can encounter sub-optimal scheduling delays when processors are busy.

- Fixes may well involve restructuring the code and even restructuring the threading design of complex software.

- Putting a CPU into deep sleep too soon can delay a thread unnecessarily.

- Enforcing processor affinity by waiting too long can delay a thread unnecessarily.

- The half-optimal principle bounds how long it is worthwhile to spin or wait.

We will revisit this CPU-waiting topic when we look at locks and queues in later chapters.

Exercises

23.1   [50] Design a completely fair scheduler.

23.2   Improve the CPU affinity algorithm to be closer to work-conserving, rather than delaying some threads while there are idle CPU cores.

Chapter 24

Waiting for Memory

This chapter is a case study of a program that uses lots of memory and triggers paging to disk, which then results in the program sometimes being blocked waiting for memory. The paging dynamics are slightly surprising. Waiting for page-fault disk transfers could be considered either waiting for memory or waiting for disk; we choose to treat it as waiting for memory and treat user file I/O as waiting for disk in the next chapter. As a second example, we briefly look back at the process-startup Mystery 2 from the previous chapter.

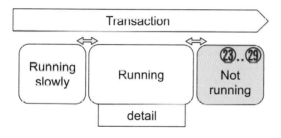

From our framework, this chapter is about not running while waiting for memory. A runnable process can wait for memory because (1) the data it wants is paged out, or (2) it needs access to a page table that some other process is manipulating. There is also the uncommon case of (3) waiting for the Out of Memory (OOM) manager to kill some processes to free up memory.

24.1 The Program

Program paging_hog has two phases. The first allocates 40MB chunks of memory continuously until the allocation fails. It then frees up the last 40MB to give the operating system a little room, and then the second phase scans all the remaining allocated memory to touch every page again. Before an allocation fails, the operating system will start paging out dirty pages from paging_hog, causing a significant slowdown and substantial memory waits. The scanning phase will then bring those pages back in.

Recall that when a program does a heap malloc, the operating system simply builds page tables pointing to the kernel's all-zero page; it does not allocate any new memory initially. To defeat this behavior, immediately after successfully allocating each 40MB chunk paging_hog writes a byte to each page. This takes 10,240 page faults, each of which allocates main memory and does a copy on write (CoW) to zero the page before returning to the user-mode byte write. The net effect is to make every page dirty.

To help keep track of the execution dynamics, the program inserts a KUtrace marker at each successful 40MB allocation.

24.2   The Mystery

What do you expect the dynamic interactions between paging_hog and the operating system's memory management routines to look like? Will paging_hog start waiting for page-out activity before main memory is exhausted, or will it run with no waits until an allocation fails and then perhaps wait for a long time? Once memory space is tight, how will the operating system manage and schedule page-outs and page-ins? Which processes will have to wait for memory access? Are there additional CPU overheads that occur only when memory is tight, and if so, do these create significant additional slowdowns? Are there any surprises?

24.3   Exploring and Reasoning

Running on a system with 8GB of RAM, we expect paging activity to start sometime before 8000MB/40MB = 200 successful allocations of 40MB each. The actual start in the trace of Figure 24.1 is just after allocating 177 chunks, 7.08GB. On the left, paging_hog is running on CPU 2 taking 10,240 page faults to zero pages. Then in the middle kswapd0, the swapping daemon, starts up on CPU 0. It runs CPU-bound for nearly the rest of the diagram. It also makes helper thread kworker0/0 runnable at time 044.6 msec, but that kernel worker process doesn't run for another 10.4 msec, at time 055 msec.

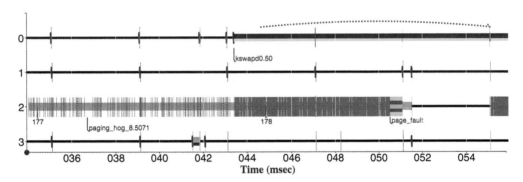

Figure 24.1   **A 20 msec overview of `paging_hog` at its transition from running entirely in memory up past chunk 177, to the start of swapping to disk before chunk 178**

Main memory has not been completely exhausted when kswapd0 starts, but the free space is low enough that the swapper starts up, trying to get ahead of the ongoing memory consumption. Soon thereafter, chunk allocation 178 succeeds and starts taking its 10,240 page faults. Then at time 051 seconds, a single page fault takes almost a millisecond followed by paging_hog not running for 3.5 msec until time 055. There is no waiting for memory until the long page fault.

There is almost always interesting information at the *boundaries* between two different behaviors. Figures 24.2a and 24.2b show both ends of the 3.5 msec execution gap. Figure 24.2a shows the end of the long page fault on CPU 2 that started at time 051 and the beginning of the long execution gap. The page fault took 573 usec before a timer interrupt at 51.085 (not shown) and another

403 usec afterward. Then at the very end it makes three other processes runnable: kworker/1:2 on CPU 1, kworker/2:2 on CPU 2, and kworker/3:0 on CPU 3. The paging_hog process is suspended and does not resume until 3.5 msec later, in Figure 24.2b. Meanwhile, kswapd0 is CPU-bound on CPU 0 the entire time, with the wakeup of kworker0/0 still pending. This is the situation when the very long page fault *blocks* waiting for something.

Figure 24.2b shows the other end of the long execution gap. On CPU 0, kswapd0 is still running at the top left, but then the timer interrupt context switches CPU 0 to the pending kworker0/0 process and back again 35 usec later. It is kworker0/0 that wakes up paging_hog again to complete the very long page fault and then pick up again with short page faults.

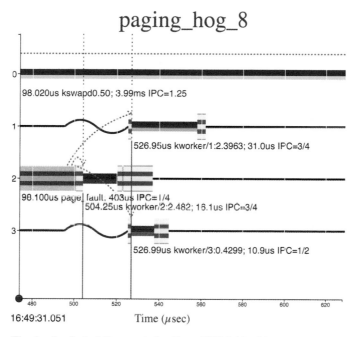

Figure 24.2a **The beginning of the page fault on CPU 2 blocking**

To summarize, the CPU-bound millisecond page fault blocks after making three worker threads runnable and remains blocked until a timer interrupt 3.5 msec later wakes up a fourth worker thread kworker0:0, which in turn restarts the long page fault. The page fault quickly completes and returns to paging_hog, which continues with many short page faults. This worker thread appears to be keeping track of how much main memory kswapd0 has made available again, and it unblocks the page fault on CPU 2 when there is enough. The fact that a timer interrupt awakens kworker0:0 after ~10 msec suggests that the strategy is to sample the state of free memory every 10 msec when the operating system has a severe memory shortage.The first phase allocation and byte-per-page writing goes on for about 185 chunks until a malloc finally fails. At that point, the second phase scanning of all the allocated chunks starts, again with a marker at the beginning of each chunk.

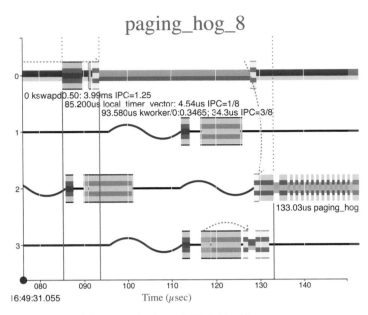

Figure 24.2b   **The end of the page fault on CPU 2 blocking**

Figure 24.3 shows chunk 5 of the scanning phase, running from the ⑤ marker on the left to the ⑥ marker on the right. The vertical lines show all the disk interrupts. The chunk has 10,240 pages, and these are being paged back in from disk over the course of 4.5 seconds. There are about 1500 disk interrupts during this time period. A quick mental calculation of 10240/1500 ~= 100/15 ~= 6.67 suggests that the pages are being read in groups of about 7 pages each.

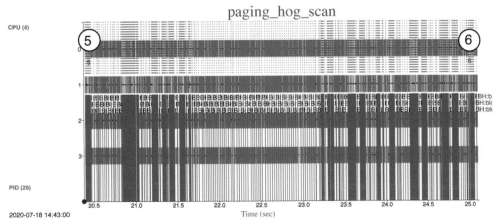

Figure 24.3   **Scanning one 40MB chunk after filling memory, showing about 1,500 disk interrupts that are unevenly spaced**

Figure 24.4 shows the initial 100 msec portion of Figure 24.3. On the left there is a group of 13 disk interrupts about one millisecond apart, a 2 msec gap, a group of 11, and then gaps of 7, 31, 29, and 15 msec in front of single disk interrupts. The closely spaced interrupts reflect pages that are close together on disk so need minimal seeks, while the larger gaps reflect longer seeks.

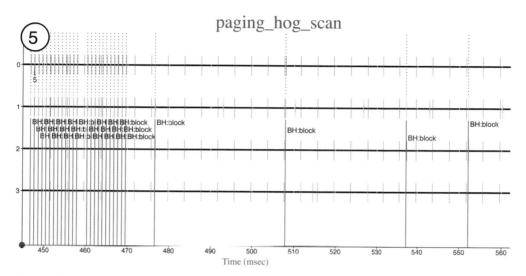

Figure 24.4   The leftmost part of Figure 24.3, showing the spacing of the first 28 disk interrupts

Recall from Chapter 5 that our sample server has old slow 5400 RPM disks. One revolution takes 11.1 msec, which is nearly exactly the elapsed time for each of the two groups of interrupts at the left in Figure 24.4. This suggests that the leftmost two groups of pages to be paged in are on two full adjacent disk tracks. After that, other pages are scattered about.

Figure 24.5 shows a further expansion of two disk interrupts in the first group of 12, spaced 0.92 msec apart. Each interrupt is delivered on CPU 1, followed immediately by the bottom-half interrupt handler `BH:block` running on CPU 1. This handler wakes up the paging_hog program that was suspended on CPU 0 in the middle of a page fault. That page fault completes, and then there are seven more quick page faults before the eighth sequential fault blocks waiting for disk again. So we can see directly that each disk access brings in eight pages, consistent with our rough estimate of 7 earlier. Doing estimates as you go can confirm that you understand the dynamic interactions when the estimates are good or can suggest that your reasoning got off track somewhere, either in the estimate or in understanding the observed data (or in observing the wrong thing).

In total, the scanning phase pages-in data that had been paged out during the allocation phase, after main memory began to fill up. Each disk transfer is eight pages. The transfers are spaced irregularly in time as a reflection of the seek time to get to the next group in the paging file. The paging_hog program waits for disk during all the gaps and then spends over 80% of its time in the page-fault routine during each little burst of execution.

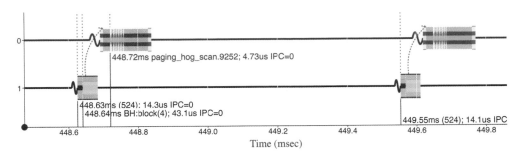

Figure 24.5   **Two disk interrupts and the page faults they resolve**

24.4 Mystery 2: Access to a Page Table

In the previous chapter we looked at scheduler behavior and waiting for CPU. The second mystery concerned waiting for CPU during the startup of multiple subthreads. We looked there at the CPU delays coming out of power-saving idle. We look here at the adjacent memory delays waiting for other threads to set up page tables.

Figure 24.6 is a more detailed version of Figure 23.4 of the previous chapter. The main program `bash` clones four sub-threads at step ① and then blocks or gets preempted in `mprotect`. The first sub-thread `schedtest.3573` runs at step ② but immediately page faults. The `page_fault` routine wakes up `bash` again and blocks waiting for it to finish setting up the shared page tables. The `mprotect` system call in `bash` resumes at step ③ and then wakes up threads 3575, 3576, 3573, and 3574 in that order. Sub-thread 3573 resumes at step ④.

24.5 Mystery 2 Understood

Look now at the bottom-half of Figure 24.6, showing where those threads wait for memory. The thin brown lines ending in dash-dash three times (Morse code for MMM) indicate waiting for memory, while the thin orange lines ending in triple dash-dot-dash-dot (Morse code for CCC) are waiting for CPU. When `bash` blocks in `mprotect` at time 406.97, it is not clear why it blocked. But when the page fault in `schedtest.3573` makes it runnable again at step ②, we know it was waiting on memory: page-table manipulation. The `bash` time from 406.97 to 417.53 usec is thus marked M, and the time from there to actually running again at 447.86 usec is marked C: waiting 30.3 usec for CPU 2 to execute its first instruction coming out of idle at step ③.

Near step ②, the four `schedtest` sub-threads all block in `page_fault` and wait for memory until `bash`'s `mprotect` resumption at step ③ wakes them up. Then they wait on CPUs to come out of idle (3575, 3576, and 3573) or to be assigned a CPU at all (3574). As we discussed in the previous chapter, thread 3574 waits 11.9 milliseconds before it runs.

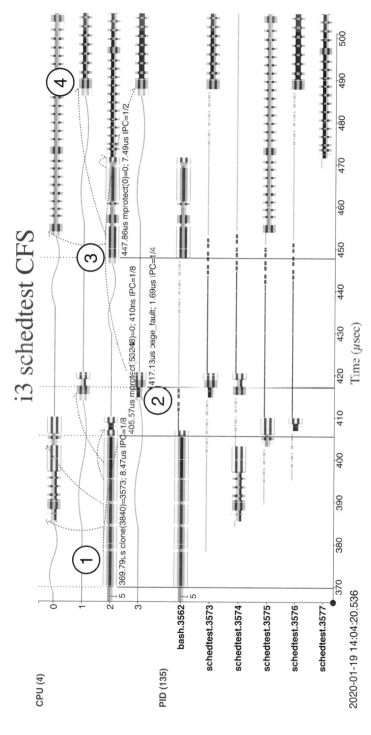

Figure 24.6 Expanded sub-thread startup showing waiting reasons for each thread (PID) when it is not executing

24.6   Summary

Because paging can produce 100x slowdowns, production systems are often designed to avoid paging altogether, partly through enforcing per-process memory allocation limits so that one process does not severely impact unrelated processes.

- Memory delays—threads blocked for virtual-memory paging activity—can be substantial.

- Even page faults that are entirely resolved in main memory with no page-file activity can consume significant CPU time, a hidden form of delay.

- Operating system swapping software algorithms are difficult to design because they need to anticipate future memory behavior across unknown programs.

- Page-file layout and management is also difficult and often fails to hide substantial seek times.

- Transferring groups of multiple pages to/from disk is helpful, but finding a good balance of group size is difficult.

- Management of shared page tables can produce delays, but they are substantially smaller than disk paging delays.

Exercises

24.1   Would it improve the performance of a program like paging_hog if the operating system transferred groups of 16 pages (64KB) instead of groups of 8?

24.2   How about groups of 128 pages (512KB)?

24.3   What are the design considerations in choosing the group size?

Chapter 25

Waiting for Disk

This chapter is a case study of a program that writes and then reads 40MB from disk and from SSD, similar to the program in Chapter 5. The delays waiting for disk are slightly surprising.

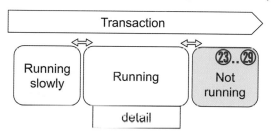

From our framework, this chapter is about not running while waiting for disk. A runnable process can wait for a disk because it is reading data that has not yet arrived or because it is writing data that can no longer be buffered in memory by the file system. We will force both to happen.

25.1   The Program

Program mystery25 initializes a 40MB array to random bytes, writes it to disk, synchronizes the file system, and then reads the file three different ways. The first read is 40MB all *at once*, the second is 10,240 individual 4KB reads *sequentially* from the beginning to the end of the file, and the third is 10,240 *random* 4KB reads. These give a variety of access patterns to understand. The program uses O_DIRECT files so that we can observe the disk activity for each step, not just the file-system in-memory buffering activity.

We look at four different runs of mystery25: (1) using a disk drive for the file storage, (2) using an SSD for the file, (3) running two copies simultaneously with two different files on disk, and (4) running two copies simultaneously with two different files on SSD.

25.2   The Mystery

From Chapter 5, about how long would you expect the disk write of 40MB to take to get the data all the way to disk? Would you expect the 40MB disk read to take just about the same time? Would you expect the sequential 4KB reads to take shorter, about the same, or longer than the 40MB read? About how long should the 4KB random reads take? Scribble down your estimates in milliseconds or seconds. Do similar estimates and write them down for an SSD.

What would you expect to be different when running two copies simultaneously? Would you expect the disk pair to take about the same amount of elapsed time, twice as long, or something in between? How about the SSD pair? Jot down your notes before continuing.

25.3   Exploring and Reasoning

The mystery25 program first allocates and initializes a 40MB array. This takes about 21 msec, of which 15.1 msec is spent in mystery25 itself, and 5.8 msec is spent in page fault handling. There are no further page faults in the rest of the program. (See Chapter 24 for details of the initial memory management issues.) The program then does the writes and reads. Here is the data measured by the program on our sample server's slow disk:

```
$ ./mystery25 /tmp/myst25.bin
opening /tmp/myst25.bin for write
  write:      40.00MB  0.008sec 4741.02MB/sec
  sync:       40.00MB  0.836sec 47.84MB/sec
  read:       40.00MB  0.673sec 59.47MB/sec
  seq read:   40.00MB  1.470sec 27.20MB/sec
  rand read:  40.00MB 68.849sec  0.58MB/sec
```

In Chapter 5 we measured this disk as transferring about 60 MB/sec, so writing or reading 40MB should take about 2/3 of a second; transferring a single 4KB block takes about 67 usec at the disk head. Also in Chapter 5, we measured about 173 4KB blocks per track, or about 692KB per track. Forty megabytes allocated in one contiguous extent on disk would cover about 60 tracks and thus take about 60 revolutions at 11.1 msec each = 667 msec. We expect non-sequential disk seeks to take about 10–15 msec. This arithmetic will be relevant for cross-checking when we look at traces of the reads and writes.

The initial `write` of 40MB does not touch the disk, even though we specified O_DIRECT. It just buffers all the data in kernel file-system main memory, such that the user's 40MB buffer is free to be modified when the `write` system call returns after about 8.5 msec. The following `sync` operation does the actual transfer to disk and does it about 25% more slowly than disk speed, *not* because the disk spins more slowly while writing (disk rotation speeds don't vary) but because the writing within `sync` is done less efficiently and occasionally misses a disk revolution—about 15 in total.

We see that the single read of 40MB indeed transfers about 60 MB/sec, but the other disk operations are slower. The 10,240 sequential 4KB reads are less efficient, taking about twice as long total as the single read. The random reads take almost 50 times longer; they are seek-bound since each requires a seek to a different block on disk. The other three runs have similar measurements with mostly similar patterns. We will get to those in a little while.

Writing and sync of 40MB. As usual, we use KUtrace to examine the dynamic behavior of this code, this time looking at the interactions between the user code, the operating system, and the disk itself. Figure 25.1 shows the overall `sync` operation. The mystery25 program does a system call to `sync`, which quickly blocks and does not return until a little over 900 msec (0.93 seconds) later. During this delay, there are 60 disk interrupts, or more specifically 60 invocations of `BH:block`, the bottom-half interrupt handler for block devices, that are fairly evenly spaced. This looks like one interrupt per disk revolution and hence per full track written.

Oddly, just 12 of these make the mystery25 program's sync code runnable, and these are quite *unevenly* spaced, as shown by the 12 vertical lines in Figure 25.1. The first one is just the startup of the sync system call, and the last one finishes the sync system call. The other 10 continue the sync but with a quite unexpected dynamic interaction—each has bursts of 70-odd wakeups of mystery25.

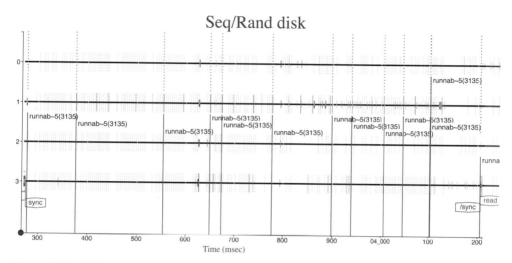

Figure 25.1 **Writing 40MB to disk via the sync system call. There are 12 disk interrupts that make the mystery25 program runnable.**

Figure 25.2a shows the disk interrupt at time 376. The interrupt occurs on CPU 1 followed by the bottom-half handler, only a portion of which is shown. It runs for 845 usec (!) total, while making mystery25 runnable 74 times.

As you can see on CPU 3, mystery25 runs for a little segment each time, consisting of (i) the scheduler switching out of idle, (ii) the kernel-mode sync system call continuing but not finishing, and (iii) the scheduler switching back into idle. This pattern repeats 10 times from time 376 near the left of Figure 25.1 to time 103 near the right. Figure 25.2b shows the very last disk interrupt, near time 206 in Figure 25.1, which causes the sync system call finally to finish and return to user-mode mystery25.

In total, the sync system call runs in 726 little segments, on average about once every 14 disk blocks. The bottom-half handler is copying data to disk, apparently in 4MB chunks (hence the middle 10 disk interrupts for writing 40MB), and updating the sync system call about its progress. I don't know why the spacing is so irregular.

Notice that almost 80% of the non-idle CPU 3 execution time is spent in the scheduler, not in sync. While this may not matter on an idle machine, the ten bursts of 70-odd pairs of context switches will slow down any other programs executing on CPU 3. Spending 80% of the time context switching is highly inefficient, violating the Half-Useful Principle stated in Chapter 5.

In our example here, it would be more efficient for the bottom-half handler to run the sync code less often, so that each sync segment is at least as long as two context switches, and perhaps run it as infrequently as just once per disk interrupt.

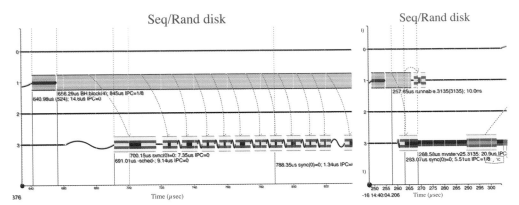

Figure 25.2a   **Disk interrupt with bottom half making `sync` system call resume multiple times**

Figure 25.2b   **Last disk interrupt running `sync` system call that finally completes and returns to mystery25**

25.4   Reading 40MB

The first of the three disk-read patterns is a single read of the entire 40MB file. Thanks to `O_DIRECT`, this read actually goes to disk instead of just copying out of the file-system cache. Figure 25.3 shows the behavior. The mystery25 program does a system call to `read`, which runs for 3.4 msec and then blocks and does not return until a little over 680 msec later, when it finishes up for 1.6 msec and returns finally to mystery25 at time 890. During this delay, there are 59 disk interrupts with 59 `BH:block` soft interrupts, essentially one per track. They are slightly irregularly spaced in time but average about 11 msec apart. In other words, one interrupt per disk revolution. The initial part of the `read` system call locks the 40MB of user buffer into main memory. The bottom-half handler then transfers data from disk directly to the locked-down user buffer, and the finishing-up part of the read system call unlocks the 40MB user buffer.

How do we know that the `BH:block` handler doesn't transfer into a kernel file-system buffer like the `write` system call does when going the other way, leaving the transfer into the user buffer up to the tail end of the `read` call? There are two reasons. First, the `read` system call tail end, after the last disk interrupt, is only 1.6 msec, which is *too short* to transfer 40MB in memory—compared to the 8 msec this transfer takes in the `write` call. Second, and completely definitively, we found in Chapter 5 that blocks from disk showed up *in the user's buffer* throughout the read, not just all at once at the end.

In total, the single read of all 40MB does what we expect from Chapter 5—it reads the entire file at the maximum disk surface rate of 60 MB/sec.

Looking at CPU time for this transfer, it takes up about 1% of the total CPU time on one core (680us/6.3ms). So we don't expect CPU time to be a bottleneck for big single reads.

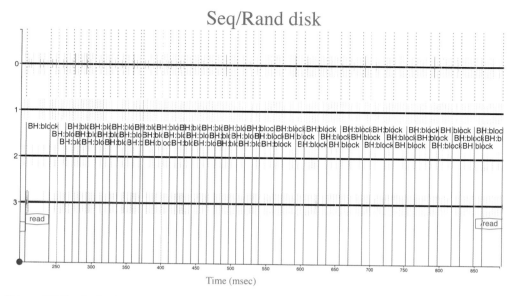

Figure 25.3 **A single read of the entire 40MB file**

25.5 Reading Sequential 4KB Blocks

The second disk read pattern is a loop reading 4KB blocks sequentially across all 10,240 blocks of the 40MB file. Figure 25.4 shows this behavior.

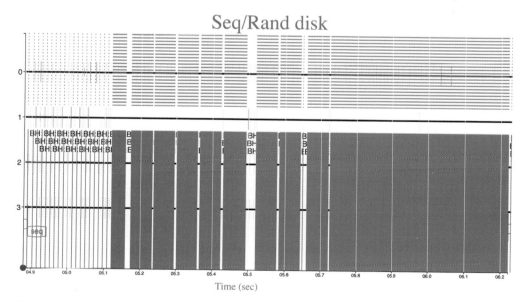

Figure 25.4 **Sequential reads of 10K disk blocks, each 4KB**

The first 18 blocks generate interrupts about 11 msec apart, i.e., once per track, and then the behavior changes, and the interrupts are spaced densely only about 150 usec apart. The dense interrupts have occasional gaps of 5–30 msec, giving 10 dense groups overall (the last is 500 msec long). Figure 25.5 shows three of these tightly spaced interrupts, from time 5.127 in Figure 25.4.

Each hard disk interrupt runs the usual bottom-half handler, which this time wakes up not only mystery25 but also a kernel worker thread, kworker/1:1H. The worker runs for a very short time and blocks again. The mystery25 program completes one read and then 3 usec later starts the next one. The time from starting each read to finishing it is about 110 usec. The data transfer is from the track buffer inside the disk drive, which at a SATA speed of 300 MB/sec (remember this is a $17 old slow disk) takes about 13.7 usec. The rest of the time is spent getting the I/O request out to the disk hardware and waiting for its microcode to find the right place in the track buffer, do the transfer, and then post the interrupt.

How do we know the transfer is not directly from the disk surface? Because if it were, by the time the next read is started, the block to be read would have passed under the disk's read/write head and we would only be able to read one block per disk revolution instead of an average of about 80 blocks per revolution. How do we know that the blocks are not simply two-way interleaved on the disk to allow enough time for the second read to start before the next block arrives? Because if that were the case, each full-track transfer would take two disk revolutions instead of one, so 30 MB/sec, not the observed 60 MB/sec maximum transfer rate.

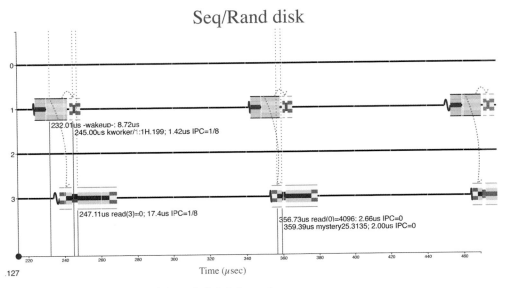

Figure 25.5   **Three sequential-read disk interrupts**

In total, the sequential read of 4KB blocks does about what we expect—it reads the entire file but at about half the maximum rate. Transferring a single 4KB block takes about 67 usec at the disk head but an average 143 usec here including all delays. At least this reduced rate still qualifies as (almost) Half-Useful.

Looking at the non-idle CPU time instead of elapsed time, the sequential 4KB reads take up about 24% (323ms/1332ms) of the CPU time on one core, which is large enough that we need to pay attention to CPU time as a possible bottleneck. Sequential 4KB reads by themselves can interfere with other programs even though the other programs are not touching disk.

25.6   Reading Random 4KB Blocks

The third disk-read pattern is a loop reading 4KB blocks at random locations across all 10,240 blocks of the 40MB file. Figure 25.6 shows this behavior, but only for the first 7.5 seconds and 1148 reads; the entire trace of this portion is over a minute long, but we don't learn anything new after the first few seconds.

Random 4KB reads require the disk to seek before each read, taking time for the seek and also defeating the readahead behavior of a track buffer. The spacing of the random reads is irregular, with times that range from 0.114 msec to 67.3 msec, with half the spaces between 2.9 and 9.9 msec and a median of 6.3 msec. This spacing simply reflects some short seeks and some very long seeks, but all within our single 40 MB file. Seeks scattered across the entire disk instead of just one small file will have a higher average seek time in the 10–15 msec range.

Figure 25.7 gives the detail of one disk interrupt. It differs from the sequential 4KB reads only in the explicit `lseek` system call and the longer millisecond-scale delay before the next interrupt. Actually, there is a second difference: the time to come out of deep sleep and the individual execution times are longer by about a factor of four. This almost surely reflects the CPU clock running at 800 MHz for the random reads instead of 3900 MHz for the sequential reads whose interrupts are close enough together to avoid low power modes. I say "almost surely" because in both cases the CPU itself reports running at 800 MHz.

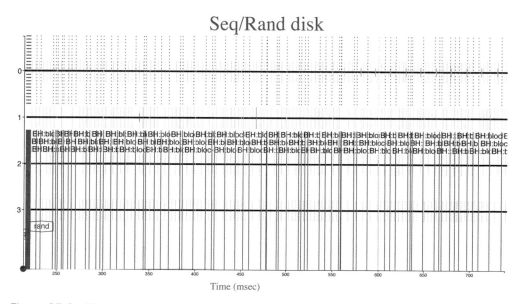

Figure 25.6   **The beginning of 10,240 random 4KB disk reads**

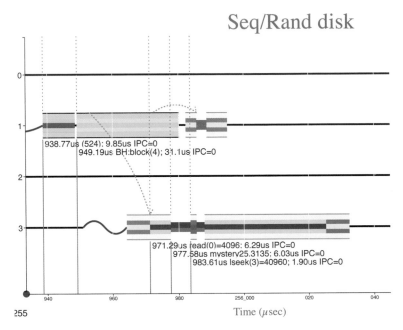

Figure 25.7   **Detail of one random 4KB read from disk**

In total, the random read of 4KB blocks does about what we expect—it spends over a minute seeking. Transferring a single 4KB block takes about 67 usec at the disk head but 6300 usec here for seek plus read. Only about 1% of the elapsed time is useful data transfer. To meet the Half-Useful Principle with seeks of perhaps 13 msec ranging across the entire disk, we would have to read about 13 msec of data at 60 MB/sec or about 780KB each time, not 4KB.

The total CPU time for all 10,240 blocks is about 1420 msec (1.42 seconds), about 4.4 times the CPU time for sequential reads. This would be a CPU bottleneck except that it is spread across more than a minute of elapsed time due to the seek delays.

We have finished with a fairly long look at disk traffic. The next three sections will only briefly touch on observed differences for SSD and for accessing two files at once.

25.7   Writing and Sync of 40MB on SSD

As you would expect, the data transfer rate of the solid-state drive is about 10 times faster than the rotating disk drive, about 700 vs. 60 MB/s. The random "seek" time is about 100x faster: 89 vs. 13000 usec. Here is the data measured by the program on our sample server's cheap SSD:

```
$ ./mystery25 /datassd/dserve/myst25.bin
opening /datassd/dserve/myst25.bin for write
  write:   40.00 MB  0.009sec 4623.53 MB/sec
  sync:    40.00 MB  0.068sec  587.07 MB/sec  1.42x slower than read 40MB
  read:    40.00 MB  0.057sec  706.00 MB/sec  base (5.5us per 4KB block)
```

```
seq read:40.00 MB  0.548sec 72.95 MB/sec   9.68x slower than read 40MB
rand read:40.00 MB 0.909sec 43.98 MB/sec   1.66x slower than seq.
                                           4KB reads (89us each)
```

This particular SSD generates interrupts under multiple interrupt numbers sent to multiple CPU cores, sometimes appearing to be a disk and sometimes appearing to be an Ethernet adapter. It is attached via the PCIe bus instead of a SATA cable, and these have different interrupt structures. The design of spreading out the interrupts across multiple CPUs allows higher transfer rates than possible with a single bottleneck CPU handling all the interrupts.

25.8 Reading 40MB on SSD

The single read of all 40MB runs at the full SSD transfer rate of 706 MB/sec, or 5.5 usec per 4KB block. But the sequential 4KB reads are almost 10 times slower. Why?

Figure 25.8 shows the spacing between two 4KB sequential transfers. Each group starts with an interrupt (mis-labeled eth0 by KUtrace due to combined network and SSD PCIe interupts), the scheduler, the end of one read, mystery25 user code, the beginning of the next read, and the scheduler. Then mystery25 blocks and waits for an interrupt at the end of the transfer. The entire sequence repeats every 54.27 usec.

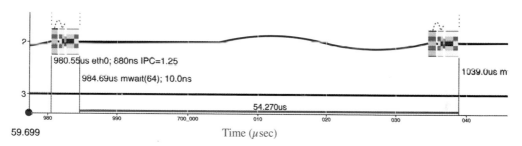

Figure 25.8   **Spacing between two 4KB sequential SSD reads**

But look! When mystery25 blocks, there is an mwait just 200 nsec (!) into the idle loop to put the CPU to sleep. This causes the extra 30 usec (30000 nsec) red sine-wave delay coming back out of sleep, reducing the transfer rate by over a factor of two. *This* is the real cost of violating the Half-Optimal Principle discussed in Chapter 23. Without the over-eager mwait, sequential reads should be about 150 MB/sec. Note that the long sleep delay might not occur on a busy machine with lots of other processes. If so, this run of mystery25 would be faster on a busy machine than on an idle one—somewhat counter-intuitive.

The CPU time for each 4KB block is 4 usec, so 10,240 of these is 41 msec of CPU time spread across 548 msec of elapsed time, or about about 7.5% of one CPU core. This is reasonable, but suggests keeping an eye on CPU time for transfers on newer faster SSDs.

The random 4KB reads from this SSD take 89 usec each, of which 5.5 usec is spent transferring data (as seen in the single 40MB read earlier). To meet the Half-Useful Principle with "seeks" of 89 - 5.5 = 83.5 usec, we would have to read about 15–16 blocks or about 64KB each time, not 4KB.

25.9   Two Programs Accessing Two Files at Once

Running two copies of mystery25 simultaneously, as suggested in Chapter 22, will reveal any saturated hardware. For disk, writing (to memory, not disk yet) gives an aggregate 6.4 GB/sec vs. 4.7 GB/sec for a single copy, meaning that two simultaneous 40MB writes get about 35% more total memory bandwidth than one write. Only a partial bottleneck here.

The sync and read disk transfers take twice as long total compared to a single copy, meaning that the single disk read-write head is saturated—it can service blocks from only one program at a time, as we would expect. The reads are in fact about 2.2x slower. The extra 10% slowdown (2.2 not 2.0) comes from extra seeks between the two different files involved. This is an example of *superlinear slowdown*—running two copies in parallel takes more elapsed time than running them sequentially one after another, because the two in parallel not only split some saturated resource in half, but they also cause each to do *additional* work (more seeks in this case, more cache line or TLB refills in other cases).

For SSD, running two copies of mystery25 simultaneously reveals a few more wrinkles. The write, sync, read all, and read 4KB sequentially behaviors are all similar to disk. But the random read of 4KB blocks barely slows down at all, so in aggregate the two programs transfer 82.36 MB/sec compared to 43.98 MB/sec for one copy. Why are the random reads so fast but the sequential reads are not?

```
One copy on SSD (from above):
  seq read:  40.000MB   0.548sec 72.95 MB/sec
  rand read: 40.000MB   0.909sec 43.98 MB/sec

$ ./mystery25 /datassd/dserve/myst25.bin & ./mystery25 /datassd/dserve/myst25a.bin
[2] 3479
opening /datassd/dserve/myst25.bin for write
opening /datassd/dserve/myst25a.bin for write
  write:      40.00 MB  0.010sec 4126.69 MB/sec
  write:      40.00 MB  0.016sec 2449.33 MB/sec
  sync:       40.00 MB  0.161sec 247.68 MB/sec  2.32x slower than single run
  sync:       40.00 MB  0.155sec 258.78 MB/sec
  read:       40.00 MB  0.109sec 368.64 MB/sec  1.94x slower      "
  read:       40.00 MB  0.112sec 356.62 MB/sec
  seq read:   40.00 MB  0.944sec 42.36 MB/sec   1.72x slower      "
  seq read:   40.00 MB  0.942sec 42.48 MB/sec
  rand read:  40.00 MB  0.971sec 41.18 MB/sec   1.07x slower      "
  rand read:  40.00 MB  0.971sec 41.18 MB/sec
```

Notice that with one copy of mystery25 running, sequential SSD reads transfer 72.95 MB/sec, while two copies transfer a total of 42.36 + 42.48 = 84.84 MB/sec. With one copy of mystery25 running, random SSD reads transfer 43.98 MB/sec, while two copies transfer a total of 41.18 + 41.18 = 83.36 MB/sec. These numbers suggest that about 84 MB/sec is the best that one of these SSDs can do when going through the full operating system and disk interrupt path (Figure 25.8) for every block, the combined hardware-software path's bandwidth limit. So sequential 4KB reads in one copy saturate the resource, meaning that two copies see almost no net speedup.

While random 4KB reads in one copy saturate access time ("seek" time) to random blocks, they use only about half the combined hardware-software path's bandwidth. When running two copies, there is enough bandwidth available for both.

But what about access time? Ah. As we saw in Chapter 5's Figure 5.18, SSDs often have multiple independent banks of flash memory. Each has an access delay (83.5 usec here), but multiple banks can be accessed simultaneously. Our two simultaneous runs of mystery25 almost perfectly keep two banks busy all the time, so see no substantial slowdown and thus transfer twice as much data in about the same time as a single run.

25.10   Mysteries Understood

With careful attention to the numeric values measured and with some exploration of the dynamic behavior as captured by KUtrace, we are able to explain most of the observed timings. Along the way, we found several examples of violations of the Half-Useful Principle for data transfers, and one example of a serious 2x slowdown due to violation of the Half-Optimal Principle from Chapter 23.

25.11   Summary

- Like most operating systems, Linux has high performance when transferring large chunks of data between memory and storage devices such as disks or SSDs.

- In contrast, transferring small 4KB blocks one at a time involves longer software, hardware, and device paths with performance losses that range from a factor of 2 to a factor of 100.

- An SSD can transfer data about 10x faster than a disk, and its access or seek time is about 100x faster.

- To achieve Half-Useful performance for any operation that has a startup time, the useful work must take at least as long as the startup.

- For disks, this means reading or writing roughly 1MB per seek.

- For SSDs, this means reading or writing roughly 64KB per seek.

- Keep this in mind when designing software that accesses external storage—tiny transfers are death for performance.

- Running two copies of a program in fact reveals saturated hardware resources—memory bandwidth, disk/SSD bandwidth, and seeking.

- Sometimes sharing a resource causes a superlinear slowdown.

- Fixing the idle-loop `mwait` problem described in Chapter 23 would double the bandwidth of tiny 4KB sequential SSD reads for our sample server.

- Avoiding deep sleep can make a program faster on a busy machine than on an idle one.

Exercises

25.1   Find another anomaly in the HTML files for the four traces in this chapter. Specify the time range, what looks odd, and your thoughts and reasoning about what likely is going on. How would you improve the performance?

Chapter 26

Waiting for Network

This chapter is a case study of network remote procedure call (RPC) delays. Using our RPC client and server programs from earlier chapters, we will examine unexpected round-trip delays.

From our framework, this chapter is about not running while waiting for network. A process can wait for the network because it is waiting for offered work, waiting for a response from another machine, or waiting for congested network hardware.

This chapter draws on the RPC framework introduced in Chapter 6. We assume that RPCs are done through a common library that creates timestamped logs of each request and response message. The library provides a message header with a pseudo-random RPC ID number for

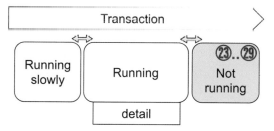

each RPC and for nested RPCs the parent's RPC ID. A distinctive message header with RPC ID allows packet capture software tools such as tcpdump [Tcpdump 2020] or Wireshark [Wireshark 2021] to identify the beginnings of multi-packet request and response messages. This should be the minimal instrumentation for any production RPC environment.

26.1 Overview

We will again use the same T1..T4 timestamps of Chapter 6, Figure 6.6, carried over here as Figure 26.1.

Figure 26.1   **Diagram of one RPC, showing the four times: T1 client sends request; T2 server receives request; T3 server sends response; T4 client receives response. w1 indicates the time the request hits the network, and w3 the time the response does.**

Our RPC library also creates KUtrace entries bracketing the user-mode CPU work for each RPC request and for each RPC response, allowing us to correlate RPC logs with the corresponding CPU execution.

In this environment, a process that is not executing because it is merely waiting for work in the form of an RPC request is straightforward to identify with logs—just after it wakes up, it time-stamps and logs the incoming RPC. We will not further discuss this case.

A process that is not executing because it is waiting for an RPC response from another machine is also straightforward to identify, but the delay could be from remote server execution delays or from request or response communication delays including network congestion. Server execution delays are straightforward to identify with server-side logs.

That leaves communication delays. This is the topic we explore in detail in this chapter.

RPC messages originate in user-mode code, are sent though kernel-mode code and network hardware, are received in kernel-mode code, and are finally delivered to user-mode code. Our T1..T4 timestamps are all created by user-mode code, but some of the delays involved happen in either client kernel code or server kernel code, or in the interfaces between user code, kernel code, and network hardware. To understand these latter delays, it is necessary to have observation tools that go deeper than just user-mode behavior.

The phrase "on the wire" as used in this chapter refers to the time RPC message bits are actually transmitted across the underlying network hardware links. These links might be Ethernet wires, Ethernet fibers, or radio transmissions such as Wi-Fi [Wikipedia 2021v] or Bluetooth [Wikipedia 2021w]. The path between two computers may use several layers of network switching and routing. Within a datacenter room, we expect only small transmission delays (microseconds) in the hardware itself, but long-distance transmissions can have delays of tens or hundreds of milliseconds. We use "on the wire" to refer to all the physical network hardware involved in moving bits. As we shall see, the interesting delays are usually between a user-mode call to the kernel and getting bits onto the wire or between bits arriving on the wire and getting them to user-mode code.

Unfortunately, without hardware packet tracing on (or near) the wire itself to give the w1 and w3 times, it is always ambiguous whether a delayed transmission after the user-mode sender software timestamp and before the user-mode receiver software timestamp occurs on the sending machine or on the receiving machine, or (rarely) in the network hardware itself.

Four experiments follow, to reveal some of the dynamics involved in waiting for network data. We will use `tcpdump` and KUtrace to observe network traffic.

26.2   The Programs

Program client4 (from Chapter 6) sends RPCs in various patterns while the program server4 receives and processes them. We look first at sending 20,000 requests of 4KB each between two machines, then at sending 200 requests of 1MB each between two machines, and finally at running three parallel clients on one machine sending 4KB requests, 1MB requests, and 1MB requests to servers on three different machines. In this last case, the total offered request traffic exceeds the bandwidth available for the single Ethernet link on the client machine, so we can study the congestion dynamics. The fourth experiment explores retransmission delays.

26.3 Experiment 1

The client4 program sends 20,000 requests of 4KB each to the server4 program on a second machine. Both machines have 1 gigabit per second (1 Gb/sec) Ethernet links, and they are connected through a multi-port 1 Gb/sec Ethernet switch. Each link can carry an idealized 1,000,000,000 / 8 = 125MB per second of data, but that calculation ignores 90 bytes of TCP/IP packet headers, hardware packet checksum, and required space between packets. The achievable link speed is between 110 and 120 MB/sec.

Figure 26.2 shows a picture of the standard Ethernet IPv4/TCP maximum-size packet. Of the 1,538 bytes sent on the wire, 1,448 (94%) contain user data. Thus, the maximum data rate user code will see is 94% of 125 MB/sec, or about 117 MB/sec. Shorter TCP/IP packets have the same 90 bytes of overhead on the wire, so achieve lower bandwidth. For detailed information on the internals and complex dynamics of the TCP protocol, see the excellent Fall and Stevens book [Fall 2012].

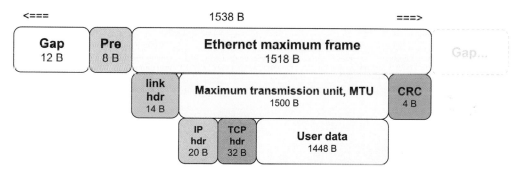

Figure 26.2 **Standard Ethernet packet layout (for a default Linux TCP header with 12 bytes of options). Gap: required 96 bit-times between packets; Pre: preamble bit pattern to synchronize receiver clocks; link hdr: destination MAC address, source MAC address, Ethertype; CRC: cyclic redundancy check; IP hdr: IPv4 source and destination addresses, protocol type of next header (the IPv6 header is longer); TCP hdr: TCP port numbers and sequence numbers.**

An RPC message of 4,100 bytes will take up three packets containing 1,448, 1,448, and 1,204 bytes of user data, and occupying 1538+1538+1294 bytes on the wire, or 34,960 bits or nearly 35 usec on the wire. Each maximum-size packet will take about 12.3 usec on the wire.

The RPCs we use in the experiments for this chapter have a method type of "sink," which tells the server to simply throw the incoming request data away and send a minimal success response. The purpose is to minimize any server-side or response-message delays so we can focus our experiments on the client side.

26.4   Experiment 1 Mystery

For a program sending RPCs of 4,100 bytes, we might naively expect a new one to go out every 35 usec, and that 20,000 of them would therefore take 35 * 20,000 usec = 700 msec. In fact, the program runs over 10 times slower than that, taking 8,094 msec (8.1 seconds) total to complete and achieving about 10.1 MB/sec on the wire, not 117 MB/sec. As usual, the mystery is "Where did all the time go?"

For this experiment, we gathered three kinds of data:

1. RPC logs as we saw in Chapter 6

2. Packet traces from `tcpdump` for both machines

3. Execution traces from KUtrace for both machines

The RPC logs give us a beginning. Using them, Figure 26.3 shows the first 5,000 RPCs with time of day on the x-axis and RPC number 1–5000 on the y-axis. They just march along regularly with nothing surprising. Figure 26.4 shows the same data by elapsed time within each RPC.

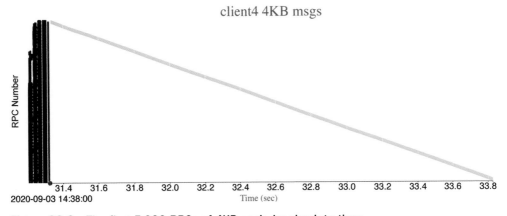

Figure 26.3   **The first 5,000 RPCs of 4KB each, by absolute time**

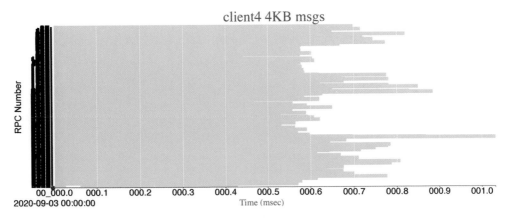

Figure 26.4   **The first 5,000 RPCs of 4KB each, by elapsed time**

Most RPCs run 400–600 usec, with a few out to 800 usec or more and no obvious pattern of when the slow ones appear, except there is some bunching into three broad groups of slower round-trips. We focus first on why the average is so large and in later experiments look at the variance.

Figure 26.5 shows several RPCs near the front of the trace. The server clock has been aligned with the client clock, using the alignment program developed in Chapter 7. The RPCs are shown from T1 = client request sent to T4 = client response received timestamps. Each takes about 400 usec. The expected very short server time, from T2 = server request received to T3 = server response sent, is shown as the downward notch about 3/5 of the way in, and the synthesized *approximate* time for data on the wire is shown in white (the 88-byte response blip is hardly visible).

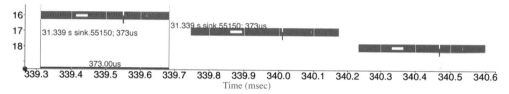

Figure 26.5   **Three RPCs sending messages of 4KB each, time aligned to client time of day**

From this simple figure we can observe several important timing aspects:

1. The overall time of 400 usec is about 10x the time on the wire for the request + response.

2. The time on the server T3 - T2 is appropriately small.

3. The requests take 240–260 usec T2 - T1 to arrive at the server, and the responses take 130-160 usec T4 - T3 to arrive back at the client.

4. The time between receiving one response and sending the next request is about 60 usec.

So there is an extra 100–200 usec delay of unknown cause between the user code outbound timestamps and the corresponding user code inbound timestamps. This could be in kernel software or in network hardware. There is also some delay in the client code between requests. Why all these delays?

26.5   Experiment 1 Exploring and Reasoning

We look first at the transmission delays and second at the between-RPC delays.

The TCP/IP networking code is fairly complicated, dealing with simultaneous flows originating on multiple CPU cores and delivered on the other end to software on multiple machines, while also managing each TCP window (the amount of sent-but-not-yet-acknowledged packet data) and doing retransmissions as needed for dropped or corrupted packets. Both network hardware and software may do packet fragmentation or coalescing. Optimizations may deliver interrupts to different CPU cores and packets to multiple ring buffers tied to different CPU caches. To handle heavy flows, packet arrival interrupts may be coalesced and delivered less frequently.

The request RPC goes through a path of many software and hardware layers to get from client to server, as shown in Figure 26.6. Starting with user code on the left, the request message goes to a `write()` system call (or `sendmsg`, `sendto`, etc.), which runs the kernel TCP/IP transmit code for forming a list of packets that are then inserted into a transmit queue, along with possibly other packets from other programs. The queued packets are placed into a main-memory ring buffer from which the sending network interface card (NIC) fetches them and sends them over the physical link, the "wire."

On the other end, the receiving NIC places incoming packets into a main-memory ring buffer and posts an interrupt for the CPU. When the hard interrupt routine runs, it immediately schedules the soft interrupt routine `BH:rx` and exits. The soft interrupt routine runs the TCP/IP receive code that forwards the data to a pending `read()` system call (or `recvmsg`, `recvfrom`, `poll`, etc.) that blocked earlier waiting for data. The `read` call passes the data on to waiting user code. If there is no `read` call outstanding, the packet data is buffered in the kernel.

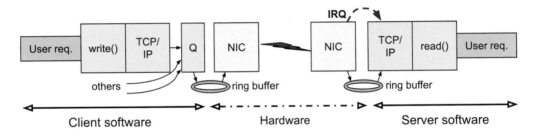

Figure 26.6 **RPC request path from client user-mode software to server user-mode software**

On this path, there are four timestamps applied as shown in Figure 26.7, using four *different* clocks:

1. Client-machine user-mode `gettimeofday`

2. Client-machine kernel-mode `ktime_get_real`

3. Server-machine user-mode `gettimeofday`

4. Server-machine kernel-mode `ktime_get_real`

Figure 26.7 **Timestamps applied on the RPC request path**

On the left, the client user-mode RPC library adds a KUtrace entry giving the RPC ID and its method name, timestamped T1. Somewhat later, `tcpdump` code in the kernel captures a portion of each outbound packet and applies a timestamp w1 soon before the packet is transmitted. The outbound `tcpdump` timestamp is recorded when a packet goes into the transmit queue or ring buffer. Exactly when the NIC hardware subsequently pulls out a packet and puts it on the wire is not visible to software.

On the server, `tcpdump` captures a portion of each inbound packet and applies a timestamp soon after the packet is received. Inbound `tcpdump` applies a timestamp when the TCP/IP protocol code processes that packet. Finally, the server user-mode RPC library adds a KUtrace entry giving the RPC ID and its method name, timestamped T2. The response message is similar.

The client machine has two concepts of time of day. KUtrace postprocessing maps the client-machine T1 timestamp to that machine's user-mode `gettimeofday` time base. The client `tcpdump` uses kernel-mode `ktime_get_real`, which is calculated from the timer-interrupt jiffies, the cycle counter, and a slope and offset; it can differ by several hundred microseconds from the user-mode version. The server machine also has two concepts of time of day, kernel and user, and these can differ from the client machines' by dozens of milliseconds.

Along the complete RPC request path, there are two common places to encounter noticeable delays, shown in Figure 26.8. On the client machine, an outbound packet may wait for a while in the software transmit queue if the NIC buffer is full. Or it may wait in the NIC hardware ring buffer. On the server machine, interrupt coalescing may delay for tens to hundreds of microseconds before signaling a CPU that a packet has arrived. Once noticed, a packet may be held in a kernel software queue for data coalescing, for avoiding out-of-order delivery, or for other reasons. Software or hardware flow control may also intrude and cause packet queueing.

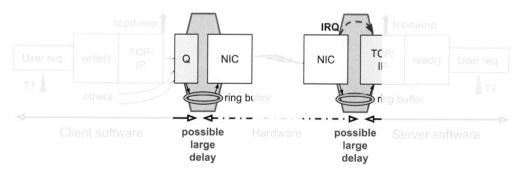

Figure 26.8 **Common places for transmission delays, one on the sending side and one on the receiving side**

To use the `tcpdump` trace and the KUtrace data, we need to do more time alignment.

As mentioned, we used the timealign program from Chapter 6 to rewrite the client-side RPC log to move the server T2 and T3 times to the client time base used for T1 and T4. The server machine's actual `gettimeofday` is about 7.176 msec earlier than the client machine's.

But `tcpdump` uses kernel time on each machine, so we have to align that also. We use the `tcpalign` program to remap `tcpdump` times to KUtrace times on each machine, adding JSON lines to the KUtrace output for each message-start packet, but ignoring other individual packets.

When all this is done, the resulting Figures 26.9a and 26.9b show the processing of a typical 4KB sink RPC—Figure 26.9a on the client machine and Figure 26.9b on the server machine, with its timeline shifted by 7.176 msec to align reasonably closely with client time. Network traffic is shown above CPU 0. Outbound messages (tx) slant slightly upwards away from CPU 0, and dashed lines indicate approximate packet spacing. Inbound messages (rx) slant slightly downward toward CPU 0. Messages can be multiple packets (three for the 4KB request here, about 690 for a 1MB request), but we only keep a timestamp for the first packet, containing the message header.

At the left of Figure 26.9a, the client records a KUtrace request entry for RPC 20591 at the first `sink.2~1` vertical line, and `tcpdump` timestamps the first outbound request packet at the first `rpc.20~1` vertical line. At the right, `tcpdump` timestamps the incoming response packet at the second `rpc.20~1` vertical line (the 20~1 notation is RPC 20591 elided) and KUtrace timestamps the response at the second `sink.2~1` vertical line. In the middle, on CPU 3, there is an Ethernet interrupt that is processing the not-displayed TCP ACK packet sent from the client after receiving the three request packets. The Figure 26.9a time scale makes it difficult to see the gaps between the three client packets.

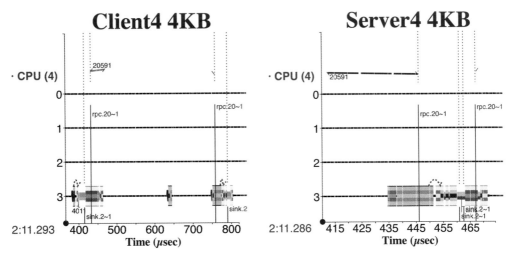

Figure 26.9ab   a) Client sending one 4KB request and receiving response. Aligned tcpdump packets at top. b) Server receiving that 4KB request and sending response. Aligned tcpdump packets at top.

In Figure 26.9b, we see the three request packets arrive at the server and see the interrupt handler wake up the server program. There again are four vertical lines: `tcpdump` incoming timestamp, KUtrace request and response timestamps, and `tcpdump` response timestamp. At the far right of the server diagram, the not-displayed TCP ACK packet for the response arrives, causing the interrupt processing at time 600 on its CPU 3.

The careful reader will note no sine-wave coming out of idle on the server. The server is an AMD Ryzen, and its idle loop does not sleep as aggressively as on the

Intel client machine. The reader might also note that the server-side execution intervals all seem shorter than on the client side. That is because the client machine is idle enough that it is running 5x slowly at 800 MHz (as we saw in Chapter 22), while the server machine is running at a full 3.5 GHz.

Why the transmission delays? With no contending network traffic at the client, there is nothing to trigger a large delay before sending the request packets. But there can well be a delay after the packets arrive at the server before the NIC posts an interrupt to the CPU, after which `tcpdump` sees them. How big a delay? The reason to delay posting an interrupt is to prevent overloading a CPU with back-to-back interrupts occurring faster than they can be processed. Instead, *interrupt coalescing* accumulates a batch of packets and allows a CPU to process each batch efficiently.

There is a clear blog explanation of the tuning parameters involved in [Damato 2016]. Using the referenced `ethtool` [Broughton 2011] command line, we find our machines have a default receive interrupt (rx) delay of up to 200 usec or four packets, whichever occurs first. By fluke, I picked a sink RPC message size that fits into only three packets, so the 200 usec parameter dominates.

```
$ sudo ethtool -c enp4s0
Coalesce parameters for enp4s0:
  ...
rx-usecs: 200   <============
rx-frames: 4    <============
rx-usecs-irq: 0
rx-frames-irq: 0
```

It looks like the request packets in fact crossed the wire at about server time 250, not 450, but the server-side interrupt was delivered only around time 450. The response delay at the client is not so long; it may have to do with the ACK packet that arrived less than 200 usec before.

In any case, a 200 usec delay in delivering network interrupts may be a reasonable desktop default, but it is about 10 times too large for network traffic within a time-constrained environment with fast processors. Reducing it can substantially improve the throughput in Experiment 1.

26.6   Experiment 1 What About the Time Between RPCs?

Recall that the time from the end of one RPC to the beginning of the next is about 60 usec in the RPC logs. The root cause is an unneeded `nanosleep` call. The client4 source is

```
// The double-nested command loop
for (int i = 0; i < outer_repeats; ++i) {
  if (sink_command) {kutrace::mark_d(value_padlen + i);}
  for (int j = 0; j < inner_repeats; ++j) {
    SendCommand(sockfd, &randseed, command, ... value_padlen);
    if (key_incr) {IncrString(&key_base_str);}
```

```
    if (value_incr) {IncrString(&value_base_str);}
  }
  WaitMsec(wait_msec);
}
```

and the command line for it is

```
./client4 dclab-1 12345 -rep 20000 sink -key "abcd" -value "vvvv" 4000
```

The command sets the outer repeat to 20,000, the inner repeat to 1, both increment tests to false, and `wait_msec` defaults to 0. Do you see any problems?

In retrospect, to be more efficient I could have set the outer repeat to 1 and the inner repeat to 20,000 instead of the other way around. But I wanted the `mark_d` numbers to be in the trace. I didn't think much about the call to `WaitMsec`. But look at the gap between two RPCs recorded by KUtrace, as shown in Figure 26.10.

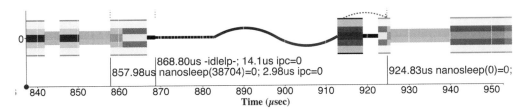

Figure 26.10   **The client execution time between finishing one RPC and starting the next**

After recording the prior response at time 852, the client code calls `WaitMsec`, which is just a wrapper around the `nanosleep` system call at time 857.98. Even though the requested delta is 0 nanoseconds, this system call goes ahead and sets a hardware timer and then blocks, context-switches to the idle process, drops into deep sleep at time 869 (the beginning of the dotted part of the idle line), and then about 12 usec later gets the timer interrupt and comes back out of deep sleep to process it and context-switch back to finish the `nanosleep`. This entire `nanosleep` behavior takes about 60 usec, adding that unnecessary time between RPCs. Simple performance bugs like this are common. They are difficult to spot in code reviews and easy to spot in traces of the actual software dynamics.

To speed this up now that we see the root cause, either `WaitMsec` could avoid calling `nanosleep` with an argument of zero, or the `nanosleep` system call could be changed to return immediately without two context switches whenever its argument is zero.

In summary, we have identified three sources of delay in this simple RPC, as shown in Figure 26.11. The delays total about 350 usec out of about 400 usec for the entire RPC, so they

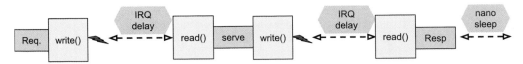

Figure 26.11   **One complete RPC, with three sources of delay identified**

explain the root causes for each RPC taking about 10 times longer than the raw time on the wire. The interrupt delays can be reduced by changing the `rx-usecs` parameter in `ethtool`, and the gap between RPCs by avoiding the degenerate `nanosleep(0)`.

26.7   Experiment 2

This time, the client4 program sends 200 requests of 1MB each to the server4 program on a second machine. At 117 MB/sec maximum speed on the wire, the RPC request should take about 8.5 msec to transmit. Figure 26.12 shows a picture of two such RPCs. The tiny notch of each server time is barely discernable. The total time for each RPC is about 9.1 msec, and the time between RPCs is about 500 usec, much of which is spent copying the 1MB message in memory twice before sending it. As we discussed in Chapter 6, reducing user-mode message copying can improve this.

The client4 program reports transmission speed of 110.4 MB/s overall, so it comes close to the maximum achievable 117 MB/s. This is all good.

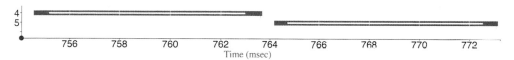

Figure 26.12   **Two RPCs sending messages of 1MB each, time aligned to client time of day**

There in fact is nothing new here that we did not already find in Experiment 1, but it gives us the baseline behavior for 1MB requests and confirms that longer messages can achieve close-to-line-rate network bandwidth.

26.8   Experiment 3

For this experiment, we run three copies of client4 on one machine and send RPCs to three different servers. One copy of client4 sends 20,000 RPCs of 4KB each as in Experiment 1, while the other two send 1MB RPCs each as in Experiment 2, structured as short bursts of four RPCs and then a delay of 550 and 600 msec, respectively (so they sometimes overlap and sometimes not), before repeating.

Figure 26.13a shows a normal 4KB request, while Figure 26.13b shows a 4KB request a little while later that overlaps a 1MB request. In the first case, the request packets hit the wire (more precisely, are timestamped by `tcpdump` code in the kernel) almost immediately, but in the second case they are delayed about 200 usec until a later Ethernet interrupt on CPU 3 causes the `BH:tx` soft interrupt handler to put more packets into the ring buffer.

The combination of `KUtrace` and `tcpdump` lets us observe the dynamic interaction between user software and the Ethernet hardware, pinpointing network congestion as a source of delay.

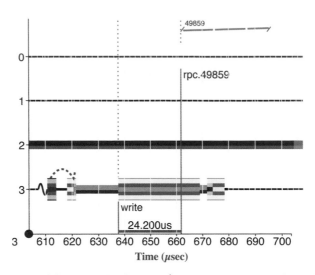

Figure 26.13a   **Normal 24 usec delay from `write()` to packets outbound**

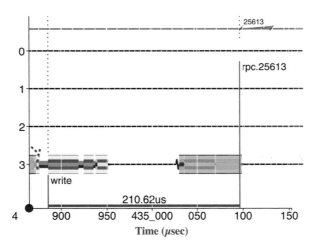

Figure 26.13b   **Long 210 usec delay from `write()` to packets outbound because of congestion from a continuing 1MB message**

26.9   Experiment 4

In our final experiment, we noticed in a different Experiment 3 trace an unusual delay in completing two scattered RPCs. Figure 26.14 shows one of them—a number of short RPCs along the top edge, then a gap of 208 **msec**, and then short and long RPCs continue. What is causing such a huge gap?

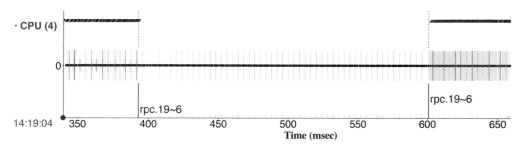

Figure 26.14   **An unusual 208 msec delay in completing rpc.19166**

Looking in detail at the client-side tcpdump packet-by-packet trace reveals a retransmission delay, something not directly observable in KUtrace. The normal packet-by-packet behavior for RPC ID 22169 is shown first in the following code. Three outbound packets of 1,448, 1,448, and 1,204 data bytes carry the request to the server. The server sends back an ACK packet with zero bytes of data and immediately sends back a response packet with 88 bytes of data. In addition to all the other timestamps, the default Linux TCP configuration includes a TCP option field with a millisecond counter used as a timestamp. This is the "TS val **1367909791**" part of the 22169 response packet, for example.

The abnormal behavior occurs in the following RPC 19166. Its three request packets starting at time 14:19:04.392731 and their acknowledgement from the server at time 14:19:04.393019 occur normally, but the server response is troubled.

Normal behavior

```
Request rpc.22169; three packets out from client dclab-2, then an ACK coming back
from the server declab-1

14:19:04.392731 IP dclab-2.48484 > dclab-1.12345: Flags [.], seq 66452801:66454249,
ack 1426305, win 229, options [nop,nop,TS val 4263427150 ecr 1367909791], length
1448

14:19:04.392732 IP dclab-2.48484 > dclab-1.12345: Flags [.], seq 66454249:66455697,
ack 1426305, win 229, options [nop,nop,TS val 4263427150 ecr 1367909791], length
1448

14:19:04.392732 IP dclab-2.48484 > dclab-1.12345: Flags [P.], seq
66455697:66456901, ack 1426305, win 229, options [nop,nop,TS val 4263427150 ecr
1367909791], length 1204

Response: ACK all three above
14:19:04.393018 IP dclab-1.12345 > dclab-2.48484: Flags [.], ack 66456901, win
1390, options [nop,nop,TS val 1367909791 ecr 4263427150], length 0

Response rpc.22169
14:19:04.393019 IP dclab-1.12345 > dclab-2.48484: Flags [P.], seq 1426305:1426393,
ack 66456901, win 1402, options [nop,nop,TS val 1367909791 ecr 4263427150], length
88
```

Abnormal behavior

Request rpc.19166; three packets out from client dclab-2, then an ACK coming back from server dclab-1

14:19:04.393125 IP **dclab-2.48484** > dclab-1.12345: Flags [.], seq 66456901:66458349, ack 1426393, win 229, options [nop,nop,TS val 4263427150 ecr 1367909791], length 1448

14:19:04.393125 IP **dclab-2.48484** > dclab-1.12345: Flags [.], seq 66458349:66459797, ack 1426393, win 229, options [nop,nop,TS val 4263427150 ecr 1367909791], length 1448

14:19:04.393125 IP **dclab-2.48484** > dclab-1.12345: Flags [P.], seq 66459797:66461001, ack 1426393, win 229, options [nop,nop,TS val 4263427150 ecr 1367909791], length 1204

Response: ACK all three above
14:19:04.393514 IP dclab-1.12345 > **dclab-2.48484**: Flags [.], ack 66461001, win 1390, options [nop,nop,TS val **1367909792** ecr 4263427150], length 0

   ... GAP of 207.5 milliseconds ...

Abnormal behavior (continued)

Response rpc.22169 from server dclab-1, and its DUPLICATE, then the selective ACK (sack) from the client to tell the server what happened

14:19:04.601061 IP dclab-1.12345 > **dclab-2.48484**: Flags [P.], seq 1426393:1426481, ack 66461001, win 1402, options [nop,nop,TS val **1367909792** ecr 4263427150], length 88
                (copy ① sent at millisecond ...**9792**)

14:19:04.601088 IP dclab-1.12345 > **dclab-2.48484**: Flags [P.], seq 1426393:1426481, ack 66461001, win 1402, options [nop,nop,TS val **1367909999** ecr 4263427150], length 88
                (copy ② sent at millisecond ...**9999, 207 msec later**)

14:19:04.601104 IP **dclab-2.48484** > dclab-1.12345: Flags [.], ack 1426481, win 229, options [nop,nop,TS val 4263427358 ecr 1367909999,nop,nop, **sack 1** **{1426393:1426481}**], length 0
                (selective ACK ③ specifying both copies received)

The server sent a response packet ① at millisecond "TS val **1367909792**," but the client either did not see or did not process this response, so did not acknowledge it. This sort of hiccup occurs daily in network transmissions. It remains ambiguous *when* this response packet actually crossed the wire, but cross it did.

After a 200 msec *retransmit timeout*, the server sent another copy ② with a new 207-msec-later "TS val **1367909999**" sender-side timestamp.

Why 200 milliseconds? A little groping around in the Linux source pool reveals that this is the minimum retransmit timeout in `tcp.h`: `#define TCP_RTO_MIN ((unsigned)(HZ/5))`.

This time, the client received and processed *both* of them back to back. It then sent a selective ACK (sack) ③ back to the server to report the duplication. This selective ACK can cause the server side of the connection to drop back into TCP "slow start," which could delay the next response or two. There was no extra delay in this particular case, but it is a dynamic that can mean that transmission trouble during one RPC slows down the *following* one or two RPCs.

I once tracked down a persistent case of TCP delays at Google. It stemmed from a mis-configured kernel that delayed sending ACKs for up to 30 msec, but the other end timed out after only 25 msec, sending duplicates whenever that happened and triggering the slow-start behavior. Once we observed the dynamic interaction, it was a 20-minute fix—plus the extensive time to roll out new kernels to the entire fleet worldwide. It was the only time in my career that I have found a problem in action N to slow down not action N + 1 but N + 2.

The combination of KUtrace and `tcpdump` lets us observe the dynamic interaction between user software and the TCP software stack, pinpointing retransmission as a source of delay.

26.10 Mysteries Understood

Using logs, packet traces, and CPU traces, we identified interrupt delivery latency as a significant slowdown in Experiment 1, along with a degenerate `nanosleep` mistake that added delay between successive RPCs. We briefly mentioned user-mode message copying in Experiment 2. We identified network congestion—more outbound traffic offered than the wire could accommodate undelayed—as a significant slowdown in Experiment 3. In Experiment 4 we identified packet retransmission as the slowdown.

Reducing the default large interrupt delivery delay helps Experiment 1, as does removing the degenerate `nanosleep(0)` call. Reducing user-mode message copying can help Experiment 2.

Nothing simple directly reduces network congestion, as in Experiment 3, when there are multiple independent programs offering messages at a faster rate than a network link can accommodate, or the mirror-image problem of multiple inbound messages converging at a faster rate than a network link can accommodate. In practice, bandwidth quotas per program and transmission priorities are used to reduce congestion delays in production environments.

Reducing the default retransmission timeout helps Experiment 4, along with reducing the default delayed ACK value. Many of these defaults were set in the 1980s and have not changed significantly since. For example, RFC 793 from 1981 [ISI 1981] mentions a retransmission timeout lower bound of one second, and that hasn't changed much. Defaults can be inappropriately large for today's time-constrained environments.

26.11 Bonus Anomaly

My friend Hal Murray was experimenting with echoing nearly a million UDP packets of 80 bytes each across a 1Gb/s network link, using multiple senders to a single 12-CPU receiver machine. Receiver CPU 9 handled all the interrupt traffic, its hyperthread pair CPU 3 was forced to be 100% idle, and the other 10 CPUs ran identical echo-server threads:

```
while (true) {
  recvfrom()
  process_message()
  sendto()
}
```

The initial runs with empty code for `process_message` echoed about 850,000 packets per second, with some idle CPU time. A later run with an artificial additional five usec of time in `process_message` echoed about 1,020,000 packets per second. Counter-intuitively, slower processing in the echo code gave 20% more throughput! *Why?*

Figures 26.15a and 26.15b show 9 usec pieces of the two different echo-server loops, with an extra 5 usec of execution time in second echo-server.

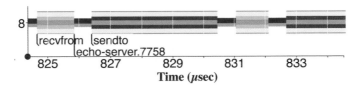

Figure 26.15a   **UDP packet loop with empty echo-server processing**

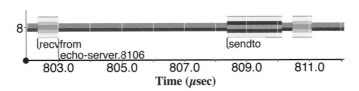

Figure 26.15b   **UDP packet loop with extra 5 usec in echo-server processing**

In the initial runs, the overall pattern had groups of packets processed for about 100 usec and then gaps of about 50 usec with *all 10* echo-server threads idle. Most `sendto()` system calls took 4–5 usec, but after each idle gap, one of the first few `sendto()` calls took an unusually long 20–50 usec, with the extra time after the UDP code added the outbound packet to the transmit queue. See Figure 26.16, which has three such groups over 450 usec. In that figure, the small black backslashes at the top show every incoming packet and the forward slashes show every outgoing packet. This is a full packet trace, not just packets that begin RPC messages. Packets often arrive in groups of eight, consistent with only generating a network interrupt every 3–4 usec.

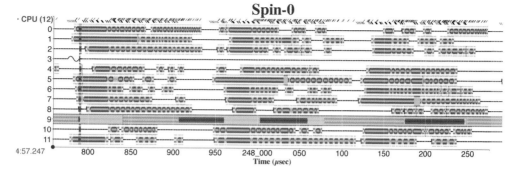

Figure 26.16   **Ten UDP packet-loop threads showing packets bunching up with idle gaps**

The fact that all 10 threads go idle at about the same time suggests that there is a common bottleneck, likely either a saturated network transmit queue or a saturated CPU 9 doing interrupt handling.

After adding an extra 5 usec processing time in the 10 echo-server threads, the pattern changes entirely, with no gaps. See Figure 26.17, which also covers 450 usec.

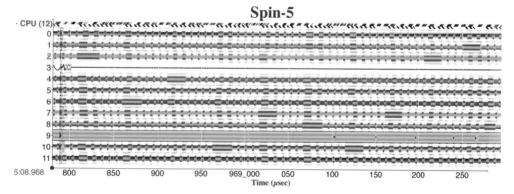

Figure 26.17   **Ten slower UDP packet-loop threads with no idle gaps**

Packets still often arrive in groups of eight, but now the CPU pattern is quite regular. Two related things have changed in the processing: first the extra 5 usec of processing time means that the echo-server threads rarely go idle, causing the second effect that the interrupt-handling code on CPU 9 rarely has to wake up a thread. In Figure 26.16 there are about 85 cross-processor wakeups in 450 usec, while in Figure 27.17 there are none. If each wakeup takes about 2 usec of CPU time in the CPU 9 interrupt handling, removing those wakeups removes an interrupt-processing bottleneck and completely accounts for the increased throughput.

Until we could observe the original bunched-up pattern in Figure 26.16, we could not understand the dynamics of the packet processing. Interested readers may want to explore *receive-side scaling* (RSS) [Herbert 2010], which enables distributing network interrupts across multiple CPUs.

26.12   Summary

- It is important to design in timestamped logs.

- It is important to design in RPC IDs.

- Careful measurement and analysis can identify major sources of delay.

- Merging data from multiple viewpoints is often needed: logs, packet traces, CPU traces.

- Network dynamics are complex, involving interactions between unrelated flows and involving state that affects future flows.

- Many mechanisms are at work to control congestion, with defaults that are sometimes inappropriate for a particular environment.

- Holding off interrupts, holding off sending ACKs, holding off retransmission, and holding off delivering packets within the TCP stack all contribute latency.

- Fixes: change delay parameters, control congestion, control interrupt delivery, reduce copying, remove simple performance mistakes.

- Observing the actual dynamics of all these interactions is the key to understanding.

Chapter 27

Waiting for Locks

This chapter is a case study of software lock delays. Using a small multi-threaded program that does fake bank transactions against a shared RAM database, locking it during updates, we will examine unexpected execution dynamics.

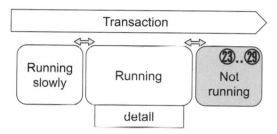

From our framework, this chapter is about not running while waiting for software locks. With two or more processes, the execution dynamics can involve excessive delays and even starvation through lock saturation and insidious lock capture. After exploring delays, we will look at fixes.

27.1 Overview

As we saw in previous chapters, software locks protect *critical sections*—pieces of code that for correctness must be executed by only one thread at a time, even on a multi-core computer with true parallel execution of different threads. As shown in Figure 27.1, each thread entering a critical section must first acquire the lock, waiting as needed if another thread holds the lock, and then when leaving the critical section releasing the lock. If other threads are waiting at lock release, the releasing thread must wake up at least one of them to try its turn at acquiring the lock.

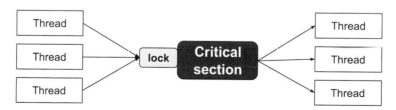

Figure 27.1   **Three threads contending for a critical section**

We focus on *contended* locks, not *held* locks. A lock can be held with no other thread trying to use it. This is the normal case. It matters when or how long a lock is held only if there is contention for that lock. So we don't directly care how long a lock is held, but instead focus on how long it takes a non-holder to *acquire* a lock. As we shall see, it is easy to end up with a design that has threads waiting a very long time to acquire a lock even though no individual thread holds that lock very long. From the point of view of transaction latency, the acquisition time is what matters, so that is what we study.

[Opper 1906]

[Wikimedia 2020b]

The execution and waiting dynamics among multiple threads using one or more locks can be complicated and not always obvious. Locking designs lend themselves to correctness mistakes, deadlock mistakes, unfair access to the critical section, starvation, and unexpected long delays acquiring a lock. In large complex software there can be hundreds or even thousands of locks protecting various data structures.

> I searched the Google source pool circa 2016 for lock declarations and found over 100,000 of them, spread across tens of millions of lines of code. In this environment, when a program ran slowly because of locking, it was difficult to identify *which* locks were involved.

In this chapter, we will look at locking execution dynamics starting with a simple two-thread lock and then touch on lock saturation before examining lock capture and starvation in multiple threads. The later portion of the chapter examines techniques for reducing locking delays.

The term *lock saturation* refers to a lock that is contended almost all the time, preventing any gain in performance from having multiple threads. The term *lock capture* refers to a single thread repeatedly acquiring and releasing a lock and then immediately reacquiring it before other threads have a chance to. The term *starvation* refers to a thread that is unable to gain access to a lock for a long time, even as other threads acquire and release that lock.

A lock is simply a shared variable that is manipulated atomically. A minimal lock is one that has two states, 0 (unlocked) and 1 (locked), and is accessed by an atomic test-and-set instruction or its equivalent. In this context, *atomic* means that the underlying hardware guaranties that a multi-step change by one CPU core is done in its entirety without interference from another core. The IBM System/360 test-and-set instruction [IBM 1967, Gifford 1987, Allen 2006] was the very first atomic operation in the computer industry. Gerrit Blaauw probably created it [Brooks 2020] before IBM built any multiple-processor System/360 computers.

The test-and-set instruction reads and keeps the old value of the lock variable and then sets the variable to 1. If two CPU cores execute the instruction simultaneously against a lock variable with value 0, exactly one of them sees an old value of 0, and the other sees an old value of 1. Which one goes first and hence acquires the lock is arbitrary. If this situation repeats many times, there is no guarantee against one CPU core always getting the lock and the other core always losing out.

Instead of executing the critical section, cores that do not acquire a lock must do something else while trying again. In the earlier chapters, we used just a simple spinlock. In this chapter we will get a little more sophisticated, which also introduces further dynamic interactions.

We use here a slightly fancy software locking library. Each declared lock has a 0/1 lock variable, a count of how many threads are waiting on a held lock, and a tiny (16-byte) histogram of how many microseconds each thread had to wait to acquire a *contended* lock. Acquisition of an uncontended lock is not measured; this is the intended normal case, and we do not want to slow it down. From the contended-wait-time histogram, the library can calculate an approximate 90th percentile acquisition time, which can be compared to a programmer-supplied expected acquisition time.

The actual histogram has only eight buckets, each covering a power of 10 microseconds of acquisition time, [0..10us), [10..100us), [100..1000us), etc. These are very wide buckets compared to a histogram with something bulky like 800 buckets spaced a factor of 1.02 apart, but these eight turn out to be sufficient to record the patterns of unexpected slow lock behavior. They allow us to calculate an approximate 90th percentile acquisition time and compare it to the programmer's expected time, often coming within a factor of 2 or 3 of the time that would be calculated by a bulky histogram.

The FancyLock class constructor places the source file name and line number of the lock declaration within the lock struct, so when there are excessive lock delays, we can know *which* lock is involved. The FancyLock destructor prints out the wait-time histogram and the 90th percentile wait. This allows programmers to compare the actual lock acquisition delay to their expectation, to track any increases in in that delay over weeks and months of software changes and/or offered-load changes, and to investigate the root causes for unexpectedly long delays.

The mechanism to acquire and release a fancy lock is a C++ Mutex class whose constructor acquires the specified lock and destructor releases it. Putting a variable of this class in a code block automatically runs that block with the lock held. This is syntactically convenient (sometimes too convenient) and guarantees that there can be no bug of failing to release a lock.

The Mutex library generates KUtrace entries for each failed acquisition of a contended lock and for the matching eventual successful acquisition, tracking the acquisition time and updating the histogram. It also generates an entry for each lock acquire and release when there are any waiting threads. At the first KUtrace entry for a contended lock, the code also places the lock's source file name and line number into the trace. This gives enough information to postprocess into an exact record of the time each thread is not executing while waiting for a lock and the source that declared that specific lock.

Figure 27.2 shows an example diagram of a contended lock interaction, and Table 27.1 gives the individual steps. At the upper left, thread 6736 is holding a lock on some shared data, shown by the pink line with arrowhead, and holds that lock until time 525.15, when it frees the lock and wakes up any waiting threads. The dashed arc shows this wakeup. The lock was declared at source line `mystery27.cc:111`, as indicated by the label near the bottom at time 528.65.

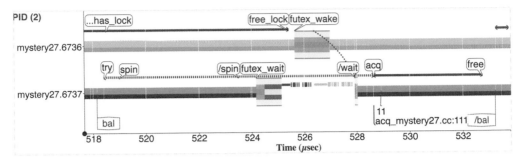

Figure 27.2   **KUtrace diagram of thread 6737 waiting on a contended lock that thread 6736 then releases**

At the lower left, thread 6737 starts a `Balance` transaction ("bal" labels), tries to get the lock and fails (because 6736 holds it), spins for about 5 microseconds trying, and then blocks via `futex(wait)`. The raised red line ending with dot-dash-dot-dot (Morse code for "L") indicates thread 6737 waiting to acquire a lock, and the raised yellow line ending in dash-dot-dash-dot ("C") indicates waiting to be assigned a CPU again.

Table 27.1   **Individual Steps of Lock Interaction Between Two Threads**

Time(us)	Thread 6736	Thread 6737	Lock held	Lock try
515.00	... started		6736	
518.15		Start Bal action	6736	
518.42		Try to get lock; fail	6736	6737
519.00		Spin for free lock	6736	6737
523.50		Stop spinning	6736	6737
524.17		Call futex(wait)	6736	6737
525.15	Free the lock			6737
526.36	Awaken waiter via futex(wake)			6737
527.64	End action			6737
527.93		Finish futex(wait)		6737
528.65		Try to get lock; success	6737	
532.75		Free the lock		
533.75		End Bal action		

At time 526.26, thread 6736 wakes 6737 up via `futex(wake)`, and thread 6737 tries again to get the lock, succeeding this time and holding the lock (pink line at 528.65) for 4.10 usec while finishing its transaction. At the upper right, thread 6736 briefly holds the contended lock again (pink line at time 533.28) while doing a subsequent transaction.

In this particular stretch of code, the total thread 6737 lock acquisition time from `try` to `acq` is about 11 microseconds, the number shown via `kutrace::mark_d` below the "acq" callout. Over a large number of such interactions with three contending threads, the acquisition-time histogram with eight power-of-10 buckets looks like Code Snippet 17.1.

Code Snippet 17.1   **Lock acquisition histogram**

```
1us    10    100    1ms 10 100    1s 10
[7689 1178 1023    23  0  0     0  0 ] = 9913 total
 Minimum            1 us
 Maximum         3375 us
 90th %ile        106 us
 Expected          50 us
```

Our 11 usec example in Figure 27.2 contributed one of the 1178 counts in the 10us bucket. Note that there are 23 counts in the 1ms bucket, which covers long delays in the range [1..10) milliseconds. The original programmer expected the 90th percentile acquisition time to be about 50 usec, but it actually is approximately twice as long at 106 usec, with a maximum observed time of 3375 usec. In the rest of this chapter we will look at locking dynamics and at techniques for reducing lock contention, thus reducing waiting time, increasing CPU utilization, and improving performance.

27.2 The Program

The mystery27 program executes fake banking transactions against a small in-memory database of 100 customer accounts. It contains several bad locking designs. Three `worker_thread` processes run simultaneously, taking out one or two locks when accessing the database. A fourth `dashboard_thread` runs every 20 msec and produces a debug HTML string of the state of the database, holding both locks while doing so (a design mistake that we will deal with).

The two global locks are named `readerlock` and `writerlock`, declared here:

```
// Readers here are mutually exclusive but quick
// We expect the reader lock to take no more than 50 usec to acquire,
// 90% of the time (the other 10% might take longer)
DEFINE_FANCYLOCK2(global_readerlock, 50);

// Writers are mutually exclusive and may take a while
// We expect the writer lock to take no more than 100 usec to acquire,
// 90% of the time time (the other 10% might take longer)
DEFINE_FANCYLOCK2(global_writerlock, 100);
```

As we shall see shortly, they are poorly used and do not quite match their names. Note that each declaration carries the most recent programmer's expectation of the 90th percentile acquisition time for that lock. In some of our experiments, these estimates will also be off-base. Among the fixes discussed later, we will expand to multiple locks so that different worker threads can work on different accounts without conflict. Right now, the two each lock the entire database.

The routine `MakeAction` produces pseudo-random transactions against the database, and the `DoAction` routine executes these transactions. The actions are called `Deposit`, `Getcash`, `Debitcard`, and `Balance`. The first three acquire both the reader and writer locks in that order, while the `Balance` action acquires only the reader lock (to make sure it has a consistent view of an account's variables). To stress the locking system, each action can include a random amount of fake work to be done while holding the locks. The `DoFakeWork` routine simply loops for approximately the specified number of microseconds. Command-line parameters can adjust the amount of fake work, adjust whether the `Balance` action uses locks at all, and adjust the locking style of the dashboard thread.

There is a lot of subtlety in any code for waiting on a lock. The `mutex` code here generates no trace events for uncontended locks and has this outer loop for acquiring a contended lock, i.e., just after finding it held by another thread:

```
kutrace::addevent(KUTRACE_LOCKNOACQUIRE, fstruct->lnamehash);
do {                      // Outermost_do
  old_locked = AcquireSpin(whoami, start_acquire, fstruct);
  if (!old_locked) {
    break;
  }
  old_locked = AcquireWait(whoami, start_acquire, fstruct);
  if (!old_locked) {
    break;
  }
} while (true);           // Outermost_do
kutrace::addevent(KUTRACE_LOCKACQUIRE, fstruct->lnamehash);
```

The two `kutrace::addevent` calls bracket the contended-lock acquisition time. The do loop repeats until one of the called routines is successful in acquiring the lock. Routine `AcquireSpin` *loops* briefly looking for the lock to be available; `AcquireWait` *blocks* and context switches elsewhere until the lock becomes available. Each then tries to acquire the available lock, but may fail if another thread gets to it sooner, winning the inherent race. When this happens, the do goes around to try again. The goal of first spinning and then blocking is to use no more than a *half-optimal* amount of CPU time waiting, as described in Chapter 23.

In this case, if it takes about five microseconds to do the two context switches involved in blocking and then resuming our thread, we first spin for about five microseconds hoping to acquire the lock without blocking. This guarantees that the amount of CPU time we use waiting for a lock to become free can never be more than twice the optimal algorithm (if we were prescient enough to know how long our future wait would be). If the lock becomes free in the first 5 usec, we stop spinning immediately, using the optimal amount of CPU time. If not, we block after 5us, costing 10us total for the spin plus two context switches, which is twice the optimal amount, had we known to initially block without spinning. It either case, our performance is no worse than half of the unrealizable optimal-choice performance.

This is the AcquireSpin loop; note that it does not generate any additional KUtrace events:

```
do {
  for (int i = 0; i < SPIN_ITER; ++i) {
    if (fstruct->lock == 0) {
      break;
    }
    __pause();            // Let any hyperthread in, allow reduced
                          // power, slow down speculation
  }
  // Lock might be available (0)
  // Try again to get the lock
  old_locked = __atomic_test_and_set(&fstruct->lock, __ATOMIC_ACQUIRE);
  if (!old_locked) {
    break;
  }
} while ((GetUsec() - start_acquire) <= SPIN_USEC);
```

The value of SPIN_ITER is chosen so that completing the for loop takes about 1 usec. The pause instruction is vital on most x86 implementations, and there are analogous instructions for other architectures. It causes a CPU core to delay issuing instructions for many cycles, with "many" not specified in the architecture but expected in the range of 10–100 cycles. The pause instruction serves three purposes:

- For a hyperthreaded core, it allows the other hyperthread(s) to use more instruction-issue cycles and more L1 data and instruction cache access cycles.

- It may allow a CPU core to save some power by spinning more slowly.

- It slows down the rate of issuing speculative instructions, which on some implementations can get 100 or more instructions ahead of the speculative branch that will eventually fail when the lock value changes from 1 to 0. Excessive speculative instructions can take dozens of cycles to flush out of the execution units, slowing the exit from the loop.

The GetUsec routine calls gettimeofday, which can do a system call. But this takes perhaps 60 nsec every 1 usec, so is not a significant delay for the overall looping structure.

The AcquireWait loop looks like this; it also generates no additional KUtrace events:

```
// Add us to the number of waiters (not spinners)
__atomic_add_fetch(&fstruct->waiters, 1, __ATOMIC_RELAXED);
do {
  // Do futex wait until lock is no longer held (1)
  syscall(SYS_futex, &fstruct->lock, FUTEX_WAIT, 1, NULL, NULL, 0);
  // Done futex waiting -- lock is at least temporarily available (0)
  // Try again to get the lock
  old_locked = __atomic_test_and_set(&fstruct->lock, __ATOMIC_ACQUIRE);
} while (old_locked);
// Remove us from the number of waiters
atomic_sub_fetch(&fstruct->waiters, 1, __ATOMIC_RELAXED);
```

The atomic add and subtract maintain an exact count of waiting threads even with simultaneous changes on multiple CPU cores. The FUTEX_WAIT call re-checks that the lock is 1 and if so blocks until it changes. If the lock is freed just after the call to `AcquireWait` and before the call to `FUTEX_WAIT` (a race condition), then `futex` will return immediately.

Unlike `AcquireSpin`, routine `AcquireWait` will return only when it has successfully acquired the lock. I could have chosen to go back to spinning if another thread gets the freed lock first, but decided that once the lock wait exceeds the spin time, it makes sense just to stick with blocking.

Finally, this is the `Releaselock` code; it generates a KUtrace event only if there are waiters to wake up:

```
__atomic_clear(&fstruct->lock, __ATOMIC_RELEASE);
if (0 < fstruct->waiters) {
  // Trace contended-lock free event
  kutrace::addevent(KUTRACE_LOCKWAKEUP, fstruct->lnamehash);
  // Wake up possible other futex waiters
  syscall(SYS_futex, &fstruct->lock, FUTEX_WAKE, INT_MAX, NULL, NULL,0);
}
```

Immediately after freeing the lock, if there are any waiters the `FUTEX_WAKE` call wakes up all of them. The usual choices of how many to wake up are 1 and `INT_MAX`. Waking one avoids a clash of many contenders for the cache line containing the lock but means that some waiting threads don't even get to try and only get another chance when the one awakened finishes. That design can be slow to recover if there are multiple waiters and can end up starving some waiters.

The experiments in this chapter explore simple locking, lock saturation, lock capture, and starvation.

- The term *lock saturation* refers to a lock that is contended almost all the time, preventing any gain in performance from having multiple threads.
- The term *lock capture* refers to a single thread repeatedly acquiring and releasing a lock and then immediately reacquiring it before other threads have a chance to.
- The term *starvation* refers to a thread that is unable to gain access to a lock for a long time, even as multiple other threads acquire and release that lock.

Sections 27.6 through 27.9 discuss possible fixes.

27.3   Experiment 1: Long Lock Hold Times

We compare the database program running with short amounts of fake work (0..15 usec) and long amounts (0..128 usec). The long work causes high lock contention.

27.3.1   Simple Locking

Figure 27.2 showed the execution dynamics of a simple pair of threads contending for one lock, with actions that have fake work that ranges from 0 to 15 usec and averages 8 usec. There is not much lock contention. With that already discussed, we move directly to an experiment in extreme lock contention using more than two threads and longer fake work time.

27.3.2 Lock Saturation

In this experiment, three worker threads execute actions that have fake work that ranges from 0 to 255 usec and averages 128 usec. Combined with non-critical-section code that takes only a few microseconds, this means that the critical section lock will be held almost all the time, stressing the locking design and in fact defeating the purpose of having multiple worker threads. This represents the extreme case of 100% sequential execution in Amdahl's law [Amdahl 1967, Wikipedia 2021x] and Gustafson's law [Gustafson 1988, Wikipedia 2020h].

We start with an estimate of the program behavior. In three seconds of wall-clock time on a four-CPU machine there is a total of 12 CPU-seconds of time. We estimate that there should be about 3 seconds of non-overlapped critical section `worker_thread` time and about 9 seconds of idle time. The locks should be saturated—held for most of the three seconds of elapsed time.

Figure 27.3 shows one second of mystery27 execution working on transactions with this setup. The full 2.7 second trace has 7.937 seconds of idle time across four CPUs and thus (2.7 * 4) – 7.937 = 2.863 seconds of non-idle execution across the three different-colored worker threads, about as expected. The reader lock is contended for 2.433 seconds, so is nearly saturated, also as expected. But the writer lock is *never* contended.

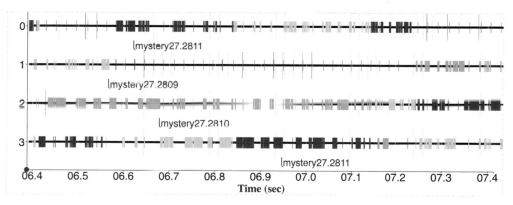

Figure 27.3   **mystery27 one second of doing 30,000 transactions in 2.7 seconds with average work of 128 usec, sorted by CPU number**

27.4 Mysteries in Experiment 1

At a gross level, the mystery27 program with an average of 128 usec of fake work per transaction has a heavily contended lock and has only one of three worker threads executing at a time, as we expected. But several details seem puzzling.

First, notice in Figure 27.4 (which is the Figure 27.3 data sorted by process ID) that thread 2810 finishes a full 0.355 seconds before thread 2811, a 13% difference in completion times. This is similar to the completion-time skew we saw in Chapter 23, but it is not because of the scheduler, as we shall see shortly.

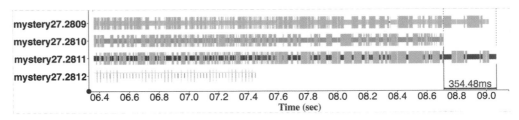

Figure 27.4 **mystery27 doing 30,000 transactions in 2.7 seconds with average work of 128 usec, sorted by process ID number**

Second, the histograms of contended lock acquisition times in Code Snippet 27.2 are unexpected, with no contention at all for the writer lock, and only 2180 out of 30,000 contended acquisitions for the reader lock.

Code Snippet 27.2 **Lock-acquire delay for mystery27, locking all transactions and averaging 128 usec hold time**

```
[mystery27.cc:115] wait zero entries

[mystery27.cc:111] 90%ile > EXPECTED
  1us 10 100      1ms 10 100    1s 10
  [219 261 1197     340 163 0    0 0 ] = 2180 total
  Minimum         0 us
  Maximum     86875 us
  90th %ile    6500 us
  Expected       49 us
```

27.5 Exploring and Reasoning in Experiment 1

Each worker thread is doing 10,000 transactions; in fact, the three threads are each doing precisely the same 10,000 transactions, because MakeAction uses the same pseudo-random generator for each worker thread. How would you expect the work to be split in time with three worker threads and a single reader lock that must be held for each transaction? One extreme possibility is thread A and then thread B and then thread C hold the lock and then threads A, B, C, A, etc., each holding the lock in round-robin fashion. The other extreme possibility is thread A, A, A for 10,000 times and then B 10,000 times and then C 10,000 times. As a software designer, you might expect something close to the round-robin interleaving with some local variation. The actual execution dynamics might surprise you.

With an average transaction time of 128 usec and maybe something close to round-robin acquisition, you could estimate that almost every transaction will wait while two previous transactions on the other two threads finish, for a contended reader lock acquisition time of about 256 usec most of the time. (The programmer, with no forethought, wrote down an expected, or more precisely hoped for, 50 usec.) The histogram would show nearly 30,000 contended acquisitions total with a big spike in the [100...1000) usec histogram bucket and a 90th percentile acquisition time of perhaps 500 usec. The measured FancyLock histograms of contended lock acquisition times in Code Snippet 27.2 are not like this at all.

The program declares the reader lock on line 111, and the writer lock on line 115 of file mystery27.cc and their constructors run in that order. The destructors run in reverse order at the end of the program and print out the contended-acquisition-delay histograms.

The writer histogram is empty because there were zero contended acquisitions. The writer lock is always available when requested inside the reader critical section. Since the reader and writer locks here are distinct and fully exclusive locks, once a thread acquires the reader lock, no other thread can then contend for the writer lock. Assuming the need for a writer lock inside the reader lock is a design mistake, but one not particularly visible in the code.

> In contrast, a traditional *combined* reader-writer lock allows multiple readers but only one writer and can have both reader and writer contention. Do not be misled by variable names.

The reader lock histogram has only 2,180 counts, not 30,000. So 93% of the lock acquisitions were *uncontended*. How can that be? Figure 27.5 zooms in on a part of Figure 27.4 and reveals the real dynamics.

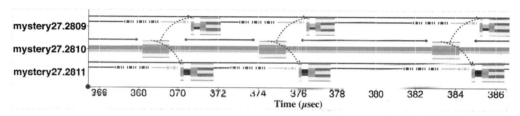

Figure 27.5   **mystery27 doing three transactions with lock capture by thread 2810**

27.5.1 Lock Capture

Thread 2810 has *captured* [Wikipedia 2021y, Shacham 1982] the lock—each time it releases the lock, it dutifully wakes up the other two waiting threads, but by the time they get scheduled on a CPU and exit from futex back to user code, thread 2810 has already *re-acquired* the lock. This pattern repeats, sometimes for milliseconds. Each re-acquire is uncontended because no other thread holds the lock at the instant that thread 2810 acquires it. The losing threads are each in the middle of a single acquisition outermost_do, which is counted just once upon successful acquire. This pattern happens almost 28,000 times over the course of the trace. Of the remaining 2,180 times, there is in fact a peak in the [100...1000) usec histogram bucket. But there are 163 instances that took [10..100) msec before a waiter finally acquired the lock—at least 80 *consecutive* delays of 128 usec each.

The worst-case delay in this trace is 84 msec, shown in the bottom row of Figure 27.6, and is also an example of lock *starvation*. The numeric markers show the number of usec to acquire a contended lock. For clarity, not all values are displayed.

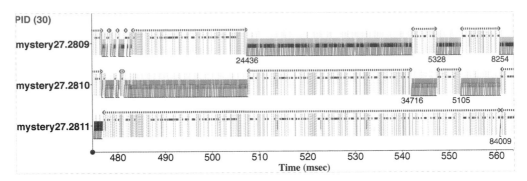

Figure 27.6   **Worst-case contended lock acquisition delay of 84009 usec for thread 2811, waiting from far left to far right**

27.5.2 Lock Starvation

The two threads 2809 and 2810 repeatedly acquire the lock, alternating from time to time which one captures the lock, and between them starving out thread 2811, even though neither of them holds the lock for very long at each acquisition.

In almost any highly contended lock execution, lock capture and starvation will play out slightly differently for each thread, but there will always be some slowest thread and some fastest thread. In this trace, thread 2811 happens to be starved out a little more often and thread 2810 a little less often. The cumulative effect is that thread 2810 finishes 13% earlier than thread 2811. This is a locking problem, not a scheduler problem.

Any lock that is nearly saturated will produce terrible performance. We therefore look in the rest of this chapter at techniques for reducing locking delays and hence reducing interference between threads and increasing overall response times.

27.6   Experiment 2: Fixing Lock Capture

Lock capture happens because the thread that frees a lock systematically re-acquires it before other threads have a chance. This is most often an issue with a (bad) locking design that has very little non-critical-section time between a repeated critical section. One brute-force fix is to impose a delay on any thread that frees a lock before it is allowed to re-acquire that lock. Another fix is to form a queue of waiters for a lock, putting new waiting threads at the back of the queue, and passing a freed lock on to the thread at the head of the queue. This is more complicated than it sounds because thread-safe queue manipulation requires locking or other atomic updates of the queue pointers themselves. Another approach, found in some hardware environments, is to have two sets of waiting-for-service bits (interrupt attention or something else), with set A actively serviced in arbitrary order by some hardware and set B accumulating new requests. When the actively serviced set is empty, the roles reverse so that set B gets serviced, while set A accumulates new requests.

In Experiment 2, we look at the dynamics of a brute-force fix: looping or otherwise running non-critical-section code for 10 usec after freeing a lock. To imitate this behavior, the mystery27 run uses the command-line option -nocapture.

Figures 27.7 and 27.8 show 10 msec intervals of three worker threads contending for a single lock. In Figure 27.7 the lock is re-acquired immediately, while in Figure 27.8 there is a 10 usec delay first. The lock is still highly contended in Figure 27.8, but the dynamics have shifted entirely, such that there is very little lock capture.

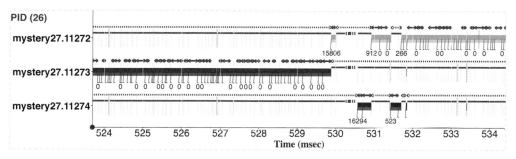

Figure 27.7   **Lock capture as in Figure 27.6**

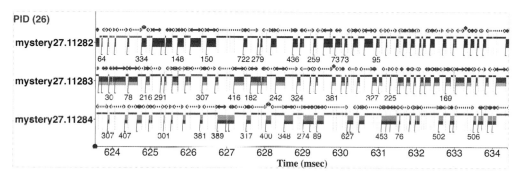

Figure 27.8   **No lock capture when each thread delays for 10 usec before trying to re-acquire a lock**

As a software designer, Figure 27.8 might be what you expected in the first place—something close to the round-robin interleaving with some local variation.

27.7   Experiment 3: Fixing Lock Contention via Multiple Locks

For this experiment, we use a common technique to reduce lock contention: multiple locks. Instead of a single overall reader lock for the entire account database, this experiment uses four locks, chosen by account number mod 4. To produce this result, I changed mystery27 by deleting the redundant writer lock as we discovered earlier, and creating four reader locks instead of one, producing program mystery27a. Both executions average 128 usec of work while holding a lock. The second one uses command-line option -multilock.

Figure 27.9 is similar to Figure 27.7 with contention for the single lock shown in cyan above the execution spans. The CPUs wait a total of 21.5 msec across 40 CPU-msec: four threads times 10 msec. Figure 27.10 shows less contention with four locks, the red, purple, green, and blue lines above the execution spans. Now the CPUs wait only 10.6 msec across 40 CPU-msec. The single dashboard update at time 691 causes about a fourth of this CPU waiting time; we will address reducing this in Experiment 5.

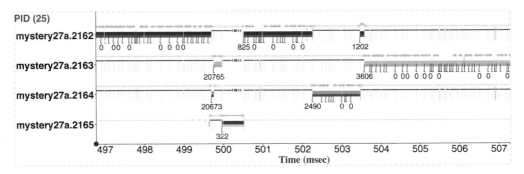

Figure 27.9   **Lock-acquire delay for mystery27a, single lock**

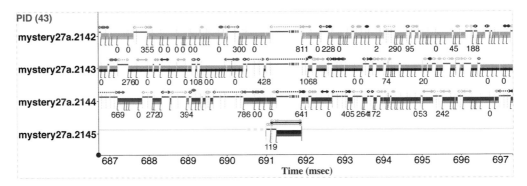

Figure 27.10   **Lock-acquire delay for mystery27a, four locks**

Table 27.2 compares the locking statistics. Using four locks reduces the 90th percentile acquisition time by about a factor of 12, from 7500 usec to 550–650 usec. The maximum acquisition time drops dramatically by about a factor of 50, from 75000 usec to 1300–1600 usec. With four locks, the total number of contended acquisitions goes up by a factor of 4.6, but they take less time to resolve. More importantly, the multiple locks allow substantial execution overlap of the three worker threads, reducing the overall runtime by almost a factor of 2.

Table 27.2 **Lock-Acquire Delay for mystery27 with Single Lock and with Four Locks**

Original design, single lock (Figure 27.9)	Multiple locks (Figure 27.10)
| ```
[mystery27a.cc:111]
1us 10 100      1ms 10 100     1s 10
[206 260 1029    338 162 0    0 0 ] sum = 1995
  Minimum         0 us
  Maximum     75000 us
  90th %ile    7500 us
  Expected       49 us
ERROR: 90%ile > EXPECTED
``` | ```
[mystery27a.cc:121]
1us 10 100      1ms 10 100     1s 10
[146 1029 930    2 0 0    0 0 ] sum = 2107
  Maximum     1313 us
  90th %ile    563 us

[mystery27a.cc:120]
1us 10 100      1ms 10 100     1s 10
[177 977 1226    6 0 0    0 0 ] sum = 2386
  Maximum     1313 us
  90th %ile    606 us

[mystery27a.cc:119]
1us 10 100      1ms 10 100     1s 10
[169 956 1238    27 0 0    0 0 ]  sum = 2390
  Maximum     1625 us
  90th %ile    650 us

[mystery27a.cc:111]
1us 10 100      1ms 10 100     1s 10
[160 1031 1182    16 0 0    0 0 ] sum = 2389
  Maximum     1625 us
  90th %ile    606 us
``` |

27.8 Experiment 4: Fixing Lock Contention via Less Locked Work

For this experiment, two techniques reduce lock contention:

- No locking for the Balance transaction, which just reads an account balance

- Less work while holding a lock for the other transactions

To do less work, imagine that a careful programmer examined the code that averages 128 usec of execution while holding locks and restructured and optimized it to average only 16 usec of locked work per transaction. She also observed that the Balance transaction needs no lock. To imitate this behavior, the mystery27 run uses command-line options -nolockbal and -smallwork.

Figure 27.11 shows the original design with all transactions using the reader lock and all doing about 128 usec of work while holding the lock. Figure 27.12 shows the improved design with the Balance transaction (about 60% of all transactions) running without a lock and all others doing about 16 usec of work while holding the lock.

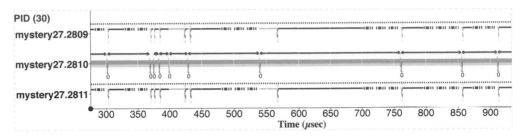

Figure 27.11   **Sample 600 usec of mystery27, locking all transactions and averaging 128 usec hold time (superset of Figure 27.5)**

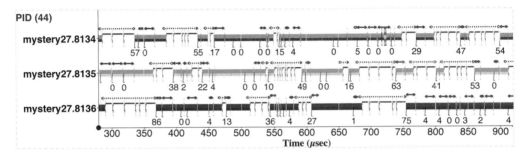

Figure 27.12   **Sample 600 usec of mystery27, no lock for Balance transactions and averaging 16 usec hold time**

Comparing Figure 27.11 to Figure 27.12, there is still some lock capture, and multiple block-wakeup-block-wakeup sequences trying to get a lock, but they are not as pronounced. With 8x less work per transaction, the lock holding times are much shorter, and many more transactions acquire the reader lock in their spin loops (the 0–5 usec acquire times) instead of blocking and later resuming. The CPUs are much busier because of this and because there is no lock required for the Balance transaction, so multiple transactions can often run in parallel. As a software designer, Figure 27.12 might be closer to your original expectation.

Table 27.3 compares the differences in lock-acquisition statistics to Code Snippet 27.2, which goes with Figure 27.11. We see that the 90th percentile acquisition time has dropped by a factor of 100, from 6500 usec to 65 usec, and the maximum (100th percentile) acquisition time has also dropped by a factor of about 100, from 86,875 usec to 750 usec.

The 90th percentile is now close to the hoped-for 50 usec, within the resolution of our histogram buckets. As expected, many more transactions—13,640 of 30,000 or about 40%—find a contended reader lock, but the wait times are short. Nonetheless, there is one more lock-contention reduction to make.

Table 27.3 **Lock-Acquire Delay for mystery27**

Original design (Figure 27.11)	Less locked work (Figure 27.12)
| ```
[mystery27.cc:111]
1us 10 100       1ms 10 100    1s 10
[219 261 1197    340 163 0     0 0 ] sum = 2180
  Minimum        0 us
  Maximum    86875 us
  90th %ile   6500 us
  Expected      49 us
``` | ```
[mystery27.cc:111]
1us 10 100       1ms 10 100    1s 10
[6717 6648 275   0 0 0     0 0 ] sum = 13640
  Minimum        0 us
  Maximum      750 us
  90th %ile     65 us
  Expected      49 us
``` |

27.9 Experiment 5: Fixing Lock Contention via RCU for Dashboard

In the previous experiments, the dashboard code holds the database locks for a long time (600–800 usec) while formatting all the account data into an HTML page. Still holding the lock, the dashboard code then tests whether a debugging flag is on and if so prints that HTML to some file. There are two flaws here: (1) **nothing** should be done at all if the debugging flag is off, and (2) all the formatting and I/O is done while **holding locks on the entire database**.

> My cohort Amer Diwan and I found precisely this code at Google in the 2009 production web-search code, in a routine called RPC_stats. That routine held a lock that blocked all other web search activity, allocated a buffer, formatted a lot of statistics into that buffer, noticed that debugging was off, freed the buffer, and freed the lock. The buffer contents thus were never used.
>
> Once we found which lock was involved in delaying all the other threads and found which routine held that lock, it was trivial to move the test for debugging to the front and exit immediately, getting production web search back up to speed. However, when system reliability engineers actually used the debug flag temporarily to see production statistics, things slowed down again. So the second fix was to take out the lock, copy the binary statistics data, free the lock, and then spend a while formatting the statistics as an HTML page.
>
> The original flaws were not particularly obvious in reading the code, and of course no one was looking for a slowdown in the RPC statistics debug code that was turned off in the pictures in everyone's heads.

In this experiment, we reduce the dashboard code lock contention to insignificance by copying the data while holding locks for just a short time. Table 27.4 shows the original and restructured code for the dashboard thread. On the left, the original code tests the debugging flag last, while on the right the improved code tests first and exits if it is off. This was just an oversight in the original code.

The more substantial change is to hold the locks just while quickly copying the binary data that the dashboard uses and then free the locks, producing a 100x reduction in lock holding time.

After that, `BuildDashString` and `fprintf` do the slow formatting, but now the worker threads are not blocked. This idea is the underpinning of the read-copy-update (RCU) technique used extensively in the Linux kernel [McKenney 2017, Wikipedia 2021z].

Table 27.4   Original and Much Improved Dashboard Code

```
void DoDebugDashboard(...) {            void EvenBetterDebugDashboard(...) {
  // Take out all locks                  if (!debugging) {
  Mutex2 lock1(whoami, ...);               return;
  Mutex2 lock2(whoami, ...);             }
  string s = BuildDashString(db);        string s;
  if (debugging) {                       Database db_copy;
    fprintf(stdout, ...);                { // Lock, copy, free
  }                                        Mutex2 lock1(whoami, ...);
}                                          Mutex2 lock2(whoami, ...);
                                           db_copy = *db;
                                         }
                                         s = BuildDashString(&db_copy);
                                         fprintf(stdout, ...);
                                       }
```

Figure 27.13 shows an example of the lock behavior across the original dashboard design and the improved one. The original design holds the reader and writer locks for 584 usec, while the improved design holds them for only 5.5 usec while doing the binary copy and then does the same ~600 usec of formatting in parallel with the three worker threads, which gain almost 1,800 usec of real work time.

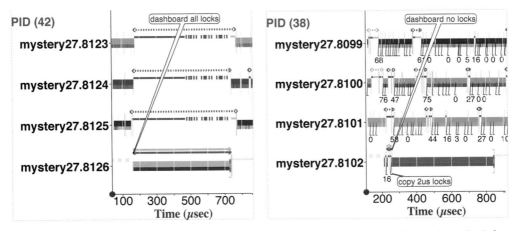

Figure 27.13ab   Original and improved dashboard execution examples. Original on the left holds locks while formatting data, and improved on the right holds them only during a short binary copy, allowing the three worker threads to continue.

This completes our five examples and our tour through some of the execution dynamics caused by software locks.

27.10   Summary

Experiment 1 revealed several bad locking dynamics. In Experiment 2 we fixed (or at least reduced) lock capture by imposing short delay after freeing a lock before trying to re-acquire it. Well-designed code does much of its work without holding locks, so it naturally contains such a delay. In Experiment 3 we reduced lock contention by using multiple locks. In Experiment 4 we reduced lock contention by doing a common operation (`Balance`) without locks at all and by moving code out of the locked region and optimizing the remaining code. In Experiment 5 we reduced lock contention by doing a locked copy of data used in a long calculation and then calculating from the copy without holding any locks.

- The term *lock saturation* refers to a lock that is contended almost all the time, preventing effective parallel execution.

- The term *lock capture* refers to a single thread repeatedly acquiring and releasing a lock before others have a chance.

- The term *starvation* refers to a thread that is unable to gain access to a lock for a long time, even if none of the other threads holds the lock very long.

- These three effects will occur in almost any heavily contended locking system unless the design explicitly counteracts them.

- Over time, lightly contended locking systems tend to become heavily contended. A lightweight technique for stating the expected lock-acquisition time and then continually comparing against that will alert code owners as delays creep up.

- Observing the actual dynamics of locking interactions is the key to understanding the slowdowns they cause.

Chapter 28

Waiting for Time

This chapter is a case study of time delays. Unlike the other case-study chapters, there is no specific program to study, but we will examine some unexpected execution dynamics.

From our framework, this chapter is about not running while waiting for a timer interrupt. A process may block waiting for a timer in order to run at periodic intervals or specific times of day, to have a timeout that checks on some other process running too long, to do timeslicing,

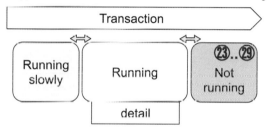

or to have a required delay accessing some external hardware.

Many programs need to wait for a certain amount of time to pass before continuing, even though this may seem counter productive from a performance point of view.

28.1   Periodic Work

Some processes, such as backups, are designed to be run only periodically or at specific times of day. Waiting to run until the next desired time frees up CPU time for other processes, so this behavior contributes to improved performance for those. Linux cron jobs, which can be programs or scripts, run on a specified recurring schedule; other operating systems have similar facilities. These facilities start up and run a complete program at specified times. The program then terminates, and the operating system starts a brand-new instance later. This use case involves nothing very complicated or error-prone from the point of view of the periodic program.

But from the point of view of *other* programs, the spontaneous arrival of a periodic program may unexpectedly consume significant computer resources, interfering with those other programs. The symptom is that some process you care about slows down periodically—every 15 minutes, every day at 2 a.m., or perhaps not quite so regularly. You want to know what just started up or what otherwise changed just as your programs slows down. Sometimes, finding this information is difficult. In a complex environment, it can be helpful to deliberately *design in* a time-stamped log of program/script startups and shutdowns. Such a log can be invaluable when you realize, after studying mysterious slowdowns for a few days, that you need to look back and see what else was happening at the slow times.

Some programs need to do periodic extra work, such as web-page refreshing within a browser. These programs typically have a separate thread that normally sleeps, perhaps via the nanosleep system call, but wakes up periodically to see if extra work is needed. Some system services, such as Read-Copy-Update (RCU) garbage collection or file system journaling, do periodic extra work. The performance issue is not the extra-work thread itself but the interference impact on other threads. Logging tools (for low-frequency wakeups) or tracing tools (for high-frequency wakeups) can show the correlation with slow execution elsewhere.

28.2   Timeouts

Some software activities need the protection of *timeouts*—a secondary action that happens if a primary activity fails to complete within a specified time. For example, the TCP network protocol has multiple timeouts—for establishing a connection, for retransmitting a packet that was not ACKed, for delaying the ACK of a packet, and so on. Many system services such as poll, recvmsg, or aio_select have timeout parameters. Some environments use software or even hardware *watchdog timers*—a timer that is supposed to be reset periodically by normally running code. If the timer expires because it was not reset, it means that the normally running code is presumed hung and needs to be restarted.

In each case, some extra piece of code runs to deal with the lack of timely completion of the primary activity. Having timeouts can be a highly important protection mechanism in time-constrained software. Designing what to do next, to actually recover, can be straightforward, or when large machinery is involved, it can be terrorizing.

One of the most famous examples of a real-time software protection mechanism occurred during the 1969 Apollo moon landing when the guidance computer became overloaded and was unable to dispatch a pending process in the last minutes of descent (there were too many interrupts from the radar unit tracking the overhead command module). It displayed error codes 1202 or 1201 and rebooted several times in those minutes, fortunately preserving the crucial downward-facing navigation data across the reboots. Margaret Hamilton, who labeled the discipline "software engineering" according to NASA, had overseen the software development and thankfully had insisted on thoughtful overload recovery [Christie's 2019, CBS 2019, Eyles 2004].

28.3   Timeslicing

One other use of timed delays is *timeslicing*—splitting up work on purpose in order to achieve some fairness or load-balancing goal. An operating system or a controlling task periodically interrupts an execution thread in order to run other threads or to assign the one thread a different piece of work. From the point of view of the interrupted work, it is not executing while waiting for time to pass—the timer interrupt that eventually allows it to run again. We saw examples of this in Chapter 23's discussion of schedulers.

Timeslicing is an important mechanism to prevent a few very long pieces of work from unduly delaying many short pieces of work. The dynamics, however, can be different from the picture in the designer's head, in a way that creates unexpected performance issues.

28.4 Inline Execution Delays

Sometimes a running program needs to delay for a fixed amount of time. This can be as low as a few hundred nanoseconds to wait for an I/O register or an external analog/digital converter to settle, or as high as several seconds to wait for just-powered-on disk drive to spin up and become functional. For delays longer than a few context-switch times, blocking via `nanosleep` or its equivalents frees up a CPU. For shorter delays, timed loops can be appropriate.

Keep in mind, however, that almost all delay times are the *wrong number* and tend to become worse over years of software use. For example, PCs have traditionally waited for several seconds during boot for disks to spin up. This was initially because there were no operating-system facilities to add a disk after booting. But even today you may encounter this delay on a PC with no hard drives at all, just electronic-speed SSDs. We saw a similar example in Chapter 26 with the default 200 msec retransmit timeout in TCP—a number that is wildly too large for network transmissions within a single datacenter building.

It can be helpful to make the numerical values of such delays easily configurable and even to have test cases designed to start failing over the years as the numbers become inappropriate for changed circumstances.

28.5 Summary

Deliberate delays waiting for a timer to expire are a useful part of many programs. Timers allow scheduling periodic work, safety timeouts, time slicing, and time for external equipment to react. Just keep in mind that they can also be sources of unexpected dynamics and performance issues.

Chapter 29

Waiting for Queues

This chapter is a case study of queuing delays. Using a small multi-threaded program that does fake "work" transactions, we will examine unexpected execution dynamics.

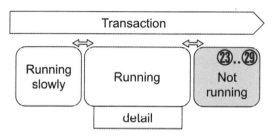

From our framework, this chapter is about not running while waiting in software queues. Any transaction may consist of several pieces of work performed by different processes: one process may do part of the work for a transaction and then queue the remaining work for another process. The execution dynamics can involve excessive queueing delays.

29.1 Overview

Imagine driving down an empty main street in the middle of the night—all the traffic lights are green, and you sail through. But in the daytime some lights are red, and there are several cars waiting in front of you—now you encounter significant delays going down the same street. So it is with software queues. We will explore queuing issues via the queuetest program that receives incoming work requests and routes each one through a short sequence of work queues, each served by a software thread. These queues represent different tasks in a complex software system such as Google search. The program strives to get in good trouble [Lewis 2016]—forcing us to confront issues and then improve them.

> Good trouble leads to good learning.

As you should expect by now, the program has several *flaws*. This chapter uses almost all of the observation skills developed in the previous chapters—RPC logs with client and server time-stamps, KUtrace diagrams, executing too much, executing slowly, waiting for CPU, waiting for locks, and waiting for time. You have learned enough to use these skills to discover root causes in complex and unexpected software dynamics. Test your skills as you follow along.

We will explore queuing issues in the context of a program that is a pretend server. The server accepts requests from a fake client (included in the program), with each request simply specifying a sequence of `<queue_number, usec_of_work>` pairs.

The server consists of several tasks/threads, each in a loop waiting for a corresponding queue to become non-empty and then executing whatever "work" the next queue entry specifies. Work in this case consists of simply spinning (doing floating-point divides) for approximately the specified number of microseconds. There are two kinds of tasks: the *primary task* serves queue 0, while the *worker tasks* serve the other queues. When done, each task places the remaining request item on the next specified queue. Figure 29.1 summarizes the flow.

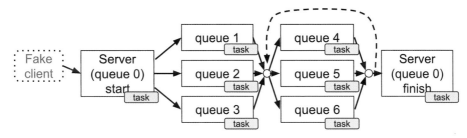

Figure 29.1   **The queue structure of this chapter's pretend server**

The fake client creates each new request, timestamps it (T1), and places it on queue 0, served by the primary task. When the primary task removes a request from queue 0, it timestamps the incoming request (T2) and then forwards the request to a worker queue. Eventually each request will return to queue 0 at the end. For finished requests, the primary task writes timestamps T3 and T4, creates the "response" (just a status code), writes an RPC log-file record that is in the same format as we used in Chapter 6, and then deletes the request.

The fake client part of the program generates N pseudo-random requests, waits for all of them to finish, and terminates. The fake client can either generate *uniform* or *skewed* requests, described next. The pseudo-random generator always starts at the same value, so for a given set of parameters the program always generates the same sequence of requests. This makes it possible to reproduce interesting execution dynamics.

The first-generated uniform request specifies this work:

First queue	Usec of "work"	Second queue	Usec of "work"	Third queue	Usec of "work"
1	74	5	2437		

The execution path for this work, shown in Figure 29.2, goes to the primary task serving queue 0, then the worker task serving queue 1, the worker task serving queue 5, and back to the primary task serving queue 0. The execution time to start is about 5 usec, to finish about 5 usec, time for queue 1's work about 74 usec, and time for queue 5's work about 2437 usec. In the absence of any competing work or other interference, we would expect this transaction to complete in about 5+74+2437+5 = 2521 usec, or about 2.5 msec.

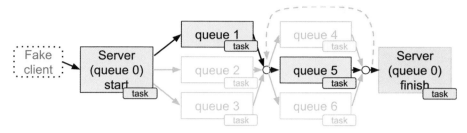

Figure 29.2 **The execution path of the first-generated uniform request**

There isn't any competing work for the very first transaction here, but by design there will be competition and interference for later transactions, some creating delays you would expect and some delays that are surprising.

29.2 Request Distribution

Uniform requests use one distribution to pick pseudo-random execution times and skewed requests a different distribution, as shown in Figure 29.3.

Uniform distribution, average = 0.5

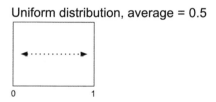

Skewed distribution, average = 0.75

Figure 29.3 **Uniform and skewed distributions**

The uniform distribution simply picks a random number uniformly distributed between 0 and 1. The average value is 0.5. For the skewed distribution, the uniform range 0 to 0.5 is used eight times out of 16, shown as half of the vertical height in Figure 29.3, 0–1 four times out of 16 shown as one-fourth the height, 0–2 two times, 0–4 one time, and 0–8 one time. There are many small values and occasional much longer ones. The average value is 0.75. The real computing world more often has execution distributions that resemble the skewed one, not the uniform one.

Uniform requests use the uniform distribution to pick times between requests and times for each queue's work. These requests pick the sequence of queues uniformly from 16 sequence patterns and pick microseconds of work for each queue uniformly from [0..1000) usec for the first queue's work and from [0..4000) usec for subsequent queues.

Skewed requests use the skewed distribution to pick times between requests and times for each queue's work, also using [0..1000) usec for the first queue's work and from [0..4000) usec for subsequent queues. They use 16 sequence patterns that are different than the uniform patterns, favor some queue sequences over others, include sequences that sometimes use queues 4–6 twice, and favor short work times over occasional longer ones.

With the uniform distribution, we expect the average request to execute for about 500 usec for the first queue's work and 2000 usec for the second, totaling about 2.5 msec per request. At that rate, we estimate that one 100% busy CPU should run about 400 requests/second, and four CPUs about 1600 requests/second.

With the skewed distribution, we expect the average request to use 750 usec for the first queue's work, 3000 usec for the second, and then one-fourth of the sequences use another 3000 usec for the third, totaling about 4.5 msec per request. At that rate, we estimate that one 100% busy CPU should run about 222 requests per second, and four CPUs about 888 requests/second.

29.3   Queue Structure

Each queue is a linked list of work items. The queue structure itself has the usual head and tail pointers, plus a count of items and a lock word used to make simultaneous insertion and deletion by different threads atomic. Figure 29.4 shows the general plan.

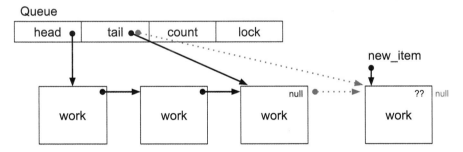

Figure 29.4   **A queue of work items. Gray shows insertion of a new item.**

Appending a new item involves updating the pointer in the existing `tail` entry and then updating the `tail` pointer itself. Removing the front item involves saving the `head` pointer and then updating it. Both operations require holding the `lock`. In contrast to the `FancyLock` class used in Chapter 27, the queues have a simple spinlock, since it has to cover only a few pointer assignments and should therefore be locked only a tiny amount of time. It is so simple that I didn't even include any observability code. But this spinlock has subtle performance flaws, as we shall see.

29.4   Worker Tasks

Each *worker task* loops forever, taking an item off its assigned queue, doing the specified work, and moving the item to its next queue. The tasks run this slightly simplified code:

```
do {
  while(myqueue->count == 0) {
    // Wait for some work
    syscall(SYS_futex, &myqueue->count, FUTEX_WAIT,
      0, NULL, NULL, 0);
  }
  Work* item = Dequeue(myqueue, ii);
  ----- Do N microseconds of work -----
  // On to the next queue
  Enqueue(item, &queue[next_q], next_q);
} while (true);
```

If there is no work pending, the worker task uses the `futex_wait` system call to wait until the count is non-zero. While waiting, a worker task's execution blocks, so it uses no CPU time. This waiting requires any task inserting into an empty queue to do a `futex_wakeup` system call.

29.5   Primary Task

The *primary task* has the same structure as the worker tasks, with the addition of timestamping, logging, and deleting each finished work item.

The primary task has one other important responsibility. If too many requests are pending when a new work item arrives, it refuses the new item by giving it a response status code of TooBusy, logging it, and then quickly finishing it. This deals in a simple way with an *offered load* that is too high. Without some overload mechanism, the queues would just keep getting longer and longer and the completion time for each request would get worse and worse. This could persist until the program completely runs out of memory or the users run out of patience.

We look next at the insides of `Dequeue`, `Enqueue`, and `PlainSpinLock`. Their details contribute to the performance delays we shall see.

29.6   Dequeue

The Dequeue operation uses a lock class to protect the few statements that must execute atomically. Remember from Chapter 27 that a lock class constructor acquires a lock and the destructor releases it, so the compiler reliably inserts locking operations at code-block beginning and ending. The dequeue routine runs this slightly simplified code:

```
Work* Dequeue(Queue* queue, int queue_num) {
  PlainSpinLock spinlock(&queue->lock);
  Work* item = queue->head;
  queue->head = item->next;
```

```
    --queue->count;
  return item;
}
```

When this removes the last item from a queue, the head becomes NULL.

29.7   Enqueue

The Enqueue operation is similar, running this slightly simplified code:

```
void Enqueue(Work* item, Queue* queue, int queue_num) {
  PlainSpinLock spinlock(&queue->lock);
  item->next = NULL;
  if (queue->head == NULL) {
    queue->head = item;
  } else {
    queue->tail->next = item;
  }
  queue->tail = item;
  ++queue->count;
  syscall(SYS_futex, &queue->count, FUTEX_WAKE,
    0, NULL, NULL, 0);
}
```

After it inserts an item into the queue, Enqueue does a futex_wake system call to unblock any waiting thread.

29.8   Spinlock

The PlainSpinLock class has these two routines, constructor and destructor, respectively, shown here slightly simplified:

```
PlainSpinLock::PlainSpinLock(volatile char* lock) {
  lock_ = lock;
  bool already_set;
  do {
    while (*lock_ != 0) {
      // Spin without writing while someone else holds the lock
    }
    // Try to get the lock
    already_set =
      __atomic_test_and_set(lock_, __ATOMIC_ACQUIRE);
  } while (already_set);
}

PlainSpinLock::~PlainSpinLock() {
  __atomic_clear(lock_, __ATOMIC_RELEASE);
}
```

The lock_ class variable carries the lock pointer value over from constructor to destructor.

29.9 The "Work" Routine

The `fdiv_wait_usec` routine does our fake work. It loops for approximately the specified number of microseconds doing constant floating-point divides (`fdiv` for short). As we measured in Chapter 2, floating-point divides on our sample servers are not pipelined and take about 15 cycles each. The `kIterations` constant is chosen to loop enough to consume one microsecond of elapsed time.

```
double fdiv_wait_usec(uint32 usec) {
  double divd = 123456789.0;
  for (int i = 0; i < (usec * kIterations); ++i) {
    divd /= 1.0000001;
    divd /= 0.9999999;
  }
  if (nevertrue) {          // Make live
    fprintf(stderr, "%f\n", divd);
  }
  return divd;
}
```

29.10 Simple Examples

Two lightly loaded examples show the expected baseline performance. The queuetest program has three main command-line arguments:

`-n <number>`	specifies the number of work transactions to do
`-rate <number>`	specifies how many transactions per second to offer
`-skew`	specifies skewed distribution instead of default uniform one

On average a *uniform* rate of 50 per second will issue a new request about every 20 msec, or 400 msec total elapsed time. The average uniform request takes about 2.5 msec of CPU execution time, so at one per 20 msec there should be little interference between requests.

Running with `-n 20 -rate 50` gives this CPU and transaction (RPC) timing, as shown in Figure 29.5.

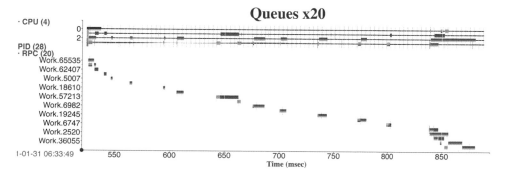

Figure 29.5 **Simple uniform execution example**

The 20 work requests are spread out fairly uniformly and usually run one at a time, with a little overlap when a few are issued quite close together. Each request does work on two different queues, not all visible at this scale. The total time is about 355 msec. This picture is reasonably close to our expectations.

On average a *skewed* rate of 50 per second will also issue a new request about every 20 msec, or 400 msec total elapsed time, but sometimes with large gaps (up to 160 msec) in between. The average skewed request takes about 4.5 msec of CPU execution time. Running with -n 20 -rate 50 -skew gives this CPU and transaction timing, as shown in Figure 29.6.

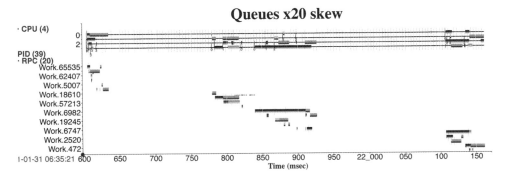

Figure 29.6   **Simple skewed execution example**

These 20 work requests happen to bunch into 3 groups with 2 arrival gaps of about 100 and 150 msec. Within each group there is substantial overlap in time. Each request runs work on two or three different queues, but again the time is sometimes too short to see clearly at this scale. The total time is about 556 msec, somewhat higher than our estimate of 400 msec.

29.11   What Could Possibly Go Wrong?

As usual, we care about the overall latency of requests. This latency can be increased, sometimes substantially, by many factors, some from interference within this program, and some from external interference. We list a number of possibilities here, and then in the next sections we will examine some longer skewed runs in detail to observe the dynamic interactions.

Interference within this program:

- There are eight tasks including the fake client, but there are only four CPU cores. Once things get busy, the dynamic interaction between the tasks and the operating system scheduler will become complex.

- Some requests will go to queues containing prior requests and will have to wait until all those finish.

- Close bursts of offered work will slow each other down.

- More offered work per second than can be finished in one second will cause queues to get longer and longer.

- Locking on queue insert/remove can delay any simultaneous insert/remove actions.

- Subtle bugs will introduce unanticipated delays.

Interference from outside sources:

- The CPU cores sometimes run at reduced clock frequency, causing execution times to stretch out by up to a factor of five.

- Programs such as `ssh` and `gedit` are running in the background during the following traces. They use some interfering CPU cycles.

- The `fdiv` instruction is not pipelined, and there are not multiple dividers in our sample servers, so two hyperthreads both doing `fdiv` loops can slow each other down.

Keep these sources of interference in mind as the following sections explore many aspects of the program and of queued designs in general.

29.12   CPU Frequency

Looking at Figures 20.5 and 20.6 in more detail in Figures 20.7 and 20.8 respectively, the added CPU frequency highlighting reveals an important variation in CPU frequency from 3900 MHz (very light green) down to 800 MHz (red).

In Figure 29.7, the CPU frequency starts at full speed on the left and drops to almost five times slower on the right. The longer request execution times from time 620–900 msec correlate with this change in frequency, not with some other interference. Without noticing the substantial frequency change, you could waste time *looking for nonexistent other sources of slowdown.*

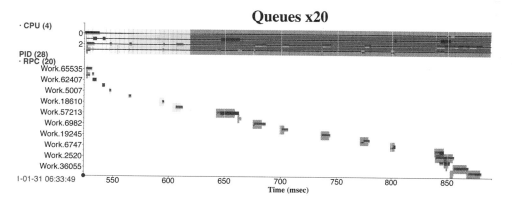

Figure 29.7   **Uniform 20 requests with CPU frequency overlay**

In Figure 29.8, the CPU frequency starts at full speed on the left and drops to almost five times slower toward the middle, and then it pops back up to about half-speed (1900 MHz) during time 900–950 before slowing down again. Execution across all four CPUs of the middle cluster of requests *triggers* the frequency increase. This dynamic interaction between code execution and CPU clock frequency is completely invisible with most observation tools. Yet it completely explains the slowdowns in the middle group of requests and why the last two in that group are not slowed as much.

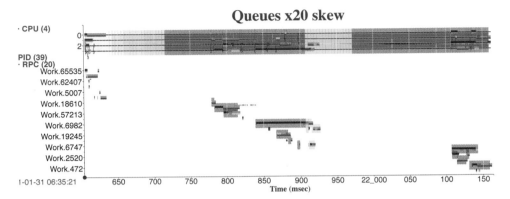

Figure 29.8   **Skewed 20 requests with CPU frequency overlay**

With modern processors varying their CPU frequency by substantial amounts over millisecond timescales as a function of recent many-core execution patterns, the performance engineer cannot afford to be blind to these changes. You can think of slow CPU clocks as a startup effect, but one that easily repeats often when CPUs are less than 100% busy. Slow clocks can slow down a transaction as a function of that program's or, worse, some other program's recent gap in execution. If the picture in your head is uniform execution of evenly spaced requests, you will miss how bursty transaction arrival can overwhelm other slowdown effects.

Fix: Long response times because of reduced clock frequency can be an issue on lightly loaded systems. If this matters, the only real cure is to change the power-saving parameters to keep clock speeds higher.

29.13   Complex Examples

The next examples use just the skewed distribution at various rates. Running with the skewed distribution and 2000 requests per second substantially outpaces the average 888 skewed requests per second that we estimated. We expect to see the queues get longer and longer, with the CPUs all 100% busy. A stress test like this can often reveal performance issues and unexpected dynamics that are still there under normal load but whose effects are subtler then.

29.14   Waiting for CPUs: RPC Log

When the number of in-process requests is above 40, the queuetest program manages the overload by *dropping* new requests. A sample run with -rate 2000 has requests arriving about twice as fast as they finish. So a run with 100 requests will start dropping requests midway through. But even before that, the high level of activity stresses the software dynamics.

Figure 29.9 shows the first 50 requests of a run using arguments `-n 100 -rate 2000 -skew` on the command line. The display is one notched line per request, as we introduced in Chapter 6. The fake client records the initial T1 timestamp when it generates a request and then places that request on queue 0. The primary task removes the request, adds the T2 timestamp, and places that request on the specified first work queue. At the end of a request, the primary task adds (nearly identical) timestamps T3 and T4 and logs it.

Running with `-n 100 -rate 2000 -skew`

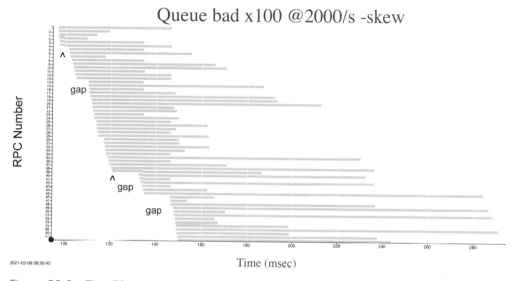

Figure 29.9   **First 50 of 100 skewed requests, some with unusual startup delays**

Looking just at the request start times, there are several gaps of 2 to 10 msec between successive starts. The nominal starting rate at 2000 requests/second is one every 0.5 msec, so the larger gaps might indicate performance issues. But also notice the notches (marked with ^) near time 100 and time 120–133 that indicate a substantial delay between the client placing a request on queue 0 and the primary task taking that request off queue 0. We might expect that delay to be only 2–10 usec, not the observed 1000 times longer 2–10 msec.

In addition to start-time delays, there are completion delays. Instead of the estimated 4.5 msec average execution time per request, we see times well above 50 msec.

The RPC log in Figure 29.9 shows us how long each RPC takes, but not *why* there are delays. For that, we take a closer look using KUtrace to see the complex (and buggy) dynamics of just the first few requests.

29.15   Waiting for CPUs: KUtrace

For the requests at the upper left of Figure 29.9, three start quickly, but the notches show that the next three get delayed reaching the primary task. The first four work requests have these queue and work schedules:

RPC ID	First queue	Usec of "work"	Second queue	Usec of "work"	Third queue	Usec of "work"
65535	3	37	4	1218	5	1898
36768	2	335	5	14000		
62407	1	452	6	3359		
54135	1	33	4	1078		

Figure 29.10 shows the execution of these requests in three vertical groups: sorted by CPU number at the top, process ID in the middle, and RPC at the bottom.

In the RPC group, the first line shows Work.65535 start with two execution blips of the client and primary tasks, then a longer red/green line showing execution of the queue 3 worker task. Surprisingly, its second piece of work on queue 4 is off the page. The light green *RPC thin dotted line* shows it waiting in queue 4, inserted but not removed. How could the very first request encounter queue delay?

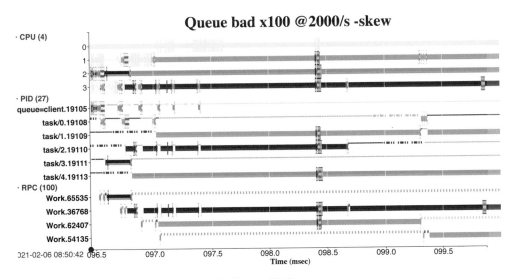

Queue bad x100 @2000/s -skew

Figure 29.10   **The first few requests in Figure 29.9**

The second RPC line shows Work.36768 start with two blips and then a long execution run on the queue 2 worker task, followed by queue 5's task at about time 098.7.

> Remember from Chapter 19 that thin lines represent lack of forward progress. In the CPU group they indicate executing only the idle process. In the PID group they indicate a process not executing while waiting on something. In the RPC group they represent an RPC waiting in a queue for some subsequent process to continue the RPC.

After the client/primary blips, Work.62407 starts on the queue 1 worker task. On the last RPC line, Work.54135 waits for queue 1 (thin dotted line) until 62407 finishes and then also runs starting about time 99.3 on the queue 1 worker task. This is normal queueing with 54135 waiting for prior work to finish. But it is *abnormal* that Work.62407 takes almost 2.5 msec to do 452 usec of work. The factor of five difference suggests the possibility of a 5x lower CPU frequency as we saw earlier in Section 29.12. Adding the frequency overlay to Figure 29.10 bears this out.

The PID group shows six processes. PID 19105 at the top is the fake client; 19108 is the server primary task; and 19109, 19110, 19111, 19113 are the first four worker tasks (the other two worker tasks are not shown). The client 19105 starts with six blips of execution, creating the first six work requests. These are spaced about 150 usec apart, somewhat closer than our nominal 500 usec spacing for 2000 requests/second. But 150 usec is not unusual for the skewed distribution.

The client puts the first six requests on queue 0, but the primary task initially takes only the first three off queue 0 followed by a 2 msec delay before removing the fourth request. We would expect the fourth request to be dequeued almost immediately after the third. What is happening?

When the primary task finishes launching the third request, it looks at queue 0 for the next one. But it is slightly *early*—the client has not yet generated the fourth request. That happens about 15 usec later. So in close succession, the primary task does a futex_wait for the fourth request, and the client task generates it and does a futex_wake of the primary. The primary becomes runnable, but as we saw in Chapter 23, the long orange line for the primary task from 97 to 99.3 msec says that it is runnable stranded but *waiting for a CPU* to run on. Call this performance issue **delay#1**. Why is there no CPU?

Look at the four CPU lines. CPU 0 is unfortunately running some unrelated program, shown in gray. CPU 1 is initially also running an unrelated program in gray. These both stop partway through the full trace, but interfere here. We are temporarily down to three CPUs.

The client task 19105 runs on CPU 2 to create the first work request and on CPU 3 to create the next five. You can see the execution blips that line up with the first PID line. The primary task 19108 runs on CPU 3 to process the first request and on CPU 1 to process the next two. Meanwhile, the first work request 65535 starts on CPU 2, running the worker task 19111 for queue 3. In a similar way, the second request Work.36768 starts on CPU 3 and Work.62407 starts on CPU 1.

Work.65535 finishes on queue 3 at time 96.8 and should move to queue 4 immediately. We see the task 19113 for queue 4 start executing as expected, but it does not remove the work item on that queue until sometime off the page to the right, leaving Work.65535 *stranded* on that queue for 10.4 msec. This is an unexpected performance bug. Call it **delay#2**.

As you can see, by time 97.0, all four CPUs in Figure 29.10 are busy. Now back to our poor primary task that is still trying to wake up. It finally does so at time 99.3 when Work.62407 frees up CPU 1. At that point, there are three requests queued up on queue 0. The primary launches all three in a row, at what looks like one wide blip but in fact is three back-to-back small blips.

These execution and non-execution dynamics are likely much more complicated than you expected, and we haven't even done six requests yet. For delay#1, as a general rule it is counterproductive to have more worker tasks than available CPUs.

We have *explained* delay#1, but we have not yet identified the *root cause*, which is related to delay#2.

Work.65535 started on queue 3 and then was moved to queue 4, which was empty. But the work was not taken off the queue. Instead, the task 19113 for queue 4 went into some form of solid execution at time 96.8, tying up CPU 2 and hence creating delay#1, but making no forward progress. By now you should have some idea what the problem might be. Scribble it down for yourself before moving to the next section.

We saw several sources of interference in this section: too much total offered load, CPUs used by other programs, waiting behind previously queued work, arrival bursts bunching up and slowing each other, and some sort of enqueue/dequeue issue. Next some fixes.

29.16   PlainSpinLock Flaw

Stuck CPU-bound trying to remove an item from a queue suggests an issue with the spinlock on that queue. Here is where we are:

Queue 3, PID 19111	Queue 4, PID 19113
	Worker task:
	```while(myqueue->count == 0) {```
	``` syscall(FUTEX_WAIT); blocks```
	```}```
Enqueue:	
{	
``` PlainSpinLock```	
``` spinlock(&queue->lock);```	
``` ...```	
``` ++queue->count;```	
``` syscall(FUTEX_WAKE);```	
}	
	Worker task:
	``` syscall(FUTEX_WAIT); finishes```
	``` Work* item = Dequeue(myqueue,```
	``` ii);```
	Dequeue:
	{
	``` PlainSpinLock```
	``` spinlock(&queue->lock);```
	``` Work* item = queue->head;```
	``` queue->head = item->next;```
	``` --queue->count;```
	``` return item; DOESN'T HAPPEN```
	}

So what is wrong with `PlainSpinLock` such that the Dequeue gets stuck? I went back and added some quick KUtrace `mark_b` calls to the code, to be able to observe the dynamics: "a" (for acquire) before the loop in the constructor, "/" (for end) after that loop, and "r" (for release) in the destructor.

A normal `Enqueue` operation does acquire and release as in Figure 29.11.

Figure 29.11   Normal Enqueue acquire and release pattern, with the `futex_wake` call notifying any task waiting on an empty queue

But the spinlock sequence at the problematic transition looks like Figure 29.12, with marks "a" and "/", but *no* release. The queue 3 task 19111 acquires the queue 4 spinlock and does a futex_wake call on the top line.

Figure 29.12   Abnormal Enqueue acquire that gets context-switched before the release

Then **BAM!** there is a context switch away from the futex_wake before the spinlock release is executed. The scheduler instead switches the CPU involved to the just-woken queue 4 task 19113, which has been waiting in futex_wait for a wakeup. That futex_wait call completes on the second line, and then the code goes into its own spinlock code at the rightmost "a", trying to acquire the not-yet-released queue 4 lock. It spins for the next **9.6 msec** until PID 19111 happens to get scheduled again and releases the lock, as shown in Figure 29.13.

Figure 29.13   Abnormal Enqueue acquire that later finally gets context-switched in again and does the release (followed by an unrelated normal acquire-release sequence). The white slashes indicate approximate KUtrace overhead in this 3 usec snippet.

29.17   Root Cause

The main flaw is that the futex_wake call is *inside* the critical section. This is an easy bug to introduce and a hard one to spot just reading code. It is much easier when you can observe the bad dynamics in action. Compiling the queuetest program with a -DFIXED parameter uses this alternate Enqueue code:

```
void EnqueueFixed(Work* item, Queue* queue, int queue_num) {
  {
    PlainSpinLock spinlock(&queue->lock);
    ...
  }
```

```
// Spinlock is now released.
syscall(SYS_futex, &queue->count, FUTEX_WAKE,
  0, NULL, NULL, 0);
}
```

Fix: The extra {...} block construct here delimits the critical section. This Enqueue change moves not only the futex call out of the critical section, but also its associated context switch. Successfully releasing the lock also removes the cascading effect that ties up CPU 2 spinning for milliseconds, using up a CPU and causing the primary task to delay starting other requests.

There is still an inherent issue with lock behavior, but it is substantially minimized. It is always possible for an unrelated interrupt to occur within Enqueue after the spinlock acquire and then context switch away before the release. Any lock system can have this problem; we have just reduced the odds. This is the motivation for using lock-free sequences with *atomic instructions* such as compare_and_swap [IBM 1983, Padegs 1981], which are more limited but use no lock. Essentially, if there is a simultaneous update, the compare at the end of an update fails, and the surrounding code tries again. More detail than that is beyond the scope of this book.

In this section we saw a subtle locking bug, dynamic interaction between tasks and the operating system scheduler, and the cascading effects (Figure 29.14) of one delay or bug causing slow completion of other work.

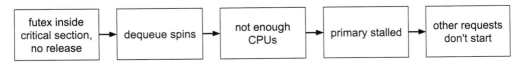

Figure 29.14   **Cascading effect of one source line out of place**

29.18   PlainSpinLock Fixed: Observability

In addition to the flaw of a futex inside the critical section, there is also the flaw of having *no designed-in observability*. That is why I had to go back and add the acquire/release marks. There is a remaining flaw we will get to later. The lesson is simple:

> Locking is complex and prone to performance bugs.
>
> If you have access to a robust and well-debugged locking library, use it rather than building your own.

With the futex moved out of the critical section, there are no delays in offering requests; queuetest performs somewhat better, still issuing a new request every 432 usec, but finishing the average transaction 37% sooner. That is pretty good leverage for moving *one line of code*.

futex Inside Critical Section	futex Outside Critical Section	Improvement
100 transactions, 12 dropped	100 transactions, 28 dropped	
Delays (usec), total = 43252, average = 432	Delays (usec), total = 43252, average = 432	
Transactions (usec), total = 4944439, average = 49444	Transactions (usec), total = 3122861, average = 31228	**37% faster**
Real 0m0.285s, user 0m0.607s, sys 0m0.006s	Real 0m0.231s, user 0m0.455s, sys 0m0.006s	**real 25% lower, user 20% lower**

Except . . . notice that the number of *dropped* transactions (whenever 40 are queued) increased substantially. In fact, the second column is doing 72/88 or 18% fewer transactions. This accounts for a good portion of the apparent improvement. Don't be misled by apparent improvements until you have cross-checked that the productive work accomplished is the same. If the offered requests were spread out a little more in time, fewer would be dropped, and the underlying performance change would be clearer.

29.19   Load Balancing

The offered requests in the skewed distribution heavily use the execution tasks for queues 4 and 5, as shown in Figure 29.15. The three-queue schedules in particular use both queue 4 and queue 5 in a single request. The times spent executing for queues 1–3 and queue 6 are relatively short. The effect is that many requests spend time waiting in queue 4 or 5 because those two execution processes are overloaded, so requests take a long time to complete. The small numbers 0 4 4 7 .. 18 along the client line show how many requests are still in progress as the client generates each new request. Remember from section 29.14 that when the number of in-process requests is above 40, the queuetest program drops new requests (returning a response error code indicating overload). This starts happening at about time 430 in Figure 29.15.

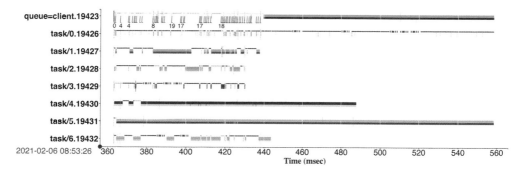

Figure 29.15   Unbalanced tasks across 100 skewed requests

The work across the queues is *unbalanced*, leading to bottlenecks at the busy queues. This is quite common and requires mechanisms to balance the work better.

Fixes: If the worker tasks are all *different*, running completely different algorithms and accomplishing different phases of a large calculation, there may be little that can be fixed. Occasionally, though, it can be helpful to create multiple copies of a bottleneck task and have them share work. This works best if there are enough CPUs available to run those multiple copies simultaneously.

If the worker tasks are the *same*, running the same code, then some systems will queue new work for the task that is least busy, equivalently queue new work onto the shortest queue. An alternate design is to have worker tasks with an empty queue *steal* work from some other queue instead of immediately blocking in a `futex` call.

29.20   Queue Depth: Observability

How deep do the queuetest queues get? How deep in normal running, and how deep during overload? How balanced are they? Which ones are bottlenecks? The simple queue structure in this program has no *observability*. There is a count kept of queued entries for each queue, but no designed-in mechanism to *show* this count. If you were building a dashboard for this program (Chapter 10), what would you display about the queues?

The instantaneous current queue depth for each one might be of interest, but more likely an average taken over the previous second, 10 seconds, minute, or 10 minutes (Chapter 9) would be more informative. A time-decaying maximum can be helpful. Showing a long and a short time-span can give a sense of now vs. normal. Comparing across queues can reveal load-balancing issues or bottleneck queues. Showing 99th percentile can highlight occasional long queues.

When you create a queue, estimate its likely depth, similar to estimating likely acquisition time for locks (Chapter 27). If you estimate that the depth is almost always zero and rarely above 2, observing a consistent depth of 5 or more can lead to some interesting learning.

29.21   Spin at the End

The client process in queuetest launches all the requests and then spins until the number of outstanding requests drops to zero. This spin is the right half of CPU 1 in Figure 29.16. It is so long because it is waiting for the queue 5 bottleneck on CPU 0 to finish.

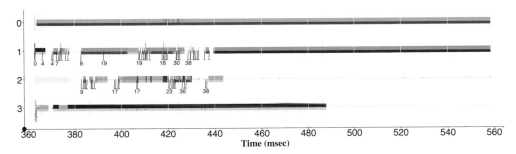

Figure 29.16   **CPU view of the same trace as Figure 29.15**

While spinning, it can slow down completion of the real work. Interactions like this between delay mechanisms are common, each producing their own little cascade of performance issues.

If the queue 5 load were better balanced, the client spin would be shorter, but it still aggravates finishing up the real work because it takes away one CPU core. There is a better way.

Fix: There is no big rush for the client to finish up the instant the last request terminates. An alternate design for the client is to issue all the requests, and then go into a loop that sleeps for several milliseconds (perhaps 20) and then checks if the outstanding requests have reached zero. If not, sleep and repeat. This frees up the one CPU core at the usually trivial expense of finishing a few milliseconds later than in the current design. In fact, the expense is usually negative because freeing up one more CPU core can allow the real work to complete sooner.

29.22 One More Flaw

Earlier, I led you down the garden path. In Section 29.2, the estimate of 400 uniform transactions per second on one CPU core is good. But the estimate of 1600/sec across four cores is not—it is off by about a factor of two. With eight CPUs, 3200/sec would be off by a factor of four. Try running with -rate 800 and -rate 1200 and see what happens. Then explain the mismatch between the estimate and your observation. When estimates and reality differ, there is always good learning.

29.23 Cross-Checking

We are almost done. After installing several fixes, it is worthwhile to cross-check the available information to see if anything else is odd. Sometimes the smallest discrepancy unravels a large hidden problem [Stoll 1989].

We looked at the CPU frequency variations earlier; look at them again via KUtrace of the fixed code. Only rarely will there be a surprise, but any that occurs is worth catching.

Look at the wakeup arcs to see if any odd patterns stand out. Look at lock-holding if it uses an instrumented library like FancyLock in Chapter 27. Look at the PC samples at every timer tick—even without routine names, are they consistent with the picture in your head?

Look at the instructions per cycle, IPC, as we did in Chapter 22. Section 29.11 mentions "two hyperthreads both doing fdiv loops can slow each other down." Figure 29.17 shows the same trace as Figures 29.15 and 29.16, with PC samples above each row and IPC triangles on top of each row.

The pink diagonal PC sample lines show the worker task loop, while the orange PC samples at the right end of CPU 1 show the client-finish loop. CPUs 0 and 2 are a hyperthread pair, as are 1 and 3. There is no obvious slowdown of the worker task loops when running simultaneously on either pair, but there could be a small change obscured by the coarse granularity of the IPC measurement. You can, however, see the speedup from 1.25 to 2.5 IPC of the client-finish loop at the far right of CPU 1 when the last queue 4 loop finishes on CPU 3. There are no real surprises here, but it is worthwhile to look.

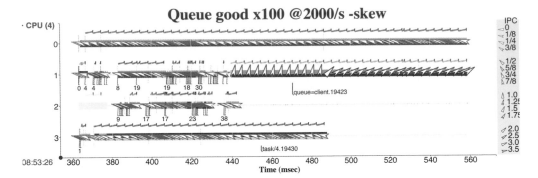

Figure 29.17   **The trace of Figure 29.16 with PC sample and IPC overlays**

29.24   Summary

- Estimate what you expect to see.

- Design-in observability of performance and dynamics.

- The picture in your head is too simple and wrong.

- Keep in mind possible sources of interference.

- Skewed distributions are more likely than uniform ones.

- Stress-test software to reveal latent performance issues.

- Avoid actions that can *block* inside critical sections.

- Expect cascading performance issues.

- Don't be mislead by apparent improvements.

- Cross-check that what you observe makes sense.

Exercises

These first few exercises use the trace files behind several of the figures in this chapter:

```
queuetest_bad_20210206_085042_dclab-2_19105_q.html (Figure 29.9)
qt_20210206_085042_dclab-2_19105.html (Figure 29.10)
queuetest_good_20210206_085326_dclab-2_19423_q.html (no figure)
qt_20210206_085326_dclab-2_19423.html (Figure 29.15)
```

Bring them up in your browser and pan/zoom as needed to examine the specified x-axis times, expanding the PID and RPC groups as needed.

29.1   Explain the large delays between times 42.120 and 42.145 in trace queuetest_bad_20210206_085042_dclab-2_19105_q.html.

29.2   Why are there longer RPC queuing delays in last half of trace qt_20210206_085042_dclab-2_19105.html?

29.3   Explain the RPC Work.36768 delay at time 26.36385 in trace
qt_20210206_085326_dclab-2_19423.html.

29.4   Explain the client delay at time 26.377 in trace
qt_20210206_085326_dclab-2_19423.html.

29.5   Explain the client delay at time 26.400 in trace
qt_20210206_085326_dclab-2_19423.html.

29.6   Explain the four RPC 36768, PID 19110 execution gaps near time 42.097 in
Figure 29.10, trace
qt_20210206_085326_dclab-2_19423.html.

29.7   It takes about 75 msec for the client to launch all the requests, instead of the
estimated 50 msec. Explain the delay, trace
qt_20210206_085326_dclab-2_19423.html.

(Hint: Across the entire trace, arrange just the row for PID 19423 onscreen by shift-
clicking its y-axis label to highlight it, collapsing the PID group to just highlighted rows,
and collapsing the CPU and RPC groups; then search for wait_time, wait_cpu, etc., and
look at the Matches total time.)

29.8   When running the fixed version of queuetest, what **goal** would you choose for the
90th percentile queue depth using the uniform distribution? The skewed distribution? In
each case, why?

29.9   Given your previous goal, measure what request rate per second the program can
sustain over 1,000 transactions. Datacenter capacity for a service is often empirically
determined this way.

29.10   In a copy of queuetest.cc, change kSkewedWorkPattern[16] so that instead of
four patterns that use queues 4 and 5, have two of them use queues 4 and 5 and two use
queues 4 and 6. Trace over 100 transactions and comment on what this does to change the
load balance and overall performance.

Chapter 30

Recap

Here we are: the last chapter. What have you learned, and what might you do next?

30.1   What You Learned

In Part I, "Measurement," you learned to make informed estimates of how long a piece of code should take. Your careful measurements of CPU, memory, disk, and network activity inform those estimates. Estimates give you some idea of what to expect when you observe the actual behavior of a program. When the estimated and actual performance differ, there is always something to learn—why your estimate was unrealistic, why the program is slower (or faster) than it should be, or a little of each.

Along the way, you learned a little more about how modern complex processor chips work and how they interact with operating systems and user software.

In Part II, "Observation," you learned of the existence of several common tools for observing program performance. You also learned how to design-in ways to observe the overall behavior and health of demanding time-constrained software systems. Logging and dashboards are key design ideas for built-in observability. Once you have even simple logging and dashboards in place, it is easier to add some more detail as you come to understand the dynamics of a complex software system and thus come to understand what other data items are most useful (just avoid slowing everything down too much).

Part II also introduced the contrast between sampling and tracing: the former gives low-overhead snapshots of what a program is doing via counts, PC samples, and such; the latter gives a blow-by-blow accounting of everything a CPU system is doing while executing one or more programs. Sampling is useful for observing the overall behavior of a software system and especially for understanding its normal or average behavior—*what* is happening. Tracing is useful for observing actual instances of unpredictable slow dynamics, either by observing long enough to have a trace contain many examples of slow behavior or by tracing continuously (flight-recorder mode) until software detects some bad performance and then stops tracing in order to capture the events leading up to and including the bad behavior. These instances lead to understanding *why* software is sometimes slow.

Along the way, you also learned more about the dynamic execution of request-driven time-constrained software.

In Part III, "Kernel-User Trace," you learned how to construct kernel hooks to capture the fundamental transition events between kernel-mode execution, user-mode execution, scheduler execution, context switches, and idle. You learned how to keep the overhead of these hooks incredibly low—less than 1% CPU and memory overhead for 200,000 events per second per CPU core. This part also taught how to construct a loadable module to do most of the work underlying the kernel hooks and how to construct a simple user-mode library to control tracing. These hooks are available as open-source code for Linux on common x86 and ARM processors.

You learned the value of recording a little extra information: the first argument and return value of system calls: wakeup events that make a blocked thread runnable again; instructions per cycle to reveal execution interference from related threads, unrelated other programs, and the operating system itself; low-power idle states that can cause delays restarting execution; PC samples to give insight into long execution paths either within kernel code or user code; CPU clock frequency to avoid looking for other explanations of 5x slower than normal execution speed; and simple network stack packet timestamping to disambiguate whether a long delay from machine A user code to machine B user code occurred before A's kernel code sent a message or after B's kernel code received it, or in the network itself.

Starting with raw traces and postprocessing them, you learned how to extend small timestamps to full-size ones and how to turn first-use event names into running human-readable names for every trace item.

From the expanded events, you learned how to turn transition timestamps into execution spans that cover 100% of the time on every CPU core in a trace and to produce readable JSON files that can be further modified, embellished, and searched. Finally, you learned how to turn the JSON files into dynamic HTML files that the user can pan and zoom, for examining execution dynamics at any desired level of detail. Several side programs can be used to trim traces, add kernel routine names, add user routine names, and add timestamped tcpdump packet information.

With traces from two or more communicating machines, you learned how to align the timestamps via postprocessing software even when the original machines' time-of-day clocks are out of sync by tens of milliseconds, all without requiring fancy high-precision hardware.

The last portion of this part explained how to use the existing HTML user interface in a browser to find and display the events, execution dynamics, and interactions that lead to slow performance. Observing exactly where all the time went in an instance of a slow time-constrained request leads directly to an understanding of the root cause(s) that make it slow—not just the *what* but the *why*.

In Part IV, "Reasoning," we went through several case studies, learning how to reason about instances of the nine common mechanisms that can slow down time-constrained software. Throughout these examples, you also learned more about what to look for as you approach a performance mystery. The examples draw upon most of the concepts covered in the first three parts of the book, giving you the opportunity to practice using them and to consolidate your learning from those chapters.

30.2 What We Haven't Covered

There is nothing in this book about graphics processing units (GPUs) or neural network processing chips (TPUs). Typically, these are processors that are external to a standard CPU. To the extent that external processors occasionally slow down latency-sensitive requests or transactions, the tools in this book can show those slowdowns from the point of view of the attached CPU—slow IPC from memory interference, late interrupts from GPU-finishing delays, and similar high-level interactions. But there is nothing here about instrumenting GPU or TPU software itself to turn the *what* of unexpected slowdowns into *why*. Perhaps one of you will pursue building extensions in this area.

There also is nothing in this book about virtual machines—using a hypervisor to run multiple guest operating systems and their user programs. In such an environment, one could focus either on the performance of guest operating systems or on the performance of the hypervisor itself.

Focus on the guest operating systems could be as simple as running existing performance observation tools, including KUtrace, on those guest operating systems. That would tell guest users about the dynamics of their code and operating system, based on virtual time. But it would be *blind* to all the real CPU time spent running other guests and running the hypervisor itself. Such a picture of execution might well be so incomplete that it is useless for understanding root causes that are outside one user's guest environment.

Focus on the hypervisor itself could involve KUtrace-like patches to capture all transitions in and out of the hypervisor, giving insight to the possibly unexpected execution dynamics between the real hardware, the hypervisor, and the guest operating systems. Tracing at this level can give a complete picture—nothing missing—of all the real CPU time. Using KUtrace-like patches for all the system calls, interrupts, and faults that are handled by the hypervisor *on behalf of the guests* would allow tracing the dynamics of operating systems, such as Windows, that have no native KUtrace support.

But doing so could be more appropriate for the virtual machine owner, not the user of one guest instance who normally is rigorously prevented from observing any other guests. Someone who builds hypervisors might extend the tools discussed here to observe the hypervisor itself. Perhaps one of you will pursue building extensions in this area.

30.3 Next Steps

I have tried to bring to this book most of what I have learned while working over 55 years on performance issues near the hardware-software boundary—CPU architecture, CPU implementation, network interface implementation, operating system design, disk-server design, compiler design, and design of complex high-level software that is time-constrained or latency-sensitive.

You now have many mental tools for approaching hard intermittent performance issues in time-sensitive software. Some of you will use these tools in your normal work, designing in better observability and reasoning from observed behavior about what causes slowness and how to fix it. Infect your own environments with better techniques for building observable complex software, and teach others how to reason about the observations.

Others, I hope, will react to some of this book by saying "I can do better." Do so—build better (but not slower) observation tools, extend the tools here to other environments, or propose and write about better approaches.

30.4   Summary (for the Entire Book)

- Estimate what performance and dynamics you expect to see.

- Design in observability of performance and dynamics.

- The picture in your head is too simple: execution dynamics are complicated; seek to observe those dynamics.

- Keep in mind possible sources of interference.

- Skewed distributions are more likely than the uniform ones we imagine.

- Stress-test software to reveal latent performance issues.

- Expect cascading performance issues.

- When you find delays, ask *why*.

- Seek *root causes*, not symptomatic fixes.

- Don't be misled by apparent improvements.

- Cross-check that what you observe makes sense.

- When estimates and reality differ, *there is always good learning*.

Congratulations. You are now a skilled professional software performance engineer.

Live long and prosper.—Mr. Spock

Appendix A

Sample Servers

This book is intended to be used by programmers who actively run the programs in the exercises. Understanding software performance is best learned by doing. All the examples and software for this book are developed for Linux x86-64, kernel version 4.19 Long Term Support (LTS), the Ubuntu distribution, and are built by the included gcc compiler collection.

To have concrete measurements for the example programs in in the book, all of them have been run on two sample servers assembled from parts. Throughout the book are references to measurements, traces, and performance numbers on these servers. The KUtrace operating system patches that observe kernel-user transitions are implemented on these servers. In addition to the two sample servers, one or two other machines are needed to produce the network loads used in the later chapters. These can be any convenient Linux boxes and do not need the KUtrace kernel patches.

These servers are small-scale proxies for larger datacenter servers, but they are sufficient to create and understand all the performance issues in this book. If you use different processors, your answers to the exercises will of course vary from those in the book, as they always must in our fast-changing field. But the insights gained will carry over from machine to machine.

A.1   Sample Server Hardware

The sample servers are named dclab-1 and dclab-2. The additional machines for generating extra network traffic are named dclab-3 and dclab-4.

The AMD Ryzen 3 chip in dclab-1 has four physical cores, not hyperthreaded. It has three levels of cache:

- L1 I-cache 64KB, 4-way associative, 64-byte line, per physical core

- L1 D-cache 32KB, 8-way associative, 64-byte line, per physical core

- L2 cache 512KB, 8-way associative, 64-byte line, per physical core

- L3 cache 4MB, 16-way associative, 64-byte line, shared across all cores

The Intel Core i3 chip in dclab-2 has two physical cores, each two-way hyperthreaded, so four logical cores. It has three levels of cache:

- L1 I-cache 32KB, 8-way associative, 64-byte line, per physical core
- L1 D-cache 32KB, 8-way associative, 64-byte line, per physical core
- L2 cache 256KB, 8-way associative, 64-byte line, per physical core
- L3 cache 3MB, 12-way associative, 64-byte line, shared across all cores

See Table A.1.

Table A.1   **Sample Server Characteristics**

Server	CPU	RAM	Boot Drive	Data Drive	OS	Kernel
dclab-1	AMD Ryzen 2200G, 3.5 GHz	8GB	250GB disk	250GB disk	Ubuntu 18.04	Linux 4.19.19 LTS w/KUtrace
dclab-2	Intel i3-7100, 3.9 GHz	8GB	250GB disk	250GB disk 128GB SSD	Ubuntu 18.04	Linux 4.19.19 LTS w/KUtrace
dclab-3	Any Linux box					
dclab-4	Any Linux box					

Either configuration is sufficient to observe and measure many forms of cross-CPU, cross-cache, and main-memory interference. With two cores hyperthreaded on one server and four full cores on another, the 2x difference in CPU cycles and cache space can be observed and measured. With a second-drive SSD on one server and a second-drive hard disk on the other, differing data rates and access patterns can be observed and measured. With at least a third computer, interfering network traffic can be observed and measured. These are the motivations for the particular configurations above.

The C programs will also run with minor changes (mostly for reading the clock) on other operating systems and CPU architectures. An ARM64 port with the KUtrace patches is available for the 64-bit 8GB Raspberry Pi-4B.

Someone skilled in the art could move the operating-system patches to other Linux distributions, other Linux kernel versions, other open-source operating systems, or 32-bit architectures.

A.2 Connecting the Servers

The servers have 1 Gbit/sec Ethernet links. I recommend connecting them via their own small local Ethernet switch, with one extra switch port connected to the rest of your building's Ethernet fabric, as shown in Figure A.1. This allows experiments that send heavy traffic between the servers (as we do in Chapters 6, 7, and 26) to run without overloading the rest of the building.

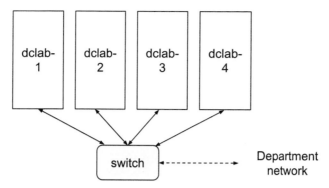

Figure A.1   **Sample server network connections**

Appendix B

Trace Entries

This appendix defines all the trace entries for KUtrace. The entries occupy one or more `uint64` words. Most entries are one word, but name entries are two to eight words. The first word of every entry has the format shown in Figure B.1, or a slight variation thereof. The name entries have additional words to hold the text name itself.

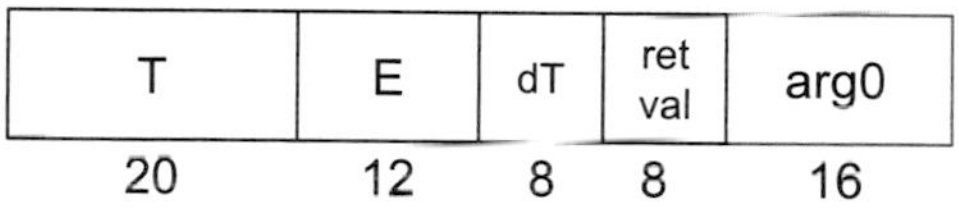

T	E	dT	ret val	arg0
20	12	8	8	16

Figure B.1 **Fight-byte trace entry with argument and return values for optimized call/return pair**

The five fields in an eight-byte trace entry are:

- T: 20-bit timestamp for the event, incrementing approximately once every 10–40 nsec and wrapping every million counts, 10–40 msec

- E: 12-bit event number, detailed below

- dT: 8-bit delta-time for an optimized call/return pair; the return time is T+dT; zero indicates a not-optimized call

- retval: low 8 bits of an optimized syscall return value, signed -128..+127; large enough to hold all normal Linux error codes -1..-126

- arg0: low 16 bits of the first parameter to a syscall, often containing a file ID or byte count or something else useful; low 16 bits of the return value for a non-optimized sysreturn; additional argument for other events

B.1   Fixed-Length Trace Entries

Event numbers 0x000 and 0x200-0xFFF are single-word trace entries.

Nop. Event number 0x000 is NOP, used for padding traceblocks (Figure B.2).

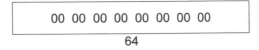

Figure B.2 **The all-zero NOP trace entry**

Point events. Event numbers in the 0x200 and 0x300 range specify point events in time, not transitions between execution states. They have either a 16-bit argument number in the arg0 field of a trace entry (Figure B.3a) or 32-bit arguments using a wider field (Figure B.3b).

Figures B.3ab **Point entries with arguments**

B.2 Variable-Length Trace Entries

In general, the first time a new syscall/irq/fault or new process ID is encountered, the trace will contain a name entry for that event followed by the event itself. For simplicity, constant syscall/irq/fault names are bulk-inserted at the beginning of the trace; PID names are inserted the first time there is a context switch to a previously unseen PID. The name for a process is the 16-byte command name held in the kernel's `task` structure.

Event numbers **0X1–1XF** are variable-length name entries of two to eight words (Figure B.4). The first word of every entry has the same format as one-word entries, followed by one to seven words of text, zero-padded. The event numbers all have the entry size in words as bits entry<7:4>, the middle hex digit. Bits <11:8> and <3:0>, the first and last hex digits, specify the kind of item being named. The arg0 field of the first word specifies the particular item number being named.

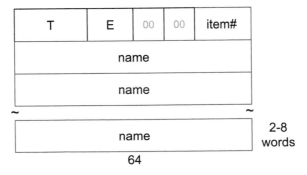

Figure B.4 **Multi-word trace entry for names**

The item numbers follow the design of the corresponding main entries: the low 16 bits of a PID, 8 bits of fault number, 8 bits of interrupt number, and 9 bits of syscall number. For example, Figure B.5 shows the name entry for the nanosleep() syscall.

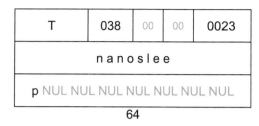

T	038	00	00	0023

n a n o s l e e

p NUL NUL NUL NUL NUL NUL NUL

64

Figure B.5 **Example name entry of nanosleep**

The entry number, 0x038, specifies a variable-length trace entry of three words, with item kind 008, syscall64. The arg0 field, 0x0023, specifies syscall64 number 23 hex or 35 decimal (see file /usr/include/asm/unistd_32.h). The nine-character name is spread across the next two words, padded with seven NUL characters.

Multi-word entries never cross traceblock boundaries—if an entire entry will not fit in the current traceblock, that block is padded out with NOPs, and the entry is put in the next block.

B.3 Event Numbers

The KUtrace 12-bit event numbers consist of a few high bits indicating the type of entry and the remaining low bits giving a specific number for that type, as shown in Figure B.6. The code points are somewhat sparsely assigned but even if densely assigned would need at least 11 bits. The complete list of KUtrace event numbers is in file kutrace_lib.h .

000 Variable length (names)		200 Point events	300 Point events
400 Fault	500 Interrupt	600 Fault return	700 Interrupt return
800 syscall_64		A00 sysreturn_64	
C00 syscall_32		E00 sysreturn_32	

Figure B.6 **Overview of hex 12-bit trace entry number assignments (The C00-FFF 32-bit compatibility syscalls are not currently implemented.)**

Kernel-mode KUtrace kernel patches insert most trace entries. User-mode libraries or inline code insert others. Postprocessing code inserts a few more into the JSON file.

B.3.1   Events Inserted by Kernel-Mode KUtrace Patches

Event 000 NOP.   Fills out unused trace-block words.

Events 0X1 to 1X6 names.   The kernel patches insert names for processes, system calls, interrupts, and traps; the middle hex digit is entry size 2..8 in eight-byte words.

Event 121 PC_TEMP.   Sampled program counter value at timer interrupts.

Events 1X2, 1X3, 1X4 KERNEL_VER, MODEL_NAME, HOST_NAME.   Traced machine identification inserted at trace startup.

Event 218 MBIT_SEC.   Traced machine network link speed; used only in post-processing to draw approximate packet times.

Events 400-4FF TRAP.   Fault entry (just page fault implemented); technically, traps never return while faults do.

Events 600-6FF TRAPRET.   Fault exit.

Events 500-5FF IRQ.   Interrupt entry.

Events 700-7FF IRQRET.   Interrupt exit.

Events 800-9FF SYSCALL64.   System call entry.

Events A00-BFF SYSRET64.   System call exit.

Events C00-DFF SYSCALL32.   System call entry (32-bit unimplemented).

Events E00-FFF SYSRET32.   System call exit (32-bit unimplemented).

Event 200 USERPID.   Context switch: arg0 is the low 16 bits of the new user-mode process id (pid=0 is the idle loop), inserted by scheduler code.

Event 206 RUNNABLE.   Process A makes blocked process B in arg0 runnable, inserted by scheduler code.

Event 207 IPI.   Interprocessor interrupt sent to CPU arg0; received IPI is one of 500-5FF IRQs.

Event 208 MWAIT.   Low-power idle hint in arg0, inserted by idle code.

Event 209 PSTATE.   Sampled CPU frequency in arg0 (MHz), inserted by timer-interrupt or frequency-change-notification code.

Event 214 RX_PKT.   Incoming packet payload hash in 32-bit arg, inserted by TCP or UDP code.

Event 215 TX_PKT.   Outgoing packet payload hash in 32-bit arg, inserted by TCP or UDP code.

B.3.2 Events Inserted by User-Mode Code

Events 201-203 RPCIDREQ, RPCIDRESP, RPCIDMID.   RPC request, response, and middle processing, inserted by a user-mode RPC library.

Events 20A-20D MARKA, MARKB, MARKC, MARKD.   Arbitrary text (ABC) or number (D) entries manually inserted by any user code; text is limited to six base-40 characters [a-z0-9./-] packed into 32 bits, and numbers are 32 bits.

Events 210-212 LOCKNOACQUIRE, LOCKACQUIRE, LOCKWAKEUP.   Software lock behavior, inserted by a user-mode locking library.

Events 216-217 RX_USER, TX_USER.   Incoming and outgoing message payload hash, inserted by a user-mode RPC library; hashes will match corresponding kernel-mode RX_PKT and TX_PKT.

Events 21A-21B ENQUEUE, DEQUEUE.   Active RPCs placed onto and removed from a software queue, inserted by a user-mode RPC library .

Event 0X3 METHODNAME.   RPC method name, inserted by a user-mode RPC library.

Event 0X7 LOCKNAME.   Software lock name (currently source declaration file-name:line), inserted by a user-mode locking library.

Event 1X5 QUEUENAME.   RPC queue name, inserted by a user-mode RPC library.

B.3.3 Events Inserted by Postprocessing Code

Event 204 RPCIDRXMSG.   Incoming RPC message duration (drawn above CPU 0 row).

Event 205 RPCIDTXMSG.   Outgoing RPC message duration (drawn above CPU 0 row).

Event 282 LOCK_HELD.   Lock holding duration (drawn above PID and RPC rows).

Event 282 LOCK_TRY.   Lock attempted acquire duration (drawn above PID and RPC rows).

Events 280-281 PC_U, PC_K.   Sampled PC values or names for user-mode and kernel-mode PCs, respectively.

Events 300-319 WAITA-WAITZ.   Reasons for PIDs or RPCs to be waiting.

Event -3 ARC.   Wakeup arc drawn from waker's RUNNABLE event to wakee's first subsequent execution event.

Event -4 CALLOUT.   Manually inserted label bubble, drawn wherever the user placed it.

Glossary

Abusive offered load A larger offered load than covered by normal RPC response-time agreements.

Access, memory Collective term for a memory read or write.

Assembly language A symbolic representation of individual computer instructions.

Asynchronous read/write An input/output operation whose initiator continues execution without waiting for a response.

Asynchronous RPC A remote procedure call whose caller continues execution without waiting for a response.

atime, directory field The last accessed time for a file

Average The arithmetic mean of a set of values.

Bursty Occurring at intervals in short sudden episodes or groups. Relating to or denoting the transmission of data in short separate bursts of signals.

Cache memory A hardware or software mechanism providing an auxiliary memory from which high-speed retrieval is possible.

Client program A computer program that requests functionality from other programs, called *server programs*.

Client-server A remote computing paradigm in which client programs sent work requests over a network to server programs, which in turn eventually return responses.

Core, memory An obsolete form of computer main memory constructed from small ferrite doughnuts (cores).

Core, processor An individual instruction-processing unit within a CPU chip.

Counters Observation tools that simply count events, such as instructions executed, cache misses, transactions performed, or elapsed microseconds.

CPU Central processing unit.

CPU time Elapsed non-idle CPU execution time for some specified processing.

Critical section A piece of code that accesses shared data in a way that would not behave correctly if more than one thread does so concurrently. See *Software lock*.

Cylinder, disk A set of disk tracks that are all at the same radial distance from the center.

Dashboard An observation tool that displays real-time status for some collection of computers or programs.

Datacenter   A large group of networked computers in a single building, communicating with users (people) and other computers that are geographically remote from that building.

Dependent instruction   An instruction that can only start its execution phase after receiving the result of a previous instruction.

Design point   The approximate offered load, or other metric such as data size, that a software service is designed to handle gracefully, i.e., within some specified response time distribution. An offered load 10 times or more from the design point is likely to have performance issues.

Destructive readout, memory or SSD   Reading a location destroys the information there, so it must be rewritten.

DIMM   Dual inline memory module. A small circuit board containing DRAM chips.

DRAM   Dynamic random-access memory, commonly used for computer main memory; slower but cheaper than SRAM.

Dynamics, of a program or collection of programs   The activity over time—what pieces of code run when, what they wait for, what space they take, and how different programs affect each other.

ECC bits, memory disk or SSD   Error correcting code, used to fix read errors in a small number of bits.

Embedded servo, disk   Hidden information of radial position recorded between disk sectors.

Erase cycle, SSD   The time taken erasing a block of flash memory.

Execution skew   The varying completion times of parallel execution paths; high skew reduces the effectiveness of parallel execution.

Execution, software   The alternating process of performing sequences of computer instructions and waiting with no (useful) instructions performed.

Extent, file   A contiguous set of disk blocks used to record a portion of a disk file.

Fill, cache line   The act of bringing new data into a cache, replacing some previous data.

Flight-recorder-mode   A tracing system that runs continuously, usually wrapping around as needed in a fixed-size recording buffer. Tracing is stopped when some software-detected error or event occurs, thus giving a trace of the events leading up to that point.

Frequency distribution   A set of values and how many times each occurs.

Fundamental resources   The five important shared resources in datacenter computer systems: four hardware (CPU, memory, disk/SSD, network) and one software (critical section).

GHz   GigaHertz: 1000 * 1000 * 1000 cycles per second.

Golden age of computing   The 1950s.

Histogram   A display of statistical information that shows the frequency of data items in successive numerical intervals. Equal-size intervals form a linear histogram, while multiplicative-size intervals form a logarithmic histogram.

Hindered transaction   One that is the subject of interference, slowing down its completion.

Hit, cache   An access to a cache that successfully finds the desired data, giving high-speed retrieval. See *Miss, cache*.

HTML   Hypertext Markup Language. The language used to construct web pages.

Hyperthread   An Intel term for its proprietary simultaneous multithreading.

Hz   Hertz, the unit of frequency: one cycle per second.

Idle time   Elapsed CPU time during which only the idle process is executing.

Instruction execution phase   The act of performing the specified action of a previously fetched instruction.

Instruction fetch phase   The act of reading an instruction from memory, typically from a level-1 instruction cache.

Instruction latency   The number of CPU cycles from starting the execution phase of an instruction and starting the execution phase of a dependent instruction.

Interference   Temporarily preventing a process or activity from continuing or being done properly.

Intrinsic function   A built-in function for a particular language compiler; may not be portable to other compilers.

IOMMU   Input-output memory management unit. Hardware that does virtual address mapping for I/O devices. May also provide memory access protection.

IP   Internet protocol. A standard set of rules for sending and receiving data over the Internet.

IPv4   IP version 4, with 32-bit IP addresses.

IPv6   IP version 6, with 128-bit IP addresses.

Issue cycle   The point at which an instruction is committed for execution.

JSON   JavaScript object notation. A standardized text format for interchanging data.

Kernel-mode   The CPU privileged execution state in which parts of the operating system run.

Latency   The elapsed wall-clock time between two events. It is important when carefully discussing latency to specify which two events. Transaction latency: see also *Response time, transaction*.

LBA   Logical block address. The address of a disk or SSD block, which may be remapped inside the device to a physical block address.

Level-1 cache   The smallest and fastest cache memory in a hierarchy of several caches.

Level-2 cache   The second-smallest and second-fastest cache memory in a hierarchy of several caches.

Level-3 cache   The third-largest and third-fastest cache memory in a hierarchy of several caches. In a hierarchy of exactly three levels, this is the largest and slowest cache, also termed the *last-level cache*.

Line, cache   A fixed-size block of memory that is entirely transferred to or from a cache, typically 16 to 256 bytes.

Lock capture   A single thread repeatedly acquiring and releasing a lock and then immediately reacquiring it before other threads have a chance to.

Lock saturation   A software lock that is contended almost all the time, preventing any gain in performance from having multiple threads.

Log   An observation tool that records, typically to a disk file, a timestamped list of transaction requests and responses and any informational software messages. Usually designed to handle a thousand events per second or fewer.

Logical block address   See *LBA*.

Long tail   The portion of a probability distribution having a number of occurrences far from the central part or mean of the distribution. See *Tail latency*.

LRU cache replacement   Least recently used, a common cache replacement policy that is near-optimal for most access patterns. See *Random cache replacement* and *Round-robin cache replacement*.

MAC address   Media access control address, a 48-bit unique hardware identifier for a network interface controller.

MB   Megabytes: 1024 * 1024 bytes.

Mb   Megabits: 1000 * 1000 bits.

Median   The midpoint of a frequency distribution of values; the 50th percentile value.

Message, RPC   A variable-length request or response, typically transmitted over a network as multiple packets.

MHz   Megahertz: 1000 * 1000 cycles per second.

Miss, cache   An access to a cache that fails to find the desired data, resulting in access to a slower memory. See *Hit, cache*.

MLC   Multi-level cell: a type of flash memory that stores more than one bit per cell.

msec   Milliseconds.

NIC   Network interface controller, the hardware that connects a processor to a network.

Non-blocking RPC   A remote procedure call that does not wait for its result before continuing execution of the caller.

nsec   Nanoseconds.

O(n)   Notation for "On the order of n". Used in this book to characterize the approximate numeric size of estimates, with n typically a power of 10 or 2.

Offered load   The number of transactions (RPC requests) sent to a server program per second; when this exceeds the transactions processed per second, response time suffers, sometimes dramatically.

Order of magnitude   An approximate measure of the size of a number. A *decimal* order of magnitude gives an estimate that is the nearest power of ten—1, 10, 100, . . . while a *binary* order of magnitude gives an estimate that is the nearest power of two—1, 2, 4, 8, and so on.

Payload   The portion of a network transmission that is actual data, as opposed to descriptive and routing headers.

Percentile   A measure used in statistics indicating the value below which a given percentage of observations in a group of observations fall. Thus, 90 percent of a group of observations fall below the 90th percentile value.

Pipelining   Overlapped execution of computer instructions, such that one instruction starts before the previous one has finished.

Prefetch   Transfer data from slow storage to faster storage in readiness for later use.

Profile   An observation tool that quasi-periodically samples some value, such as program counter, queue depth, or system load.

Program counter, PC   The address of the next instruction to be executed by a processor; also known as instruction counter, IC.

Query   An input message to a computer system that must be dealt with as a single unit of work; a request.

Random cache replacement   A cache replacement policy that replaces arbitrary lines within a cache set. See *LRU cache replacememt* and *Round-robin cache replacement*.

Refresh, memory   Periodic rewriting of memory information to preserve it.

Register update cycle   The last execution stage in a pipelined computer implementation; the instruction result is written to a CPU register, at which point the instruction is done and said to be retired.

Remote Procedure Call   A form of network message passing, used to execute work on another computer server.

Request/response model   A remote computing paradigm in which client programs sent work requests over a network to server programs, which eventually return responses.

Response time, transaction   The time elapsed between sending a transaction request message and receiving its result.

Restore, memory   Rewriting of memory information that was just destructively read.

Round-robin cache replacement   A common cache replacement policy that sequentially replaces lines within a cache set, independent of the access pattern. See *LRU cache replacememt* and *Random cache replacement.*

RPC   Remote procedure call.

SATA   Serial ATA (AT attachment). A hardware interface used to connect ATA hard drives to a computer's motherboard.

Sector, disk   A subdivision of a track on a magnetic disk, storing a fixed amount of user-accessible data.

Server (hardware)   A single computer system executing transactions.

Server (software)   A computer program that provides functionality for other programs, called *clients.*

Service   A collection of programs that handle one particular kind of transaction.

Set-associative cache   A cache divided into sets of N cache lines. A particular memory location can be cached in only one set, derived from its address, but in any of the N lines within that set. Such a cache is called *N-way associative.*

Simultaneous multithreading   A computing architecture that makes one physical CPU processor core appear as two or more logical cores; essentially multiple program counters and register files use a single processor core and its cache system.

Slop   Unidentified communication time in network transmission; a delay between sending and receiving that exceeds the transmission time needed in the network hardware itself.

Software dynamics   Changes in software execution over time, varying what executes, or how quickly it executes, or what it waits for. The factors may be contention for shared hardware and software resources; delays in responses from mechanical devices or from other computers; and interactions with parallel threads in a single program, with other programs, or with the operating system.

Software execution   The alternating process of performing sequences of computer instructions and waiting with no (useful) instructions performed.

Software lock   A software construct that allows only one thread at a time to execute a critical section, with any other thread forced to wait to enter the critical section.

Socket   A software construct for a single network connection.

SPEC   Standard Performance Evaluation Corporation, which develops benchmark suites.

SRAM   Static random-access memory, commonly used for computer cache memory; faster but more expensive than DRAM.

SSD   Solid-state disk; also known as *flash memory* or *flash drive.*

Starvation   A thread being perpetually denied resources to continue, typically because it is unable to gain access to a software lock, even as multiple other threads acquire and release that lock.

Stride   The number of locations between successive memory accesses within an array.

SUT   System under test.

Synchronous RPC   A remote procedure call that runs to completion before the caller continues execution. See *Non-blocking RPC*.

System time   Elapsed kernel-mode CPU execution time.

System under test   A hardware-software combination whose performance is observed while processing some offered load.

Tag, cache   The address associated with the data in a cache line.

Tail latency   The longer events in a group of latency observations, often characterized as those longer than the 99th percentile value of the probability distribution.

> The tail-flick test in pain research starts a timer and applies heat to an animal's tail; when the animal flicks its tail, the timer stops and the elapsed time recorded as *tail latency*.

TCP   Transmission control protocol. A standard for reliable network communication. See *UDP*.

Thrash, cache   Continuous eviction of useful data by two or more agents, causing all to make very slow or no progress.

Timestamp   A representation of the wall-clock time at which some event occurs.

TLB   Translation lookaside buffer; sometimes just called *TB*. A cache of virtual- to physical-memory address translations.

Trace   An observation tool that records time-sequenced events such as disk seek addresses, transaction requests and responses, function entry/exit, execute/wait transitions, or kernel/user mode execution transitions. Usually designed to handle tens of thousands of events per second or more.

Track, disk   That portion of a disk which passes under a single head during one rotation.

Transaction   An input message to a computer system that specifies a single unit of work, giving a result.

Transaction latency   See *Response time, transaction*.

Translation lookaside buffer   See *TLB*.

UDP   User datagram protocol. A stateless communication protocol primarily used for establishing low-latency and loss-tolerating connections. See *TCP*.

Unreasonable offered load   See *Abusive offered load*.

usec   Microseconds.

User-mode   The CPU unprivileged execution state in which normal programs run.

User time   Elapsed user-mode CPU execution time.

Virtual memory   A memory management capability that allows mapping a large apparent (virtual) memory space to a smaller physical memory space, allowing some data to be held in secondary storage.

Wall-clock time   Time of day: hours, minutes, seconds, fraction.

Wear-leveling   A technique for prolonging the service life of flash memory by spreading writes across all physical blocks.

References

[Agarwal 1986]   Agarwal, Anant, Richard Sites, and Mark Horowitz. "ATUM: A New Technique for Capturing Address Traces Using Microcode," in *Proceedings of the 13th Annual Symposium on Computer Architecture*, June 1986, pp. 119–127. https://dl.acm.org/doi/abs/10.1145/633625.52422

[Allen 2006]   Allen, K. Scott. "Atomic Operations," 2006. https://odetocode.com/blogs/scott/archive/2006/05/17/atomic-operations.aspx

[Amdahl 1964]   Amdahl, G. M., G. A. Blaauw, and F. P. Brooks. "Architecture of the IBM System/360," in *IBM Journal of Research and Development*, vol. 8, no. 2, April 1964, pp. 87–101. https://dl.acm.org/doi/10.1147/rd.82.0087

[Amdahl 1967]   Amdahl, Gene. "Validity of the Single Processor Approach to Achieving Large Scale Computing Capabilities," in *Proceedings of the Spring Joint Computer Conference*, 1967, pp. 483–485. https://dl.acm.org/doi/10.1145/1465482.1465560

[Aniszczyk 2012]   Aniszczyk, Chris. "Distributed System Tracing with Zipkin," June 7, 2012. https://blog.twitter.com/engineering/en_us/a/2012/distributed-systems-tracing-with-zipkin.html

[Anonymous 1896]   Anonymous. "A New Automatic Telephone Exchange System," *Engineering News*, vol. 35, p. 52, Google Books Result. January 23, 1896, "Busiest Hour of the Day," p. 52, col. 2, line 5. https://books.google.com/books?id=HVAyAQAAMAAJ&pg=PA52&lpg=PA52&dq=early+bell+telephone+%22busiest+hour++of+the+day%22&source=bl&ots=17ac5k-Xi2&sig=Bo8b4Ehx_l-QDqoMSRdzswxYN6g&hl=en&sa=X&ved=0ahUKEwiequO3nvLaAhULj1QKHcYVCwIQ6AEITTAI#v=onepage&q=early%20bell%20telephone%20%22busiest%20hour%20%20of%20the%20day%22&f=false

[Anonymous 1905]   Anonymous. "A Study in Traffic: *Telephone Journal*, January 14," *Telephony*, vol. 9, p. 122, Google Books Result. February 1905, "Busiest Hour of the Day," p. 122, col. 2. https://books.google.com/books?id=yOLmAAAAMAAJ&pg=PA122&lpg=PA122&dq=early+bell+telephone+%22busiest+hour+of+the+day%22&source=bl&ots=fdP1jabNXx&sig=s8RG7srWE9gHB7wbzES0AU2066c&hl=en&sa=X&ved=0ahUKEwjvmKKLmPnaAhWQFHwKHYqcB2gQ6AEITzAJ#v=onepage&q=early%20b

[Babcock 2015]   Babcock, Charles. "'Leap Second' Clocks In on June 30," June 17, 2015. https://www.informationweek.com/software/information-management/leap-second-clocks-in-on-june-30/d/d-id/1320850?page_number=1

[Blake 2015]   Blake, Geoffrey, and Ali G Saidi. "Where Does the Time Go? Characterizing Tail Latency in Memcached," 2015. http://ieeexplore.ieee.org/document/7095781/

[Borg 1990]   Borg, Anita, R. Kessler, and David Wall. "Generation and Analysis of Very Long Address Traces," in *Proceedings of the 17th Annual International Symposium on Computer Architecture*, May 1990, pp. 270–279. https://dl.acm.org/doi/abs/10.1145/325164.325153

[Bostock 2020]   Bostock, Mike. "Data-Driven Documents," 2020. https://d3js.org/

[Brooks 2020]   Brooks, Fred. Private communication, October 9, 2020.

[Broughton 2011]   Broughton, Jayson. "Fun with ethtool." *Linux Journal*, May 25, 2011. https://www.linuxjournal.com/content/fun-ethtool

[CBS 2019]   CBS. "Margaret Hamilton: MIT Software Pioneer Who Helped Save Apollo 11 Moon Mission," June 28, 2019. https://boston.cbslocal.com/2019/06/28/margaret-hamilton-apollo-11-software-pioneer-interview/

[Chesson 2006]   Bignose internal tool at Google by Greg Chesson, no public reference.

[ChipsEtc 2020a]   The SRAM was invented at Fairchild Semiconductor in 1964 by an electrical engineer named John Schmidt. It was a 64-bit MOS p-channel SRAM. http://www.chipsetc.com/sram-memory.html

[ChipsEtc 2020b]   The DRAM was invented at IBM by Dr. Robert H. Dennard in 1966. http://www.chipsetc.com/dram-memory.html

[Christie's 2019]   Christie's. "Margaret Hamilton: The Woman Who Wrote the Software That Put Man on the Moon," July 2019. https://www.christies.com/features/Software-pioneer-Margaret-Hamilton-on-Apollo-11-9947-3.aspx

[Comcast 2018]   Comcast. "Dapper Style Distributed Tracing Instrumentation Libraries," December 6, 2018. https://github.com/Comcast/money

[Conti 1969]   Conti, J. "Concepts for Buffer Storage," *Computer Group News*, March 1969, pp. 9–13.

[CVE 2017]   Common Vulnerabilities and Exposures. "CVE-2017-5753," 2017. https://cve.mitre.org/cgi-bin/cvename.cgi?name=CVE-2017-5753

[Damato 2016]   Domato, Joe. "Monitoring and Tuning the Linux Networking Stack: Receiving Data," June 22, 2016. https://blog.packagecloud.io/eng/2016/06/22/monitoring-tuning-linux-networking-stack-receiving-data/

[Dean 2009]   Dean, Jeff. "Numbers Everyone Should Know," 2009. http://www.cs.cornell.edu/projects/ladis2009/talks/dean-keynote-ladis2009.pdf

[Dean 2010]   Dean, Jeffery. "Building Software Systems at Google and Lessons Learned," November 2010, slide 36. https://research.google.com/people/jeff/Stanford-DL-Nov-2010.pdf

[Dean 2013]   Dean, Jeff, and Luiz Barroso. "The Tail at Scale," 2013. https://research.google.com/pubs/pub40801.html

[Dixit 1991]   Dixit, Kaivalya M. "Overview of the SPEC Benchmarks," in *The Benchmark Handbook*, Morgan Kaufmann Publishers, 1991. ISBN 978-1558601598. http://jimgray.azurewebsites.net/benchmarkhandbook/chapter9.pdf

[Dixit 2021]   Dixit, Harish Dattatraya, Sneha Pendharkar, Matt Beadon, Chris Mason, Tejasvi Chakravarthy, Bharath Muthiah, Sriram Sankar. "Silent Data Corruptions at Scale," submitted on February 22, 2021. https://arxiv.org/abs/2102.11245

[Emer 1984]   Emer, Joel, and Douglas Clark. "A Characterization of Processor Performance in the VAX-11/780," in *Proceedings of the 11th Annual International Symposium on Computer Architecture*, January 1984, pp. 301–310. https://dl.acm.org/doi/abs/10.1145/800015.808199

[Eyles 2004]   Eyles, Don. "Tales from the Lunar Module Guidance Computer," 2004. https://www.doneyles.com/LM/Tales.html

[Fall 2012]   Fall, Kevin R., and W. Richard Stevens, *TCP/IP Illustrated, Volume 1* (Second Edition). Addison-Wesley, 2012. ISBN 0-321-33631-3.

[Fram 1972]   Fram oil filter commercial, 1972. https://www.youtube.com/watch?v=OHug0AIhVoQ

[Friedenberg 1964]   Friedenberg, S. E., R. L. Brockmeyer, M. J. Stoner, J. R. Friend, and T. R. Battle."1410/7010 Operating System Timing Report," prepared by Evaluation Technology Department, Programming Systems, DSD Poughkeepsie, July 30, 1964. http://ibm-1401.info/Pics1/ibm_1410_7010_Adobe.pdf

[Geng 2018]   Geng, Yilong, Shiyu Liu, Zi Yin, Ashish Naik, Balaji Prabhakar, Mendel Rosenblum, and Amin Vahdat. *Exploiting a Natural Network Effect for Scalable, Fine-Grained Clock Synchronization*, NSDI '18, pp. 81–94. https://www.usenix.org/system/files/conference/nsdi18/nsdi18-geng.pdf

[Ghemawat 2003]   Ghemawat, Sanjay, Howard Gobioff, and Shun-Tak Leung. "The Google File System," 2003. https://ai.google/research/pubs/pub51

[Gifford 1987]   Gifford, David, and Alfred Spector. "Case Study: IBM's System/360-370 Architecture," *Communications of the ACM*, vol. 30, no. 4, 1987. https://dl.acm.org/doi/10.1145/32232.32233

[Goldsmith 2010]   Goldsmith, Belinda. "Mother's Day Sees Highest Call Volumes of Year: Study," Reuters Life! May 6, 2010. https://www.reuters.com/article/us-mothers-survey/mothers-day-sees-highest-call-volumes-of-year-study-idUSTRE64611R20100507

[Google 2008]   Google. " Protocol Buffers—Google's Data Interchange Format," 2008. https://github.com/protocolbuffers/protobuf/blob/master/src/google/protobuf/stubs/logging.h

[Google 2012]   Google. "ptrace-tools," July 11, 2012. https://code.google.com/archive/p/ptrace-tools/

[Google 2021]   Google. "Protocol Buffers," 2021. https://developers.google.com/protocol-buffers/

[Gregg 2021]   Gregg, Brendan. *Systems Performance* (Second Edition). Addison-Wesley, 2021. ISBN 0-13-682015-8. Also see http://www.brendangregg.com/perf.html

[Gustafson 1988]   Gustafson, John. "Reevaluating Amdahl's Law," *Communications of the ACM*, vol. 31, no. 5. https://dl.acm.org/doi/10.1145/42411.42415

[Hennessy 2017]   Hennessy, John L., and Patterson, David A. *Computer Architecture: A Quantitative Approach* (Sixth Edition). Morgan Kaufmann, 2017. ISBN 978-0128119055.

[Herbert 2010]   Herbert, Tom, and William de Bruijn. "Scaling in the Linux Networking Stack" (undated; describes 2010 Linux 2.6.35 patches). https://www.kernel.org/doc/Documentation/networking/scaling.txt

[Hildebrand 2021]   Hildebrand, Dean, and Denis Serenyi. "Colossus Under the Hood: A Peek into Google's Scalable Storage System," April 19, 2021. https://cloud.google.com/blog/products/storage-data-transfer/a-peek-behind-colossus-googles-file-system

[Hochschild 2021]   Hochschild, Peter H., Paul Turner, Jeffrey C. Mogul, Rama Govindaraju, Parthasarathy Ranganathan, David E. Culler, and Amin Vahdat. "Cores That Don't Count," Workshop on Hot Topics in Operating Systems (HotOS '21), May 31–June 2, 2021, Ann Arbor, MI, and New York. https://dl.acm.org/doi/10.1145/3458336.3465297 or https://sigops.org/s/conferences/hotos/2021/papers/hotos21-s01-hochschild.pdf

[Hoff 2012]   Hoff, Todd. "Google: Taming the Long Latency Tail: When More Machines Equals Worse Results," 2012. http://highscalability.com/blog/2012/3/12/google-taming-the-long-latency-tail-when-more-machines-equal.html

[IBM 1959]   "1402 Card Reader/Punch," 1959. http://www.computerhistory.org/collections/catalog/X233.83B

[IBM 1967]   IBM. "System/360 Principles of Operation A22-6821-7," p. 74, 1967. http://www.bitsavers.org/pdf/ibm/360/princOps/A22-6821-7_360PrincOpsDec67.pdf

[IBM 1970]   IBM. System/370 Model 145. http://www-03.ibm.com/ibm/history/exhibits/mainframe/mainframe_PP3145.html

[IBM 1983]   IBM. "IBM System/370 Extended Architecture Principles of Operation," Publication SA22-7085-0, March 1983. http://bitsavers.trailing-edge.com/pdf/ibm/370/princOps/SA22-7085-0_370-XA_Principles_of_Operation_Mar83.pdf

[IBM 2021]   IBM. "pthread_trace_init_np(): Initialize or Reinitialize Pthread Tracing," June 2021. https://www.ibm.com/support/knowledgecenter/ssw_ibm_i_71/apis/users_h1.htm

[IEEE 2021]   IEEE. "Organizationally Unique Identifier," June 2021. https://standards.ieee.org/products-services/regauth/oui/index.html

[Intel 2021]   Intel. "Intel® 64 and IA-32 Architectures Software Developer's Manual Volume 3B," Chapter 18, 2021. https://software.intel.com/content/www/us/en/develop/download/intel-64-and-ia-32-architectures-sdm-combined-volumes-1-2a-2b-2c-2d-3a-3b-3c-3d-and-4.html

[ISI 1981]   Information Sciences Institute. "RFC 793, Transmission Control Protocol," September 1981. https://tools.ietf.org/html/rfc793

[Keatts 1991]   Keatts, Bill, Subra Balan, and Bodo Parady. "030.matrix300 Performance Considerations," SPEC Newsletter, December 1991. https://inst.eecs.berkeley.edu/~cs266/sp10/readings/keatts91.pdf

[**Knuth 1971**]   Knuth, Donald, and Richard Sites. "Mix/360 User's Guide," Stanford University Computer Science Report STAN-CS-71-197, 1971. http://i.stanford.edu/pub/cstr/reports/cs/tr/71/197/CS-TR-71-197.pdf

[**Kocher 2019**]   Kocher, Paul, Jann Horn, Anders Fogh, Daniel Genkin, Daniel Gruss, Werner Haas, Mike Hamburg, Moritz Lipp, Stefan Mangard, Thomas Prescher, Michael Schwarz, and Yuval Yarom. "Spectre Attacks: Exploiting Speculative Execution," 40th IEEE Symposium on Security and Privacy S&P '19, 2019.

[**Krohnke 2011**]   Krohnke, Duane W. The IBM Antitrust Litigation, 2011. https://dwkcommentaries.com/2011/07/30/the-ibm-antitrust-litigation/

[**Lamport 1977**]   Lamport, Leslie. "Concurrent Reading and Writing," CACM 20:11, pp. 806–811, 1977. https://lamport.azurewebsites.net/pubs/rd-wr.pdf

[**Lee 2016**]   Lee, Ki Suh, Han Wang, Vishal Shrivastav, and Hakim Weatherspoon. *Globally Synchronized Time via Datacenter Networks*, 2016. http://fireless.cs.cornell.edu/publications/dtp_sigcomm16.pdf

[**Lewis 2016**]   Lewis, John. Bates College Commencement Address, May 29, 2016. https://www.bates.edu/news/2016/05/29/civil-rights-hero-john-lewis-to-class-of-16-get-in-trouble-good-trouble/

[**Linux 2021a**]   Linux. "malloc_hook(3) Linux manual page," March 2, 2021. https://man7.org/linux/man-pages/man3/malloc_hook.3.html

[**Linux 2021b**]   Linux. "CFS Scheduler," June 2021. https://www.kernel.org/doc/html/latest/scheduler/sched-design-CFS.html

[**Lipp 2018**]   Lipp, Moritz, Michael Schwarz, Daniel Gruss, Thomas Prescher, Werner Haas, Anders Fogh, Jann Horn, Stefan Mangard, Paul Kocher, Daniel Genkin, Yuval Yarom, and Mike Hamburg. "Meltdown: Reading Kernel Memory from User Space," 27th USENIX Security Symposium Security 18, 2018.

[**Liptay 1968**]   Liptay, J. S. "Structural Aspects of the System/360 Model 85, II: The Cache," *IBM Systems Journal*. vol. 7, issue 1, 1968. https://dl.acm.org/doi/10.1147/sj.71.0015 and http://www.cs.umass.edu/~emery/classes/cmpsci691st/readings/Arch/liptay68.pdf

[**Longbottom 2014**]   Longbottom, Roy. "Whetstone Benchmark History and Results," October 2014. http://www.roylongbottom.org.uk/whetstone.htm

[**Longfellow 1904**]   Longfellow, Henry Wadsworth. *There Was a Little Girl*. https://www.bartleby.com/360/1/120.html

[**McKenney 2017**]   McKenney, Paul E., and Jonathan Walpole. "What Is RCU, Fundamentally?" December 2017. https://lwn.net/Articles/262464/

[**Metcalfe 1976**]   Metcalfe, Robert. "Ethernet," 1976. http://www.ieee802.org/3/ethernet_diag.html

[Naur 1968]   Naur, Peter, and Brian Randell, eds. "Software Engineering," Report on a conference sponsored by the NATO Science Committee, Garmisch, Germany, October 7–11, 1968. https://eprints.ncl.ac.uk/file_store/production/158767/AB6BCDA7-F036-496B-9B5C-2241458CB28D.pdf

[NIST 2020]   NIST. "Leap Seconds FAQs," February 11, 2020. https://www.nist.gov/pml/time-and-frequency-division/leap-seconds-faqs

[Ousterhout 2018]   Ousterhout, John. "Always Measure One Level Deeper," *Communications of the ACM*, vol. 61, no. 7, July 2018, pp. 74–83. https://dl.acm.org/doi/pdf/10.1145/3213770

[Padegs 1981]   Padegs, A. "System/360 and Beyond," *IBM Journal of Research and Development*, vol. 25, no. 5, pp. 377–390, September 1981, doi: 10.1147/rd.255.0377

[Painter 1998]   Painter, Rich. "C Converted Whetstone Double Precision Benchmark," March 22, 1998. https://www.netlib.org/benchmark/whetstone.c

[PaX 2003]   Linux PaX project. "Address Space Layout Randomization," March 15, 2003. https://pax.grsecurity.net/docs/aslr.txt

[Perl 1996]   Perl, Sharon, and Richard Sites. "Studies of Windows NT Performance Using Dynamic Execution Traces," USENIX 2nd Symposium on OS Design and Implementation, October 1996. http://usenix.org/publications/library/proceedings/osdi96/full_papers/perl/perl.ps

[Rothenberg 1999]   Rothenberg, Jeff. "Ensuring the Longevity of Digital Information," February 22, 1999. http://www.clir.org/wp-content/uploads/sites/6/ensuring.pdf

[Rubstov 2021]   Rubtsov, Artem. "HDD Inside: Tracks and Zones," 2021. https://hddscan.com/doc/HDD_Tracks_and_Zones.html

[Shacham 1982]   Shacham, Nachum, and V. Bruce Hunt. "Performance Evaluation of the CSMA/CD (1-persistent) Channel-Access Protocol in Common-Channel Local Networks," in *Proceedings of the IFIP TC 6 International In-Depth Symposium on Local Computer Networks*, 1982.

[Saive 2015]   Saive, Ravi. "20 Command Line Tools to Monitor Linux Performance," January 3, 2015. https://www.tecmint.com/command-line-tools-to-monitor-linux-performance/

[Schmidt 1965]   Schmidt, J. D. "Integrated MOS Transistor Random Access Memory," *Solid State Design*, vol. 6, no. 1 (1965-01), pp. 21–25.

[Schmidt 1964]   Schmidt, John. "Schmidt Patent Notebook (#290)," http://www.computerhistory.org/collections/catalog/102723020

[Scott 2015]   Scott, Tom. "Why Leap Seconds Cause Glitches," June 30, 2015. https://www.youtube.com/watch?v=Uqjg8Kk1HXo

[Sigelman 2010]   Sigelman, Benjamin H., Luiz Andre Barroso, Mike Burrows, Pat Stephenson, Manoj Plakal, Donald Beaver, Saul Jaspan, and Chandan Shanbhag. "Dapper, a Large-Scale Distributed Systems Tracing Infrastructure," Google Technical Report dapper-2010-1, April 2010. https://research.google.com/archive/papers/dapper-2010-1.pdf

[Sites 1972]   Sites, Richard. "Algol W Reference Manual," Stanford University Computer Science Report STAN-CS-71-230, 1972. http://i.stanford.edu/pub/cstr/reports/cs/tr/71/230/CS-TR-71-230.pdf

[Sites 1988]   Sites, Richard, and Anant Agarwal. "Multiprocessor Cache Analysis Using ATUM," *ACM SIGARCH Computer Architecture News*, May 1988. https://dl.acm.org/doi/abs/10.1145/633625.52422

[Sites 2004]   Sites, Richard. Thoth internal tool at Google, no public reference.

[Sites 2017]   Sites, Richard L. "KUTrace: Where Have All the Nanoseconds Gone?" Tracing Summit 2017 in Prague; https://tracingsummit.org/ts/2017/files/TS17-kutrace.pdf, video https://www.youtube.com/watch?v=UYwWollxzAk

[Sites 2018]   Sites, Richard. "Benchmarking Hello World," *ACM Queue Magazine* 16 5, November 2018. https://queue.acm.org/detail.cfm?id=3291278

[Sites 2020]   Sites, Richard. "Anomalies in Linux Processor Use," *USENIX ;login: Magazine*, Summer 2020, pp. 22–26. https://www.usenix.org/publications/login/summer2020/sites

[Stoll 1989]   Stoll, Clifford. *The Cuckoo's Egg: Tracking a Spy through the Maze of Computer Espionage*. Doubleday, 1989. ISBN 978-0385249461.

[Tcpdump 2020]   Tcpdump and Libpcap. "Tcpdump and Libpcap," December 2020. https://www.tcpdump.org/

[Tufte 2001]   Tufte, Edward R. *The Visual Display of Quantitative Information* (Second Edition). Graphics Press, 2001. ISBN 978-1930824133.

[Valgrind 2021]   Valgrind. "Helgrind: A Thread Error Detector," June 2021. http://valgrind.org/docs/manual/hg-manual.html

[Weaveworks 2017]   Weaveworks. "The Long Tail: Tools to Investigate High Long Tail Latency," 2017. https://www.weave.works/blog/the-long-tail-tools-to-investigate-high-long-tail-latency/

[Wikimedia 2008]   Wikimedia. "Extinction Intensity," May 21, 2008. https://upload.wikimedia.org/wikipedia/commons/0/06/Extinction_intensity.svg

[Wikipedia 2019a]   Wikipedia. "IBM Advanced Computer Systems Project ACS," https://en.wikipedia.org/wiki/IBM_Advanced_Computer_Systems_project

[Wikipedia 2020a]   Wikipedia. "IBM 709," December 16, 2020. https://en.wikipedia.org/wiki/IBM_709

[Wikipedia 2020b]   Wikipedia. "IBM 360/91," February 26, 2020. https://en.wikipedia.org/wiki/IBM_System/360_Model_91

[Wikipedia 2020c]   Wikipedia. "GE 645," December 26, 2020. https://en.wikipedia.org/wiki/GE_645

[Wikipedia 2020d]   Wikipedia. "IBM 360/85," October 2020. https://en.wikipedia.org/wiki/IBM_System/360_Model_85 28

[Wikipedia 2020e]   Wikipedia. "DEC Alpha 21464 EV8," December 2020. https://en.wikipedia.org/wiki/Alpha_21464 13

[Wikipedia 2020f]   Wikipedia, crediting William Regitz and Joel Karp. "Intel 1103," December 16, 2020. https://en.wikipedia.org/wiki/Intel_1103

[Wikipedia 2020g]   Wikipedia. "Work-Conserving Scheduler," August 2, 2020. https://en.wikipedia.org/wiki/Work-conserving_scheduler

[Wikipedia 2020h]   Wikipedia. "Gustafson's Law," December 18, 2020. https://en.wikipedia.org/wiki/Gustafson%27s_law

[Wikipedia 2021a]   Wikipedia. "IBM 7094," March 31, 2021. https://en.wikipedia.org/wiki/IBM_7090#IBM_7094

[Wikipedia 2021b]   Wikipedia. "IBM 7030," May 24, 2021. https://en.wikipedia.org/wiki/IBM_7030_Stretch

[Wikipedia 2021c]   Wikipedia. "CDC 6600," May 20, 2021. https://en.wikipedia.org/wiki/CDC_6600

[Wikipedia 2021d]   Wikipedia. "Manchester Atlas," May 12, 2021. https://en.wikipedia.org/wiki/Atlas_(computer)

[Wikipedia 2021e]   Wikipedia. "IBM 360/67," March 14, 2021. https://en.wikipedia.org/wiki/IBM_System/360_Model_67

[Wikipedia 2021f]   Wikipedia. "IBM RISC System/6000," May 22, 2021. https://en.wikipedia.org/wiki/IBM_RISC_System/6000.

[Wikipedia 2021g]   Wikipedia. "DEC Alpha 21064," January 22, 2021. https://en.wikipedia.org/wiki/Alpha_21064

[Wikipedia 2021h]   Wikipedia. "Intel Pentium," April 24, 2021. https://en.wikipedia.org/wiki/P5_(microarchitecture)

[Wikipedia 2021i]   Wikipedia. "IBM Power4," February 1, 2021. https://en.wikipedia.org/wiki/POWER4

[Wikipedia 2021j]   Wikipedia. "Hyper-threading," February 3, 2021. https://en.wikipedia.org/wiki/Hyper-threading

[Wikipedia 2021k]   Wikipedia. "Cray-1 Computer," February 20, 2021. https://en.wikipedia.org/wiki/Cray-1

[Wikipedia 2021l]   Wikipedia. "MIPS R4000," April 18, 2021. https://en.wikipedia.org/wiki/R4000

[Wikipedia 2021m]   Wikipedia. "Robert H. Dennard," April 30, 2021. https://en.wikipedia.org/wiki/Robert_H._Dennard

[Wikipedia 2021n]   Wikipedia. "Interpacket Gap," March 11, 2021. https://en.wikipedia.org/wiki/Interpacket_gap

[Wikipedia 2021o]   Wikipedia. "Network Time Protocol," https://en.wikipedia.org/wiki/Network_Time_Protocol

[Wikipedia 2021p]   Wikipedia. "Coordinated Universal Time," May 30, 2021. https://en.wikipedia.org/wiki/Coordinated_Universal_Time

[Wikipedia 2021q]   Wikipedia. "Cyclic Redundancy Check," May 28, 2021. https://en.wikipedia.org/wiki/Cyclic_redundancy_check

[Wikipedia 2021r]   Wikipedia. "Protocol Buffers," May 8, 2021. https://en.wikipedia.org/wiki/Protocol_Buffers

[Wikipedia 2021s]   Wikipedia. "Extinction Event," May 12, 2021. https://en.wikipedia.org/wiki/Extinction_event

[Wikipedia 2021t]   Wikipedia. "Advanced Format," May 17, 2021. https://en.wikipedia.org/wiki/Advanced_Format

[Wikipedia 2021u]   Wikipedia. "Punched Card," May 30, 2021. https://en.wikipedia.org/wiki/Punched_card

[Wikipedia 2021v]   Wikipedia. "Wi-Fi," May 30, 2021. https://en.wikipedia.org/wiki/Wi-Fi

[Wikipedia 2021w]   Wikipedia. "Bluetooth," May 31, 2021. https://en.wikipedia.org/wiki/Bluetooth

[Wikipedia 2021x]   Wikipedia. "Amdahl's Law," May 6, 2021. https://en.wikipedia.org/wiki/Amdahl%27s_law

[Wikipedia 2021y]   Wikipedia. "Carrier-Sense Multiple Access with Collision Detection," January 6, 2021. https://en.wikipedia.org/wiki/Carrier-sense_multiple_access_with_collision_detection

[Wikipedia 2021z]   Wikipedia. "Read-Copy-Update," January 20, 2021. https://en.wikipedia.org/wiki/Read-copy-update

[Williams 2019]   Williams, Don. "Theoretical/Operational Hourly Ride Capacity at WDW—FP+ analysis," July 31, 2019. https://crooksinwdw.wordpress.com/2013/12/14/theoreticaloperational-hourly-ride-capacity-at-wdw/

[Wireshark 2021]   https://www.wireshark.org/

[YouTube 2016]   "1940 Tacoma Narrows Bridge Collapse (A.K.A. Galloping Gertie)," https://www.youtube.com/watch?v=KRutAt0FlGA

Photo Credits

Chapter 3

[Wikimedia 2010]   Scholz, Hans-Peter. Ferrite core memory. https://commons.wikimedia.org/wiki/Category:Core_memory#/media/File:Ferritkernspeicher_detail_01.jpg

[Wikimedia 2016]   Nguyen, Thomas. https://commons.wikimedia.org/wiki/Category:Intel_1103#/media/File:Intel_C1103.jpg

Chapter 5

[Wikimedia 2013]   https://commons.wikimedia.org/wiki/File:35-Desktop-Hard-Drive.jpg

[Wikimedia 2012]   https://commons.wikimedia.org/wiki/File:ReadWrite_Head_of_SyQuest_SQ3270S.jpg

[Wikimedia 2005]   https://commons.wikimedia.org/wiki/File:Cylinder_Head_Sector.svg

[Wikimedia 2006]   https://commons.wikimedia.org/wiki/File:Flash-Programming.svg

[Sites-Bowen 2021]   Sites-Bowen, Connor. 2021.

Chapter 6

[Boggs 1976]   Boggs, David R., and Robert M. Metcalfe. "Ethernet Diagram," 1976. http://www.ieee802.org/3/ethernet_diag.html

[Wikimedia 2020a]   Wikimedia. "Ethernet Type II Frame Format," October 2, 2020. https://commons.wikimedia.org/wiki/File:Ethernet_Type_II_Frame_format.svg

Chapter 7

[Wikimedia 2021]   Wikimedia. "16 MHz Crystal," February 13, 2021. https://commons.wikimedia.org/wiki/File:16MHZ_Crystal.jpg

Part III

[Thurber 1933]   Thurber, James. "For Heaven's Sake, Why Don't You Go Outdoors and Trace Something?" 1933. https://www.cartoonstock.com/cartoon?searchID=CC19035

Chapter 27

[Opper 1906]   Opper, Frederick Burr. Public domain, 1906. https://upload.wikimedia.org/wikipedia/commons/4/4b/Alphonsegaston.jpg

[Wikimedia 2020b]   Wikimedia, Zwergelstern. "File:Niagara Falls Switch Yard.jpg," cropped and brightened, June 19, 2020. https://commons.wikimedia.org/wiki/File:Niagara_Falls_Switch_Yard.jpg

Index

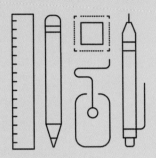

Photo by izusek/gettyimages

Register Your Product at informit.com/register

Access additional benefits and **save 35%** on your next purchase

- Automatically receive a coupon for 35% off your next purchase, valid for 30 days. Look for your code in your InformIT cart or the Manage Codes section of your account page.

- Download available product updates.

- Access bonus material if available.*

- Check the box to hear from us and receive exclusive offers on new editions and related products.

Registration benefits vary by product. Benefits will be listed on your account page under Registered Products.

InformIT.com—The Trusted Technology Learning Source

InformIT is the online home of information technology brands at Pearson, the world's foremost education company. At InformIT.com, you can:

- Shop our books, eBooks, software, and video training
- Take advantage of our special offers and promotions (informit.com/promotions)
- Sign up for special offers and content newsletter (informit.com/newsletters)
- Access thousands of free chapters and video lessons

Connect with InformIT—Visit informit.com/community

the trusted technology learning source

Addison-Wesley · Adobe Press · Cisco Press · Microsoft Press · Pearson IT Certification · Que · Sams · Peachpit Press

 Pearson

KUtrace HTML Legend

Execution (measured)

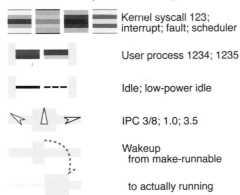

Kernel syscall 123;
interrupt; fault; scheduler

User process 1234; 1235

Idle; low-power idle

IPC 3/8; 1.0; 3.5

Wakeup
  from make-runnable

to actually running

Non-execution

Waiting for CPU

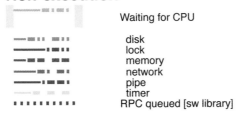

disk
lock
memory
network
pipe
timer
RPC queued [sw library]

Synthesized (approximate)

Exiting low-power idle

KUtrace overhead: diag.
white lines (10-50ns)

Time-aligned data

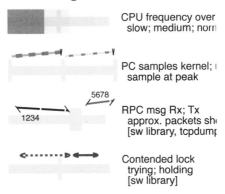

CPU frequency over
  slow; medium; norm

PC samples kernel;
  sample at peak

5678

1234

RPC msg Rx; Tx
  approx. packets sh
  [sw library, tcpdum

Contended lock
  trying; holding
  [sw library]

Manually-inserted

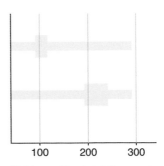

Hi   there

Callouts

Markers a; b; c; d

A   B   C   123

[also execution RPCIDs,
lock try/acquire/release,
queued from sw libraries]

Annotations

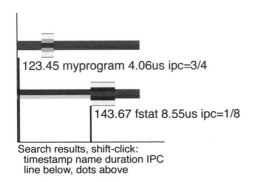

123.45 myprogram 4.06us ipc=3/4

143.67 fstat 8.55us ipc=1/8

Search results, shift-click:
  timestamp name duration IPC
  line below, dots above

Grid

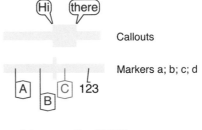

100   200   300

Light gray X-axis gridline overlay